D1474158

Co-operative culture
and the politics of
consumption in England,
1870-1930

Dedicated to my parents
Noreen Madeline Gurney and Henry James Gurney

Co-operative culture and the politics of consumption in England, 1870–1930

Peter Gurney

Manchester University Press
Manchester and New York
distributed exclusively in the USA by St. Martin's Press

141642

Copyright © Manchester University Press 1996

Published by Manchester University Press
Oxford Road, Manchester M13 9NR, UK
and Room 400, 175 Fifth Avenue,
New York, NY 10010, USA

Distributed exclusively in the USA by
St. Martin's Press, Inc.,
175 Fifth Avenue, New York, NY 10010, USA

British Library Cataloguing-in-Publication Data
A catalogue record for this book is available from the British Library

Library of Congress Cataloging-in-Publication Data
Gurney, Peter
    Co-operative culture and the politics of consumption in England,
    1870-1930 / Peter Gurney
        p. cm
    Includes bibliographical references.
    ISBN 0-7190-4950-4
    1. Consumer co-operatives-Great Britain-History. I. Title
    HD3325.A4G87 1996
    334'.50941-dc20   96-16160

ISBN 0 7190 4950 4 *hardback*

First published in 1996

00 99 98 97 96   10 9 8 7 6 5 4 3 2 1

Printed in Great Britain
by Bookcraft (Bath) Ltd, Midsomer Norton

Contents

List of appendices

List of abbreviations

ASE	Amalgamated Society of Engineers
AUCE	Amalgamated Union of Co-operative Employees
BSP	British Socialist Party
CWS	Co-operative Wholesale Society
ICA	International Co-operative Alliance
ILP	Independent Labour Party
LRC	Labour Representation Committee
NUDAW	National Union of Distributive and Allied Workers
PATA	Proprietary Articles Traders' Association
RACS	Royal Arsenal Co-operative Society
SDF	Social Democratic Federation
SSA	Social Science Association
TDA	Traders' Defence Association
UCSC	Union Cold Storage Company [Vesty]
WCG	Women's Co-operative Guild
WCPF	Workers' Co-operative Productive Federation
WEA	Workers' Educational Association
WEC	War Emergency Workers' National Committee

Acknowledgements

I have lived with this project for ten years and have accrued many personal and intellectual debts along the way. Jeff Carpenter gave me my first glimpse of 'people's history' before I left home and when I got to Sussex University in the early 1980s John Rosselli and Eileen Yeo provided much encouragement and good advice. Stephen Yeo supervised the doctoral thesis from which this book developed and was generous with ideas and imagination. Many other historians also helped sustain the work including John Benson, Ellen Furlough, Donald Gray, Victoria de Grazia, J. F. C. Harrison, Bill Lancaster, John Lowerson, Edward Royle, Gill Scott, John Walton and Michael Winstanley. My copy-editor at MUP, Gerard Hill, improved the manuscript with some excellent suggestions. Helen Rogers read and commented on the work at every stage and helped me to finish it.

At the start money came from the British Academy in the form of a Major State Studentship but I must also thank Ian Kershaw and the history department at the University of Sheffield for awarding me the Douglas Knoop Fellowship in Economic and Social History which gave me the space I needed to write the manuscript in 1993-4. Staff at the following libraries made the job much easier: Sussex University Library (particularly Inter-Library Loans); the British Library; Colindale Newspaper Library; the Bishopsgate Institute; Goldsmith's Library, University of London; the London School of Economics and Political Science; Public Libraries in Birmingham, Brighton, Leeds, Manchester and Sheffield; Co-operative Union Library, Holyoake House, Manchester. Roy Garrett, the late librarian of the Co-op Union, was an inspiration and I am sorry that he did not live to see the published version.

This book is small recompense for the trouble I have been to friends; many fed me, put me up and tolerated my obsessions. Kevin Crisp, Karen and Ann Dunn, Martin Evans, Jacqui Maurice, Mandy Morris, John Reiners, Richard Rodgers, Kevin Sheehy, Carl Talbot, Patrick Tobin and Bonita Webb were most patient. Vanessa Powell reminded me that there is more to life than books, for which I am grateful.

The book is dedicated to my mother and father who now prefer to shop at Sainsburys' but who tried to teach me what co-operation might mean.

The conflict between capitalism and socialism is now commonly seen in terms of a competition in productive efficiency, and we need not doubt that much of our future history, on a world scale, will be determined by the results of this competition. Yet the conflict is really much deeper than this, and is also a conflict between different approaches to and forms of socialism. The fundamental choice that emerges, in the problems set to us by modern industrial production, is between man as consumer and man as user.

Raymond Williams, 'Advertising: the Magic System',
New Left Review, 4, 1960

1

Introduction:
Co-operation and the historians

The breakthrough of the new political economy of the free market was also the breakdown of the old moral economy of provision. After the wars all that was left of it was charity – and Speenhamland. The moral economy of the crowd took longer to die: it is picked up by the early co-operative flour mills, by some Owenite socialists, and it lingered on for years somewhere in the bowels of the Co-operative Wholesale Society.

> E. P. Thompson, 'The Moral Economy of the English Crowd in the
> Eighteenth Century', *Past and Present*, 50, 1971

I

The practice and history of co-operation have perplexed and exasperated, but also excited, many intellectuals since the mid-nineteenth century. These ambivalent attitudes were particularly marked amongst those on the left who regarded this highly visible working-class movement as both a problem and an opportunity. Researching her influential defence of consumers' co-operation published in 1891, the young Beatrice Webb read the movement press until her eyes ached. The damning remarks provoked by this experience were symptomatic of a wider impatience:

> A grind and no mistake! Six hours a day reading and note-taking from those endless volumes of the *Co-operative News*. A treadmill of disjointed facts, in themselves utterly uninteresting and appallingly dry, and not complete enough to be satisfactory.[1]

Leonard Woolf, who published sympathetic studies in 1918 and

1921, also said some harsh things later. In his autobiography Woolf
adopted a haughty and distant tone. He described the movement as
the creation of the 'working class human ant' and referred to the
'dingy Co-op grocery store in some rain-sodden street in a hideous
grimy northern industrial town'. The movement was dull and life-
less, lacking any lofty idealism: 'a great deal of the co-operative
spirit which moves the vast co-operative machine is as drab and
dreary as its material surface', he concluded.[2]

The condescending, partial nature of this common representation
of working-class culture need not be laboured; like so much else,
dominant ways of seeing consumers' co-operation in the late nineteenth and early twentieth centuries have been filtered through middle-class spectacles. Although both Webb and Woolf recognised the
potential of co-operation they tended to view it largely in relation to
their own particular social and political visions. Thus they were
both disappointed with the movement, though for different reasons;
as we shall see, many co-operators resisted the subordinate role assigned to their movement by collectivists like Webb and had little
enthusiasm or hope for the state-supported co-operation advocated
by Woolf. Fabian socialists generally urged the movement to do
more, to rediscover its spirit or idealism and believed that what was
needed was the advice and guidance of outside 'experts'; left to their
own devices working people would merely pursue narrow material
interests. Thus Woolf and Webb articulated the notion – which professional historians have subsequently accepted as axiomatic – that
workers were attracted to co-operation mainly for what they could
get out of it, particularly the 'divi'.

This book questions and where necessary contests these widely-
held assumptions and argues for a more appropriate reading and
context; consumer co-operation was neither drab nor dreary for the
thousands of men, women and children who made the English
movement the largest and most successful in the world by the First
World War and it deserves to be placed at the centre of explorations
of working-class associational and community life. For many it was
a vital way of making ends meet, certainly; for a significant number
of co-operative ideologues it simultaneously promised a revolutionary re-ordering of economic and social relationships. We cannot be
certain that these constituencies (the customers and the ideologies)
were clearly separated and scholarship has often failed to deepen
our understanding. The 'strategy of condescension' noted above is,

with minor exceptions, still prevalent (though not as obvious perhaps) and is a major obstacle blocking a proper, critical appreciation of this important location of working-class creativity and
practice.[3] Before we consider the movement itself an examination of
the marginalisation of this subject within academic discourse demands our attention.

II

Although an increasing number of academic historians became interested in the history of labour after the First World War, histories
of the Co-operative movement were written largely by activists and
tended to be bland and celebratory.[4] G. D. H. Cole, who tried to
build bridges between co-operators and professional historians, was
the exception which proved the rule. Cole had dismissed the movement somewhat cursorily in his first major work, *The World of
Labour* (1913): 'It will continue alongside Capitalism; but it will do
nothing to overthrow it', he concluded.[5] He soon changed his mind.
Rejecting the Webbs' vision of a collectivist state, Cole fully converted to the theory of Guild Socialism during the war. He was particularly encouraged by the entry of the Co-operative movement
into politics in 1917 and was also stimulated by Woolf's work on
the subject.[6] Henceforth he believed that the future of democratic
socialism lay in a marriage between Guild Socialist and co-operative
organisation which would regulate the rights and interests of
producers and consumers. Cole hoped that this would furnish an
institutional framework for a society owned and controlled by the
working class in practice as well as in theory. We can see him working through these problems in *Self-Government in Industry* and in
the preface written for the 1919 edition of *The World of Labour* he
asserted that: 'The relation of the great Co-operative Movement of
consumers to the theory of Guild Socialism is the most immediate of
the unsolved problems before us'.[7]

Cole spent a great deal of time and energy over the next thirty
years trying to arrange such a marriage. *A Century of Co-operation*
(1945) testified to this interest. In the preface Cole noted that he had
been collecting material for a study of the movement for many years
before being invited to write the centenary history by the Co-operative Union. As one would expect, this dense, sympathetic narrative
was marked by a concern with relations and conflicts between

producers and consumers. By this time Cole strongly rejected the
view that voluntary associations of producers could transform capitalism without state intervention; that was the hard lesson of the
enthusiastic experiments which had followed the First World War.
In the chapter on 'Guild Socialism and the Building Guilds' he also
reminded readers that the CWS Bank had withdrawn its support as
soon as the Guilds' financial position had been undermined and that
'the Guild Socialists found many of their strongest opponents
among leaders of Consumers' Co-operation . . . .' Noting the fall-off
in trade per member, Cole also criticised the movement for failing to
adapt to changing patterns of working-class demand. What was ur-
gently needed, he argued, was a little less 'solid common sense' and
a good deal more 'imagination'.[8]

One rather minor sub-theme in Cole's centenary history provided
an influential legacy. Cole had referred to the gradual shift away
from community-building and argued that this transformation was
apparent within the Rochdale Pioneers' society by the mid-1850s.
However, this change was little more than a necessary and fairly
unremarkable change of emphasis:

> The Pioneers had settled down to develop Co-operation not apart
> from the world as it was but in that world and subject to its limiting
> conditions. They had become realists, even if they had not shed their
> idealism.[9]

In an essay included in the *Festschrift* published shortly after Cole's
death, Sidney Pollard took up this notion and drew a clear-cut, rigid
distinction between the 'idealism' of the Owenite phase and the
'self-interest' which characterised the post-1844 period. Pollard
maintained that the Pioneers' decision to pay dividends on purchases, 'represented the first major breach with Owenism, and one
that proved fatal to its ultimate ideal'.[10] As we shall see, this teleological view – although it rests mainly on a few highly selective
quotations taken from the *Co-operator* and completely marginalises
the utopianism of late nineteenth century co-operators – has been
repeated *ad nauseam* by professional historians ever since.

This was not Pollard's fault of course; historical hypotheses need
to be sharpened and tested by debate but there was very little interest in the subject. Pollard himself contributed an excellent essay on
'The Foundation of the Co-operative Party' to the second volume of
Essays in Labour History (1967) but the most talented of the post-

war generation of labour and Marxist historians, including Eric
Hobsbawm, John Saville, E. P. Thompson, Christopher Hill, Gwyn
Williams, J. F. C. Harrison and Royden Harrison among others,
were drawn either to the more 'heroic' phases of popular or working-class struggle (English Revolution; working-class formation;
Owenism, Chartism, and so on) or else to the history of the Labour
Party and the trades unions, institutions whose power and influence
were clearly demonstrated in post-war Britain. There was ideological heterogeneity here surely, but all these historians were on the left
in a broad sense and many also had links with the world of adult
education.[11]

Despite these (albeit fairly tenuous) connections, labour history
gradually became 'routinised' or professionalised after the Second
World War. Courses on the history of labour became more and
more common within the expanded university sector and consequently the history of the labour movement became almost completely detached from the movement itself. This is a gross
simplification of what was in fact a long and uneven process but the
broad contours are clear enough; the rearguard action fought (and
lost) by the History Workshop movement against this trend from
the mid-1960s bears this out. Specialists in this field of knowledge
increasingly functioned as cultural producers within what the
French sociologist Pierre Bourdieu has referred to as the domain of
'Homo Academicus'. Their goods were bought and sold in a different market.[12] The rest of this section will focus on the role assigned
to co-operation within the burgeoning academic literature generated by this transformation.

Scholars influenced by the theory of the labour aristocracy
showed some interest in the subject of co-operative history. In an
article which first appeared in 1954, Hobsbawm re-worked the
Leninist notion which argued that the upper stratum of British
workers had been 'bribed' with a portion of the super-profits made
from imperialist expansion. This purported explanation of working-
class 'reformism' was tested and refined in a spate of books which
appeared in the 1970s. John Foster's *Class Struggle and the Industrial Revolution* (1974) was an early, important intervention. Foster
accepted Lenin's reading and within his work co-operation figured
as the province of a small, selfish stratum of the working class, the
respectable, sober artisans or labour aristocrats who had turned
their backs on revolution once and for all.[13]

Adopting a more nuanced, Gramscian perspective, Geoffrey
Crossick's study of Kentish London, *An Artisan Elite in Victorian
Society* (1978) moved beyond Foster's economism to stress the cultural and ideological underpinnings of mid-Victorian social stability.[14] Crossick accepted Pollard's thesis that the dividend
represented a profound caesura and like Foster emphasised the
fairly narrow social background of the majority of local co-
operative leaders. However, Crossick also drew attention to the
complexities and ambiguities of co-operation in Kentish London
and the persistence of a certain, albeit limited, idealism. For
Crossick, as for Gray and Tholfsen, bourgeois hegemony in this period depended on consent as well as coercion, and co-operation was
an important locus for ideas and values (respectability, self-help,
thrift, improvement, progress, and so forth) which although distinctively working class could nevertheless be easily bent to a specifically bourgeois vision of the social order. But despite the hesitations
and qualifications, co-operation retained its anti-revolutionary hue;
taking shares in the co-op and regularly collecting the dividend gave
certain workers a material stake in capitalism and the continuation
of capitalist social relations.[15]

The theory of the labour aristocracy was eventually subjected to
telling criticism and left quietly to expire.[16] Nevertheless – and this is
of more pertinence to my theme – alternative accounts which con-
vincingly rejected the theory adopted a similar reading of the Co-
operative movement. Neville Kirk's *The Growth of Working-Class
Reformism in Mid-Victorian England* (1985) is a good example.
Kirk demonstrated the fairly extensive occupational base of the co-
operative leadership in the North West and even deployed evidence
which pointed to the continuing and perceived 'revolutionary' potential of co-operation in the 1860s drawn from the pages of the *Co-
operator*.[17] Despite this he accepted the notion that the dividend
replaced the New Moral World in the minds of many working-class
co-operators and that the movement thus aided the largely uncon-
scious 'drift into reformism'.[18] This way of plotting the movement's
history begs a great many questions, some of which will be considered in a moment.

First it is worth drawing attention to a dominant trope within the
literature on working-class politics and culture during this period,
perhaps best captured by the phrase 'a life apart'. Many scholars
have stressed the self-enclosed, defensive and subordinate nature of

the majority working-class culture in this period. Passivity and intra-class divisions are key features within this schema and, to parody the argument, all most workers wanted to do – apart from those whom Richard Hoggart once referred to as 'the earnest minority' – was to keep their heads down and live for family and friends, a few pints on a Saturday night and a song and a laugh in the music hall.[19] Decisions were made above their heads – at Westminster, in the company board room, in the trade union headquarters. A great deal of writing about the working class shares these common assumptions. They can be found in Orwell's work in the 1930s; in Hoggart's seminal study of working-class culture written in the 1950s; and even in Anderson and Nairn's polemics of the 1960s.[20] Stedman Jones' notion of a 'culture of consolation' is best seen in this tradition. By the close of the nineteenth century, according to Stedman Jones, there was widespread belief that capitalism had become a permanent system – an 'immovable horizon':

> The main impetus of working-class activity . . . was concentrated into trade unions, co-ops, friendly societies, all dictating a 'de facto' recognition of the existing social order as the inevitable framework of action.[21]

Co-operation, supposedly, was just another facet of an enclosed, conservative world, a way of making ends meet rather than a way of changing society. Even if it did not exactly turn workers into bourgeois mirror-images, it certainly mitigated and defused actual and potential class-conflict.

This interpretative framework has gained considerable support recently; in fact it is in danger of becoming a new orthodoxy.[22] Jay Winter's preface to Henry Pelling's *Festschrift* can be read as a kind of informal manifesto which proclaimed and celebrated the shift from labour to working-class history. Winter contrasted the institutional focus of the first generation of labour historians with the broader concerns of contemporary scholars. The social history of the working class now had to take full account of apathy as well as activism and although Winter claimed that the aim was to 'complement rather than supersede' earlier research one was left in little doubt that recent work was qualitatively superior. The terms used to describe Pelling's own achievement are revealing: Pelling helped replace a mythologised and whiggish interpretation of labour history with 'a rigorous and accurate . . . painstakingly-researched and documented historical analysis.' All this was accomplished without fuss, 'quietly and authoritatively', as befits a cool, independent scholar.[23] Even allowing for the context of a *Festschrift*, such an assessment is nonetheless either very naïve or disingenuous: all texts are ideological in the sense that they articulate a set of positions and arguments, whether explicitly or implicitly, by means of language. This is as true of history as it is of literature.[24]

These observations are not intended to impugn the quality of Pelling's empirical research. All that is being urged here is that the shift described by Winter was not neutral: Pelling was writing for a different market, was functioning in a different domain than were other, more 'committed', writers. The career of Edward Thompson, especially his early New Left activist-historian phase, provides a suggestive contrast. Unlike Pelling, Thompson had a direct if often critical *relationship* with the labour and socialist movement: *The Making of the English Working Class* (1963) certainly helped to establish the scholarly reputation of its author (though not immediately), but it was also specifically designed to make socialists and inspire them with the antinomian spirit. Consequently this text gained a wide audience outside as well as within the universities, both in this country and abroad.[25] Winter's uncritical celebration of the movement from labour to working-class history merely obscures complex sociological processes which can only be gestured towards here. Briefly, writing the history of the working class became, for more and more professional academics, primarily a way of making a living rather than a way of helping to change the world. This transformation was bound up with (though not merely determined by) a number of interconnected factors; not least of which by the late 1970s was the related triumph of Thatcherism and the 'crisis' of labour.[26]

One text in particular, strongly influenced by this trend, deserves consideration here: Paul Johnson's *Saving and Spending: The Working-class Economy in Britain 1870–1939* (1985). Although admitting that consumers' co-operation was an overwhelmingly working-class practice Johnson is in absolutely no doubt as to the primary motivation: 'The mass of the members were more interested in money than in social development . . . .' His argument turns on a rigid distinction between leaders and led; activists may have articulated a vague utopianism but the rank and file were excited more by large dividends than by the notion of a 'Co-operative Common-

wealth'. Moreover, the practice of credit trading within the movement became more and more widespread, despite constant condemnation from the leadership. This potentially illuminating discussion
is reduced to a simple, misleading dichotomy: 'Ideals were all very
well, but they were too costly for most co-operators to take too
seriously'.[27]

Much of the work discussed above has been valuable: close attention to the distinctive and independent nature of working-class culture has shed new light on crucial questions. However, as far as the
history of the Co-operative movement is concerned the tendency has
been to close down or at least seriously hinder new research. In this
connection, two major though related problems need to be addressed. The first is the pivotal, deradicalising role frequently assigned to consumers' co-operation. Even if connections with a
'labour aristocracy' are no longer taken for granted, the notion that
the movement encouraged the 'drift into reformism' is accepted *a
priori* by many. Within this schema the spread and popularity of
consumers' co-operation is supposed to help explain the decline of a
revolutionary alternative in Britain post-mid-century. The difficulty
here is that 'reformism' is a vague catch-all, effectively criticised by
David Beetham who has questioned

> whether a conceptual strategy is acceptable which rolls all working-
> class and socialist politics into one bundle, and treats them as equiva-
> lent, whatever their character – oppositional or acquiescent,
> aspirational or mundane . . . it ignores distinctions and complexities
> that are important both for recovering the richness of a tradition and
> to political practice itself.[28]

Beetham rightly argues that 'revolution' must be understood as a
deviation from the norm of 'reformism' in capitalist societies and
not vice versa. So we need to be discriminating with regard to working-class institutions and ideologies if we are to appreciate fully, and
not just efface from the historical record continuing patterns of
working-class resistance.

The second problem is the assumed separation of ideals and material interests, of heads from bodies, and the common condemnation
of the dividend which goes with this. This goes back a long way; in
the mid-nineteenth century Christian Socialists like Thomas Hughes
denigrated the 'gut's gospel' of co-operation and Neale's biographer
has rehearsed this view uncritically. As a narrative strategy which

purports to explain working-class 'incorporation' this antinomy runs through Thomas Cooper's autobiography in the early 1870s to Theodore Rothstein's study fifty years later.[29] Interestingly enough private traders in the late nineteenth century also attacked consumers' co-operation from this angle. R. Walker of the Scottish Traders' Defence Association launched an indignant attack on the materialistic basis of the movement in a public debate in 1889: 'we must decidedly protest against the delusive dividend system, as at present carried on . . . which appeals so strongly to the most sordid passions in human nature', he declared.[30] The problem of course was that from Walker's point of view the dividend was not undermining working-class radicalism, it was undermining his business.

Clearly we need to re-think this dualism. I would suggest that one reason why it has been accepted by so many scholars is that intellectuals naturally tend to equate 'ideals' with texts and an explicit and fully-articulate body of knowledge, a thorough and recognisable if not necessarily always coherent theory which has its locus in the mind rather than the body. Pierre Bourdieu's recent reflections are apposite here:

> There is a sort of *de facto* division of labour of social production with respect to major varieties of experience. Very often the people who are able to speak about the social world know nothing about the social world, and the people who do know about the social world are not able to speak about it.[31]

Bourdieu refers to the 'practical knowledge' shared by workers and their inability to articulate this knowledge, because of inequalities in the distribution of cultural as well as economic capital. The habits of the intellectual and his or her investment and trading in the sphere of cultural capital make it more and not less difficult to understand this knowledge.

'Ideals' can easily be found within Owenism of course, but we have too readily assumed that they were squeezed out of the later Co-operative movement because of the success of the dividend; in fact, as I argue below, late-nineteenth-century co-operation produced its own brand of utopianism based on the principle of the dividend. And of course the dividend itself was an 'ideal' despite the fact that it put food in bellies and clothes on backs. Was it not likely that many rank-and-file members gradually recognised that profit-making was unnecessary or even immoral after they had traded at the store for a while? We cannot say for sure, but this would help explain the fierce loyalty generated by the movement and the determination to overcome the many setbacks (including unemployment and economic crises, strikes and traders' boycotts) which bedevilled the majority of local societies from the start. This is not to dismiss the existence of real and complex contradictions between ideals and commercial success; these were present from the movement's inception. But to freeze this problem in an abstract and ahistorical fashion – 'burgeoning wealth generated indifference' as one scholar bluntly puts it[32] – is very unhelpful and may serve only to engender a thoroughly pessimistic response to all strategies of social transformation built piecemeal from below. The dividend was part of the 'practical knowledge' used by working people to cope with and simultaneously reconstruct capitalist social relations. There are many reasons which help explain the failure of the movement to fulfil its utopian potential in the long term, which will be discussed in the chapters which follow, but the popularity of the dividend is not one of them.

Although a number of historians have sought to eschew the marginalising assumptions outlined above[33], the 'passivity school' continues to make converts, indeed some have moved significantly beyond the earlier position. Alastair Reid has recently thrown down the gauntlet to those old-fashioned social historians who still work within the framework of a theory of domination and subordination; that is, those who continue to emphasise the inequitable distribution of power and the contests, both overt and hidden, generated by these inequalities. Reid himself prefers the social democratic fiction that British society after 1850 was 'held together by a more positive form of consent' and opines, rather presumptuously, that the next decade will decide the issue.[34] As this book demonstrates, the history of the Co-operative movement provides a very rich source of evidence with which to counter this view, but it would be useful at this juncture to briefly trace the origins and development of co-operative praxis in the earlier period.

III

As Edward Thompson suggested in the passage quoted at the beginning of this chapter, the Co-operative movement grew out of the critique and rejection of an increasingly individualistic, market-ori-

entated and competitive mode of production/consumption in eight-
eenth-century England. Bread was the staple diet of the common
people and the conflicts which arose over its production, distribution and exchange were often intense during the eighteenth century;
mills were frequently the target for food rioters. Co-operative flour
mills were established by the urban poor – often aided by sympathetic members of the local gentry – in various localities from at
least the mid-eighteenth century; the dockyard workers of
Woolwich and Chatham founded a co-operative mill as early as
1760. The grain crisis precipitated by the Napoleonic Wars encouraged the spread of co-operation; flour clubs (co-operative retailing
schemes) were established by friendly societies in an effort to keep
prices down and the latter also sponsored a number of the successful
co-operative corn milling societies which were established at Sheffield, Hull, Birmingham, Hereford, Whitby, Brentford, Nottingham
and Wolverhampton.[35] These forms have attracted little scholarly
interest though they represented an important alternative to capitalist modes of industrialisation; shares could be purchased in instal-
ments (usually on a sliding scale) and the societies were run by an
elected committee.[36]

The mill established in Hull in 1795 (a year of acute agricultural
distress) was called, appropriately enough, the Hull Anti-Mill Co-
operative Society. The intention was to provide working people
with cheap, unadulterated bread and free them from the fraudulent
practices of the local millers and shopkeepers. The number of original members of the society was 1,435 and each subscribed 1s 1d
per week for four weeks, then 6d per week for a further four weeks.
The mill was so successful that in 1810 local millers indicted the
society as a nuisance; the following year a Yorkshire jury which
'considered poverty a still greater nuisance' found in its favour. The
co-operators of Hull received donations from the local gentry to the
tune of about £350 when they began; with the French Revolution
troubling their peace of mind the gentry was happy to support an
association which they hoped would encourage social harmony and
loyalist sentiment.[37] This pattern was repeated elsewhere; large
fixed capital outlays meant that financial help from 'gentlemen' was
usually necessary. The theme of class collaboration was important
and runs through the latter history of the Co-operative movement; I
deal with it at length in chapter six. Here we may briefly note the
resultant tensions which threatened the stability of these early ven-

tures. Although Matthew Bolton disputed the claim that the Birmingham Union Mill was a philanthropic enterprise, the poorer members of the society were shut out from management by the rule that required committee members to hold at least five one-pound shares. Sometimes this situation provoked open hostility between working men and their social superiors who ran the mill.[38] The success and longevity of the Hull Anti-Mill – in 1891 it had over 5,000 members and had sold £37,000 worth of flour over the preceding year – may be partially due to the fact that it was one of the most open and democratic organisations: share prices were as low as 6s 4d and there was a limit of five shares per member.

Co-operative initiatives punctuated the early nineteenth century as different groups of workers were squeezed by the process of industrialisation: in an effort to cut out big hosiers and middlemen, framework knitters in Nottingham, for example, founded a producer co-operative in 1818, a desperate remedy which quickly collapsed through lack of funds.[39] The important turning point came in the 1820s with the Owenite movement and modern social historians have recovered some of this rich history in recent years; we know a good deal about early Owenite co-operative stores and labour exchanges.[40] Importantly during this phase 'co-operation' and 'socialism' were synonymous terms. Co-operative stores were seen as a practical route to 'Community' by George Mudie as early as 1821. In 1828 Dr William King published the Co-operator in which he promulgated a similar strategy. Owenites recognised that changes in business organisation (joint-stock companies were allowed to form without the expense of charters of incorporation after the repeal of the Bubble Act in 1825) would revolutionise the socio-economic landscape but argued that workers themselves should take advantage of the opportunities which were opening up. King wrote:

> There might as well be a company of workmen as a company of capitalists. A joint-labour company is as simple as a joint-stock company . . . there was a time when joint-stock companies did not exist. Capitalists were too ignorant to form them. As the knowledge of capitalists increased, they formed joint-stock companies; and as the knowledge of the working classes increases they will form joint-labour companies . . . They will keep the enormous profits in their own hands . . . This is the first and obvious advantage of co-operation.[41]

According to the Co-operator some 300 co-operative trading associations had been established by 1830. The Owenite stores indicated that working-class associations could be built in the sphere of consumption, profits accumulated and later ploughed back into production. This mode of social transformation was preferred to Owen's idiosyncratic mixture of millenarianism and patronage. These stores in many localities were forerunners of the later, 'modern' co-operative stores.[42]

Shopkeeping was undoubtedly linked to utopian aspirations during this period but it also served more immediate ends: adulteration and truck were omnipresent during the early nineteenth century and by setting up their own shops workers sought to free themselves from these particular forms of exploitation. Although limited government intervention attempted to curb the worst excesses in 1831, truck persisted throughout the century, particularly in more isolated regions like the South Wales valleys.[43] Again Thompson's insight is helpful; co-operation, which sought to regulate market relations according to customary notions of justice, referred back to and extended the praxis of 'moral economy' within an urban, industrial environment. Co-operative trading thus enjoyed widespread appeal amongst working-class radicals; it was enthusiastically adopted by more overtly 'political' Chartist groups for example. Owenism, especially on the theoretical level, tended to eschew the political sphere and regarded political agitation as diversionary. In contrast, Chartism prioritised this arena and sought creatively to relate the economic, the political and the social. Chartist strategy – most effectively outlined in the so-called 'Ulterior Measures' recommended in the May Manifesto of 1839 – consisted of an imaginative mixture of direct and indirect tactics aimed at undermining the state. These ranged from general arming, through the 'Sacred Month' or general strike, to 'exclusive dealing' – only trading with shopkeepers sympathetic to the democratic cause. The latter was regarded as a way of undermining the 'shopocracy' and had been advocated in the radical press since the middle class 'betrayal' of 1832.[44] It was also widely acknowledged that the threat of a general strike would remain hollow unless the working class could provide for their own immediate needs.

Exclusive dealing led rapidly to the formation of Chartist co-operative stores, again sometimes explicitly regarded as a way of building a way out of the competitive world but always closely connected to the question of state power. Bradford had a co-operative society which functioned as a Chartist association in its own right. In Nottingham in 1840 the local Chartist leader James Sweet advocated co-operation in the pages of the *Nottingham Review* in the following uncompromising manner:

> To you who are of the slave class, who have no part in the constitution – to you who know and feel the miseries of the poor, who wish to be free in reality and not in name only – who wish your homes to be comfortable, your wives happy and your children educated – who wish to labour and enjoy the fruits thereof – I would point out a large part of your duty which you have too long neglected, and urge you to adopt it [exclusive dealing] without delay, and overthrow the tyranny that oppresses you and redeem your class from slavery, want and woe.[45]

Consumption was therefore regarded as an intensely political sphere. As the working-class domestic economy was usually controlled by women it is not surprising that they were particularly active in this crucial phase of co-operative development.[46]

The late 1830s and early 1840s were marked by moments of acute confrontation between an increasingly interventionist capitalist state and a well organised working class. Chartist co-operation took on greater importance after the failure of direct, insurrectionary tactics in 1839. The defeat of the general strike in 1842 and the subsequent 'show trial' of Chartist leaders forced the lesson home further and also set the parameters for a visibly 'modern' system of labour/state relations. Strict divisions were made between economic, social and political activity during the trial; subsequently trades unions could only legitimately pursue the former. After this date direct confrontation with the state became less prominent within working-class transformative ideology and practice. Labour's political and cultural revolution was fractured as the former seemed less and less feasible in the foreseeable future.[47]

An increasing amount of associational activity was channelled into 'economic' and 'social' solutions to the inequality and oppression engendered by competition; Chartist decline and co-operative success were synchronous in many localities as recent studies have demonstrated.[48] Working-class co-operators colluded in the separation of spheres of activity sketched above. The original rules of the Rochdale Pioneers (1844) emphasised that politics should be kept out of co-operation; despite the mythology it was this feature of the

Rochdale model that was truly innovative and 'modern', not the discovery of the 'dividend'.[49] Such collusion was understandable given the recent failure of direct, confrontationalist tactics. But the central point is that co-operation increasingly became a 'social' project which closed its eyes to the question of state power. The 'short' political revolution (on the level of the state) and the 'long' cultural revolution (building collective, social forms) were deliberately separated and named by the capitalist state – described as legitimate or illegitimate – after a series of violent social conflicts before mid-century.[50]

The 1840s was also a key decade in the history of the relationship between the state and emergent capitalist forms of association; it is important to remember that capital as well as labour was disciplined during these years. To speak of the 'relative autonomy' of the state from the capitalist class (at least in the short term) at this time is rather an understatement; the state actively policed fractions of capital and also attempted, with a good deal of success, to reconcile antagonistic interests within what Poulantzas used to refer to as the 'dominant bloc' – capitalist agricultural, commercial and industrial interests which dominated mid-Victorian society but which were often bitterly divided over particular issues of policy.[51] Peel's Bank Act of 1844 stabilised and regulated the money supply and the Company Acts passed the same year simplified the incorporation of joint-stock companies (which now had simply to register with the Board of Trade) and drastically cut the cost of company organisation. The prospectuses of registered businesses could henceforth be supervised by a government department, ensuring some measure of accountability, if not to the 'public', at least to state servants. (Although partners or investors were still liable for the debts of their companies, limited liability was eventually conceded by Gladstone in 1856). The celebrated repeal of the Corn Laws marked the highwater mark of *laissez-faire* ideology and expressed the 'ideal' separation of economic and political domains; the former was henceforth properly left to the self-regulation of the market mechanism – the 'laws' of supply and demand.[52] As we shall see in later chapters, Free Trade finance was to have profound repercussions on co-operative theory and practice.

This *modus vivendi* between the English bourgeoisie, the capitalist state and organised labour was clearly symbolised by the Industrial and Provident Societies Act of 1852. Drawn up mainly by the

Christian Socialist J. M. Ludlow, who was keen to 'humanise' and regulate the new urban 'masses', the Act was vigorously supported by J. S. Mill.[53] It simultaneously conferred certain privileges and set certain limitations on co-operative practice. The early stores had been bedevilled by their uncertain legal position; officials frequently defrauded societies causing insolvency and sometimes ruin. The 1852 Act placed co-operative societies in a similar position to Friendly Societies, which meant that their funds were now protected against fraud. Societies were forbidden, however, to engage in banking, mining or wholesaling or to hold land. In 1855 the Act was amended making land-owning legitimate but disallowing expenditure on education. Limited liability and the right to establish a wholesale society was not granted until 1862.[54] It seems likely that during the 1850s the formal eschewal of 'politics' became generally accepted in co-operative circles; that was why sympathetic outside observers like Marx and his English disciple Ernest Jones – who both recognised the potential of co-operation – repeatedly argued that the movement must once again engage directly on the terrain of politics (and production) if the idea of a democratic and mutualistic future society was to become more than just a romantic dream.[55]

It should be stressed, against the orthodox view, that the reason working people expended more effort organising consumption from mid-century had more to do with changes in the capitalist mode of production than with any loss of vision. To adopt Marx's schema, up until mid-century and beyond, industrial capitalism was changing in character from a system of production based on the artisan and handicrafts to one based on large-scale 'machineofacture'. As the 'social forces of production of labour' were developed, the capitalist required a larger minimum amount of capital to function *qua* capitalist. Workers' formal subordination of labour under capital now became real, and their power over the labour-process consequently weakened.[56] This was a very long drawn-out, uneven process[57], but it was one which made it more difficult (though not impossible) for the working class to undertake productive ventures, because of the large amounts of capital employed, in certain sectors of the economy. Strategies which highlighted the sphere of consumption acquired a particular urgency against such a background; there were good material reasons to initially embark on shopkeeping. Kropotkin recognised the usefulness of this strategy at the end of the century. Co-operative expansion he argued was 'fully accounted for by the network of distributive societies which they (co-operators) have at their command. The sale has been simplified, and production has been rendered possible by first organising the market.'[58]

The organisation of the market for basic commodities – flour, tea, sugar, bacon, cheese, butter and so on – was the key to early co-operative success. This was no mean feat: although the general adoption of the dividend on purchases from the mid-1840s encouraged the spread of co-operative stores, the long-term stability of these ventures – notwithstanding the example of the Rochdale Pioneers – was not assured. Indeed the initial failure rate was very high in the textile districts of Lancashire and West Yorkshire, the heartlands of the shopkeeping movement; about two-thirds of societies founded in 1851–2 collapsed within a decade. The early 1860s witnessed the most impressive wave of expansion in Yorkshire, the North-West and the coal mining districts of the North-East. In 1881 the British Movement could claim 971 distributive societies and 547,000 members; this had risen to 1,438 societies with almost 1.8 million members twenty years later. In 1901 approximately 67 per cent of all co-operators in England and Wales were concentrated in the North-East, the North-West and Yorkshire; by contrast the South-East had only 4.6 per cent. By the outbreak of the First World War the number of societies in Britain had contracted slightly to 1,385 though membership had increased to well over 3 million.[59]

Most retail co-operatives had been set up by and for workers whose wages were usually regular, if not necessarily high, and by the end of the century large numbers of railwaymen and miners, textile and engineering workers, had been converted to the co-operative cause. Many workers benefited from the gradual, if halting, rise in money wages in the second half of the nineteenth century and this helped stimulate demand. G. H. Wood's index shows that money wages increased from 100 in the base year 1850 to 180 by the turn of the century, though this long-term trend conceals major fluctuations as wages moved in line with the trade cycle. Prices of many foodstuffs remained fairly stable after mid-century, then fell by approximately 40 per cent from the mid-1870s to the mid-1890s, the years of the 'great depression'. From 1896 prices rose again and by 1912 had reached the level of 1850.[60] However, despite these favourable conditions, even in the industrial North there were areas which proved inimical to co-operation: ports and holiday resorts like Liverpool and Blackpool for example, witnessed only sporadic, small-scale advance because of the prevalence of casual labour and irregular earnings. Southern England as a whole, apart from industrial centres such as Gloucester and Plymouth, continued to be largely untouched by co-operation. Likewise despite its massive potential London – where casualism and a shifting population presented major obstacles – remained a 'co-operative desert' until after the First World War.[61]

Although individual societies were deeply rooted within specific localities they shared certain basic characteristics and were part of a movement which had a national organisational structure by the early 1870s. Profits were divided between members according to the value of goods purchased during a quarter; membership was conferred by the ownership of a £1 share which could be bought with accumulated dividend. Stores were run democratically – members had the same voting rights regardless of the number of shares held. They also supplied education and recreation (financed from the trading surplus) which was arranged by elected educational committees which regularly held delegate meetings throughout the country. Women were particularly active in these areas and in 1883 set up their own independent organisation, the Women's Co-operative Guild, a body which could claim over 30,000 members – mostly working-class married women – by the First World War. The Co-operative Union was the central, federal organisation which furnished legal advice, published literature and propaganda and promoted co-operative education. Its structure was as follows: Britain was divided into eight sections, and societies in each section elected Sectional Boards. These organised conferences and together constituted the Central Board which prepared an extensive report of co-operative activity annually. This report was discussed at the Annual Congresses, organised by the Co-operative Union and held every spring from 1869. A committee consisting of two representatives from each Sectional Board elected the United Board which was the executive governing body. The Union was supported by subscriptions from local societies.

Most societies were also members of the English or Scottish Co-operative Wholesale Societies (established in 1863 and 1868 respectively) and subscribed to these bodies according to the size of their membership and elected the boards of directors. In 1883 the annual net sales of the English CWS already amounted to over £4.5 million.

In contrast competitive retailers were poorly organised and it was not until multiple shop retailing expanded, particularly from the 1880s, that the benefits of similar economies of scale were felt.[62] During the late nineteenth century the English CWS invested heavily in productive ventures, and although ignored by Payne in his important survey, it was one of the largest companies in the world by the early 1900s. If we take capital as a guide (as Payne does) the CWS was the sixteenth largest company in Britain in 1905 with almost £4.4 million in capital, way ahead of Lever Brothers, Huntley and Palmers or Brunner Mond. By 1914 annual net sales stood at nearly £35 million and total capital had increased to approximately £9.9 million.[63] The movement's visibility in the late Victorian and Edwardian periods contrasts vividly with its marginalisation by recent historians: the numerous stores in working-class neighbourhoods; the elaborate central emporia with their libraries, concert halls and reading rooms in the centres of northern towns; the boot and shoe, soap and jam, biscuit and hosiery factories made the Co-operative movement a central feature of the urban landscape. Many commentators, across the political spectrum, debated the significance and meaning of this phenomenon, for had not all this been achieved without the help or intervention of either experts or capitalists?

IV

A re-assessment of the cultural politics of the Co-operative movement in the late nineteenth and early twentieth centuries is clearly long overdue, for not only is this subject of major importance to students of labour and working-class history generally, it also has a direct bearing on a growing area of recent scholarly debate – the origins and growth of the so-called 'consumer society'. The sphere of consumption has only latterly attracted serious attention. Economic and social historians have tended to concentrate on forms and relations of production; consumption has usually been treated negatively, as merely the end point of a prior and more important process. On the Left, consumption has too often been regarded as merely a sordid and seductive sphere, necessarily generating new modes of 'false consciousness' and totally distinct from production, the latter a source of authenticity and 'species being'. For many, a causal connection between increases in consumption and the decline of revolutionary fervour has simply been assumed.[64] This notion, usually mixed from the 1930s onwards with a good dose of anti-Americanism and a rejection of 'modernity', has been very unhelpful and has seriously hindered our historical and political understanding of the relationship between working-class consciousness and consumption practices. In recent years scholars across a wide range of disciplines have become increasingly dissatisfied with earlier dismissive treatments and it would be useful to briefly outline how some of their work has influenced and provoked my own thinking.[65]

From a position firmly within the tradition of Marxist economics, Michel Aglietta has attempted to overcome the disabling opposition between production and consumption. In his suggestive theoretical study Aglietta argued; 'As long as capitalism transforms the labour process by the creation of collective means of production, but without re-shaping the mode of consumption, accumulation still progresses only in fits and starts.'[66] According to Aglietta mass production and mass consumption are internally related and the stabilisation and expansion of the American economy between the wars was made possible by 'the capitalist production of the mode of consumption'. Fordism reduced the unit cost of articles of mass consumption and aided by increased credit facilities and New Deal welfarism which cushioned demand, helped create a 'social norm of working-class consumption'. Thus the triumph of American capitalist civilisation depended as much on transformations in the sphere of consumption as production.

More recently, in his postmodernist treatment of the commodity form, Thomas Richards has drawn attention to the specificities of what he has termed the 'commodity culture' of Victorian England and proposes a solution to the production/consumption antinomy, a solution derived mainly from critical theory. Richards takes up Baudrillard's insight that modern culture is quintessentially a commodity culture complete with its own sign system and adds Debord's emphasis on 'spectacle' as a rhetorical mode of exaggeration and excess which encouraged consuming subjects to interpret this material culture in particular ways. Thus, for Richards, 'In the spectacle production and consumption are paired moments in a single moment of commodity representation.'[67] It is the modern art and industry of advertising which enlisted spectacle in the service of the commodity, and in a set of fascinating essays, Richards explores the meanings of the sign system manufactured by advertising within various domains: exhibitions, monarchy, empire, the body.

As will soon become apparent I have found both these approaches useful though far too functionalist; the dominance of commodity culture and the production of a particular mode of consumption is regarded as an inevitable though deplorable occurrence. There are echoes of Weber's notion of capitalism as an 'iron cage' here. Within such schemata, consumption once more becomes part of the larger tragedy of modern life, a site of mystification and disillusionment. Though anthropologists like Daniel Miller have suggested a different approach – one that celebrates commodity culture and stresses the agency of consumers and their ability to manipulate meaning or 'recontextualise' particular commodities – this merely bends the stick too far in the other direction and ignores questions of power, difference and association.[68] Instead we need to discover and explain the social organisation of consumption, to put consumption back into the whole social process as Douglas and Isherwood have correctly insisted.[69]

In this book I argue that the dominant modern mode of mass consumption which emerged in England in the late nineteenth and early twentieth centuries should not be regarded as inevitable or the only available alternative and this is why the neglected social history of co-operation is so important. The Co-operative movement developed a transformative social and economic strategy based on the association of workers within the sphere of consumption.[70] Participation and membership were counterposed within co-operative discourse to the passive and homogenised 'masses' so beloved by capitalist entrepreneurs. Co-operation, as I argued above, attempted to moralise economic relations. G. J. Holyoake, for example, praised co-operators who had fully grasped the idea that 'morality has material conditions'; Edward Jackson, the historian of the Bristol Society, suggested that the medieval idea of industry was 'essentially moral' and asserted that 'the Co-operative movement of today sets out to exhibit the same spirit of fraternity' as had the local guilds.[71] This vision frequently clashed, in theory as well as in practice, with capitalist understandings of consumption, hence my key hypothesis: that the constitution of a particular mode of consumption generated fierce and protracted social conflicts which were just as heated and important, though often not as visible, as those which occurred around production.[72]

Admittedly there has been some valuable historical work on consumption in this period but it also tends to be whiggish; Fraser's general overview is a good example here. Benson's recent introduction to these themes is a marked advance but makes only cursory reference to the co-operative alternative to mass consumption.[73] The problem with Fraser's work in particular is that it takes for granted what should be a central problem for analysis, namely the constitution of the 'mass market'. It is certainly true that the language and institutional forms of 'mass society' – which included the 'mass market' and 'mass consumption' – were refined and generalised during this period, but these forms did not fall from the skies, nor were they the only alternative on offer. As Supple has argued, 'Mass markets (like any other sort) are created as well as discovered . . . .'[74] As many workers enjoyed higher earnings during the late nineteenth century they were faced with a bewildering array of commodities from which to choose. And the choice between Sunlight Soap, Lipton's Teas or the products of the Co-operative Wholesale Society, the choice between being a co-operator or a 'mass consumer', was a cultural and political choice of major consequence. No object of material culture was necessarily anti-revolutionary; what really mattered was how the consumption of particular goods was organised socially through different and competing forms of association.

The Co-operative movement was deeply involved in the construction of a culture or 'way of life', a rich and complex 'signifying system', and this culture provides the major focus for this study.[75] The songs co-operators sang at their soirées, the newspapers they read and classes they attended, their attitudes to the past and the future, the quality of their social relations with each other, the bread baked in co-operative bakeries, were all components of this 'signifying system' and can furnish important insights into what it actually meant to be a co-operator in this period. For the local and national leadership the purpose of this movement culture was to create an active membership and thus generalise the moral economy of co-operation. Although the ideal invariably outran the reality, to see this intervention merely as part of a 'culture of consolation', which helped defuse and contain revolutionary potential, seems particularly wrong-headed.

However, we must be careful not to read the evidence left by activists uncritically: the notion of culture must not be used to efface difference. Most of the voices that were heard in the local and national co-operative press and on co-operative platforms were those of a minority within the working class and it would be incorrect to assume an easy fit between working-class and co-operative culture. As a number of historical sociologists have insisted, cultural hetero-geneity characterised the former and there were also important overlaps between class-cultures.[76] Co-operative culture had to be actively made, fashioned from the symbolic and organisational cul-tural resources with potential use-value for labour, though some of the most useful resources such as self-help, thrift, respectability, time-management and so forth, were also deeply embedded within middle-class culture at this time. The project therefore involved building with these resources and re-forming, 'educating' the work-ing class through a 'dialogical' association – one which not only aggregated the individual resources of its members but also defined a collective identity.[77] We cannot be completely sure to what extent the majority of members consciously affirmed the collective identity I have sought to reconstruct in the chapters which follow and I shall return to this problem (which bedevils all analyses of popular move-ments) on more than one occasion below.

Individual societies were deeply rooted within their local environ-ments, and social profile, ideology and cultural life could differ sig-nificantly between societies depending on the specificity of political traditions and socio-economic determinants. Case studies are an in-valuable way of exploring these differences and I point out where this type of work would be most useful. Moreover, although I con-centrate mainly on the English movement, its geographical concen-tration in this period means that most of my argument derives from northern societies, particularly those in Lancashire and Yorkshire. However, local peculiarities should not blind us to the fact that the movement saw itself, and was often perceived by its enemies, as a national phenomenon. The culture of the movement was a national culture and it seems reasonable to present, therefore, an analysis of the national movement. The project of this book is to convey the reach and ambition of co-operators in this period and argue a case, against the historiographical orthodoxy, for taking the movement seriously: hence a general approach is appropriate.

Consequently I have painted a picture with broad strokes and an overlapping chronology, both within and between chapters. The varieties of cultural construction I am interested in cannot be squeezed easily within a highly specific and linear time-span; co-operation was effecting a 'long revolution', a transformation which

was faltering and uneven but very different in conception and practice to ideologies which emphasised *the* revolutionary moment. Co-
operators, I shall argue, moved beyond 'trade union consciousness',
not by means of a Bolshevik Party or an elite of Webbian experts,
but by utilising and extending the 'art of association'. Most of my
material and argument relates to the period 1870–1930. By 1870
the movement had established its own national press and an increasing amount of money was expended on the cultural activities which
concern me most. By 1918 co-operators had a clearer idea of the
type of transformation they hoped to effect, and by the end of the
war this vision seemed concrete, realisable in the near future. By the
late 1920s this optimism had almost completely evaporated. I trans-
gress the chronology at various points, when earlier and later connections are most important.

The following chapter analyses the relationship between education and the ultimate utopian goal – the Co-operative Commonwealth. I consider the strengths and weaknesses of co-operative
strategy, especially the tensions which resulted from an over-optimistic assessment of the power of knowledge and peaceful persuasion, a belief shared by many autodidacts in the nineteenth century.
Chapter three explores the movement's social life, details the conflict between co-operators and private interests in this sphere and
stresses the potentially alienating effect of the 'improving' discourse
employed by many co-operative ideologues. Chapter four highlights
the internationalism which was such an important constituent in co-
operative culture, but tempers this ambition with a consideration of
the prevalence of nationalist and pro-imperialist sentiment which
co-existed and competed with the wider 'patriotism'. Chapter five
unravels co-operators' historical consciousness via an examination
of the work of G. J. Holyoake, the movement's first historian, and
the jubilee histories of local co-operative societies.

Moving beyond this hermeneutic reading of the movement culture, chapter six considers middle-class responses to co-operation
(as concept and practice), especially attempts to view co-operation
as a moderating, 'civilising' influence. I explore the linguistic inter-
sections and contradictions between some co-operative spokesmen
and middle-class moral reformers and argue for the limits to, and
ultimately the rejection of, this middle-class embrace. Chapter seven
asks why co-operators and late-nineteenth century socialists often
failed to find a common ground, fingers points of contact and mo-

ments of struggle between leading state socialists and co-operators, and emphasises the movement's commitment to anti-statist, associationist forms of economic and social transformation. Chapter eight explains how the challenge represented by the Co-operative movement was met and contained by private capital – organised increasingly along monopoly lines – and the state, particularly in the years which immediately followed the First World War. Finally chapter nine summarises the main arguments and presents a number of reflections on the experience and meanings of defeat and suggests avenues for future research.

Part one
Co-operative culture

2

Co-operative education and social transformation

Let them promote the diffusion of that knowledge and the boon of education which would extinguish superstition and jealousy, and they would have that bond of united interest which no power on earth could break asunder – they could free themselves from the toil and misery which oppressed them; they could make for themselves a heaven upon earth. *(Cheers)*

J. T. W. Mitchell in the *Co-operative News,* 7 April 1877

I

Co-operative ideologists in the second half of the nineteenth century hoped that their movement would eventually transform competitive, capitalist society into a society based on the principles and practices of mutual association. Of course there was no single or agreed doctrine which mapped out this transition, and the timing and exact nature of social change continued to generate debate. Nevertheless, a number of commentators have noted the persistence of a utopian tradition during the 1860s and 1870s.[1] Whether this ambition can be properly understood as merely 'residual' or 'rhetorical' need not detain us at this stage; the focus here is on how co-operators sought to achieve the substitution of one form of society and economy by another. Like the Owenites before them, co-operators eschewed the violent and sudden conquest of state power and believed that the key to social transformation in the present and the future lay in the sphere of education. The goal, pursued and articulated throughout the period under consideration, was an educated and active membership organised around, and empowered by, consumption.

We know a good deal about the Owenite and Chartist roots of this strategy and the centrality of the notion of 'really useful knowledge' within early English radicalism.[2] Although Brian Simon observed long ago that Owenism continued to inform co-operative praxis 'in a somewhat attenuated form' there has been little exploration of the connections and mutations involved.[3] This chapter does not attempt to analyse educational provision in detail – that would necessitate a separate study. Instead it interweaves and considers two major themes which recur in this book: the relationship between 'education' and the movement's transformative ambition. I argue that co-operators extended the earlier radical critique of competitive knowledge and constructed alternatives which were deeply anchored within working-class autodidact culture. As we shall see, these roots were a mixed blessing and helped undermine as well as strengthen co-operative advance.

The context for a transformative strategy based around education had changed radically since the early nineteenth century. The most important development was large-scale state intervention in this sphere and a brief consideration of the attitudes of co-operators to the emerging system would be instructive. 'Cramming' or rote learning provoked a torrent of criticism from the start; G. J. Holyoake maintained that Forster's Act of 1870 should be called 'a Bill for National Instruction', as it had little to do with education but was concerned rather with the inculcation of a rigorous, military discipline.[4] Suspicions were reinforced by the House of Commons decision in 1878 to restrict the Board School curriculum to the three Rs. Samuel Bamford, editor of the *News* between 1875 and 1898, denounced this as a sign of class exclusivity and inveighed against Members of Parliament who 'regard the children of the labouring classes as animals of a different species from the more favoured bipeds who ride in Rotten Row and hang about West End clubs.'[5] Issues of class control repeatedly surfaced. The Reading co-operator W. T. Carter put the matter very bluntly at a conference a decade later:

> They would never get a proper system of education until the working-classes took it out of the hands of the state, and [put it] under their own management. [6]

The problem with the Board Schools was that they were anti-co-operative in both form and content. As power clearly lay in the School Boards before their abolition in 1902, co-operators on a local level attempted to gain control over these bodies during the last decades of the nineteenth century. A survey of 107 societies (out of a total of 1,420) in 1892 revealed that there were 164 co-operators on School Boards and 124 school managers in England.[7]

The state system which, as Gardiner has demonstrated in a marvellous work of historical recovery, also marginalised and drove out initiatives which had developed from below in the form of private or 'dame's schools'[8], came under increasing critical scrutiny from the turn of the century. The Balfour Act of 1902 – passed by a Conservative administration to 'rationalise' the state system, and supported by Fabians like Sidney Webb – abolished the School Boards and was fiercely opposed by co-operators. It was anti-democratic, they maintained, as it replaced an elected with a nominated body and would weaken working-class participation. It also discriminated against women who could not sit on local councils. Further, it drew a sharp division between 'elementary' and 'higher' education, reserving the latter for the deserving middle-class. As the *News* declared over the Cockerton judgement of 1900:

> The upper classes are still largely convinced that education in any real sense is a social qualification to be kept for the making of gentlemen. Their interest in the matter, then, is to keep down the cost of educating the masses, which seems to them to be going too far.[9]

The Act abolished the system of grants to Higher Grade and Continuation Schools which seriously affected the movement. As a representative from the Preston Society pointed out to the Liberal leader Campbell-Bannerman in a deputation in 1901, local co-operators ran seventeen schools with 2,500 scholars. Half of these were adults, and grants amounting to £1,961 were earned which would be lost if the Bill was passed.[10]

This is not the place for a detailed history of the 1902 Act or the response it generated within the Co-operative movement[11], but we may briefly note how the critique of state education sharpened following this legislation. An article in the 'Women's Corner' of the *News* in 1906 opined that, 'the schools are ruining the people wholesale', because they functioned as a sort of prison-house for the teaching of individualist dogma: 'the worst of compulsory school attendance', remarked the author, 'is that it hands over the children, bound hand and foot, to the unholy influences of greed and trick-ery.'[12] In an article in the *Manchester and Salford Co-operative Herald* in 1911, James Haslam attacked the controllers of 'public' education, who made schools mystify and obscure rather than aid working-class understanding. Children were taught to believe that the social system was 'timeless' and 'natural' rather than historically specific and thus transformable. Why was this so? Haslam asked:

> Simply because those who controlled our schools during the private-profit making period of the nineteenth century didn't want working-class children to learn these things. They do not want them to learn these things today. They want working-class education and environ-ment to be such that make workers wage-slaves, and not thinkers and free men and women.[13]

Many co-operators argued that state education performed an im-portant ideological function, helped to structure and reinforce capi-talist relations of production and reproduction and rendered the working class dependent and divided. The Board Schools had been specifically designed to teach the competitive ethic and it was up to the movement to teach the superiority of alternative principles to its members regardless of their age. That was why co-operators were so active in this field and developed such an extensive repertoire of educational forms to meet this challenge. Some of the content of these forms will be discussed later in this chapter; first it is necessary to briefly sketch the general pattern of development.

II

Libraries and reading rooms had long occupied a prominent place in the traditions of radical education; in 1842, for example, twenty Owenite branches had libraries throughout the country.[14] Co-op-erators inherited and developed this emphasis in the second half of the nineteenth century. Perhaps the most famous co-operative library was the one opened by the Rochdale Pioneers in 1849. By 1876 the library held 12,000 volumes and the central newsroom supplied 27 daily and 55 weekly papers.[15] There were at least 55 libraries and newsrooms in Lancashire, Durham and Yorkshire in 1879 which cost £9,200 a year to maintain and stocked over 121,000 volumes. Lancashire led the field with 36 libraries, proof of the movement's strength in the North-West. These were tailored to fit working-class needs; most opened in the evenings and on Saturday afternoons, though some larger libraries employed full-time staff and were open all day.[16] Despite the fact that state initiatives expanded in this area in the last two decades of the nineteenth century (a development considered in more detail below), the scale of this provision continued to grow apace. The survey carried out by the 'Special Committee of Enquiry on Education' which reported to the 1897 Congress revealed that 376 reading rooms were maintained by 95 societies, and 131 societies supported libraries which stocked nearly 350,000 volumes and cost £16,600 per annum to run.[17] Libraries and reading rooms not only encouraged literacy but also helped root the co-op store firmly within working-class neighbourhoods.[18]

During the 1850s and 1860s there was a dearth of specifically co-operative literature to read in these institutions: libraries stocked pamphlets and Holyoake's early histories of Rochdale and Halifax, but up-to-date news about the movement was hard to come by. In the 1850s Holyoake's paper the *Reasoner* had devoted some space to these developments but it was concerned mostly with Secularist matters. In the 1860s Henry Pitman's journal the *Co-operator* had attempted to fill this lacuna and reach a national audience, but it was financially weak and never fulfilled this promise. The leaders of the movement believed that a national newspaper would be a vital means of propaganda and education and consequently from 1871 the *Co-operative News and Journal of Associated Industry* was published weekly in Manchester. Sold at the 'workingman's price' of 1d., the circulation of the paper disappointed the hopes of many. Climbing gradually from the 10,000 mark when it was first issued, by the turn of the century 50,000 copies were sold every week; this figure doubled by the end of the First World War.[19] Heavily subsidised by local societies, the *News* was a difficult and demanding read with a decidedly 'improving' tone.

A flood of co-operative periodicals appeared during the late nineteenth century. Many local societies produced their own monthly or quarterly 'records' which were distributed free to members with their groceries; there were at least 32 of these issued in all parts of the country by 1900 with a combined circulation of over 384,000 per month. This item accounted for a large proportion of local societies' educational expenditure before 1914.[20] From 1896 the CWS published a monthly entitled the *Wheatsheaf* which eventually supplanted or rather incorporated these records: the CWS supplied the inner sixteen pages and local societies not served by their own journals contributed news, reports and notices of events. This was by far the most successful journal in this period; by December 1902 over 208,000 copies were distributed to 366 societies. This included nearly 1,200 local pages which took 35 compositors about three weeks to set; the printing time was 200 hours for the inner 16 pages and 300 hours for the local material. By the end of World War One the circulation of this paper had reached 500,000.[21]

The co-operative press was regarded as a superior alternative to the vulgarity and anti-working-class bias which characterised capitalist productions.[22] Thoroughly didactic in tone, the informal education it furnished was of particular benefit to working-class housewives whose support largely determined the success of the stores. Spare time to devote to more formal instruction was a luxury for these women, but the *News* and other co-operative literature made it possible for many of them to learn about the wider movement within the home. Mrs Wrigley, who joined the Oldham Society in the mid-1870s, was a typically over-worked woman who managed to piece together her understanding of co-operation in this way: 'I can't say that I have read many books as I had no time', she later recalled, although 'I have learnt a great deal through newspapers.'[23] The Oldham Society recognised the importance of mobilising this constituency early on; the central library featured a popular Ladies' Room in the 1890s.[24]

Co-operative knowledge was also communicated by means of lectures and classes. Lectures had played a prominent role from the beginning: the speaking tours of Holyoake in the 1840s and 1850s had helped spread news of the Rochdale model throughout the country. In the later decades a phalanx of lecturers toured the national circuit; old stalwarts like Holyoake and E. O. Greening were joined by popular CWS officials like J. T. W. Mitchell, William Lander and Ben Jones who regularly denounced competition. The movement also developed formal and systematic instruction in co-operative classes from the 1880s. These were pioneered by Ben Jones and the Liberal MP Arthur Acland, who organised and taught a course on co-operative history and ideology during the spring of 1883 in order to train co-operative teachers for class work.[25] Classes did not flourish as expected, however, and only 75 pupils were taught throughout the country in 1887. The real impetus came after the publication of the 'Special Committee of Inquiry on Education' in 1897 which recommended that classes in co-operation be placed at the top of the educational agenda. The result was a sharp increase in the number of adult students, from 405 in 1896 to nearly 1,664 in 1902. On the eve of the First World War almost 5,176 students were enrolled in co-operative classes. The largest expansion however, was in classes for junior co-operators; at the turn of the century 1,967 children attended classes in junior co-operation and this figure had risen to 16,777 fourteen years later.[26]

Despite the Owenite and Chartist legacy, it would be a mistake to assume that educational advance was either guaranteed or inevitable. Initially co-operators had had to face down hostile state legislation: in 1855 the Industrial and Provident Societies Act was amended making expenditure on recreation and education illegal. The ban, ignored by most societies, was eventually lifted in 1862.[27] By the late nineteenth century competition rather than coercion had become the norm[28]; as noted above, the state colonised 'elementary' education during this period which limited the reach of democratic alternatives. Although many co-operators were clearly very unhappy about this shift and argued for greater popular control, most accepted that the responsibility for teaching basic literacy and numeracy had been taken out of their hands. Although evidence suggests that at least one society, Wallsend in the North-East, swam against this current and ran its own elementary school in the early 1870s, unlike the Owenites – and Johnson's observations are pertinent here – the common aim was no longer the substitution of an entirely different system to the one provided by the state but more often its supplementation with an education in co-operative history and theory.[29]

III

Obstacles were also encountered within the movement. Some local activists dismissed education as a waste of time and money and maintained that business success should be the overriding concern. This philistinism (it was regularly denounced in these terms) was gradually defeated as the preceding sketch suggests. Co-operative educationalists deployed various arguments to buttress their case and articulated a particular educational philosophy to which we must now turn. It is possible to identify four overlapping components of this philosophy. Firstly co-operators stressed that knowledge ought to be accessible to all, regardless of birth or status, and like all other goods necessary for human existence, knowledge should be produced, distributed and consumed in a democratic fashion. J. T. W. Mitchell, most often remembered as the pragmatic chairman of the English CWS between 1874 and 1895, never tired of repeating this notion. He has been portrayed by one modern scholar as a crude materialist, a working-class capitalist interested only in increasing the power and profits of the CWS and opposed to the idealism of middle-class Christian Socialists like E. V. Neale.[30] His advocacy of co-operative education clearly reveals the partiality of this view. At the Annual Meeting of the Oldham Society in 1876 Mitchell launched this stinging attack on educational inequalities:

> Now co-operators believed education to be one of the best elements in their system. They not only wanted to make money, but they desired to make themselves into men and women, and to cultivate their minds. By education they could make themselves equal to the highest and noblest in the land. Why should the children of any of those whom he saw before him have an inferior education to the Queen upon the throne. *(Hear, hear)* Working people and their children ought to possess as great a share of the luxuries of this world as any nobleman that breathed . . . [31]

Mitchell continued that co-operators should not accept a second-rate education but should strive to 'supply an education that was equal to any that could be got at any of the universities either in Oxford or Cambridge'.

Logie Barrow's concept of a 'democratic epistemology' helps us unravel Mitchell's mentality. In his study of plebeian spiritualism in nineteenth-century England, Barrow argues that particular spiritualist and medical discourses and practices depended on a democratic theory and definition of knowledge. Such definitions were open to everyone, favoured empiricism over abstract theory and encouraged suspicion toward established intellectuals and professions. Not surprisingly, these definitions were in conflict with, and struggled against, increasingly dominant elitist epistemologies.[32] Co-operative knowledge can be usefully read from this angle. It was inclusive and no democratic epistemologist could have been more 'empirical' or unimpressed by outside 'intellectuals' than J. T. W. Mitchell. Professor Long, an American agriculturalist, attended a quarterly meeting of the CWS in 1887 and Mitchell welcomed him in the following ironic manner:

> We are all pleased, in these days of British Associations and other grand institutions, to have men of learning in our midst. *(Hear, hear)* We rejoice in all the theories they promulgate, and so far as we are able we put them into practice; but if we cannot put them into practice we put them on one side. *(Laughter)* I never have, and hope I never shall, express universal condemnation of theorists. Theories are the basis of universal practice; and while the theorists think and we act, we trust that there will be a permanent and beneficial association between the thinker and the actor as long as the Co-operative movement shall stand. *(Applause)*[33]

An ardent Congregationalist and Sunday-school teacher, Mitchell was also active on the Educational Committee of the Rochdale Society. His line was that academic understandings or 'theories' were fine, but unless ideas were grounded in practice they were of little value. The movement had its own 'grand institutions', including the CWS, which itself performed an important educative function – a point I shall return to below.

Accessibility and inclusivity were key characteristics then: co-operative 'truths' could be easily summarised and co-operative knowledge performed a demystifying function, further requirements of a democratic epistemology according to Barrow. In their early textbook, *Working Men Co-operators* (1884), Jones and Acland stated that they wanted to encourage working people to be critical and summed up the aim of co-operative education thus:

> Its sole object would be to encourage 'thinking'. Many of our best art and science teachers will tell us that their difficulty is to prevent the work done under them to be mere 'cram', that is, an unintelligent packing of knowledge learnt by rote, and just enough of it to secure a certificate. Such work does little good.[34]

They went on to advocate discussion groups, much like those which had been used by mutual improvement societies; ideas had to be communicated in a dynamic way, not killed by dogmatic assertion. This ideal was frequently contrasted with the state system, which as Jones pointed out a few years later, imparted competitive knowledge and enforced 'cramming in certain specified subjects . . . .'[35] For Jones, competitive pedagogic practices were constitutive activities which reinforced the overall dominance of competitive economic and social forms. Co-operators continually pointed to the differences between these modes and their own educational practice.

Secondly, in a related emphasis, co-operative educationalists repeatedly urged the importance of independence in this sphere. The American radical H. D. Lloyd, who toured co-operative productive works in Britain in 1897, correctly observed that;

> It is a general thing among co-operators to furnish themselves with their own halls. They think the care and expense which they go to in the provision of their own books and newspapers, and library rooms to read them in, the best of investments, as rendering them entirely independent of local influences, which might seek to hamper them. At the beginning of the movement, the hostility of the vested and business interests often manifested itself in denying them meeting places, and the censorship of the parson and squire is still remembered and resented. Co-operators began establishing free libraries long before the Free Libraries Act. At a very early period in the movement, co-operation set before itself the task of becoming mentally independent as being quite as important as that of becoming independent in its groceries.[36]

The Public Libraries referred to by Lloyd, established after the Acts of 1850 and 1855, raised the issue of 'independence' explicitly. These Acts, as Corrigan and Gillespie have pointed out, sought not only to encourage literacy, but hoped also to 'capture' existing literate working men and make them respectable members of the 'Public'. William Ewart, chairman of the Select Committee which investigated state provision in 1849, later wrote that the most important effect of the Acts was that they had 'turned the people from Alehouses and Socialism.'[37] In reality the immediate effects were slight as the Acts were permissive and relatively few libraries were built. Various factors help account for this inaction, not least of which was that the threat posed by an insurgent working-class receded from mid-century; moral and intellectual leadership did not have to be fought for quite as vigorously in the 'age of equipoise'. Though it pulls us dangerously close to the notion of 'social control', it is tempting to posit some kind of relationship between the rise of independent working-class educational and political bodies in the last decades of the nineteenth century, especially the development of co-operation and socialism, and increasing state provision. It may have been purely coincidental that between 1887 and 1900 an average of 16–17 libraries a year were established compared to only 3–4 a year between 1847 and 1860, but this seems unlikely.[38]

Many co-operators at the time read this development as an ominous sign and argued that philanthropic provision was usually informed by the intentionality of class interest. Fears were heightened by the sale of a number of co-op libraries in the 1880s and 1890s.[39] This was not the general pattern, however, as most educational committees were keen to keep their libraries. In a letter published on the front page of the *News* in 1902, G. J. Holyoake fulminated against the practice of dispensing with co-operative libraries and asked, 'Can it be true that they [the societies] are giving up this source of priceless independence?' Holyoake worried that co-operators had no control over which texts were bought by the 'Public' libraries and the contemporary social and political context provided no reassurance; the orchestrated jingoism of the Boer War and the anti-democratic nature of educational reform served to underscore the dangers involved:

> New controllers of the public library will arise, who will dislike the books the stores have given them, will keep the books out of the catalogue, or never replace them when they are worn out. We see what revolts of opinion and practice are going on under Imperialistic influences. We see the disruption of our schools, and the alienation of our liberal teaching. Public libraries will soon share the same fate.[40]

This question was raised by W. R. Rae at the 1904 Congress at Stratford. He argued that more use should be made of the Public Libraries Act but that co-operators should ensure that their literature was stocked in these libraries. If inadequate provision was made then co-operators could establish specialised libraries. To be fair to Rae the impulse behind his recommendations was the desire to shift educational funds from this area to work in the classroom – they were a response to scarcity of funds.[41] In the discussion which followed Rae was repeatedly criticised. Free libraries were increasing in some areas like Woolwich[42], and the RACS had cut their expenditure on general literature already and concentrated on the acquisition of social, political and economic texts. But in the North public libraries were not so common. Henry Vivian remarked: 'The business of the state was to organise the rearguard of education; but co-operators should organise the advance guard of education.'[43]

Rae's paper continued to provoke condemnation. At a meeting of the North-West Educational Committees Association at Failsworth at the end of the year Mr Jepson (Darwen) thought that Rae's proposals 'would do more harm than good', and the meeting voted against the dissolution of libraries.[44] The North-West Sectional Conference of the Co-operative Union at Hebden Bridge also voiced its disapproval. Mrs Williams (Sheffield) stated that she had difficulty in obtaining co-operative books from public libraries, and Mr Crompton (Eccles) noted that there were no free libraries in his town.[45] Rae's advice was ignored by the majority of societies, and in 1912 when the Plymouth Society opened a new reading-room and library opposite its central departments, a local activist reflected on the importance of these institutions:

> Some people asked, 'What do you want reading-rooms for? What good are they in these days, when we have such splendid opportunities for reading and recreation?' These might be alright in their way, and he did not say a word with regard to the opportunities the town afforded with regard to libraries. In these places, however, there was little or no co-operative literature, while in their own reading-rooms there was as much literature of that nature as could be desired, so that our members could make themselves more conversant with the co-operative movement than previously.[46]

Between 1911 and 1915 the cost of maintaining reading-rooms and libraries by the Leeds Society was consistently one of the top four items in the educational expenditure account. Although in the long-term the outlook looked bleak as the number of Public Libraries continued to grow – Rae's assessment was sound – before the First World War co-operators doggedly held on to their own libraries.[47]

Independence in the educational sphere, it was hoped, would enable successful association. 'Education' broadly conceived was deeply ingrained in the democratic structure of the movement: joining a local society, attending meetings and events, brought people into contact with co-operative principles and practices. Activists believed that a specifically co-operative education would help strengthen the affective bonds which developed between members within the sphere of consumption. From this perspective, co-operative knowledge was more than just the accumulation of certain ideas and facts but implied a particular sensibility, one which emphasised humanity's *social* nature. Holyoake frequently articulated this idea:

The education fund created by the Pioneers was to prepare members for 'companionship'. They did not require classical, scientific and historical knowledge in order to sell oatmeal and candles. It was the *social education* [my emphasis] which goes before and after which they had primary need. Education is not co-operative because it is given to co-operators by co-operators, unless it is conducive to the formation of the co-operative mind . . . No one will accuse me of undervaluing general education. The education of the schools is of supreme service in public citizenship, but co-operation is a school of social citizenship, with requirements which erudition does not supply.[48]

Note the separation of 'public' from 'social' in this context; this points again to the fact that the earlier strategy of substitution – a strategy in which Holyoake himself had played a full part as an Owenite lecturer – had faded by the late nineteenth century. Nevertheless, a 'social education' which went beyond mere 'erudition' was still a vital necessity for co-operators: Holyoake's aim was to encourage the formation of active 'associates' rather than passive, individual 'consumers'.

Many shared this vision, including J. T. W. Mitchell. In his address to the Leicester Congress in 1877 quoted at the start of this chapter Mitchell, employing a characteristic religious idiom, argued that education would secure 'that bond of united interest' which would allow co-operators to create 'a heaven upon earth.'[49] Much later, in a somewhat drier vein, Harry Snell, a Fabian member of the RACS asserted that

education teaches combination. The lower you go in the scale of intelligence the less the power of association. On the other hand the most intelligent of the people are always found in Co-operation, Trade Union, Socialist or Reform movements. Who can doubt that as education – real education – advanced, these movements would grow in numbers and strength.[50]

Snell's tone was assuredly 'improving' – a point I shall return to presently – and lacked Mitchell's millenarian passion, but the drift was similar. Association without education was inherently unstable and therefore liable to collapse at the first hint of crisis.

The final aspect followed naturally: a social education, it was argued, supplied by an independent and organised working-class, would eventually result in liberation from 'the toil and misery which oppressed them', as Mitchell put it. At the Oxford Congress in 1882 Ben Jones argued that the success of co-operative education 'means the reduction of the profits of capital as capital, and the gradual emancipation of labour, till it occupies its true place in the world, and is crowned with the dignities which its necessity and its usefulness demand for it.'[51] At a conference later that year he maintained that what working people needed was an understanding of 'political economy'; but not the liberal-bourgeois variety with its arid gospel of supply and demand, which only shored up capitalism and attempted to 'explain' existing inequality and suffering as 'natural' aspects of an otherwise perfect system. Instead Jones argued for a co-operative political economy which challenged the shibboleths of the market place and the capital/labour relationship:

> The essence of the whole problem was this, that the great bulk of the wealth of this country belongs to the few, and the work has to be done by the many . . . If working men would but get the necessary knowledge they might very soon put this right . . . This showed the necessity of the education of co-operation.[52]

Jones's conception of 'political economy' bore more resemblance to the Owenite notion of 'social science' – indeed he often referred back to this phase – than it did to the teachings of Alfred Marshall.[53] Perhaps he preferred this term because by the 1880s 'social science' had been effectively displaced from its earlier radical location and was now a site of organisation and practice for middle-class intellectuals; notably in the Social Science Association discussed in chapter six. Whatever the reasons, for Jones co-operative political economy was a form of 'really useful knowledge' which would allow workers to both comprehend and challenge the domination of capital. Soon after this he put the matter very bluntly. It was only by means of an education in co-operation, he asserted, that working men and women could secure the 'emancipation of labour from the thraldom of capital.'[54]

Both Mitchell and Jones had the highest aspirations for their movement. For them co-operative education and working-class liberation were inextricably connected; they did not accept that greater education was always beneficial, regardless of context or intention, but believed that knowledge had always to inform associational practice. This helps explain their critical attitude toward outside intellectuals who made a living from the production of what we might call purely 'scholastic' knowledge. Some academics were very keen on the movement's 'educational' potential – an issue which will be considered in detail later – and frequently urged co-operators to develop this field; many of them viewed the movement as a vehicle for individual working-class 'improvement'.[55] Co-operators in the main refused to separate 'education' from the material and social progress of the movement in this way. Mitchell's ironic deflation of academic theorists was noted above but sometimes the reaction was much more impatient. Jones maintained that lectures from University men were all very well but what co-operators really needed was an education which would help them to work together to build a new social and moral order. This keen student of history – his monumental *Co-operative Production* was published in 1894 – sometimes adopted a deliberately provocative tone to drive home the point: 'It was more important to working men to make history than to learn of what had been made.[56]

So for activists like Jones and Mitchell co-operative education was part of the general transformative strategy of the movement and could not be treated discretely. The question of strategy had been a key problem for Owenites and Chartists before mid-century as Johnson has suggested: it was generally understood that education had to be 'allied to some kind of power . . . [and have] some purchase on authority' if it was to maintain its radical trajectory.[57] Lacking an adequate social agency, Owenite educationalists had been forced time and time again to appeal to middle-class philanthropists for material help, often with disastrous results.[58] By the late nineteenth century, however, independent working-class education was firmly tied to a most powerful engine of social and economic change – a burgeoning movement which was regulating and moralising consumption in the interests of labour. The most successful and dynamic sector of this movement was represented by the CWS which expanded its operations enormously under Mitchell's chairmanship.

Mitchell himself never doubted the utopian potential of co-operation. At a meeting of the Gateshead Society in 1880 he speculated that if co-operators monopolised the country's trade, within fifty years the CWS 'could buy up the whole of the land in England.' He assured his audience that 'this was no exaggeration theory, but practical fact.'[59] Seven years later at the Carlisle Congress Mitchell declared:

Profit was made by the consumption of the people, and the consumers ought to have the profit . . . He advised co-operators never to be satisfied until they got control of the entire producing, banking, shipping, and every other interest in the country.[60]

Mitchell's vision was a reconstruction of the Owenite dream of worker ownership and control of the means of production and consumption. He believed that co-operation regulated exchange relations and moralised the market; profit (or 'surplus') accumulated by co-operative trade could be used to educate members and finance productive and commercial ventures through the CWS. Ultimately these enterprises would expand to swallow and transform the capitalist mode of production and consumption. He consistently emphasised that the relationship between knowledge and material power was symbiotic and that the success of the wholesale demonstrated that this symbiosis was now a 'practical fact'.

Despite Beatrice Webb's opinion of Ben Jones – she described him as a 'high-minded grocer' in her diary – he too shared this utopian vision. In his history of co-operative production, which trod a careful and conciliatory path between the advocates of co-partnership workshops on the one hand and the champions of the wholesale on the other, Jones reached back to the Owenite community-building phase. According to Jones modern co-operators followed

> the philosophy advocated in the Brighton tracts of 1828–9; which was, to begin with what they could do, however small, and gradually go on from this, until they co-operated for everything. When this is accomplished we shall, though it may not be in the form usually understood, then have a co-operative community.[61]

Commenting on the debate between 'individualism' and 'collectivism' from the 1880s to the First World War, Stefan Collini has written that: 'In the immense literature which was thus generated, the older Utopian tradition was largely eclipsed by the newly-imported State Socialism.'[62] Though this is undoubtedly correct in terms of Collini's chosen texts, it could be argued that the utopian tradition and the language of 'community' persisted within, or rather was re-invented by, the Co-operative movement. Jones certainly employed a neo-Owenite discourse.

Examples can easily be multiplied. The President of the National Co-operative Festival in 1907 was William Openshaw of the London branch of the CWS. At the opening of the exhibition of co-operative productions Openshaw enthused about the growth of co-operation and noted that:

> Almost every variety of the necessaries of life was now co-operatively produced, but co-operators had a long way to go before they reached the end they had in view, viz., to become a practically self-supporting and self-employing community, co-extensive with the limits of the civilised world.[63]

The same year Thomas Tweddell, vice-president of the CWS, explained to that grand body the British Association that 'when his movement succeeds in embracing the whole community then socialism will be triumphant'.[64] From the 1890s and more especially from the turn of the century the eventual goal came to be commonly referred to as the 'Co-operative Commonwealth' within the movement; no doubt the appeal of the notion of a 'Commonwealth' lay partly in its proximity to the older, Owenite language of 'community'.[65]

CWS officials, the prophets of universalised co-operation, readily adopted this term. Opening new buildings for the Birkenhead Society in 1909, Miles Parker denounced private capitalism and offered the following advice:

> Co-operators needed to husband all their financial resources, so that they might secure for themselves the instruments of labour, which hitherto had been monopolised by the capitalists. But there were great financial forces against them, and it was only by standing shoulder to shoulder that they would succeed in obtaining the real co-operative commonwealth, in which all the necessaries of life would be made secure as well as every provision for old age. *(Applause)*[66]

Local as well as national activists often cited the spectacular success of the CWS as material proof that theirs was a perfectly rational utopia. The editor of the local record of the Burnley Society reflected on the progress of this institution in 1912 and believed that it presaged a time 'when everything we need may be supplied through co-operative channels'. This would realise the movement's original ambition which was to establish 'the ideals of the Co-operative Commonwealth in our midst'.[67] The Middlesbrough co-operator, D. Lang, pointed out in 1914 that co-operation aimed to abolish profit and that this 'means that the ultimate object of co-operation is to abolish the capitalist and capitalism and to establish a co-operative commonwealth'. The expansion of the CWS had proved that capitalists were totally unnecessary.[68]

It would be over-simplistic to portray the CWS as the unproblematic bearer of Owenite ideology and practice. The community idea and the Co-operative Commonwealth coexisted with a strong collectivist impulse which threatened to undermine the more libertarian aspirations and I shall return to this problem in chapter seven. It is also impossible to quantify the desire for a Co-operative Commonwealth in the movement before the First World War or accurately assess the appeal of this notion amongst the rank-and-file. Universalistic aims, however, were commonly articulated and should not be marginalised as 'residual' utopianism or mere 'rhetoric': critical outside observers often drew attention to this aspect. The Russian anarchist Kropotkin, who had a detailed knowledge of the movement, emphasised that many co-operative ideologues thought that co-operation would lead 'mankind to a higher harmonic stage of economical relations' and noted that

> it is not possible to stay in some of the strongholds of co-operation in the North without realising that the great number of the rank-and-file hold the same opinion. Most of them would lose interest in the movement if that faith were gone . . . .[69]

Individuals like Jones and Mitchell were educationalists precisely because they believed in a rational utopia which had been made possible by utilising the advantages of large-scale production and consumption for labour and redistributing profit or rather 'surplus' to working-class families. Within this strategy, 'intellectual' and 'economic' reform were two sides of the same coin, both equally necessary to assure full emancipation.

IV

I wish now to turn to some of the problems and contradictions generated by this strategy. The first concerns the social identity and role of many of the promulgators of co-operative education. In the late nineteenth century nearly all emerged from what is usually referred to as the autodidact tradition. Though Edward Thompson recently urged caution here, as the somewhat patronising term 'autodidact' has been over-used and tends to obscure the fact that hardly any individual workingmen were 'self-taught' in a straightforward sense, nonetheless the notion of an autodidact tradition remains useful so long as we recognise that learning both within and outside the working-class family always took place within a complex web of social relationships.[70] 'Autodidacts', as David Vincent has insisted, depended upon and constructed a sophisticated network of institutions and associational forms throughout the nineteenth century.[71] Most of the enthusiasts quoted thus far in this chapter shared many formative experiences: the most important of these were a common experience of poverty and early work and a dedicated quest for knowledge and 'self-improvement', often fuelled by nonconformist religion. Some examples will illustrate these themes.

Born at Wardle near Rochdale in 1846, Samuel Bamford – who later became the editor of the *News* – worked as a half-timer in a cotton mill and only managed to attend a dame school two evenings a week. Bamford's real education was picked up in the local Methodist chapel and was later directed into co-operative channels after he attended evening classes instituted by the Rochdale Pioneers' Society in 1874. Ben Jones, the son of a dyer's labourer and a power-loom weaver, was born at Salford in 1847. After a short period at a National School, he started work in a cabinet-maker's shop at the age of nine. Jones later attended evening classes at Owens College and the Mechanics' Institute in Manchester which eventually helped him secure a position as an assistant bookkeeper with the CWS in 1866. J. T. W. Mitchell, born at Rochdale in 1828, the illegitimate son of a working woman, became a piecer in a cotton mill at the age of ten. Besides the local National and Sunday school, the young men's class at the Providence Independent Chapel in the town, as well as the Pioneers' Society which Mitchell joined in 1853, provided most of his formal education.[72] He taught Sunday-school classes in a Congregationalist chapel throughout most of his adult life.

Like many other workingmen, co-operators often had a passionate love of books. Admittedly Mitchell's reading was fairly restricted – the Bible, co-operative statistics and a dash of John Bunyan[73] – but Bamford and Jones read widely, especially in history, politics and economics. The long reviews of the 'book of the week' in the *News* were aimed at those who shared this interest. Featured texts were invariably demanding works of non-fiction: Marx's *Capital*, Shaw's *Fabian Essays in Socialism*, Kropotkin's

Fields, Factories and Workshops. The Plymouth co-operator T. W.
Mercer, who also had utopian hopes for the movement, later de-
scribed in detail the library he had built up before the First World
War. Books were living things for Mercer, who owned an impres-
sive collection of Owenite texts including works by Robert Owen,
William Thompson, E. T. Craig, Henry Travis and G. J. Holyoake.
He was particularly fond of his copy of Thompson's *Distribution of
Wealth*, which had been signed by Robert Owen himself: 'I did not
begrudge one penny of the price I paid for my copy', Mercer wrote,
'although it cost me the larger half of a month's salary.'[74]

A similar earnest sensibility is found time and again in the biographies of late nineteenth-century co-operators. As I have argued,
such individuals found it difficult to disentangle material deprivation from intellectual deprivation and argued therefore that the
movement must supply the educational as well as the bodily needs
of its members. There can be no doubt that the moral rectitude,
determination and self-sacrifice of these activists partly accounts for
the remarkable success of co-operation in this period. These qualities were deeply embedded within the culture of the nonconformist
chapels to which most leading local and national co-operators belonged; a rough measure of this influence can be gauged from the
entries for the 110 co-operators included in the first two volumes of
the *Dictionary of Labour Biography* who were active in this period.
Of these the religious affiliations of 47 per cent are known and the
overwhelming majority were nonconformists of one sort or another:
39 per cent of the total sample or 83 per cent of the group whose
beliefs are recorded. The largest denominations were Methodists
and Congregationalists, which comprised 35 per cent and 15 per
cent of the known group respectively.[75] Although he does not pursue
connections with co-operation, Robert Colls has argued convinc-
ingly that Methodism broadly construed effected a 'cultural revolution' in the mining communities of the North East in the first half of
the nineteenth century. Methodism attempted to reform working-
class manners and morals and inculcated the self-discipline and self-
reliance essential for successful association.[76] However, this
nonconformist reforming zeal may also help explain some of the
movement's apparent weaknesses and failures, for many rank-and-
file co-operators simply could not always maintain or afford the
necessary level of enthusiasm. When their devotion wavered, as it
often did, co-operative ideologues were often quick to castigate and

condemn.

The so-called 'apathy' of the majority of members was a constant cause for complaint. This criticism was undoubtedly warranted, in as much as the quantitative evidence that exists demonstrates that participation in the formal structures of societies (the election of Educational and Management Committees, attendance at Quarterly Meetings and so on) was confined to the few. Figures collated from the *Leeds Co-operative Record* for the period 1902–1918, for example, indicate that the total number of people attending ward meetings rarely exceeded 2,000 or between four and five per cent of the total membership. However, the 'earnest minority' very rarely considered that they themselves might be at least partly responsible for this inertia although occasionally a critical voice did break through: a correspondent in the *Burnley Co-operative Record* in 1914 pointed out that the same people invariably dominated the society's meetings and bored the less confident and articulate.[77] It is tempting to agree with Logie Barrow who has suggested – in a fascinating discussion of the decline of autodidact culture before the First World War – that the educated working-class minority may have intimidated more people than it attracted. According to Barrow such individuals often functioned as 'stupefiers' rather than 'energisers'.[78]

The negative impact of these 'stupefiers' can be traced in various internal debates. Take for instance the controversy over the status of fiction within the movement. Serialised fiction did appear in the co-operative press but was always didactic and invariably illustrated the superiority of co-operative principles.[79] Less 'serious' and 'improving' forms of popular literature – especially romance and melodrama – were frequently denigrated as diversionary and left largely in the hands of competitive suppliers. But despite the machinations of the Co-operative Union, members proved recalcitrant and fiction was always the most popular category in co-operative libraries.[80] Not that we should infer from this that these libraries offered only 'shallow' entertainment or that users were not interested in the more 'demanding' texts.[81] After all, the works of Dickens, or even Marie Corelli, could quite easily be read in oppositional ways: their views of the world broken down, rearranged and interpreted anew, when rubbed against the specificities of working-class experience. Moreover, such reading habits could often lead on to non-fictional texts, a point made by the old Owenite J. C. Farn in a paper at a conference

of Northern Co-operative Societies in 1874. Farn argued that novel-
reading should not be regarded as worthless and opined that

> amusement in reading is not only not bad in itself, but has a tendency
> to improve itself, and hence should be provided for in co-operative
> libraries.[82]

That these libraries stocked theoretical and historical texts useful for
labour, as well as popular novels, was important and marked them
off from 'public' libraries which tended to avoid the former. Unfortunately, within the culture of the movement this was regarded by
many as a source of weakness rather than strength.

There was also a steady stream of criticism from the movement's
leaders concerning the failure of members to support the *Co-operative News* whole-heartedly. Will Crookes defended the paper
against its critics at the Oldham Congress in 1885:

> I have heard leading men say it was too dry reading but such is not my
> experience, and I rather believe the reason for the dryness was more in
> the lack of interest in true co-operation in the reader than in the mat-
> ter contained in the paper.[83]

The charge of 'dry reading' contained enough truth to cause widespread concern. The Women's Co-operative Guild fully appreciated
the temptation that less demanding, non-co-operative literature represented for working-class women who were usually too busy or
tired to reflect upon co-operative theory and statistics. At a debate
at the WCG Congress at Oxford in 1910 a resolution was passed
urging local guild branches to increase sales through the society's
committees. Mrs Tomlinson noted that the present circulation of
80,000 was not bad considering that it was 'a class paper' (the language is revealing) though Mrs Elliot, who acknowledged the educative function of the *News*, confided that she had 'lost some
readers to whom she supplied it because there was not enough fiction in it.'[84]

The problem of how to educate *and* reach a popular audience was
ever-present and Mrs Tomlinson's apology did not solve this dilemma which continued to bedevil the movement. In her autobiography Linda McCullough Thew, who grew up in the mining village
of Ashington in Northumberland between the wars, remembered
that her grandfather always took the *News*, though

he never read a word of it. My grandfather was a shot-firer. He liked
the *Co-op News* for making his shots: the page was just the right size
and the paper the right weight.[85]

Both grandparents preferred to read the *News of the World* or
Reynold's News when they got the chance and many working
people moved back and forth between 'high' and 'low' forms of literature in a way which dumbfounded those who had swallowed
'improvement' whole. In the late nineteenth century, Garnett had
accurately described the *News* as a 'grand text-book' but how many
working-class individuals had the time, training or energy to read it
thoroughly after hard labour?[86] The same question could be put to
the *Millgate Monthly*, published by the CWS from 1905. The tone
of this magazine was also 'high class' but it did not even dent the
huge circulations of miscellany periodicals like Newnes's penny *Tit-
Bits* or Northcliff's *Answers*.[87] To turn up one's nose at 'low class'
productions simply did not help matters.

The subjects taught in co-operative classes also raise important
issues concerning the ideology and motivation of the 'earnest minority'. The most popular classes were those in technical subjects, like
book-keeping and management. In the 1913–14 session, for example, 2,886 adults entered for classes in technical subjects compared
with 1,608 who entered for courses in co-operative economics, history and theory.[88] The popularity of the former subjects can be read
as evidence of the pragmatic, instrumental way in which workers
who desired to raise their own individual social position used the
movement; a qualification in book-keeping might increase one's
chances of self-advancement in the labour market generally.
Though the success of the movement also depended on technical
and administrative expertise – it was, after all, a business – there is
probably some truth in this claim of self-advancement: once again
the entries in the *Dictionary of Labour Biography* provide some useful leads. Although only a very crude guide, the 87 wills recorded
show that a significant number of co-operative leaders left fairly
substantial estates; 31 per cent of the total left more than £5,000
although only 3 per cent left over £15,000. More had achieved comfort rather than prosperity: 44 per cent left less than £2,000 and
many of these – 12 per cent of the total – left effects valued at less
than £500. It would be rash to generalise from these figures and the
relationship between the movement and patterns of social mobility

warrants detailed study. But we can say that even if co-operative officials were not in it just for the money the business experience afforded by the movement meant that some measure of financial advancement was not an unwelcome possibility, for a few at least. Even Ben Jones continued in business on his own account after he retired from the CWS in 1902. At the time of his death forty years later (he was 94) Jones owned an hotel, a number of cafés and a bakery business in Bournemouth; the estate was valued at £10,011.[89]

If divisions and sources of possible antagonism between the leadership and the rank-and-file deserve our attention we must be careful not to freeze this notion, *pace* Robert Michels, into an ahistorical 'iron law'.[90] The mentality traced in broad terms above may help to explain why co-operation failed to attract and hold the poor working class before the First World War, though it is likely that low wages and material insecurity made the greater difference.[91] At the local level, social and ideological distinctions between activists and ordinary members may not have always been that great and we need more case studies of local societies like Smith and Walton's work on the Sabden Co-op in Lancashire, which uncovered a broad-based membership, encompassing unskilled as well as skilled workers, in a slightly later period.[92]

And we ought not to forget that even the most self-respecting co-operators often had to negotiate a narrow path between sufficiency and scarcity. In his autobiography, Jack Lawton recalled how, after his family joined the Newcastle Society sometime in the mid 1890s,

> that respectable society's cart came to our door regularly and proclaimed to all the world that we were *bona fide* members who paid for our groceries and looked the world in the face.[93]

Lawton was a miner (as well as a Methodist) and his family lived on a street near the Boldon colliery. Within this tight-knit community, membership of the store was a laudable ambition which conferred a certain measure of 'respectability', but this was understood as a fluid and changing condition rather than a fixed state. Lawton narrated this change with irony – 'we were getting to be really respectable members of society' – and closed with bathos: 'sad to relate, our family finances would still not stretch to the Store for everything we needed.'[94]

V

The second major problem with this consumption-based strategy stemmed, ironically, from its inclusiveness; although it undoubtedly contained a utopian impulse, the 'ideology of consumption' lacked a theory of social change based on the concept of 'class'. The Co-operative Commonwealth, it was thought, would be achieved by means of the gradual diffusion of co-operative knowledge and trade amongst the whole of the 'community'. The latter term may have harked back to the Owenite legacy but it also served to mask the dynamics of class. The social basis of co-operative praxis was universal, J. T. W. Mitchell insisting, for example, that consumption was something that everyone had in common, regardless of their class, creed or colour. This was the beauty of the consumptionist strategy, which did not merely focus on the organisation of men at the point of production like trade unions, or men in the 'public' sphere like most political associations, but on the organisation of whole families through consumption. According to Mitchell the 'distribution of profits on consumption was the most Christian principle in the world. It was a divine principle . . . .'[95]

Mitchell accepted (and sometimes celebrated) the fact that co-operation was predominantly a working-class phenomenon. However, this did not mean that individual members of other classes could not participate and indeed a number of the movement's most visible national advocates in the late nineteenth century, including Arthur Acland, Joseph Cowen and E. O. Greening, came from middle-class backgrounds.[96] In fact Mitchell very rarely used the term 'working class' at all but preferred 'industrious classes' or, more usually, 'working people' or even 'the people'. His model of social structure was pyramidal; the key problem was that 'profit', the result of 'industry', was being monopolised by the 'upper 10,000' rather than going into the pockets of 'the people' as a whole.[97] From this angle Mitchell, and a great many other Victorian co-operators, make ideal candidates for Patrick Joyce's 'populist' reading of social relations in England in this period. When Mitchell or Ben Jones used the term 'class' it was often in a negative way; in 1889 the latter recommended political involvement in order to 'purify' local and national government 'from the baneful effects of class'.[98] Both Mitchell and Jones (like most other co-operative leaders) were staunch, albeit not uncritical, supporters of the Liberal Party and free trade but they also had utopian hopes for their movement and were virulently anti-capitalist. They thus pose insuperable problems for the 'populist' label and it has proved far easier to forget them.

Mitchell did not believe that the existing class basis of the movement was fixed or absolute and preferred to pitch his appeal towards 'humanity'; nonconformist religion was a shaping factor here. A passage from a speech delivered at Tynemouth in 1884 makes this clear:

> In co-operation there were no class interests. Co-operation took humanity as it found it, and declared that all mankind was equal. There might be a difference of education, but co-operation tended to destroy even that. Co-operation was the one true redemption for the social evils of human life, because it declared that the profits made by every kind of industry belonged to the people who made them. *(Applause)*[99]

To Mitchell, co-operation was the working-out of a religious ideal ('one true redemption') in the secular world: 'it ran on lines that God made all men alike'.[100] The appeal to all humanity was a common theme within the movement. That E. O. Greening found it congenial causes no surprise perhaps[101]; but many leaders who were much closer to the realities of working-class life also frequently employed this discourse. For example, at the 1910 Congress W. H. Watkins argued for working-class education and criticised the old practice of inviting Lords to preside over these annual events. He quickly qualified this with the following remark:

> Co-operation knows no class. And in this connection it will perhaps be of service to again proclaim that the Co-operative movement countenances no policy of exclusion or class division.[102]

Such sentiments tended to obscure the fact the co-operation was an overwhelmingly working-class association which was in conflict with the ideas and practices of other classes and within which intra-class struggles were being waged. Lacking a sociology of class or class-conflict, many co-operators succumbed to the appeal of an abstract 'humanity'.

This problematic exerted a strong influence on educational thought and practice. I stressed above co-operators' re-working of the idea of 'really useful knowledge' and argued for the radical implications of 'independence' in this sphere, but the full picture is rather more complex than this.[103] As various historians have pointed out, universalist categories derived from the Enlightenment exerted a strong attraction on working-class intellectuals in the nineteenth century[104]; many co-operators similarly argued for 'Knowledge' in the broad sense and rejected explicitly partisan understandings. Thus links with middle class reforming educational initiatives were always possible; the alliance between co-operators and Christian Socialists during mid-century was built partly on the terrain of 'Knowledge' and this terrain continued to be a site of compromise and conciliation between the classes throughout the second half of the nineteenth century and on into the twentieth. In the 1870s and 1880s co-operators gave limited support to the University Extension Movement; and some of its leading lights, including Professor Stuart and Arnold Toynbee, regularly addressed co-operative gatherings during these decades. One of the movement's first text-books, as we noted above, was co-authored by Arthur Acland, another devotee of University Extension. Although such links were fragile and eventually disintegrated this did not rule out collaboration absolutely.[105]

The foundation of the Workers' Educational Association in 1903 raised these issues once again. Co-operators supported and were involved in the development of early WEA branches in localities such as Bristol and Reading and the founder, Albert Mansbridge, was himself an ardent co-operator.[106] Mansbridge's understanding of the forms and institutions of knowledge was thoroughly apolitical and his spiritualised, uplifting vision fitted in nicely with the views of middle-class intellectuals and reformers who regarded education as a salve which would help heal the wound of class conflict. Three years before the WEA was set up Mansbridge naïvely stated that 'in a university you are comparatively free from political influences'.[107] It was a position he was to maintain despite mounting criticism. The alternatives emerged clearly in the wake of the Ruskin College strike and the establishment of the Central Labour College in 1909. In an article in the *News* the following year Mansbridge admitted that universities should be made more democratic though he remained convinced of their value.[108] George Sims quickly responded with a penetrating question:

> Is the educational teaching of the Universities – in social science, i.e. history, economics, and political science – in line with the emancipation of labour, viz., the abolition of private trading and the substitution by co-operation?[109]

Scholarships provided by the movement had failed as a contributor to this debate in the *News* explained, because Oxford turned working-class students 'into prigs against their own class.'[110] A few even went as far as W. T. Carter who reckoned that the 'universities had been captured by another class . . . .'[111] At the Plymouth Congress in 1910 Mr W. Stevenson praised Ruskin and the Central Labour College and suggested that co-operators link up with these bodies and teach 'working-class knowledge'. Frank Maddison, the Liberal MP, alternatively recommended the WEA and the desire for 'truth' instead of partisan knowledge. In a heated exchange Mr McCarthy rounded on Maddison:

> In regard to working-class ideas, there was a right side and a wrong side; there were working-class economics and capitalists' economics. In politics, the two ideas of the rich and poor, – the possessed classes and the dispossessed – were absolutely antagonistic. Mr Maddison represented a dying cause in this movement.[112]

Mansbridge spoke in support of Maddison and tempers frayed until W. R. Rae diplomatically placated the situation.

Four years later at the Dublin Congress, Mr J. D. McDougall laid out the alternatives very clearly indeed:

> They could go to the universities and ordinary schools to get economics taught from the point of view of the employer of labour. It was the duty of the Co-operative Union to teach economics from the point of view of themselves and such must be the economics of Marx and his successors.[113]

Rae, representing more closely the mainstream position, replied that the movement was already 'teaching the economics of co-operation', though more should be done. It would be wrong to suggest that these tensions were easily resolved – they recurred. Although McCarthy's description of Maddison as 'a dying cause' was widely shared in many respects – and I shall return to this theme in later chapters – in terms of the educational praxis of the movement it was fairly wide of the mark. Local societies tended to support the WEA after the First World War rather than the labour colleges, and although we should be wary of reading too much into this – the WEA at the level of the local tutorial class was very different to the conception in Mansbridge's head[114] – the pattern was significant. The movement was shot through with heterogeneous ideological currents which sometimes intersected, and sometimes ran into each other. By 1914 the language and imagery of class frequently intruded but the earlier rhetoric, especially the appeal to 'humanity', was far from dead and continued to exert a particularly strong influence on the movement's educational strategy. As we have seen this generated fierce internal debate, but it also made it more difficult to pull together with potential allies within the growing socialist movement who shared a commitment to the Co-operative Commonwealth but questioned whether this utopia could really be achieved by an educational strategy, albeit one driven by the undeniable power of the Wholesale Societies.

3

The means of social life

There was no culture that could surpass the culture of the co-operative
store.

J. T. W. Mitchell in the *Co-operative News*, 1 October 1881

I

In recent years social historians have broadened our understanding
of both the forms and meanings of 'popular culture' in the late nineteenth and early twentieth centuries. Many groups of workers in this
period, particularly those who were skilled and in regular employment, enjoyed a gradual reduction in their working week and a con-
sequent increase in available leisure time. Coupled with a steady rise
in real wages between 1880 and 1900 – a faltering and uneven phenomenon admittedly – this meant that there was an expanding market for commercialised forms of pleasure and entertainment in
Victorian England.[1] This transformation was read in various ways.
For leisure entrepreneurs the development of a mass market for
leisure represented new and exciting opportunities for enterprise and
profit.[2] Bourgeois moral reformers, on the other hand, were deeply
concerned about this change and its presumed effects on working
people and, as Peter Bailey has ably demonstrated, campaigned for
the diffusion of 'rational recreation' which they hoped would act as
a civilising counter to the vulgar, debasing delights of the music hall
or the betting shop and serve to promote harmony between the
classes. Bailey contends that this attempt to 'police' and regulate the
use of workers' leisure time from within, by members of the reforming middle class, was ultimately unsuccessful.[3]

Within this context, historians of the organised working class have drawn up their own agenda and have offered various interpretations of the politics of culture. Stephen Yeo, for example, has argued that making a democratic, egalitarian 'culture' was a central concern for 'new life' socialists during what he terms the 'religion of socialism' phase in the social history of socialism, that is from about the mid-1880s to the mid-1890s. During these years, according to Yeo, the 'politics' and 'culture' of socialism were intimately connected in what was an eclectic, utopian critique of the existing system. Thereafter 'politics' became increasingly channelled toward and understood in terms of parliamentary advance and the 'culture' of the Socialist movement soon became depoliticised; within his account the Clarion movement degenerated into a purely recreational society from about 1895.[4] Extending Yeo's temporal framework and specific argument, Chris Waters has recently investigated the dynamics of socialist culture before the First World War and has particularly underscored the reforming zeal of its leaders. Water's discusses the changing meanings of terms like 'leisure', 'recreation' and 'popular culture' and argues that what workers did with their spare time continued to be contested throughout the period.[5] Finally, in an influential article Ross McKibbin has suggested that one of the reasons why Marxism or socialism failed to attract a mass following before 1914 was that much of the available cultural space was already occupied by working-class voluntary associations which pre-dated the introduction of Marxist ideology in the early 1880s. According to McKibbin working-class cultural practices had a diversionary rather than narcotic effect as they 'dissolved the proletariat into clubs, societies, informal association, sporting loyalties, and private hobbies, and put many working men outside the activities and claims of the official political parties.'[6]

Much of this work is highly pertinent to the themes of this chapter but McKibbin's argument furnishes the most appropriate point of entry. To buttress his case he makes a direct contrast between the British experience and the German Social Democratic Party which organised an impressive range of social and cultural activities before the First World War. The SPD was able to build a mass membership by means of its choirs, gymnastic societies, cycling clubs and so forth, although the effects of this initiative have been variously interpreted by German scholars.[7] McKibbin's comparison is useful up to a point, but it would make more sense to compare the culture of

the SPD with that of the British Co-operative movement in this period; the scale of co-operative provision was remarkable and makes
the better-known activities of the Clarion Clubs look like very small
beer indeed. To give just one example; 10,000 co-operators from all
over the country made up the United Choir which sang at the National Co-operative Festival at the Crystal Palace in 1897, yet we
know very little about this or any other of the movement's interventions in this sphere. In this chapter, I argue that the Co-operative
movement was deeply involved in the construction of an alternative
and sometimes oppositional culture or signifying system designed to
create active 'members' rather than passive 'consumers'.[8] Educational initiatives reached significant numbers, but more important
as far as the majority were concerned was the expansive social life
constructed around the stores. Again the intention is not to be exhaustive and instead two key questions structure the discussion
which follows: what did the culture of the movement mean to its
members? and why did co-operative activists consider it so important to intervene in the cultural sphere?

II

As one would expect, the second question presents less problems for
the historian that the first. As I stressed in the introduction, most
modern historians, looking through the distorting lens of Christian
Socialism, have implicitly or explicitly berated the movement for its
'materialism'. From this perspective the motivation of the majority
appears fairly unproblematic; the dividend or 'divi' which they received every quarter. This dismissive approach has not only diverted
attention away from the cultural life constructed around the stores,
but has also rigidly separated the theory and practice of consumers'
co-operation in a way which would have appalled J. T. W. Mitchell.
Material success made educational and recreational provision possible certainly, though to abstract the economic from the ideological
or cultural is very misleading. A potentially more fruitful approach
is opened up if we recognise that the production of a new culture
was not a secondary and subordinate concern but was itself intimately bound up with the production of a new form of moral
economy. The Italian Marxist Antonio Gramsci made this point
succinctly when he wrote: 'the programme of economic reform is
precisely the concrete form in which every intellectual and moral

reform presents itself.'[9]

To put the matter more straightforwardly: shopping at, and then becoming a member of, the store was the most important point of entry to the movement culture. For a great many perhaps, co-operation meant shopping and the 'divi' first and foremost, but these consumption practices were highly specific – co-op stores were not private shops run for profit – and the practice, ritual and symbolism of co-operative trading constituted co-operative culture in a fundamental sense. This was what J. T. W. Mitchell implied when he remarked: 'There was no culture that could surpass the culture of the co-operative store.' The historical significance of shopping at a co-operative store is a serious problem for analysis yet the historiography relies on little more than bland assumption and tired cliché. If, however, we bear in mind Douglas and Isherwood's suggestive definition of consumption as 'a ritual process whose primary function is to make sense of the inchoate flux of events' in order to construct an intelligible 'universe of values', we can begin to get a fuller sense of the significance of co-operative shopping.[10] And in the main it was working-class married women, the so-called 'women with the basket' who controlled the domestic economy, that built co-operative culture from the ground up and created a distinctive universe of values via the rituals of co-operative consumption.

Some concrete examples would be instructive, but immediately we encounter serious problems. Most rank-and-file members rarely contributed to the national or local press or addressed co-operative gatherings and consequently it is very hard to ascertain how they experienced shopping at the stores. Given the lack of sources it is legitimate to draw on oral and autobiographical evidence which relates to a later period as it seems likely that there were strong continuities over time. Molly Weir's autobiography, for instance, which describes her childhood in a poor working-class neighbourhood in Glasgow during the inter-war years, sheds some light on this subject. Almost as soon as she could walk Molly ran errands for her mother and grandmother and quickly learnt many of the varied and ingenious ways women made ends meet on very limited budgets: 'We children of the tenements were aware of the economy of daily living.'[11] Women handled material constraints creatively, conjuring nutritious and appetising meals out of the cheapest ingredients and children, especially girls, were schooled in this knowledge at a very early age.

The co-operative store, as Weir stresses, was an integral part of this economy of daily life. For a start it offered credit, as indeed did most other societies, despite the protestations of the national leadership.[12] But more than that, the store was a social nexus and a defining feature of working-class community and neighbourhood life which generated fierce loyalties:

> There was a Co-op about every five hundred yards in our district, but you got to know your own Co-op as though it were a club, and how alien other Co-ops seemed if you were sent there by a neighbour. But your own! Ah, that was different. So cosy. So chummy.[13]

The notion that the local store was more like a 'club' is supported by oral testimony. Miss Haigh, who was born in Huddersfield in 1903, clearly recalled the social atmosphere of the Scapegoat Hill Society before and after the First World War:

> Up at Scapegoat Hill there was a distant relative of ours that was in the drapery department. D'you know mornings they used to go and they had a nice chat and they talked – it was like a coffee morning but they hadn't the coffee![14]

Women and children not only shopped in the stores, they also met their friends and discussed the neighbourhood news there; in fine, co-operative shopping was a social event.

The local corner shop run by private traders could and often did serve a similar social function – this helps explain their long popularity[15] – but differences were important. Firstly, working people owned both the local co-operative store and the factories which produced most of the goods found in them. The CWS manufactured a vast array of staple commodities by the late nineteenth century and these were emblazoned with the wheatsheaf design. This logo had been chosen, as an early editorial in the *Wheatsheaf* magazine pointed out, because it symbolised both the essential role of wheat in the daily life of the common people and the power of association.[16] Whether most members got this message every time they opened the larder door is open to question but many societies believed that it was essential that the majority fully recognised that they owned the movement, most especially the impressive factories and workshops run by the CWS. Consequently, day trips to CWS works were a common and popular feature of co-operative culture throughout my period and beyond. In the inter-war years films showing the production of co-operative goods in CWS plants were regularly screened in co-operative halls.[17]

Secondly, shoppers were usually treated differently in the co-op store. There was no attempt made to hoodwink the customer into purchasing unnecessary items or spending more than was originally intended. This was a stock theme of co-operative discourse, nicely captured in an anonymous Lancashire dialect poem in the mid 1890s:

Of course yo'll not find that fal-der-dal stuff
    Yo get i'these private consarns,
Wheer they deal i' soft soap an' a' sorts o' puff
    So lung as yo' swallow their yarns.
Yo'll get no palaver like that at the Store,
    Ther's noane o' that snake i' the grass;
They'll sarve yo' wi' what yo' may want an' what's more,
    They'll give yo' good value for th' brass.

An' then, when yo've spent what yo' set eawt to spend,
    Yo need not be feart they'll say –
Now anything else can I sell you my friend,
    I've some splendid butter today.'
They tak' it for granted yo' know what yo' want,
    Witheawt so mich fuss or ado;
They'll never persuade yo' wi' blarney or cant,
    To spend a'yo'r brass like a foo'.[18]

As members as well as customers, working people were treated civilly, though not deferentially, no matter how meagre their income or expenditure. This was a very important consideration, especially when it came to the purchase of relatively expensive articles of furniture or dress. For people on low or restricted incomes, shopping for such commodities could be a highly traumatic experience, a potential source of embarrassment and shame if one's desire outstripped one's purse. Although Molly Weir loved her local store, wider perspectives opened up when her mother took her to the grand central branch to buy her a new pair of shoes. She recalled that, as this was an important outlay, they took their time making up their minds: 'Nobody felt rushed, for we all knew that shoes had to last for a very long time, and money was scarce and we couldn't afford to make a

mistake.'[19] This archetypal ritual of consumption nicely demonstrates how shopping at the co-operative store strengthened the
pride, self-confidence and independence of working-class women
and their families. Shopping in this context made them powerful.

Many of these larger purchases were paid for out of accumulated dividend. The 'divi' appealed strongly to working-class
women, though how we interpret this popularity is a difficult
question. Rather than regarding the 'divi' *a priori* as evidence of
'embourgeoisement' and the successful penetration of working-
class culture by capitalist ideology, a more sympathetic reading
may perhaps be suggested. The dividend was distributed every
quarter or half year by local societies and the ritual of the 'divi
day' lent a specific rhythm which regularly punctuated the annual
cycle of working-class community life. It was a time of celebration
and excitement for those who could afford a little luxury and relief
for many others who sorely depended on the extra income to meet
pressing needs. An anonymous contributor to the *Failsworth Co-
operative Messenger* struck a common chord in 1913:

> I thank the day I became a co-operator. I have been a widow for fif-
> teen years, and had to earn my own living, and thankful that I have
> my 'divi' to draw at the quarters' end – it pays for coal . . . The advice
> of my mother, a staunch co-operator, who died at the age of ninety-
> one, was 'keep true to the store and the store will keep true to you.'[20]

Working-class married women frequently negotiated a narrow
path between scarcity and survival and found the 'divi' invaluable,
part of the 'common sense' passed from generation to generation,
mother to daughter, which informed their family and community
life. Joining a store and getting a check number was a rite of passage
which usually coincided with getting married and setting up home
independently. Women were often remarkably adept at 'rational
forecasting', budgeting and maximising their 'divi' in the short and
long term.[21] The 'divi' was put to different uses, depending on the
particular family circumstances – whether the husband was employed, family size and so forth – and the life-cycles of individual
households. Those who were slightly better off or better organised
often let their 'divi' accumulate and used it to finance an annual
holiday. Mrs Scrimshaw explained why her mother, who had two
children but a husband who only gave her 18 shillings a week out of
his low wages, let the 'divi' accumulate with the Leeds Society be-

tween the wars:

> Mother always left hers in to go on holiday with. And perhaps it'd be about £5 for the whole year, perhaps not that sometimes depending on how much the 'divi' was and we used to go to Blackpool for a week on that 'divi' . . . She wouldn't draw the 'divi' because, no, this had to be for the holiday. She couldn't save money out of dad's wage. This was the only way.[22]

Regardless of these particular uses, the 'divi' encouraged and made possible a less fatalistic attitude to time. The future was no longer a matter of chance and luck but could, within limits, be planned, predicted and constructed.[23] Women knew where the next pair of shoes or delivery of coal or even a holiday was coming from. But that was not all; by remaining 'true to the store' these women were making the culture of co-operation every time they shopped at the co-op or queued for their 'divi'.

III

Although the rituals of co-operative trade constituted the basis of the movement culture, a wide range of recreational activities were organised around the social nexus of the store including tea parties and soirées, festivals and choirs, field days, galas and outings, demonstrations and marches. Activists generally agreed that the movement should supply not only honest goods and co-operative knowledge but should also try to meet the recreational and social needs of its members. James Clay, for example, emphasised that the Coventry Society had sought to propagate co-operative ideas and provide members with 'the means of social life' from the mid-1870s when the first Educational and Recreational Committee was established.[24] Why did co-operators think it important to develop the social life of the movement? A number of reasons stand out, not least of which was the desire to demonstrate the superiority of co-operative forms of trade to as wide an audience as possible. Private capitalist traders employed advertising to secure custom but these modes were rejected by the movement's local and national leaders, who were extremely hostile towards what J. T. W. Mitchell once called 'the Barnum wickedness of the competitive world'.[25] If anything this hostility increased after the advertising industry was revolutionised and professionalised in the 1880s and 1890s in conditions of large-

scale capitalism.[26] To co-operators advertising was nothing more
than a legalised form of fraud and trickery and had no place within
a reconstructed moral economy.

One of the main functions of the social life of the movement, then,
was propagandism and the commonest form of recreational activity
– also employed by Chartists and Owenites in the 1840s – was the
tea party or soirée.[27] In his jubilee history of the Leeds Society G. J.
Holyoake noted that the free tea parties organised by the society
during the mid-1860s were regarded as an alternative to the 'pre-
vailing system of trade-puffing and advertisements'. Holyoake recorded that over 2,500 members were entertained and believed that
the parties had helped to create 'a new social feeling' among the
members.[28] At these events, usually held during the winter months,
tea and other non-alcoholic refreshments, sometimes a meal, were
served to members and their guests, followed by a programme of
music and dancing. Co-operators in Halifax also held their first tea
party in 1865 and the society's historian recorded that they consumed 300lb of ham and 100lb of beef alone![29] By the early 1870s
co-op teas were a regular feature of working-class life, especially in
Lancashire and Yorkshire. In 1873 the *Co-operative News* commented: 'The soirées that have taken place have been so numerous
during the present season that space will compel us to curtail our
notices of them.'[30]

Local societies spent a substantial portion of their educational
funds subsidising these events. The Halifax Society, for example,
spent £38 15s 0d on three free tea parties and two socials in the
winter of 1900.[31] Cost was usually on a sliding scale with a lecture
invariably sandwiched between musical entertainment in an effort
to combine instruction with pleasure. The Leeds Society commenced its social season in 1900 with a 'grand tea and concert'
which included an address by W. R. Rae, a member of the Central
Board of the Co-operative Union. The cost was 9d for adults, 6d
for children or 3d without the tea. The usual cost for concerts, if
anything, was 1d.[32] The previous year the secretary of the Manchester and Salford Society described how thousands of men,
women and children had participated in these events and proudly
observed that 'the speaker has frequently won as much applause as
the artistes.'[33] This form remained popular up until the First World
War although some commentators believed that its importance
was gradually declining. In the long run the conviviality offered by

the pub, the music hall and later the cinema, proved more seductive, though co-operators did not accept these developments passively.[34]

Exhibitions of co-operative productions served a similar propagandist role. Again, this form was not new but dated back to the exhibitions of industrial goods organised by the Mechanics Institutes in the 1830s which had been designed to inculcate 'better taste' in the 'lower orders'.[35] Local co-operators made increasing use of this cultural form from the 1870s, though with different intent: exhibitions were indices of material success and simultaneously dramatised the potential of co-operative production. As Jackson remarked of an exhibition held at Bristol in the mid-1890s:

> The Exhibition of Co-operative Products did much to open the eyes of members and the general public to the vastness of the Co-operative movement; moreover it stimulated many members to show more loyalty to the principles of co-operation by demanding goods of co-operative manufacture from the store.[36]

Displays were carefully arranged and large numbers of members were involved in their organisation. A report of the Midland Exhibition (a joint affair organised by societies in this section) held at Rugby in 1897 noted that 'so great was the crush at one time that the doors had to be closed against the public – but only temporarily of course, because in our exhibitions, like our movement, we want everybody to come in.'[37]

The largest exhibitions were arranged under the auspices of the National Co-operative Festival held annually at the Crystal Palace at Sydenham Hill between 1888 and 1910. Edward Owen Greening was the driving force behind what G. J. Holyoake referred to as a 'brilliant extension of the Exhibition idea.'[38] At least 140 societies subscribed to the 1889 Festival and funds of £1,300 were raised. Festival day commenced at 9 a.m. on Saturday 24 August and the exhibition was opened at 9.30 a.m. by Hodgson Pratt. The rest of the day's activities included a demonstration of Edison's phonograph, a testimonial to Mrs Lawrenson of the Women's Co-operative Guild, members' arts and crafts exhibitions, a gigantic flower show, athletics and a balloon ascent. The Handel Orchestra and a choir consisting of 5,000 voices gave a concert between 4 p.m. and 6 p.m. Performing elephants, backed by a brass band, entertained in the gardens, followed by a spec-

tacular fountain display. A play was performed in the theatre at
7 p.m. while E. V. Neale delivered the presidential address in the
great concert hall. As dusk fell the gardens were illuminated and at
8.30 p.m. a floral ballet entitled 'A Golden Dream' was performed
outdoors. The day ended with a bang – a great fireworks display,
the crowning attraction of which was a flaming co-operative
wheatsheaf. The 'hymn' used for the festival had been written the
year before by Lewis Morris and was entitled 'The Triumph of Labour'. Over 32,000 people attended.[39]

Greening conceived the festival as a stimulus to co-operative
growth in London and the South, a region often described as a 'co-
operative desert' at this time. Moreover, it served to demonstrate
the movement's importance to society at large and it was a great
success in this respect. From 1888 onwards, 'the press awoke to
the fact that working-class co-operation was a power in the land,
and the movement secured a large increase of public recognition
and respect.'[40] This was almost an understatement, for the London
press coverage of the festivals was exhaustive, in contrast to the
relatively muted response of Northern newspapers, where co-operation was already an integral part of working-class life. Determined efforts were made to make the festival accessible and cost
was kept down: in the 1890s the rail fare from London was 1s 6d
including admission, for children it was half price. Arrangements
were made with railway companies to secure reduced rates for
parties from the provinces.

In 1893 the festival was extended from one to five days, Tuesday
to Saturday. By 1895 it could be described as

> the great object lesson in co-operation. The tens of thousands of co-
> operators – perhaps themselves the greatest sight of all – the exhibi-
> tions of productions, the gigantic choir, the flowers and fruits from
> workmen's gardens, the speaking, the sports, make up a day not to be
> forgotten. Nothing else helps one to realise the movement as a great
> living organism.[41]

The attendance in 1896 reached 41,755 for 'Festival Saturday'
alone, and visitors travelled from over 100 miles (160km) away,
arriving from 8a.m. at the Palace. New features were continually
introduced. Children's sports, musical drill and choir contests, grew
in size and importance. By the late 1890s over 5,000 exhibits were
sent to the flower show. The senior choir grew as local societies were

prompted to establish choirs to send to the festival; the United Choir numbered 10,000 in 1897. Cricket matches were arranged between societies and photographic displays began to appear.[42] This festival was clearly an important and highly visible phenomenon in England in the late nineteenth and early twentieth centuries.

The principle of inclusion deeply informed the social life of the movement. Tea parties, exhibitions and festivals were aimed at working-class families as a whole and were intended as alternatives to the male-dominated world of the pub or the betting shop. Although women were excluded from most 'public' terrain, whether middle or working-class, they could and did participate in the creation of the movement culture. Only a few reached managerial positions but many more were active on the educational and recreational committees of local societies: by 1889 at least 42 women sat on these committees, while two years later the figure had risen to 73 and by 1904 a total of 238 women from 108 societies in the Co-operative Union held this position.[43] Family-based forms of pleasure which included children were considered vital to the long-term success of co-operation. The Worcester Society, for example, organised a tea party for members' children in the mid 1890s. Over 500 attended, attracted by the magic lantern show as well as the CWS buns, and a report of the proceedings noted that:

> Mrs Aylett took the chair, supported by the members of the Women's Guild, 38 in number, and the general committee (or board of directors) with their wives and daughters, a true co-operative family.[44]

The culture of the movement did not simply confer power on working-class women but also constrained them within prescribed gender roles – as the proverbial 'woman with the basket' – and moments such as these should not blind us to the fact that the head of the co-operative family was usually male. Nevertheless, co-operative culture did make available a range of possibilities, a certain social space, within which women could mobilise and articulate their own vision of a reconstructed social life.

The social education of children was a continuing concern. The provision of classes was noted above but informal modes were also employed to secure the loyalty of the next generation. Most societies held special Children's Days, which featured sports and singing as well as refreshment, from the late nineteenth century; in 1907 the *Co-operative News* complained that it had been inundated with

written accounts and photographs of children's galas and if all were
published they would take up the whole of the paper. Reports had to
be greatly condensed, though this caused complaint.[45] This mush-
rooming activity helped launch the movements' youth paper, *Our
Circle*, in October that year. Four years later the editor remarked:

> I have been to several of these meetings lately, and no one can possibly
> gather from the accounts which appear in cold print in the *News* the
> strength and converting power they exercise over our movement. Talk
> of enthusiasm! there are waves of it at these galas.[46]

The young were also encouraged to participate through drama by
members of the Women's Co-operative Guild. Nellie Dawson described in the pages of *Our Circle* the plays and concerts staged by
the Abbey Wood Junior Guild in 1907. The West Hartlepool Society
put on an operetta the following year in which fifty children took
part.[47] These initiatives account for the publication in 1909 of a play
written especially for young co-operators by a Lancashire Women's
Guild member, Miss Evelyn Pilkington.

Entitled *The Dawn*, this play was warmly received and quickly
became a favourite. It dramatised the co-operative message in a
mythical way: two goddesses, 'Co-operata' and 'Commercia', struggle to control the fortunes of a working-class family. They finally
call a truce and useful industry is harnessed to democratic association: thus the economy is 'moralised'. The first performance was
given by the Abbey Wood Young People's Circle at the Working
Men's College in London in October 1909. The organisation of
drama groups was a lengthy process, but just over a year later reports of performances can be found in the *News*. Between February
1911 and December of that year at least eleven societies – mostly in
Lancashire and Yorkshire – performed the play. The Chester Society's drama group toured the district; it was estimated that over
4,500 adults and children attended nine performances. This type of
activity was to flourish in the inter-war years.[48]

The social life of the movement served as an alternative to commercial forms of advertising and was highly inclusive; co-operative
activists also insisted that 'the means of social life' ought to be self-
provided. In this sphere as elsewhere 'independence' was a major
preoccupation. Local societies were repeatedly encouraged to supply all their own needs; music for example – which played such a
central role in co-operative culture – was considered a necessity. An

editorial in the *News* in the summer of 1884 entitled 'Music for the Millions' advocated the establishment of sol-fa classes and glee clubs linked to the stores. It was hoped that these would generate indigenous talent and render expenditure on 'outside' vocalists unnecessary.[49] Progress was slow, however, and twenty years later, at a meeting of the North-West Choral Association, Mr Booth voiced the same complaint:

> At the present time music at the various societies' concerts was always secured at a very great cost . . . frequently the musicians were strangers, whose spirit, sentiment and interest were quite foreign to co-operation and whose chief concern was the excellence of their terms. Not a word or a sentiment was expressed in harmony with, or in furtherance of, the objects of co-operation.[50]

In 1905 seventeen societies in Lancashire and Yorkshire were members of this Association, whose objects were to form singing classes for adults and children, establish string bands, compile a register of choirs and soloists and plan the interchange of choirs between societies.

Four years later the CWS published a list of 170 approved musical artists and set up a booking agency.[51] By this time co-operative songs were often performed; the Co-op Union had published its first song book over a decade before. This text included poems by William Morris – 'March of the Workers', 'All for the Cause', 'The Day is Coming' – and co-operative 'hymns' such as 'The Triumph of Labour'. These were chosen to propagate the 'ethical principles on which the movement is based' and combat 'middle-class materialism'.[52] Both the ambition and quality of local choirs was impressive. The Failsworth Society, for example, staged large-scale productions of oratorios by Handel and Haydn, *Messiah* and *Creation*, in their Co-operative Hall in 1910. The entrance fee was 4*d*.[53] Co-operators also took part in open competitions with non-co-operative bodies: the Burnley, Colne and Nelson Co-operative Choirs, for instance, competed at the popular Morecambe Music Festival in 1905. Amateur choirs from all over the North took part and were judged by a panel which included Sir Edward Elgar. The *News* reported that all the choirs performed well and that the ladies of the Colne Co-operative Choir won first prize in the Female Voice Competition.[54]

This commitment to independence also helps us make sense of the internal conflicts which marred the success of the National

Festival. Briefly, the festival was the brain-child of, and propaganda vehicle for, advocates of profit-sharing and co-partnership, many of whom like Greening came from middle-class backgrounds. Individuals like Greening and E. V. Neale tended to regard co-operation primarily as an antidote to class struggle and anathematised the 'ideology of consumption' and the Wholesale societies. These connections are explored further in chapter six; here we may note that goods produced by the CWS – which had abandoned profit-sharing in the mid-1870s – were always marginalised if not totally excluded from the showpiece exhibition. This generated much acrimony and convinced many that it was necessary to wrest control away from these distinguished patrons: from about 1896 alternative regional festivals were held in the North and the Midlands and these expanded as the cost of travelling to London increased.[55]

One of the largest of these was organised by the Manchester and Salford Society in 1900 and took place in the Botanical Gardens at Old Trafford. A correspondent in the *Wheatsheaf* sounded the following class-conscious (and regionalist) note:

> It seemed only fitting, therefore, that the Co-operative Festival should have been held here in the North, because it is the home of the mass of the working people of this country and co-operation is ideally a movement of the working-classes.[56]

The festival lasted four days and was attended by about 60,000 people. Northern societies rallied support – the Pendleton Society alone sent 5,000 members. The cost was 4*d* for children and 1*s* for adults and almost thirty concerts were held over the four days. Friday was 'Children's Day' and several schools in the area were forced to close as over 15,000 children enjoyed the free entertainment and refreshment provided.[57] The aim of the large exhibition was to present a 'thoroughly representative' display of co-operative productions and consequently CWS goods were highlighted. At the opening ceremony John Shillito, chairman of the English CWS, emphasised that this democratically-controlled body was an integral part of the movement. As a sign of unanimity, J. C. Gray, general secretary of the Co-op. Union, also lent his support and dismissed the National Festival as a gathering 'of irresponsible nobodies in London'.[58]

Finally, it was widely believed that in order to achieve its real potential local societies had to generate what Holyoake referred to as 'a new social feeling'. Unless members were bound together by mutualism as well as self-interest their association would be irredeemably weakened, or so the argument ran. The notion that the movement was a *social* institution was constantly emphasised and carried an emphatic opposition to the 'individual' and 'individualist' theories of society.[59] The round of tea parties, festivals, concerts and so on were not only useful from a business point of view but were also conducive to fellowship. The case of music is again instructive. James Johnston, speaking before the North-West Choral Association in 1910, ranked music higher than painting or sculpture as it tended to produce 'finer feelings'. According to Johnston co-operative choirs would

> foster and strengthen a feeling of fellowship amongst the members . . . in the practice of choral music they had a good illustration of the subservience of the individual to the whole body . . . the formulation and carrying on of choirs fostered the spirit of working together more fully and practically than any other form of organisation.[60]

This was a typically balanced mix of theory and practice, though sometimes idealism got the upper hand. For some harmonic singing actually prefigured the coming utopia. Four years later, at another of the Association's meetings (it now had 36 member societies) held in the Bolton Co-operative Hall, the president Mr Fairbrother observed that the movement received 'a great impetus from the musical side of its work . . . . They wanted co-operative festivals to be the prophets preparing the way for the Co-operative Commonwealth.' The meeting was entertained by the Bury Society's juvenile choir which sang 'Comrades Song of Hope'.[61]

It is very difficult to assess whether the social life of the movement lived up to these grandiose expectations: there is very little evidence which conveys directly the experience of participants. But there is some. Historians of leisure have drawn attention to the increase in working-class demand for holidays and outings during the late nineteenth century, facilitated by a shorter working week, higher wages and the reduced cost of rail travel.[62] As one would expect, local societies tried to meet this demand; co-operative holidays were promoted in the *News* from the early 1870s and became common during subsequent decades, especially the day-trip – the most popular and accessible form. In the summer of 1898, for example, the RACS organised an annual excursion to Hastings and St Leonards.

The trip took place on a Saturday and the return rail fare was 3s 6d for adults and 1s 9d for children under twelve. In 1900 the society arranged a trip to Folkestone and Dover. Over 1,200 members went and it took two trains to accommodate them all.[63] This pattern was repeated every year. For many working people the store supplied the only holiday that they could afford. In her autobiography Mary Bentley recalled the trips organised by the Manchester and Salford Society before the First World War:

> The most they could expect was a day's outing with the Co-op. trip to Southport or Blackpool. They would take seats that were reserved for them on the train very early in the morning, have all the fun of the fair and come back late at night with the children having to be wakened up to get them off the train. Though only one long day, the Co-op. outing was looked forward to with great excitement, money found for a bucket or spade, sandcastles built – it was wonderful what could be done in a day.[64]

Bentley's father was a foreman cooper who earned relatively good wages – about 28 shillings a week – but with four children to feed and clothe, Mary's mother found the 'divi' invaluable. Co-operation put new shoes on the children's feet but also supplied 'all the fun of the fair' and was remembered as a source of happiness as well as material aid. The editor of the *Wheatsheaf* who desired to make 'the store the hub of pleasure as well as profit' would have heartily approved.[65]

IV

When co-operative activists wrote about the role of recreation they drew on a number of intellectual traditions which deserve to be explored in more detail. Waters has perceptively argued that socialist discourse on music in this period was inflected both by the project of middle-class social reform and the utopian heritage of the earlier Owenite movement. Not surprisingly, a similar dialectic informed co-operative discourse on recreation. These traditions – the philanthropic and the utopian – were not mutually exclusive but, as Waters points out, had roots in Enlightenment assumptions concerning the possibility of, and the relationship between individual and, social change.[66] There were differences though. Broadly speaking the reforming impulse was driven by the desire to harmonise relations

between the classes within the existing capitalist social formation
and tended to view the moral reformation of the individual worker
as an end in itself. Occasionally this project was mapped out in the
most blatant terms – witness Francis Fuller before the Social Science
Association in 1875:

> It is a point of self-interest and self-protection for us to exert ourselves
> to improve the tone of popular amusements to induce men to cultivate
> the 'leisure hour' for the good of mind and body. Our safety, the secu-
> rity of society, of our homes and families, in the long run, are con-
> cerned with the form in which they take their recreation.[67]

Within the utopian tradition, on the other hand, the transformation
of individual taste and behaviour was regarded as a stepping-stone
to the anti-competitive, New Moral World of the future.

Let us track these traditions within the Co-operative movement.
For the movement's ideologues to be most effective recreation had
to be 'of the right stamp', or 'improving' in character. In 1874 the
old Owenite, J. C. Farn, denounced the increasing commercialisation of music and song in the pages of the *Co-operative News*. Farn
believed that music was a natural human need but that at the moment 'bad', competitive forms abounded. This had serious implications, especially for the young who 'need, from imperfect education,
the prompting, the guiding, and the governing of song . . . as an aid
to the educational forces at work for good or for evil upon them.'
Farn reckoned that co-operators should compose their own songs
which condemned adulteration, honoured truth and told of the inhumanity and waste of international war. 'Enough has been said to
show that there is some need for reform in the singing amusements
of the multitude', he concluded.[68]

This attitude was widely shared. In the early 1880s Samuel
Bamford, the editor of the *News*, noted how

> co-operative enjoyments are usually marked by the prevalence of a
> fairly high tone, both as regards the audiences and the nature of the
> entertainments. Commonness, clap-trap and spuriousness would be
> out of place in a co-operative hall, the atmosphere of which would
> prove deathly to what may flourish in the music hall or drinking sa-
> lon.[69]

Bamford's words focus many of the key issues. First there is a commitment to the reform of working-class manners and morals. The

co-operative hall is a cultural space qualitatively different from the pub or music hall. There is the evaluative commentary, co-operative recreation is of a 'fairly high tone', and does not depend on 'commonness, clap-trap and spuriousness' for its success. But the virulence of the language used to describe this project mirrors middle-class injunctions to the profligate and degenerate poor. Not only are the enjoyments of a 'fairly high tone', but so too are the audiences; the writer buttressed his argument by accepting and strengthening divisions within the working class – a fault line around 'high' and 'low' culture. This area was very problematic, and the reforming ambition understandable and necessary if co-operation was to achieve its wider aims, yet the impulse could quite easily slide into exhortations which did little more than create distance and suspicion amongst the less secure and financially stable strata of the working class. This contradiction, as I noted in the previous chapter, also frequently informed debate within the sphere of formal education.

If anything the tone of voice became shriller as the commercialisation of leisure gathered pace over the following decades. By the early 1900s the Huddersfield co-operator and secularist, Owen Balmforth, was losing his patience. Criticising the growth of music halls he petulantly observed that 'too much leisure time is nowadays spent in a manner which is extremely questionable'.[70] In 1903 an editorial in the News had noted approvingly that co-operative audiences always set 'a good example of refined and rational entertainment'. Six years later Mr Bank of the Colne Society deplored the fact that the 'land is covered with music halls . . . but the great social and economic inequalities remain.' Quotations could be multiplied here; co-operative activists invariably contrasted the 'purifying' and 'elevating' effects of the social life of their movement with the degenerate and vulgar forms of mass entertainment peddled by leisure entrepreneurs. The latter, it was maintained, tended to debase popular taste and demoralise working-class consumers. Noting the threat from this quarter William Bamford, who succeeded his father as editor of the News in 1898, argued that: 'In recreation, as well as in business, we should be pioneers and reformers.'[71]

Bailey has written informatively about the middle class supporters of 'rational recreation' who sang the praises of the sober, intelligent and respectable worker in earlier decades.[72] Their aim was to castigate the improvident, thriftless and immoral poor and inculcate 'improving' manners and morals in the rest of the population. 'Rational recreation' was construed (like co-partnership schemes explored in chapter six) as a way of building class-harmony thus securing the stability of the capitalist social order. Though this initiative generally failed and working men struggled successfully to retain their autonomy in this sphere, late nineteenth-century co-operators, like their socialist counterparts[73], also advocated rational recreation as an alternative to developing capitalist modes of pleasure and entertainment. Both industrial co-partnership and rational recreation were favourite hobby-horses of the middle-class co-operator, E. O. Greening. As noted above, Greening was the driving force behind the National Festival which embodied both these concerns. In 1896 he explained that his enthusiasm for the Festival stemmed from the fact that he was 'an advocate of recreation not of idleness . . . by recreation I mean re-creation. All our facilities are developed by use'.[74] For Greening 'rational recreation' would help check the deleterious social and political effects of the increasing division of labour which he thought, echoing Ruskin, subverted human nature and generated conflict.

Though the patronage of individuals like Greening was successfully resisted by co-operators in the late nineteenth century, this improving and complex structure of feeling continued to shape the debate within the movement right through to the First World War and beyond. In an editorial in the *News* in 1912 on the subject of holidays Bamford linked the quickening pace of industry with the modern desire for speed and novelty in recreation. The language used to describe the holiday crowd was striking: excursion trains were 'disgorging thick processions of men, women and children'. Bamford recognised the opportunities for cheap travel afforded by large parties but immediately denigrated the popular preference for 'artificial' (or 'low') over 'natural' (or 'high') pleasures – 'the engineer's water-chute to Tennyson's brook' as he tersely put it. The balance sheet, however, was not entirely negative, the crowd had been worse in the days of George IV, Bamford opined, when drunkenness and riotous behaviour were rife! He closed with a typical mixture of reproach and sympathy:

> Our masses, as masses go, are sober, more sensible, and more intelligent. They have more money, and it is not to be wondered at that they

feel like letting themselves 'go' after a year's pent-up life in a crowded workshop of swift machinery.[75]

The language is revealing; as Williams noted, there are no such things as masses, only ways of seeing people as masses.[76] They are anonymous, other people, prone to temptation and weakness. But there is also the effort to understand: the article makes interesting connections between the pace of life and the impact of competition and profit-making on the sphere of recreation as well as production.

The schoolmasterly attitude is, nevertheless, unmistakable and forms an important point of contact with bourgeois moral reformers. The often intolerant, indignant tone adopted by co-operators writing about recreation (as well as education) must have alienated and angered as many people as it attracted. Unfortunately, though understandably, it was far easier to lecture and scold recalcitrant workers than devise more effective and appealing ways of capturing their hearts and imaginations. Not infrequently a feeling of distance and coldness, a rather humourless lack of sympathy can be discerned amongst co-operators impatient with the 'failings' of the poor. The obvious attraction of 'low' domains like the music hall and the seaside resort continued to cause concern in the inter-war years and was joined by a new threat – the cinema – the appeal of which, according to an article in the *Manchester and Salford Co-operative Herald* in 1917, depended on 'rudeness, or "cheek", or vulgarity'.[77]

The interrelated utopian tradition found various expression within the movement. Some commentators like W. H. Brown believed that the reform of popular taste, especially the taste for music, was intimately connected to the democratic appropriation of past, present and future. During the First World War Brown lectured in Bolton on 'Music as a Factor in Social Reform', contended that the 'Chartists were the first social reformers to organise the people to see beauty in song', and described the co-operative choir as the direct heir to this radical tradition.[78] Walter Hampson – 'Casey' of the *Labour Leader* – a keen co-operator who often appeared on co-op platforms, had addressed the same subject a few months before. Hampson argued that like co-operation, music also depended on concord and harmony. He went on to counterpoise the 'degenerate' modernist music of the present with the 'populist' music of the past:

> From the people they had a grand record of old-time folk songs, cra-
> dle songs, songs of joy, songs of daily avocations, all representative of
> the people, sometimes in joyous mood, sometimes in jocund mood,
> sometimes in rebellious mood, furnishing a finer guide to the history
> of the past than many books that had been written. These old folk
> songs – the songs of rebellion, love and joy – were communal prod-
> ucts, the products of co-operation.[79]

Hampson followed his speech with a polished performance on the
violin. I am concerned less here with the correctness of this idealised
and naïvely authentic notion of 'popular culture' – which had of
course been a site of commercial exploitation throughout the nineteenth century – than with the emphasis placed on democratic participation and musical production. For Hampson and for Brown
choral music in particular clearly demonstrated the necessity of
working together but also allowed access to a usable past and a
transformable future.

The malleability of the social order was a common theme. Recommending co-operative plays and historical pageants in 1907 –
forms which were not fully developed until much later – Albert
Mansbridge remarked that a 'real attempt to reproduce the past is in
effect an attempt to pierce the future, in that it involves a new view
of life.'[80] For many activists co-operative exhibitions were vital precisely because they symbolised the desire to 'pierce the future' and
indeed utopian readings of these exhibitions multiplied in the years
before the First World War. In 1913 the historian of the Cainscross
Society drew the following lesson from an exhibition held by the
society in the mid-1890s:

> Up to this time local co-operators, while long familiar with a shop or
> store as a centre of Co-operative distribution had no conception that
> the working classes owned mills, factories, and all the instruments of
> production.[81]

This was a different language to the one favoured by the advocates
of co-partnership, used by those who looked forward to the time
when co-operation would replace rather than merely humanise
capitalism. At an exhibition held in the Oldham Co-operative Hall
around the same time, J. T. Taylor, Chairman of the Educational
Committee, declared that

they believed that if Co-operation must be the success which its founders desired it should be, not only must they distribute that which was
produced, but they must produce that which was distributed. The
promoters of that exhibition wished to make it an object lesson in the
study of co-operation.[82]

Goods from 25 societies were displayed and Taylor was clear about
what it all meant: one day the working class would own and control
the means of production as well as distribution. The movement constructed and articulated a specific co-operative identity, one which
expressed a commitment to open, democratic and collective cultural
forms, self-provided by the working-class. Moreover, the possibility
of a reconstructed moral economy was demonstrated both materially and symbolically by the culture of the movement.

Patrick Joyce's recent summary and critique of the work of cultural sociologists like Bernice Martin, who has investigated the symbolic ordering of working-class culture in a later period, helps us to
better situate and understand this movement culture. Martin has
drawn attention to the almost obsessive need for order and bound-
ary demarcations in the everyday life of working people, manifested
most clearly by the relentless quest for 'respectability'. From this
perspective co-operative culture can properly be seen as one element
within a more generalised 'proletarian culture of control' which underpinned the stability and advance of the labour movement over a
very long period.[83] Enough has been said to indicate just how central
the notion of order was to the success of co-operation: the practice
and rituals of co-operative trade – accumulating checks, calculating
'divi', budgeting and so on – as well as the reformation of the social
and cultural lives of the membership depended upon the exclusion
of disorderly, spontaneous elements which always threatened to in-
vade and overturn precarious lives. Rejecting the fatalism which
many commentators believe pervaded the mentality of working-
class people, co-operators sought to develop aspirations which
would remain purely speculative unless firmly based upon individual and collective discipline.

According to Joyce, Martin's rigid Durkheimian approach over-
emphasises social solidarities and tends to erase the ways in which
boundaries were always negotiated and sometimes overturned (albeit temporarily) within the forms of popular culture itself; Joyce
himself prefers what he calls a 'transactional' analysis which does

not reduce 'culture' to a fixed social base and which also pays attention to the dynamics of power. This is a useful corrective and sheds
further light on my subject. Forms of popular culture such as the
music hall or the romance narrative held both utopian and conservative meanings together in tension and were often characterised
by a tolerant, ironic attitude toward the disorder and incoherence
prevalent in working-class life, especially amongst the poor. Liminal
sites of working-class pleasure like Blackpool not only offered good
value and a packed experience but also held out the promise of
transgression: temporarily at least the social world could be turned
upside down during the annual 'off' to the seaside.[84]

Like their socialist counterparts, co-operators in the late nineteenth and early twentieth centuries failed to comprehend the appeal of such pleasures and frequently resorted, as we have seen, to
haughty condemnation. It seems likely, however, that most rank-
and-file members adopted a more flexible approach to the consumption of the movement's social life and its goods. The devotion of a
relatively small minority was unwavering, but such enthusiasm was
rare. Indeed the 'culture of control' was fairly unstable and co-existed with what can be termed a 'culture of licence'. Social identities
and patterns of behaviour were not fixed but tended to constantly
overlap and blur: one might shop at the co-op, take a holiday in
Blackpool, send one's children to the co-op gala, buy a best dress
from a private outfitters. Once again we must be careful not to con-
fuse the wish-images of national and local leaders with the complex
historical reality.

V

This chapter has considered the 'alternative' nature of co-operative
culture thus far, but increasingly from the turn of the century this
culture became more overtly 'oppositional' as co-operators began to
reach out and engage directly with economic and political interests
which constrained their subversive ambitions; this oppositional
stance provides my final focus. Cultural activities had often been
turned to political ends in the past, particularly to raise funds to
relieve workers engaged in conflict, but during the decade or so preceding the First World War the movement culture itself clashed with
private capital and the local state in a variety of contexts. Here it is
only possible to sketch a few of these important episodes. To take

antagonism from private capital first; the decline and eventual collapse of the National Co-operative Festival in 1910 was partly due,
as we noted above, to the desire to slough off middle-class patronage, but another major cause was the attack from railway companies, which commenced in 1900. Cheap excursions to the Crystal
Palace and discounts for large parties made the expansion of the
festival possible throughout the 1890s. Special excursion trains were
laid on for the great northern societies and choir singers and exhibitors were permitted to make the return journey to London for the
price of a single ticket. Exhibits and displays were also usually trans-
ported at low rates but in 1900 all these concessions were abruptly
discontinued and fares rose on average by twenty-five per cent. The
privilege of half fares for singers and exhibitors was stopped completely. This meant that for a workman, his wife and two children,
travelling from Lancashire or Yorkshire, the cost of the journey rose
from 30s to £2 10s. Moreover, Saturday excursions were cut out
altogether from some towns; and thirty-eight societies which had
sent singers to the United Choir in 1899 were absent in 1900. The
railway companies argued that these price rises were due to the increased cost of coal and labour and, somewhat ironically, to the
congestion of traffic on Saturdays. The effect on the festival was
devastating.[85]

Reaction inside the movement was prompt and highly critical –
a motion condemning the railway companies was passed unanimously at the Cardiff Congress in 1900.[86] J. C. Gray reported to
Congress the following year that letters of complaint, incorporat-
ing the resolution, had been sent to the companies concerned, but
little had been achieved.[87] G. J. Holyoake, making an effort to be
optimistic, wrote after the 1901 festival that 'though the paralys-
ing hand of the railway was laid upon its excursionists and visitors
it was a great Festival.'[88] However, the fact remained that attendance was reduced to less than 29,000 and these came mostly from
the London area. The choir was a mere shadow of its former self,
made up of 3,000 singers. Three years later Holyoake's daughter,
Mrs Emilie Holyoake-Marsh, wrote angrily of the impact of this
policy:

> The railway companies have done more to damage the great Festival
> held annually in London, by raising the fares, than any trader's soci-
> ety or boycotters could possibly accomplish. None know better than

the wives and mothers what the increased charges mean; a small additional charge of about sixpence or ninepence each is of importance when it is an excursion in which the whole family wish to join, and prohibitive at times when wages are scanty and work uncertain.[89]

As I have argued, co-operative culture drew its major strength from organising and including in its ambit whole families, not just the male bread-winner at the point of production or the male citizen in the 'public' sphere. But this strategy could also pose problems: small increases in cost could easily undermine a recreational activity that was designed to involve women and children besides men, and although the festival limped on, attendance never rose to more than 25,000 throughout the 1900s. There had been no love lost between the movement and the railway companies for a long time – individuals were victimised for their co-operative involvement and boycotts had been unsuccessfully attempted in some areas[90] – but this concerted offensive raised the temperature considerably. Whether or not this was a deliberate policy designed to hamstring co-operative culture, it was certainly perceived as such by the leaders of the movement who voted in favour of the nationalisation of the railways at the Middlesbrough Congress in 1901. Moving the motion, Ben Jones spoke for many when he declared that the movement was 'powerless to stem the tide of rampant injustice in the railway world, which was taxing co-operators severely'.[91]

Conflict at the level of the local state also became increasingly common. The Widnes Society, for example, faced strong opposition in the early 1900s because it had managed to compete successfully with local music halls. In 1906 the society was granted a music and dancing licence which was renewed until 1910. The co-operative hall specialised in 'refined' entertainment and in a few years 'it was rapidly becoming a family place of pleasure.' Thousands of working people attended every week. The music halls eventually objected to the renewal of the society's licence to the magistracy in 1910 and the society reacted by collecting 12,000 signatures (over a third of Widnes's population) for a petition deploring the action. Renewal was granted following this resistance but the following year the magistrates would not allow the hall to be used to raise money for the striking Railway Servants' Association. Even the Superintendent of Police got involved, backing the music hall and the magistrates. Undaunted, the society organised numerous public meetings to rally support, and their efforts were finally successful.[92]

Public space was often contested during this period but the outcome was rarely so clear-cut. Not surprisingly perhaps, socialists
faced hostility from municipal bodies at this time and co-operators
were also frequently discriminated against.[93] In the summer of 1909
a conflict started between the Manchester and Salford Society and
the City Council which became increasingly acrimonious and lasted
for over a decade. In June, under pressure from local traders, the
Council denied co-operators the right to use the public parks for
propaganda purposes: concerts were allowed as long as no speeches
were given. The decision provoked a virulent debate in the Council
chambers; James Johnston, a co-operative councillor, was warned
by the Mayor to refrain from the use of threatening language. An
editorial in the *News* denounced the decision and warned trade unionists, suffragettes and socialists that they might be affected next.
Co-operators were often 'first to be victimised by the covert operations of the private capitalists'.[94] At the end of the month a large
demonstration was held at Failsworth. Passions were running high
and oppositions became more explicit. A member of the Failsworth
Society expressed his anger explicitly:

> Mr Ross Clyne [a councillor] was, however, reported to have said that
> it would be 'God help England' if it was in the hands of co-operators.
> It would be God help Mr Ross Clyne and several others who voted
> with him, as there would be no room for many of the businesses which
> these gentlemen at present obtained their livelihood from.[95]

The *News* reported the affair in great detail, published cartoons
lampooning the anti-co-operative councillors and the notion of
'public' parks and detailed the position taken by individual councillors on the issue. The paper advised co-operators to bear these views
in mind in the Municipal elections on November 1st. The Co-op.
Union issued a circular to all candidates standing for election, ask-
ing them to declare their intentions. Replies were later published in
the *News*.[96]

This was not the end of the story. The Council snubbed co-operators again the following spring and still denied them the right to
spread the co-operative message in the parks. Councillor Bowie attempted to ridicule the co-operative project in a council meeting, as
Clyne had done:

> One of the co-operative directors [William Lander] said at Wakefield
> that the co-operators were out to do away with private ownership of
> the means of life, and, I submit, Lord Mayor, that that would lead us
> to a fine state of things. (*Laughter*)[97]

These middle-class spokesmen may have resorted to ridicule, but
they undoubtedly took seriously, and even feared, co-operative ambition. At the end of May the society finally defied the restriction
and held a demonstration at Boggart Hole Clough, which was attended by 1,000 people. Reports of this meeting referred back to
Peterloo and more recently, the battle waged by local socialists who
had also been banned by the Parks Committee in 1896. Councillor
Johnston referred back to this earlier incident and argued that now
it was co-operators' turn to fight exclusion and privilege. In July
another large meeting was held in Alexandra Park and as both these
gatherings were unmolested it looked as if victory had been secured.[98]

The calm lasted three years, then in July 1913 the Parks Committee refused to allow a children's gala in the parks on the
grounds that it was an advertisement for the stores. A deputation
of 27 co-operators put their case to the committee and the Council
reconsidered the decision. They again stipulated that a gala would
be allowed on condition that no speeches be given. The importance of wresting control of the local state away from private interests was a lesson repeatedly driven home in the co-operative
press. John Burns, President of the Local Government Board, was
eventually contacted, and he began to conduct a critical correspondence with the Committee.[99] Confrontation was suspended by
the outbreak of war, but when hostilities ceased, co-operators'
right to use the parks was challenged once again. In May 1919 the
City Council refused to allow the Co-operative Parliamentary Representation Committee to hold a demonstration in Platt Fields, another of the city's public parks. Co-operators complained and
resolved to ignore the ban. Representing local traders, Clyne was
again to the fore, and recommended the use of force to break up
the proposed gathering.[100]

Manchester co-operators, supported by the local Trades Council
and Labour Party, turned the event into a propaganda exercise on
the afternoon of Saturday 12th July 1919. The description which
appeared in the *News* is worth quoting at length as it provides excel-

lent illustration of the culture of the movement mobilised for mani-
festly political and class purposes:

> The procession was headed by the C.W.S. Tobacco Factory Band,
> which played stirring music. In the front of the procession was a deco-
> rated lorry sent by the Beswick Society, and two from the Manchester
> and Salford Society. The lorries displayed, on their sides, appropriate
> mottoes, which ought to be commended to the City Council. They
> were: 'Co-operation', 'Equity', 'Freedom for All'. After the lorries
> came eight brake loads of the children of co-operators, and members
> of some of the guilds. Several of the brakes displayed guild banners.
> Following the brakes there was carried the beautiful banner of the
> National Warehouse and General Workers' Union. It led the first de-
> tachment of the large army of co-operators, trade unionists and
> labourists. The rear of the procession was brought up by two of the
> Failsworth Society's lorries, with guild banners; another brake load of
> children; and a 'Co-operative News' lorry, its sides covered with the
> 'News' bill for the week, 'Co-operators Defy City Council'. Along the
> route men and boys sold a special edition of the 'Co-operative
> News'.[101]

According to the News, 'immense' crowds gathered around the
three platforms at Platt Fields and the 'whole demonstration was a
pronounced success.' This time local capitalists and anti-co-operative councillors could do nothing but accept defeat.

It is worth returning to McKibbin's thesis outlined in the introduction to this chapter for, despite Andrew Davies' rather cursory
dismissal of attempts to relate changes in working-class social life to
changes in political attitudes, the question as to whether the
associational life of the British working-class inhibited the development and popularity of a rejectionist ideology on the German model
is still very pertinent.[102] The evidence is certainly patchy and the
culture of co-operation was only one element, albeit a very important one, in a complex associational network which encompassed
chapels and angling clubs as well as trade union branches and cycling societies. McKibbin correctly stresses, pace Stedman Jones,
that this was not an 'apolitical or inert culture', but we can go further.[103] The social life of the movement, which touched the lives of
so many people, was understood, at least by co-operative activists,
as an integral part of a general anti-capitalist, sometimes utopian
strategy. At different times, within particular contexts, the

oppositional thrust of the movement culture became increasingly obvious, to the movements' bitter enemies as well as to its supporters. The culture of co-operation certainly provided consolation and may also have diverted working-class energies away from more obvious kinds of 'political' activity sometimes, but it could also open up the prospect of a very different world.

4

Internationalism

The great and final achievement of co-operation must be the substitution of the present individualistic system by a co-operative commonwealth. This must be something more than a local or national accomplishment; it must also be international.

Editorial in the Co-operative News, 30 August 1913

I

Though co-operators themselves have often emphasised the theme of this chapter, it has not attracted academics or labour activists eager to reconstruct an heroic past.[1] However, even a superficial reading of the literature suggests how deeply the movement's ideology and discourse was informed by a sense of internationalism. The discussion which follows details the nature and substance of that internationalism and its place within co-operative culture. The working hypothesis is that there was an affinity between the movement and internationalism, an affinity greater perhaps than that which existed between other mass working-class associations and internationalism.

We should not be surprised to find this affinity. After all, utopian socialism was a European, or rather an Anglo-French, phenomenon. The ideas of Owen, Fourier, St Simon, Proudhon, Thompson and Cabet were freely exchanged, and travelled to and fro across the channel. 'Community-building' was practised in France, Britain and America and the results of these experiments were debated and discussed in a variety of countries and contexts. The Owenites' self-description – 'The Association of All Classes of All Nations' –

proudly declared the universality of their vision. From its inception in the 1820s 'mutual co-operation' was contrasted in a general, international way, with the system of 'individual competition'.[2] Moreover, the European revolutions and particularly the French Revolution of 1848, helped strengthen international links. The producer co-operatives sponsored by the Provisional Government made a profound impact on many English co-operators. The Christian Socialists, especially J. M. Ludlow, propagated the notion of 'association' and established their own workshops in London under the auspices of the Society for Promoting Working Men's Associations.[3] The workshop idea and continental writings on association also deeply influenced working-class Owenites like G. J. Holyoake and James Hole at the time.

Organising around the sphere of consumption brought practical benefits. The workshops quickly collapsed in a hostile market but many co-operative distributive stores put down solid roots, thus enabling the construction of a movement culture. The continuities between this project and the Owenite strategy articulated by writers like Dr William King and William Thompson have already been emphasised; the centrality of the principle of inclusion is again important. Co-operation hoped to include everyone: women, children, men, all could associate and take part in the life of the movement in a myriad of ways. This ambition was not, in theory, contained by the nation; all consumers, in all countries, shared common interests, and could unite in a worldwide Co-operative movement. The sectional, chauvinistic interests of workers as workers or political subjects could be overcome in this way. J. T. W. Mitchell remarked in 1880 that, 'The highest form of co-operation was that which bound nations together by mutual interest and sympathy'.[4] Mitchell's inclusive 'ideology of consumption' was explored in chapter two; these principles encouraged the growth and expression of the varieties of internationalism analysed in this chapter.

II

Co-operative Congresses were marked by their high level of international content and exchange. At the very first congress, held in London in 1869, letters from foreign correspondents were read out which described co-operative developments in Europe as a whole. Denmark, France, Italy, Germany, Sweden and Switzerland all sent

details.[5] This was repeated the following year, and in 1871 the
Russian movement sent its first report.[6] Old Owenites with a passion
for education as well as internationalism were primarily responsible
for constructing and maintaining these early connections. At the
Bolton Congress in 1872, G. J. Holyoake argued that the British movement could learn and benefit from this exchange:

> He had said over and over again in the *Social Economist* what he
> knew to be true – that the diffusion of the new ideas arising on the
> continent concerning the development of social and industrial life,
> would be of the greatest advantage to the progress of this country.
> Foreigners thought of things which we never thought of; and we do
> many things which they never were able to discover the mode of do-
> ing. This international communication of information would be cred-
> itable to all concerned, and advantageous to the whole body.[7]

It was the Birmingham Owenite, William Pare, who conducted the
voluminous correspondence with continental co-operative societies,
whose growth was watched so eagerly at these early congresses. Letters were exchanged yearly, but a deputation did not appear until
the Oldham Congress in 1885, when the French movement sent
Messrs Marty and Nicole. These men, from the co-operative associations in the Seine département around Paris, were warmly received by the delegates, their speeches translated by A. H. D.
Acland.[8] From this year onwards the international presence at these
gatherings gradually increased.

An unprecedented number of foreign delegates attended the Newport Congress in 1908. Twenty-three were present, representing ten
different countries: Austria, Denmark, Finland, France, Germany,
Hungary, Norway, Russia, Sweden and Switzerland. The subject
which excited so much interest, which will be considered in some
detail later, was the feasibility of federal action by wholesale societies in different countries.[9] Foreign delegates up to this time had spoken during the morning session on the first day of Congress;
however, from this date a special evening session was convened to
afford them more time. This international session developed its own
distinctive form and style. At the Plymouth Congress in 1910, nine
countries were represented. The national anthems of each were
printed on leaflets and sung in turn, led by the individual delegates
from each country, accompanied by an organ. Co-operators sat
down to eat and drink together in a ritual of fellowship and good-

will.[10] This symbolic internationalism was to assume a greater importance after the war with the institution of an International Co-operative Day in 1923, and the Wembley Pageants held in the 1920s and 1930s to mark this event; the 1938 pageant entitled 'Towards Tomorrow' and written and directed by the communist Montague Slater, was attended by about 60,000 people.[11]

It would be instructive at this juncture to note briefly the level of internationalism at the British Trades Union Congresses before the First World War. No written communication was published in the annual reports; foreign delegates did not appear at Congress until 1895, and these were two representatives from the American Federation of Labour. This body continued to send delegates each year throughout our period. No international sessions were convened, though occasionally international questions did intrude. At the Nottingham Congress in 1908, for example, the Labour MP Arthur Richardson denounced militarism during the opening session, as did the president, D. J. Shackleton. A resolution was carried on the third day of Congress which condemned British workers who acted as blacklegs in labour disputes overseas.[12] But overall, international debate and exchange was notably absent.

European co-operators never tired of singing the praises of the British movement and its founders. Owen, but more often the Rochdale Pioneers, were singled out for their inspirational role. The Italian co-operator, Professor Vignano of Milan, declared at the Newcastle-on-Tyne Congress in 1880:

> From Rochdale had come a light – a sun that had sent its illuminating rays all over the world, raising and maturing the sentiment of universal fraternity . . .[13]

The international impact of Holyoake's *Self Help by the People: History of Co-operation in Rochdale*, was widely acknowledged.[14] The French delegate, Edouard de Boyve, read an address on behalf of the Federation of French Co-operators at Lincon in 1891, and complimented Holyoake for his propagandism:

> Have we not drawn our co-operative principles from reading the story of the Pioneers of Rochdale, whom our honourable friend Holyoake has immortalised? Do we not repeat this story to all who join us? Are we not striving to put into practice the principles of these Pioneers – justice and social emancipation?[15]

Dr Totomianz, the Russian delegate at Newport in 1908, also stressed how widespread knowledge of British co-operation was in his country:

> We translate your literature, we read your newspapers and reports, and our working men know the history of the Rochdale Pioneers as well as they know the books by Tolstoy or Gorki.[16]

The Pioneers were singled out, not because they had turned their backs on the Owenite vision of a fully-liberated humanity, but rather because they had showed how such a dream could be materially created.

The admiration was not always one way. A delegation from the Co-operative Union visited productive co-operatives (in the building trade) in Paris the following year. William Clayton reminded the delegates of the historical links between the British and French movements:

> Two of the great forces at the beginning of the last century, so far as influencing and directing the social aspirations of the working classes were concerned, were Robert Owen and Charles Fourier, and he was of opinion that a close reading of Robert Owen's time would reveal the fact that the influence of Fourier over Owen was very remarkable. (*Applause*)[17]

Two years before, Mrs Abbot had drawn attention to Belgium co-operators in the *Co-operative News*, especially those who had built the Maison du Peuple in Brussels. The social provision organised by this society – pension funds, medical aid, maternity benefit and so on – was seen as an ideal which the British movement would do well to emulate.[18]

In the late nineteenth century Holyoake was not the only British co-operator who enjoyed an international reputation. He had travelled to the first French Congress in 1885 with the Christian Socialist E. V. Neale, and they both gave advice to this body. The secretary of the Co-operative Union, J. C. Gray, attended the first German Congress in 1904, and his support was much appreciated by German delegates at the British Congresses. During our period these individual links became increasingly common, strengthened by the formation of the International Co-operative Alliance in 1895, a body largely concerned with the diffusion of information regarding co-operative progress and, in its early days, a forum for many middle-class profit-sharers.[19]

International topics were covered in detail in the co-operative press. The *News* regularly reported visits to and from overseas: in August 1908, for example, Belgium, French and Austrian co-operators toured England and their visits were described enthusiastically.[20] In 1910 the paper described a visit to Helsingfors, Finland, by delegates from the CWS and SCWS, visits by Russian co-operators to Manchester and London, and a Dutch delegation to Rochdale; and the paper carried an interview with one of the Dutch delegates concerning co-operation in Holland.[21] The Russian co-operators, led by Dr Totomianz, also visited the Leeds Society. Eighteen delegates were treated to lunch in the People's Hall and toured the society's places of business. The local record included a detailed report of the event.[22] The *Co-operative News* also included regular factual articles on continental co-operative progress, and coverage increased especially from *c*. 1910.[23] The *Wheatsheaf* carried similar features, many written by Dr Hans Muller.[24] The movement's theoretical journal, the *CWS Annual*, also published many articles on international subjects.[25]

The children's magazine, *Our Circle*, shared these concerns. The earliest editions carried lessons in Esperanto – usually a picture-story with text beneath. Later long stories in Esperanto appeared.[26] Foreign visits were described and editorials encouraged international feeling. In 1911 an International Fête of co-operative children from Germany, Belgium, Russia, France and Wales was held in Paris. *Our Circle* carried a full report, including photographs, of the event which ended with an anti-war demonstration.[27] This publication was least affected by the wave of nationalistic feeling which broke within the movement after the outbreak of war in 1914 – a topic I shall return to below – and maintained a balanced and critical tone.[28]

The press paid special attention to the congresses organised throughout Europe by the ICA. The sheer size of the European movement and its ability to stage such events generated much pride. The Cremona Congress in 1907 was reported in the *News* for a whole month; the editor of the *Millgate Monthly* attended and later published his impressions in the magazine.[29] The Leeds Society sent two delegates to this congress, and three years later the Failsworth Society sent a delegate to the Hamburg Congress who marvelled at the sight of seventeen nationalities assembled and co-operating together.[30] In 1913 the congress was held in Glasgow and the *News* published a special international edition, packed from cover to cover with written and photographic reports of the event, which assembled 600 delegates representing twenty-four countries. In his report the Failsworth delegate lamented the fact that English co-operators were so woefully ignorant of foreign languages and advised the movement to remedy this failing in the future.[31] Internationalism was then a central component of co-operative culture as this brief overview has shown. However, although fraternity and friendship were important co-operative ends, to be most effective internationalist sentiment required organisation and direction, a problem which was to become all too apparent.

III

Co-operators in England quickly took advantage of the Industrial and Provident Societies Act of 1862 – which made federal organisation legal – and established the English Co-operative Wholesale Society the following year. Wholesaling was vital to co-operative success as it reduced costs and helped solve the problem of boycotting; with a strong wholesale organisation, co-operators could buy their supplies directly from the manufacturer, thereby cutting out the capitalistic middleman.[32] The CWS expanded rapidly over the succeeding years and its business soon became international. Palm-oil supplies for the Irlam soap factory came from West Africa and the Wholesale owned tea plantations in India and Ceylon and corn-growing estates in Canada by the First World War. Key figures in the English and Scottish Wholesales, men like Ben Jones, J. T. W. Mitchell and William Maxwell travelled around the world on co-operative business. As I have argued, the national and international growth of the Wholesales during our period provided Mitchell and many of his colleagues with concrete proof of the efficacy of co-operation and the universality of its project.

From the late 1880s it became clear that co-operative trade had to be organised internationally if the European movement was to prosper as a whole. This point was articulated repeatedly at the British Congresses. During a discussion following Vaughan Nash's paper on 'Co-operation and International Commerce', at the Ipswich Congress in 1889, T. Shaw of Mosley drew this conclusion:

We must throw the 'middleman' overboard and do our trade directly with foreign co-operators through the Wholesale Societies, buying their productions and sending ours in return.

At the same meeting Frank Hardern of Oldham noted that the Wholesale's overseas expansion had been unplanned and not a conscious policy based on an ideological commitment:

Our great Wholesale Societies were penetrating into the continent in all directions . . . until their ships and agencies were trying to do for international commerce what co-operators ought to have done years ago.[33]

The time was now ripe, he maintained, for taking these matters in hand and building systematic trade links.

International co-operative trade, it was argued at the Peterborough Congress almost a decade later, would form the basis for true brotherhood, help destroy national chauvinism and replace it with an emphasis on the process rather than the place of manufacture. J. Tetley of Leeds remarked that:

He would like to impress upon his fellow working men the importance of international co-operative trading. Much nonsense has been talked about things being 'made in Germany'. The important question was not where things were made, but under what conditions they were made.[34]

A resolution was passed unanimously at the Middlesbrough Congress in 1901, urging all countries to establish their own wholesales, and that these bodies should be 'encouraged to enter into close relations for international supply'.[35] The following year an international exhibition was held as part of the ICA Congress in Manchester. The Central Board reported that it was 'by far the largest and most important exhibition ever held in connection with the movement'.[36] Housed in St James's Hall, the largest in the city, it was open for nine days in July. Exhibits from all parts of Europe were featured: corn, potatoes and other agricultural produce from Italy; boots and leather from Russia; lithographs from France; basket and wickerwork from Belgium and Holland; paints, varnish and soap from Holland. More than 50,000 people paid to see the exhibition. The pressing problem was how best to exchange these productions and thereby strengthen the European movement.

The solution eventually proposed was a federation of European Wholesale Societies, with a central administrative and advisory body. The success of the English CWS deeply impressed continental co-operators. Many visited the productive and other departments of the wholesale and put the lessons gleaned from these trips into practice back home. In this way the British movement, more fully developed than other national movements, performed an educative role.[37] By 1908 fifteen wholesale societies existed in Europe, encouraged and supported by the British wholesales. These had a total annual turnover of about £39,785,000. Following Dr Hans Muller's paper on international co-operation at Congress that year, William Lander, on Muller's suggestion, advocated a federation of wholesales, to integrate and co-ordinate the exchange and production of co-operative goods across national boundaries. A sentimental feeling which bound nations together was all very well, he argued, but it was vital to unite people's pockets as well as their hearts, vital to build internationalism on strong material foundations if effective changes were to be made.[38] At the ICA Congress held in Cremona the previous year, William Maxwell had outlined a similar scheme:

> If every country in Europe had its Co-operative Wholesale Society, would it not be possible for all to combine, exchanging the products of the various countries, and thus make the movement a world-wide federation? What has been done in England and Scotland might be extended over the globe, and, through the agency of the ICA it is, I think, that the idea might be carried into practice in a comparatively short time.[39]

This notion attracted an increasing amount of attention in the years preceding the outbreak of the First World War for a number of reasons.

Firstly, international wholesaling would be a useful way of combating boycotts organised by private traders. The history of these boycotts in Britain has not been adequately documented by social historians and this is unfortunately true for Europe as a whole. Co-operation faced determined opposition in many countries. At the Bradford Congress in 1911 the Norwegian delegate, Mr Delhi, and the Swedish delegate, Mr Rosling, detailed the traders' boycotts in their respective countries. In Norway they were well organised and published their own anti-co-operative journals (as they did in England). The Swedish movement was up against a sugar manufacturers' syndicate which refused to sell sugar to the wholesale society, forcing co-operators to import this commodity at greater expense. Mr Rosling drew this conclusion from the 'hard fighting' experienced in his country:

> The Swedish co-operators have therefore a very large interest in the co-operative international movement, and would be very glad if there could be formed an International Co-operative Wholesale. We consider the co-operative movement one of the best weapons of the working classes in their economic struggle. It would give an economical foundation for building up a better community than the present private capitalism.[40]

At the Dublin Congress in 1914, M. Helies, the French delegate, drew a similar lesson from the history of the French CWS. Established in 1906, this body would have collapsed without the assistance of the English CWS when French banks decided to boycott and refused to discount its bills. Helies was profoundly thankful:

> The English Wholesale did not hesitate in the presence of French capitalism, but at the instigation of Mr William Maxwell, the honoured president of the International Co-operative Alliance, fulfilled the office of banker to the French co-operative societies.[41]

For Helies this was a sign that co-operation was breaking down national economic frontiers and could in the future abolish totally those barriers created by 'capitalistic regimes'.

But a far-reaching historical development was also forcing international wholesaling onto the agenda: capitalism itself was organising along international lines.[42] Monopoly capitalism posed new threats, required new forms to challenge and contain. Co-operators were sensitive to these transformations and debated at great length the rise and function of trusts and syndicates. A resolution moved by W. Crooks and adopted at the Perth Congress in 1897, recommended all societies to consider the question of international co-operation. Crookes believed that this was an urgent matter as

> it was also easier now for capitalists to play one country against another. Hence the importance of a closer alliance between the working people of all countries.[43]

At Middlesbrough in 1901, Mr E. Scherling of the German CWS, advocated links between the English and German wholesales to help counter 'the concentration of enormous capital and economical power' in trusts and syndicates.[44] The following year at Exeter, Mr D. Mc'Innes recommended the exhibition described above from this angle:

> The exhibition was necessary, in these days of trusts and syndicates, to show the beginning of an international movement among the people themselves.[45]

At an exhibition of co-operative productions in Hartlepool in 1907, Mr T. Liddle pointed out that

> they did not exist as a trust to enrich an individual or a few capitalists, but they existed in order to benefit and enrich the whole of the workers of the world. (*Applause*) In conclusion, he said they had international co-operation, and they trusted it would grow until it embraced every nation on the face of the globe.[46]

The critique sharpened over time. By 1913 an editorial in the *Co-operative News* baldly stated that 'capitalism is becoming increasingly international' and warned that, as this trend continued, 'so does it become a more deadly menace to the workers'. The only remedy was to organise co-operative trade in a similar fashion: 'We must link up not only our sympathies, but also our material interests'.[47]

During the First World War the *Russian Co-operator*, published in English from London by a group of Russian activists, also emphasised the need to build international trade links. This monthly journal was the organ of the Russo-British Information Bureau, a joint committee of the English, Scottish and Irish Wholesales, Moscow Narodny Bank and the Union of Siberian Creamery Associations. *The Millgate Monthly* commented on the proposed function of this body in 1917:

> Its objects are to translate into practice the theories of internationalism in Co-operation between this country and Russia.[48]

The editor pointed out that sentiment was not enough: internationalism had to be 'built up around the framework of actual business transactions, just as co-operative sentiment was built up around the store'. The journal publicised the extent and form of the Russian movement in this country, and encouraged Anglo-Russian co-op-

erative trade. As the first editorial pointed out, such connections
were vital if the 'monopolists' were to be defeated: 'Unless co-operative organisations in various countries unite with a common purpose, the issue may be successful for the capitalists.'[49] Both the
February and October revolutions in Russia were welcomed by British co-operators, though the latter was treated with some caution
and concern for the future autonomy of the co-operative sector.[50] In
June 1918 the *Russian Co-operator* published a letter from William
Gallacher of the Scottish CWS, who described the revolution as the
initial step towards an 'International Co-operative Commonwealth'.[51]

What happened to these sanguine though critical hopes, plans and
expectations? Unfortunately, before the First World War, although
a good many resolutions were passed, no practical organisation was
established. Some progress was made, however, during and in the
immediate aftermath of the war. An International Co-operative
Trading Committee had been set up at the Cremona Congress in
1907 but had fallen into disuse during wartime. The question was
discussed at ICA Congresses in Hamburg and Glasgow and was
raised at the Inter-Allied Co-operative Conference in Paris in September 1916. The second Inter-Allied Co-operative Conference considered it again in February 1919, and an Inter-Allied Co-operative
Committee was set up to assist societies in devastated areas, and to
establish an International Co-operative Bureau of Statistical and
Commercial Information which was to study the best way of organising international wholesaling.[52] An International Co-operative
Wholesaling Society was finally constituted in 1924, but merely collected information and had no trading functions.[53] The failure really
to get to grips with international trade, a failure which was in no
small measure due to forces beyond the control of co-operators – the
waste and disruption caused by war, the uneven development of the
European movement, the attack on co-operation by the Fascists
which disorganised the Italian, Spanish, German and Austrian
movements in the 1920s and 1930s – pushed the attainment of the
International Co-operative Commonwealth further and further into
the future. Co-operators were apt at diagnosis, but the appropriate
remedy was difficult to apply.

IV

A closely related theme much discussed at Congress was the possibility of international war. The dangers were all too apparent, well before the end of the century, particularly to old Owenites like Dr John Watts and E. T. Craig. At Ipswich in 1889, Craig denounced Bismarckian foreign policy and counterpoised the co-operative ideal:

> Prince Bismarck considered war to be the means of consolidating the independence and promoting the wealth and happiness of a nation. That was an erroneous doctrine. War was destructive. International co-operation would produce a higher state of civilisation and happiness. By sympathising and fraternising with our brethren abroad, we shall render unnecessary the terrible engines of destructive war.[54]

Owenism, as I noted, was internationalist in its ideology and discourse. Competition and war were internally related for the Owenites and only a system of co-operation would usher in a 'higher state of civilisation and happiness', an era of world peace.

These antinomies recurred. As Mrs Treub, a member of the Dutch delegation to Liverpool in 1899 observed:

> The more co-operation is practised in the world, the more competition will lose ground. In this moment the heart of co-operation is beating in this hall. Therefore, I am sure you are doing even more for bringing peace to the world than the peace conference now sitting at The Hague. Your work is essentially a work of mutuality and peace.[55]

One reason why it was so essential to encourage and develop co-operative trade links was that the exchange of goods would further the cause of peace. In this way the CWS ships which ploughed the world's oceans symbolised far more than a successful business enterprise.

> The time was coming when co-operative ships sailing between the countries of the earth would weave such a web of concord and peace between the people of all nations that there would be no more war . . . [56]

declared Dr Hans Muller before the Paisley Congress in 1905. Peace and free trade of course had been sacrosanct Liberal principles, proclaimed triumphantly from Manchester by Cobden and Bright. The crucial difference was that for co-operators these aims were necessarily conjoined to the construction of an alternative socio-economic system. Competition, or capitalism, bred war; only co-operation would make matters all right.[57]

Not only was conflict endemic to a system of competition, it was also provoked and continued by corrupt and self-seeking politicians, not by the common people. Mr T. Broderick of the English CWS made this point in support of the motion on international wholesaling in 1901. He argued that if people could be drawn together through co-operation it would become increasingly difficult for 'amateur statesmen and unscrupulous adventurers to plunge the different countries into bloodshed . . . .'[58] This notion, that if only the common people could associate beneath the level of the politics of the nation state, then wars would become obsolete, was regularly voiced. T. W. Allen, president of the Newport Congress in 1908, addressed this issue directly:

> We remember that most of the quarrels that have been were not the people's quarrels at all, but those of our rulers for imaginary gain and supremacy, and we rejoice that, in some instances, in spite of monarchs and government, we are learning to take our hands from each others throats to clasp them as friends and brothers.[59]

Co-operation offered a method of construction, a way of building internationalism so that it did not merely consist of vague rhetoric about universal brotherhood. The Co-operative Commonwealth had to be made on the ground, in each specific national context, in each particular locality, and would not arrive as if by magic on the morrow of the revolution.

Co-operators' pride in the local will be discussed in the following chapter. Here we might note that there was often a pride in Englishness and the achievements of the English working-class, not just smug assurance, but a sense of uneven successes, partial victories. This sense of 'patriotism' could be turned to radical, oppositional ends. As Hugh Cunningham has suggested, the language of patriotism had been located within a radical discourse in England before mid-century, was struggled over and gradually 'captured', its meaning narrowed and restricted until the reactionary, nationalistic elements predominated.[60] Even in our period, though, it could be used in a progressive way to strengthen internationalist sentiment.

William Maxwell, a Scotsman, moved a resolution at Newcastle-on-Tyne in 1909 appealing to co-operative societies to support the ICA with annual subscriptions, and opined:

> He had been told that he was misusing his time in this work of inter-nationalism, because it would spoil his patriotism. He would bow to no man in his love of his country, but he was not less a patriot because he loved his fellow men in other countries, and not less a Scotchman because he went to Germany and France to make brethren of them.[61]

Towards the end of his speech Maxwell elaborated on this theme of 'true' and 'false' patriotism; he knew that not all its manifestations were progressive:

> Mr Maxwell rebuked the misguided patriotism of the people who demanded more Dreadnoughts and other engines of war to destroy their brethren in other countries; that was not true patriotism.[62]

Though the motion was passed unanimously, unfortunately for Maxwell and other internationally-minded co-operators, 'true patriotism' had been under attack for many years, and now stood fully in the loser's corner. 'Engines of war' were manufactured at an ever-increasing rate by both Germany and Britain from the turn of the century. The pace of the arms race and the danger of eventual conflict grew as the years passed. By 1910 Europe was poised on the knife-edge of the most bloody and traumatic war ever fought on her soil. The capitalist press in Britain inflamed imaginations with rumours of war and tales of the Kaiser's desire for European domination. At Plymouth in this year Maxwell vehemently denounced the calumnies which appeared in the newspapers. He called this anti-German propaganda 'one of the greatest crimes committed during their lifetimes'. The German delegates on the platform had no quarrel with the people of England, he continued, and would not back their government if war was declared; these co-operative gatherings made conflict more and more unlikely. He rounded off with a ringing critique of power politics and the arms race:

> The constant building of armaments and the constant trying of governments to get on top of each other, he deplored. We were not going to fight these men, but it was said that this arming was an insurance for peace. It was nothing of the kind. It was the old worn out theory of one nation wanting to get the better of the others. What was wanted

instead was more equality than we have had; an equality which would lead men to regard each other as friends and brothers instead of enemies.[63]

Five years later lines were drawn and trenches dug, and the optimism which characterised the pre-war Congresses – the belief that international brotherhood was urgent and possible – had largely disappeared. W. J. Douse, secretary of the Nottingham Society and hardly the most left-wing co-operator, was chosen to deliver the inaugural address at the first congress after the outbreak of war, held in Leicester in 1915. He gave a thoroughly nationalistic speech in which he harangued 'the fiendish ferocity of the Kaiser and his murderous Huns'. The position of the Co-operative Movement, as he interpreted it, was clearly spelt out:

> We represent some 3,000,000 of Britain's most loyal subjects, and are convinced that our Government was bound in honour to take up arms when the modern Attila tore into shreds the parchment he had signed to assure forever the inalienable rights of brave little Belgium.[64]

Douse considered that the Germans were determined to 'enslave the world' and would resort to any tactics to achieve this end. The use of poison gas, the sinking of the *Lusitania*, the poisoning of water springs were cited as evidence that Germany had departed from the 'canons of civilised warfare'. To round off this pat rendition of common accusations and official propaganda, Douse invoked God, on our side needless to say in this 'sacred cause'. That such an address was deliberately chosen as a focus for this congress indicates that the movement was not immune from the worst forms of nationalistic fervour. No international session was convened that year.[65]

Fortunately Douse's was not the only voice to be heard at the Leicester Congress. The war was discussed in some detail by delegates when the first resolution, a general condemnation of the European war, was moved by A. Taylor from the Co-operative Printing Society. He put the blame squarely on Germany's shoulders and called for the immediate evacuation of Belgium. He advocated the establishment of a tribunal to enforce international law and the rights of small nations and ended with the remark that initial doubts about the inhumanity of the enemy had been laid to rest by the report of the Bryce Commission. He saw the fight as a straightforward one between the forces of militarism and democracy.[66]

Mr A. C. Burn (W. London), who seconded the motion, added an important gloss. He made a distinction between rulers and the common people, and recognised that the struggle for economic freedom and liberty, the struggle between co-operation and competition, transcended this conflict between nation-states and would continue after the war. The middle classes, he argued, must be made to carry the financial burden of the war in all nations, and not the working classes which historically had been the case:

> History told them clearly that the workers were the first to suffer from war and the last to recover from it. The middle classes always won the gains accruing from war; they had always taken the advantage and saddled the workers with the cost of war. Therefore it was necessary that they, the workers, should concentrate their efforts on the Government of their time to see that the cost was put upon those capable of bearing the burden.[67]

This warning was often voiced on local co-operative platforms. At a concert at Didsbury in 1916, R. J. Davies declared:

> God knows you have paid for it with your blood . . . he was afraid that they would have to suffer far more serious hardships than they were undergoing at the present time. For it was the workers who would have to pay. There was no wealth but that which was created by the toilers.[68]

Although the fight for direct political involvement had intensified since the early years of the century, the war made it clear that questions of political power could not be ignored. As Pollard has argued, the movement was affected by the general swing to the left of all sections of the British labour movement in 1917 and became more and more vocal on political issues.[69]

At the 1915 Congress, Aneurin Williams, representing the ICA, delivered a paper on 'The Future Policy of Co-operation: National and International'. In this he praised the neutral stance adopted by this body and advised the movement to remain distanced from organised politics. In the discussion which followed John Penny from Sheffield made the connection between war and politics against Williams:

> Europe was devastated by this infernal war. Who was responsible for that war? Were British co-operators responsible? Did we want it? He

believed the German co-operators wanted it no more than we did. What had the co-operators of Germany and Austria done? They real-ised the menace of war, and forced their way into their parliaments and denounced militarism. They were not powerful enough to defeat the military party; but they faced the issue, and men like Liebknecht deserved a tribute for the work they did. They fought for peace in the only place that peace could be established and they looked towards Britain. They said, 'You British co-operators! You, too, professed to believe in peace'. But we waved our palsied hands and said, 'No poli-tics!' There were sins of omission as well as commission. It was cus-tomary to blame the Kaiser; but when we came to consider who was responsible for the war, let us take part of the blame upon ourselves.[70]

Such convictions, coupled with a heightened sensitivity to the threats posed by monopoly capitalism and the growth of a regula-tory, overbearing State, made possible the first steps toward direct political action in 1917, which led to the foundation of the Co-op-erative Party two years later.

V

The dialectic of internationalism/nationalism informed the move-ment's national and local press. The *Co-operative News* adopted a cautious attitude at the start of the war and continued the critique of power politics and the arms race.[71] The paper rapidly changed its line, however, and soon ran a series of articles under the heading 'Germany's Evil Genius', though its tone became more critical as the war dragged on.[72] The available evidence suggests that the pressure on the most enlightened local editor to join in the jingoistic chorus was immense. The editor of the *Pendleton Co-operative Record* was slow to apportion blame when war broke out, made the distinction between politicians and 'the people', and praised German co-opera-tors.[73] Accused of being pro-German, the editor quickly rebuked the charge and declared his support for 'the most just war in history'.[74] The *Record* also published a declaration from the Society's Board of Management in 1916, dissociating themselves from Maxwell's con-ciliatory attitude towards Germany and his desire to maintain the neutrality of the ICA The Board stated the determination of local co-operators not to shake hands with the enemy until total victory was secured.[75]

It is important to remember the contextual constraints co-operators had to wrestle with. The editor of the *Bolton Co-operative Record*, for example, drew attention to the use made of Maxwell's pronouncements by grocers in Burnley in 1916. They had exhibited bills in their windows setting out one of Maxwell's speeches as reported in the *Morning Post*, and in large letters above the text asked, 'What would those who have sacrificed their lives for their country think of this?' Co-operators were accused of disloyalty and of not doing their fair share for the defence of their country, particularly as they did not pay income tax.[76] These charges were hardly fair; local co-operators had joined up *en masse*, and all societies lost many of their male employees in the war, let alone their members. (Jubilee histories published at this time invariably included a roll-call of co-operative employees killed in action). The movement countered such charges passionately and did not brook any doubts regarding its 'patriotism'. These dilemmas were never resolved within co-operative culture and would repay further consideration.

At the Edinburgh Congress in 1883, William Maxwell proposed the toast 'The Queen and the People' in the following terms:

> It is immaterial to me whether you are a Royalist by conviction, Royalist from expediency, or Royalist from regard; whether the present form of government be your ideal or not, I am sure of this, that you will all agree with me when I say that the present Queen of Britain is all that a constitutional sovereign should be – thoroughly interested in the people's welfare, and thoroughly sympathetic with the people's bereavements.[77]

J. T. W. Mitchell followed with 'a glowing eulogism of the Queen and her children, especially the Prince of Wales . . . .' The tradition continued after Victoria's death; the monarchy was invariably the first toast given at co-operative gatherings. Continental co-operators were often taken aback. At the dinner held at the ICA Congress in Manchester in 1902, McInnes toasted the king and immediately the English delegates rose and sang the national anthem. A correspondent in the *Wheatsheaf* described the ensuing scene of embarrassment:

> The 100 guests, Socialists, Anarchists, or otherwise, felt bound to take part, by rising, in this manifestation of respect for the Sovereign who represents, to English eyes, that British Power of which they are

proud. 'A country that has such love and respect for its Government, of whatever kind, and that has so deep a religious feeling, is very strong!' said some of the foreign delegates around me. I leave my readers to furnish their own comments on English patriotism.[78]

The monarchy was frequently praised for its closeness to 'the people'; Maxwell's sentiments were also typical in this respect. The coronation edition of the *Millgate Monthly* in the summer of 1911 was filled with photographs and articles about the royal family. The editor argued that the king deserved the support of all his subjects as long as he cared for the welfare of the people (as King George did) and declared that 'Readers of this magazine will yield to none in their loyalty to the crown and constitution'.[79]

The repercussions of these attitudes were profound. As Corrigan and Sayer have argued in a discussion of the 'Englishness' of the radical tradition in this country:

This anchorage of English radicalisms within a long-standing national culture – and one easily bent, moreover, to national chauvinism – may be one reason why they have been more prone to take 'reformist' than 'revolutionary' form.[80]

This comment can be applied equally to the Co-operative movement in our period, although the reform/revolution polarity has to be treated with circumspection (as the quotation marks indicate). The editor of the *Pendleton Co-operative Record* declared in 1915 that:

We are proud to think that in this great conflict we can give the names of so many from our own employees who have responded to the call to go and fight for the honour of King and country, and who will not be satisfied until British pluck and endurance has again prevailed.[81]

Co-operation was an international project, but the national movement had a highly developed sense of its distinctive Englishness/Britishness and this should not be ignored or marginalised.

Thus on international subjects such as war and trade, co-operators were adept at abstract criticism but rather slow in taking a government to task for specific acts of imperialist intervention – most notably the Boer War, largely ignored by the co-operative press and Congresses.[82] British imperialism was never seriously scrutinised, though occasionally a critical voice did break through. An anonymous correspondent in the *Co-operative News* in 1907 remarked that:

> Our imperialistic boast of an Empire upon which the sun never sets
> has forced the stinging reminder that there are parts of our Empire
> upon which the sun never shines![83]

The more dominant note, perhaps, was sounded by the editor of the
News following the outbreak of the First World War:

> We are convinced that the main trend of British policy was defensive,
> and the main trend of German policy aggressive. In a word, British
> armaments and British diplomacy were inspired by the need of de-
> fending the British Empire; German diplomacy and armaments were
> inspired by the desire to extend the German Empire.[84]

It is worth noting, however, that the editor's trite clarification was
provoked by a debate on the merits of British democracy in the
pages of the *News*. Soon after, a correspondent justly accused the
paper of an 'anti-German bias' which he had not expected to find.[85]
The editor later condemned the Easter Rising because of the alleged
links between Sinn Fein and the German state, and lamented this
futile attempt to destabilise the British Empire.[86]

In 1913 William Lander, a director of the CWS, travelled to Sierra
Leone in order to secure a concession for the production and export
of palm oil. For nearly a decade the Wholesale had been fighting a
protracted trade war against capitalist soap manufacturers like W.
H. Lever – a conflict discussed in some detail in chapter eight – and
Lander's mission was to secure the supply of raw materials. In September the following year he gave several lectures recounting his
experiences in Africa to the Bolton Society. Lander was an articulate
advocate of the Co-operative Commonwealth and his accounts are
of particular interest because they suggest how deeply the imperialist ethos coloured the culture of the movement. He was well aware
of the legacy of the slave trade and that the white man continued to
assert 'a superiority over the black'. Signs of inhumanity were all
around; a whip used by officials was noted in the Customs House.
Despite his criticisms Lander believed that, whereas capitalists had
failed to reform a society which languished in a 'backward state of
civilisation', co-operators would effect a more lasting improvement.
He 'humorously showed the desire of the natives to wear clothing'
by means of a slide show and noted that the CWS intended to satisfy
this desire by opening a store on the site as soon as possible.[87] Back

by popular demand, Lander made this civilising mission explicit:

> England was the greatest colonising force in the world, and having taken over the colonies, those colonies should be organised and developed on modern lines, which would give the natives a chance, for he held that in the sight of God the colour of a skin did not make any difference . . . [88]

The effort to sympathise was genuine enough and a deep humanitarianism informed Lander's approach, but the notion that the 'natives' were child-like and 'uncivilised' was too deeply ingrained within the overall culture to efface easily.

Pride in Empire in the local context was common, as the material from Pendleton and Bolton suggests. The editor of the *Burnley Co-operative Record* categorically stated in the early months of the war that:

> Whatever our faults or the faults of our economic system, there are not many people who do not allow that, broadly speaking, our Empire stands for freedom and justice to all.[89]

The editor maintained this position throughout the war although he also looked forward to an international brotherhood of nations when hostilities ceased. This faith in the progressive nature of Empire was omnipresent. The working conditions of those employed by CWS undertakings overseas were never detailed, let alone criticised. The co-operative press could publish photographs of tea-pickers employed on the CWS plantations in Ceylon and take for granted the contentedness of the native workers. The *Millgate Monthly* featured photographs of black coal miners at work in the Rand coalfield in 1917 and did not raise an eyebrow.

The magazine also ran a series of photo-articles at this time on 'The Empire's Sources of Wealth' and the editor added a stirring preface to the first feature:

> The British Empire, with its thirteen odd million square miles of territory and 435 millions of people, is the greatest the world has ever seen. The present war has certainly tended to knit the colonies more closely to the Motherland, and after the present great conflict we shall undoubtedly rely upon them more than ever for our foodstuffs and raw materials . . . . The story of their discovery and development is often a fascinating romance . . . [90]

The ideological commitment to the creation of an international Co-operative Commonwealth was riven with contradictions which this chapter has explored; the most reactionary forms of nationalism and imperialism could and did co-exist with a virulent anti-capitalism and the publicly expressed desire to substitute international co-operation for monopoly capitalism. If we should be surprised at the important role internationalist ideas and practices played in co-operative culture, we must not forget the 'popular' prejudices, bolstered by the state education system, the capitalist press and 'Public' rituals, which competed with, constrained and modified co-operative ambition.

5

The sense of the past

It was only recently that we had a history of our own country. Before times it had been a history of kings and men in high places, but now we saw that it had been the working class who had made progress possible . . .

Wilson Clayton in the *Bolton Co-operative Record*, May 1917

I

In the second volume of the *History of Co-operation in England* published in 1879 G. J. Holyoake, the movement's first historian, complained that

> So little attention has been given by historians to projects of the people for protecting their industrial interests, that it is difficult to tell how early trade unions, such as we now know them, began in England.[1]

The early history of co-operative initiatives had been similarly ignored and Holyoake's general text was intended to remedy this absence. He had collected much of the material for the work over a period of more than thirty years and supplemented this with the recollections and suggestions made by many old co-operators. Holyoake had the time and the ability to complete this task of recovery but a passion for the past was widely shared amongst his contemporaries.

In the second half of the nineteenth century more and more co-operators began to look back and try to make sense of the history of their movement and that of the working class more generally since the 'dark days' of the early industrial revolution. A number of factors strengthened this tendency to think historically in an explicit and formal manner. The cataclysmic decades of the first half of the nineteenth century seemed increasingly remote: Owenite Communities and Social Missionaries, Chartist Conventions and Plug Plots, were remembered, if at all, as features which belonged to a very different world. The contrast with the present 'modern' phase of working-class association could not have been more striking. The stores were now a central institution and their stability and permanence had been palpably demonstrated during the Cotton Famine of the 1860s and the trade depression of the early 1870s. From about this time many societies, especially in Lancashire and Yorkshire, also celebrated their 'coming-of-age' or twenty-first anniversaries and these events provided ample opportunity for reflection. As the editor of the *Co-operative News* observed after the publication of the first volume of Holyoake's *History* in 1875, this text met a real need: establishing the historical lineage of the successful modern movement before it was entirely lost to view was an urgent task.[2]

Social historians have only recently begun to explore popular conceptions of the past in the nineteenth century. As David Vincent has shown, working-class autobiographers typically related their own individual stories to the history of their communities and their class. With the development and spread of print culture many recognised that a 'satisfactory alternative history' which centred around the lives of the unlettered could no longer be sustained by the old modes of oral transmission. In this context working-class autobiographers drew on the established traditions of spiritual autobiography and oral reminiscence to transmit their alternative and often frankly subversive accounts to the next generation. Factual veracity was not an obsessive concern; anecdotes and stories were frequently inserted for purposes of entertainment and instruction. In an important sense, however, these texts cannot be understood simply as 'oppositional'; they were also regarded by middle-class readers as a sign of the increasingly 'civilised' and 'pacified' nature of the working class.[3] Print culture could be both liberating and confining for working people, as Vincent repeatedly stresses both here and in his later study of popular literacy.[4]

More recently Patrick Joyce has argued that what he calls 'liberal culture' in the second half of the nineteenth century was underpinned by a particular understanding of the past: 'Past and present were intrinsically linked in the advance of liberal culture', he writes. This liberal reading of the past – which was informed by the tradition and the texts of Protestant dissent as well as by Macaulay and the Whig interpretation of history – celebrated *progress*, conceived in terms of the march of reason, the growth of political liberty and the increase in material prosperity. Workingmen leaders like Thomas Cooper, George Howell, Thomas Burt and John Wilson, so Joyce maintains, shared this orientation although they sometimes gave it a radical inflection; Joyce instances Thomas Cooper's lectures on English history delivered during the late 1840s and early 1850s which included accounts of subjects usually ignored in the Whig interpretations, such as Peterloo and Henry Hunt. Unfortunately Joyce does not examine this tension in detail as most of his discussion focuses on histories from 'above', as he himself admits, particularly local urban histories and school texts. Nevertheless, despite this methodological problem what comes through very strongly, from popular almanacs and dialect literature as well as urban histories, is the ubiquity of narratives of progress during this period.[5]

I have found this work by Joyce and Vincent useful though neither of them considers the sense of the past communicated by co-operators, and the subject has also been ignored by other prominent students of 'people's history'.[6] This is surprising given the extant material available, and this chapter explores the connections between the culture of the movement and particular understandings and representations of the past. From the start the movement was shaped by a sense of the past which was communicated by means of celebration and ritual – the anniversary of the store was the most obvious occasion here – as well as by written texts. First it is appropriate to return to the movement's early historian, G. J. Holyoake, and explore in some depth his appropriation of the radical past; particular attention will be paid to his own version of the narrative of progress, and the tensions and contradictions contained therein. Employing evidence from the many jubilee histories produced in the twenty years before the First World War to mark a society's fiftieth anniversary, I go on to suggest that the narratives of progress which underpinned liberal culture were in crisis, at least within this working-class association and by the end of the period were being increasingly displaced by what are better understood, perhaps, as narratives of emancipation.

II

W. T. Stead, the renowned journalist whose lurid and semi-porno-
graphic exposé of the 'Maiden Tribute of Modern Babylon' had
shocked and fascinated the reading public in the 1880s, interviewed
Holyoake for the *Review of Reviews* in 1901. The interview took
place at the reformers' home in Brighton and Stead was clearly fascinated by the interior: 'The whole quaint little house with all its
rooms and rambling passages and staircases was redolent of the
memories of a stormy past', he wrote. Portraits of Holyoake's
mother, Joseph Cowen and Garibaldi hung on the walls. Also
prominent were two flags presented by the latter in recognition of
Holyoake's work on behalf of Italian liberation. Holyoake confided
to Stead that he hoped that one of these flags, which were 'solemnly
aired from the windows of Eastern Lodge' during holidays, would
one day be used as the pall over his own coffin. (The wish was
granted five years later). Propped against a wall was a Macerone
pike manufactured during the Reform agitation in Birmingham in
1831 which had once belonged to James Watson, the Owenite publisher. Busts of Voltaire, J. S. Mill and Joseph Mazzini adorned the
furniture along with a bottle of 'Mr. Secretary Walpole's Tears' – a
satirical souvenir produced to mark the Hyde Park 'riots' in 1866 –
and one of the whistles used by the Radicals of Leeds to help them
keep order against Tory opponents of free speech at a meeting of
republicans in the city in 1871. Holyoake also showed Stead, not
without a touch of pride, the compasses he had made when learning
his trade as a metalworker at the Eagle Foundry in Birmingham in
the 1830s.[7]

Stead's interest in Holyoake was understandable for, by the turn
of the century, the latter was a very well known figure in Britain,
continental Europe and America. Born in Birmingham in 1817,
Holyoake quit the workshop and became an Owenite lecturer in
1840, first in Worcester, then in Sheffield. Like many of his generation his early career in the radical movement was stormy: he was
imprisoned for six months in Gloucester Gaol for blasphemy in
1842. For the next decade he made a precarious living as a radical
publisher and bookseller in London, founded the Secularist movement and in 1852 was elected onto the Chartist Executive. A prolific
writer, most of his energy thereafter was divided between the Co-
operative movement and Liberal politics.[8] Via this fascinating inter-

view Stead re-presented a set of images from a vanished past; the question is how are we to make sense of this premature obituary of the man and a particular kind of politics?

The objects so lovingly described by Stead – he preferred to call them 'relics' – belonged to Holyoake's *Musée imaginaire*. Many professional historians have since criticised Holyoake's historical studies for their inaccuracy and chronological lapses, but he is best seen as a 'collector' rather than a 'historian'.[9] His historical works are really collections of stories or anecdotes, arranged fairly haphazardly, but which nevertheless articulate, explicitly and implicitly, a set of arguments or 'morals'. (Note the affinities with autobiographies here). Holyoake's house closely resembled many other texts in his *oeuvre* and, taken together, the objects and their associations or stories communicated a particular understanding of the past. The major theme of course was progress. The present respected and comfortable (if not particularly well-off) situation of the occupant of the house and the triumph of peaceful methods of social and political change provided a vivid contrast to an earlier age characterised by poverty and violent forms of protest. The objects also tended to bathe Holyoake in a romantic light and this was surely deliberate; known for his tolerance and equanimity, for his dispassionate nature, Holyoake no doubt occasionally fantasised about the colourful life of a revolutionary leader.

Joyce's emphasis on the importance of narratives of progress to liberal culture is helpful here but we must be careful not to push it too far; the liberal vision frequently blurred or even faded entirely. True, Holyoake often read the signs of the times – especially the development and spread of education, material well-being, international understanding and so forth – as evidence of progress toward the end of his life. Nevertheless, his memorialisation of conflict and violence may have implied rather more than simply nostalgia or wish-fulfilment; some of the episodes dated from the quite recent past, after all. More than this, it could be argued that these objects and the forms of organisation and strategy they represented were merely *stored* in Holyoake's labyrinthine retreat. Working-class associations, especially co-operative societies, had clearly done much to improve the condition of the people since the first half of the century but the renunciation of a confrontationalist strategy was conditional upon the maintenance of a liberal, non-repressive, state apparatus. This was Holyoake's line: 'Those who are refused political recognition in a state, own no allegiance to it', as he had written during the Reform agitation in 1865, in a pamphlet which countenanced the use of violence to achieve political change.[10] Maybe one day, if necessary, the Macerone pike would again be pressed into service. After all the red flag was regularly unfurled. However we read this text – and my point here is that it *can* be read in a number of ways and that narratives of progress are often complex and contradictory – the nuances of meaning were lost on Stead. Predictably, the published article canonised Holyoake, quite literally. According to Stead, the 'relics' were the mementoes of a secular saint who had discovered his 'vocation' – the fight for 'truth and social justice' – at an early age and, despite persecution, had remained true to this cause until the end. Stead correctly intuited that the 'relics' were vitally important to Holyoake for whom the past was 'an ever present and vivid reality', but accepted the progressive vision of the past that they explicitly communicated quite uncritically, probably because it accorded so closely with his own.

Central to the liberal vision of the past was the notion of class co-operation and harmony – Cowen, J. S. Mill and Mazzini were prominent figures in the selective radical tradition constructed by Holyoake.[11] To unravel this aspect we need to go back fifty years to find the genesis of Holyoake's re-working of the radical past. In the aftermath of the collapse of the organised working-class movement in the late 1840s, many radical British working men struggled to find appropriate channels for their energies and ambitions. Many, including Holyoake, believed that in this changed and weakened situation, collaboration with liberal members of the middle class around specific issues (franchise reform, repeal of the taxes on knowledge, support for European liberation movements and so on) was a viable and attractive option. Consequently a conciliatory, tolerant policy was pursued. This was the message of Holyoake's funeral oration delivered at Hetherington's grave side in 1849. For Holyoake the latter symbolised an earlier, more aggressive mode of protest; 'Hetherington shrank from the rich and bland, and wrapped himself up in the integrity, and poverty, and ruggedness of his own order', he declaimed to an audience of over 2,000 people. According to Holyoake, Hetherington was 'more soldier than advocate', maintained that class co-operation led directly to political corruption and thus favoured 'assault' rather than 'exposition'.[12]

Holyoake believed that the school of politicians represented by

Hetherington, and by extension the earlier radical movement, was already 'going a little out of fashion' by 1849. Working-class radicals now needed to speak to different audiences and communicate with potential allies from across the social spectrum. This helps explain his repeated stress on the importance of grammar and the art of public speaking for working people. His *Public Speaking and Debate* which first appeared in 1849, recommended discipline of speech, method, tact and style but also stressed that form and content ought not to be divorced, that principles always informed method. Pronunciation, it was argued, needed to be refined: unaccented vowels and dropped 'h's' served immediately to distinguish the educated from the ignorant.[13] Holyoake recognised, somewhat grudgingly, that the body of the orator was always in some sense bound up with the message, that physical health and 'great volumes of animal heat' were often necessary although personally he did 'not rate this animal life very high.'[14] This was probably an oblique stab at Feargus O'Connor, another of the unfashionable old guard, from someone whose slight stature, delicate health and 'thin' voice were continual handicaps.[15]

So even before mid-century, Holyoake had perceived a rupture between 'early' and 'modern' forms of radicalism and had begun to reinforce this mode of emplotment in his own speeches and writings. This partial and one-sided view was of course perfectly compatible with liberal appropriations of the past and can easily be read as evidence of Holyoake's 'incorporation' into bourgeois culture.[16] But we must remember that Holyoake was working within and trying to make sense of a very real organisational and ideological crisis: after the failure of the General Strike of 1842 and the Chartist disarray following the Kennington Common 'fiasco' six years later, direct confrontation with the capitalist state was no longer a viable option.[17] The collapse of Owenite socialism and the community experiments had also demonstrated the difficulties involved in social transformation conceived and executed from above. Whatever the long-term implications, all this meant a profound caesura in labour movement development. Holyoake grasped the significance of this change and attempted to piece together a way forward. His strategy certainly did not rule out co-operation with middle-class radicals but it cannot be grasped in its full complexity by flattening and vague generalisations like 'incorporation' or 'populism'.[18] Moreover, the break and the lessons to be drawn therefrom could be turned to quite different ends. The discipline and regulation of the language and the bodies of working-class people by themselves, that is the self-reformation of the class, was a vital resource necessary for building a successful associational culture from below. There was and is no easy way out of this contradiction which marked the rest of Holyoake's life and which has been nicely captured by the French sociologist Pierre Bourdieu in the following paradox: 'Resistance may be alienating and submission may be liberating.'[19] Holyoake's recommendations could have both 'reactionary' and 'radical' implications, simultaneously.

It is within this context that his developing interest in the history of the retail Co-operative movement from the mid-1850s becomes intelligible. The first histories of popular movements usually appear soon after or during their collapse; R. G. Gammage's *History of the Chartist Movement* (1854) is a good example. This was not the case with the history of the Co-operative movement, the writing of which began as soon as co-operation had gained a relatively firm base in the industrial North. Indeed 'history' was intimately bound up with the success and promulgation of co-operative forms during this early phase and was construed, not merely as the product of passive reflection possible only after the struggle subsided, but as an active ingredient in a developing movement culture. Holyoake's work was central here, especially *Self-Help by the People: History of Co-operation in Rochdale* (1858) which had first appeared three years before as a series of articles in the *Daily News*. (We might note here that Samuel Smiles' famous work, which pushed an individualist version of the self-help doctrine, was published in 1859). Holyoake's work performed an important agitational and inspirational role within the movement, both in this country and on the continent.[20] Joseph Cowen, for example, read passages from the text during concerts at the Blaydon and Stella mechanics' institute in 1858 and a co-operative store was commenced soon after.[21] This pattern was repeated elsewhere; *Self-Help* served as a practical handbook for working-class activists and was concerned as much with the future as with the past. For Holyoake the twenty-eight Pioneers had founded the 'modern' movement through the successful introduction of the dividend on purchases. Although this part of the account was largely mythological, as a number of scholars have pointed out[22], Holyoake did not obscure the Owenite and Chartist credentials of the Pioneers. The dividend was not regarded as a sign of 'embourgeoisement' but rather as a stepping-stone to the co-operative community of the future.

This text was also aimed at a middle-class liberal audience: for Holyoake, the example of the Pioneers demonstrated that peaceful social change, based on independent working-class action but supported by sympathetic middle-class individuals, was eminently practicable. Dedicated to Lord Brougham, *Self-Help* furnished ample proof of the improved manners and morals of a class that had only recently threatened to overthrow the system by means of violent revolution. Drawing on this text, J. S. Mill had enthused about the future 'uplifting' effects of co-operation on the working classes in a revised edition of his *Principles of Political Economy* (5th edition 1862). In the 1860s Gladstone and Bright also employed the so-called 'Rochdale argument' in support of franchise reform. Thus this early history was implicated in the process of working-class 'pacification' and 'civilisation' after mid-century.[23] In this respect it had much in common with working-class autobiographies which were eagerly consumed by middle-class readers for similar reasons. Again, it is worth recalling Vincent's insistence that print culture and literacy was both a problem and an opportunity for working people; it made it possible to build bridges between the cultures of different social classes but such skills could also be a source of class pride and consciousness.[24]

The remarkable success of *Self-Help* established Holyoake's role as the historian of co-operation and he followed this with a history of the Halifax Society in 1867. This text also celebrated the local Owenite roots but pushed the Communist millennium far into the future: 'Co-operation . . . is the first rung of a ladder to which there are a thousand steps' he told readers in the introduction.[25] Soon after, Holyoake wrote the first general history of the movement which appeared in two volumes in 1875 and 1879. Interestingly, these works were produced privately; the movement had not completely embraced Holyoake yet, even if Holyoake had fully embraced the movement. Ill-health and lack of money meant that this project was nearly abandoned until Walter Morrison, the Liberal MP, organised financial support.[26] Volume two of *The History of Co-operation* was dedicated to John Bright, 'a friend of equity in industry'. Although it was welcomed, this tendentious work proved highly controversial within the movement for by now Holyoake had nailed his colours to the mast of co-partnership – a favourite amongst middle-class liberal reformers – and bent the history to serve this cause. He also emphasised the connections between Secularism and early co-operation, much to the chagrin of people like Lloyd Jones. Other text books on co-operative practice published around this time were similarly marked by these internal debates.[27]

Holyoake's *History* pushed the notion of class alliances very strongly indeed, and the role of force to effect social change was entirely discountenanced, at least in England. The few hotheads that had caused mischief amongst radical movements in the first half of the century, he suggested, had picked up their misguided (and foreign) faith in martial methods from the army. Holyoake had criticised the middle-class Owenite Executive for its class-bias and mismanagement of Queenwood in 1844 but retracted this criticism in the first volume of the *History*. The polemical pamphlet written after a visit to Harmony Hall had been an 'error' and, whilst working-class independence was a worthy ambition the ingrained distrust of 'gentlemen' had produced only negative, results.[28] Although the second volume did contain a critique of competition – 'a chopping-machine and the poor were always under the knife' – readers were assured that things were much better now: factory legislation had improved conditions of labour and employers generally 'have more friendliness of manner'.[29]

Soon after, in 1881, Holyoake published what was to be perhaps his clearest statement of faith in the liberal vision of history, the *Life of Joseph Rayner Stephens*. Although Holyoake did attempt to explain and justify working-class opposition to the New Poor Law in the 1830s, the workhouse (it was claimed) was no longer the terror it had once been and now only touched the lives of a small unfortunate minority. Stephens' use of violent, revolutionary rhetoric was played down and this grim phase contrasted with the prosperous and harmonious present. The main reason for this change, Holyoake asserted, was free trade which had 'brought steadier employment and higher wages to the working class' as well as more food.[30] The country had avoided the cataclysmic upheavals witnessed elsewhere through an innate and particularly *English* 'love of truth, justice and fair play.'[31] Linking the patriotic and the masculine, Holyoake impatiently declared:

> This is our English way, and it is ignorance and silliness to censure
> that manly energy of independence which is the characteristic of the

Englishman in every land in which he is found.[32]

Although Holyoake maintained that no single party monopolised these patriotic sentiments – they could be found in Tory as well as Radical hearts – they were mobilised most effectively within modern Liberalism because this political creed was future-orientated. 'Liberal glasses', he remarked, 'have a longer vision . . . and reveal things good for progress as well as party.'[33]

All this sounds as if Holyoake had swallowed the liberal cult of progress wholesale and Biagini has recently argued that Holyoake thoroughly accepted and articulated an authentic 'popular Liberalism'.[34] However, as the discussion above suggests, his contradictory class location and desire to speak to different constituencies meant that his position in various debates, including the debate on the legacy of English radicalism, was neither stable nor consistently held. The 'organisation of forgetting' certainly aided class co-operation but this was a ragged and changing process.[35] At certain times, in certain contexts, critical memories threatened to subvert the bland urbanities. Holyoake's stubborn insistence on the utopian, anti-capitalist roots of co-operative practice has already been noted. This emphasis was strongly approved by old Owenites like William Pare who wrote to Holyoake in the summer of 1867 after reading *The History of Co-operation in Halifax*. Pare explained that he liked the work because Holyoake sought to 'vindicate with discrimination the old Socialist movement – the progenitor of the present – and do not as some others who should know better speak of the grand old Owen merely as a "dreamer"!'[36] The moral bankruptcy of the competitive system repeatedly drew Holyoake's fire: 'We live in a society of thieves, whom competition licences to plunder, and he who does it most adroitly is said to have "great business capacity"', he wrote in a pamphlet in 1873.[37]

Belief in progress was conditional, and particular moments and critiques could not easily be assigned to oblivion by the liberal vision. A number of factors helped undermine any simple affirmation of faith. First, despite the improvements, poverty had not been abolished in late Victorian Britain. In a speech to the National Liberal Club Banquet in 1896 Holyoake attempted to both placate and reproach his audience in the following manner:

> The world is not fit for a gentleman to live in while undeserved misery exists in the neighbourhood of his mansion. I am no Socialist, but I

can see that honest industry is defrauded somewhere while it needs charity or state aid.[38]

Of course the tone of this passage is highly propitious: only '*undeserved* misery' is morally repugnant and the implicit ambition is working-class 'independence' – a suitably vague keyword often espoused by many Liberal leaders – rather than Tory philanthropy or State Socialism.[39] But it is all too reassuring, as if the audience needed to be reassured, over and over again, and as if Holyoake was always about to be accused of dissembling: 'I am no Socialist, but . . . .' Perhaps some of the assembled worthies had read his article, in *Subjects of the Day* six years before, which argued that co-operation was no more than Owenite Socialism in modern guise.[40] And if they had gone on to read the reports of the dinner held two years later in honour of the leader of the Social Democratic Federation, Henry Hyndman, at which Holyoake referred to 'the domination of capitalists . . . as coercive and as pitiless as hate itself', their worst fears would surely have been realised.[41]

Not only was the economic system far from perfect, but democratic politics was also under constant threat. Holyoake's qualified support for Bright and Gladstone should not blind us to the fact that he was a great nuisance to Liberal Party grandees, from his time in the Reform League in the 1860s through to his virtual retirement from active politics following the Home Rule crisis in the mid-1880s. He consistently put issues of democratic form and participation on the political agenda. This ranged from criticism of the middle-class composition of Parliament and the role of the representative, to the importance of the ballot and the increasing cost of agitation.[42] The year before his death in 1906 he lamented the decline of the platform and compared his own preference for debate to the orthodoxy which now prevailed:

> After my lectures I always invited discussion, for no truth can be fully trusted until it has been fairly discussed on equal terms. The Anti-Corn Law League first gave method to the procedure at public meetings, which has since developed to the present form with resolutions supported from the platform, but never discussed by the audience that is subsequently called upon to endorse the views expressed.[43]

Holyoake accepted that real political gains had been made for working people in the political sphere but he also believed that the existing system was a compromise and that very real losses had also been incurred. For example, working-class 'apathy' was structurally embedded in the wider network of social relationships (poverty was the greatest barrier to participation) and the country was still ruled by what Holyoake called the 'aristocracy of sex'.

This latter criticism often recurred. In the 1840s Holyoake had been on friendly terms with Owenite feminists like Frances Wright and Emma Martin and had been a strong supporter of women's social and political rights. He maintained this support throughout his life and this was one of the reasons why he held J. S. Mill in such high esteem: Mill's *Subjection of Women* was greeted with a glowing tribute in 1869.[44] Holyoake held no illusions about official Liberalism in this regard, since it tended to marginalise or simply ignore this vital issue. He admired Bright certainly, but made no bones about his political limitations:

> The idea of democracy was not in his mind, and women, as part of the human race, having political interests was simply abhorrent to him.[45]

Biagini's argument that during the 1850s Liberal politicians like Gladstone, Cobden, Bright and J. S. Mill 'had replaced the socialist leaders in the co-operators' pantheon' is at best misleading and highly simplistic.[46] The relationship between both the movement in general and Holyoake in particular, and Liberalism, was complex; the links cannot be grasped in terms of absolute assimilation or rejection. Holyoake's Owenite-derived commitment to female emancipation brought him closer to some middle-class radicals and distanced him from others. Again the limitations of an undifferentiated understanding of 'popular Liberalism' are apparent, as is the appropriateness of the progressive historical vision when the position and status of women was under consideration.

Finally, Holyoake sometimes used the confrontational nature of the earlier phase of radical history as a critical resource or political weapon in the present, to try and force concessions from above. His guarded support for violent protest during the agitation which preceded the Second Reform Act in 1867 was noted above; twenty years later the issue was raised once again, this time by the crisis provoked by Gladstone's Bill for Irish self-government. In a pamphlet published by the National Liberal Association in 1886 Holyoake reminded his readers of the turbulent Chartist times and drew a clear political lesson from this experience and the comparable events across the Irish Sea:

> What was the characteristic of Birmingham as late as 1839? The
> 'Friends of the People', as they called themselves after the manner of
> Marat, were listened to with greedy ears. The wilder the speeches the
> more they were applauded – because their extravagance implied sym-
> pathy and indignation. In the class amid which I was reared, despair
> was hereditary. Invasion itself would have excited but acquiescence.
> In any change of masters there was hope since the prospects of the
> working class could not, it was thought, be worse. Then fairness was
> regarded as feebleness. There was nothing too mad to be believed,
> nothing too malignant to be said, and that not of alien rule, but of a
> class in the same town. Hundreds made arms secretly. The riots and
> the fires of the Bull Ring occurred when I was there – not acting, but
> not wondering. Whoever judges the capacity of Birmingham for free-
> dom, tolerance and self-government by the language and acts of that
> time, would judge it as Ireland is judged today.[47]

As one would expect in this context Holyoake's remarks were very
guarded. The exclusion of the English working class from the political nation in the 1830s had not only bred despair but had also weakened the patriotic spirit: 'Invasion itself would have excited but
acquiescence.' We see him on the sidelines during the Bull Ring riots,
an informed observer rather than a participant of course. Without
self-government it was little wonder that Ireland was being torn
apart by civil strife and the only remedy was Home Rule: 'Ireland is
to us what slavery was to America', he wrote.

Enough has been said at least to render problematic Holyoake's
embrace of 'popular Liberalism' and the progressive historical vision which underpinned it. Nevertheless, there were real points of
attachment for radicals from working-class backgrounds, such as
Holyoake. The most important point of attachment, as a number of
commentators including McKibbin, Joyce and Biagini have indicated, was support for free trade.[48] Like the majority of his peers
Holyoake accepted the separation of the political from the economic realm, a division embodied in free trade finance. The policy
of cheap food dovetailed nicely with unfettered collective bargain-
ing and it was not the role of the state, so Holyoake thought, to
create monopolies of any kind or distort the workings of the market
mechanism. This did not mean that he totally ruled out state intervention to curb and regulate competition; he supported Beatrice

Webb's resolution in favour of legislation against 'sweating' at the 1892 Co-operative Congress, for example.[49] But he often inveighed against protection, with over-drawn, simplistic comparisons between the 'Hungry Forties' and a more prosperous, well-fed present.[50] Most co-operators in the late nineteenth century similarly believed that free trade was vital to the success of their enterprise, at least this side of the Co-operative Commonwealth. Support for free trade was regarded as perfectly compatible with the social aims of the movement and helps explain co-operators' reluctance to intervene directly in the political sphere to secure their interests. This view, and the historical vision on which it was based, was to be severely tested from the turn of the century by a younger generation of co-operative writers.

III

From the early 1890s it was becoming increasingly apparent to many co-operators that representations of the past shaped political practice in the present. Working-class children were now being taught a triumphalist version of the history of the English nation in the Board Schools and the story of working-class community and association was effaced by this imperialist narrative.[51] One response was to exert pressure on Schools Boards to modify the curriculum. Arthur Acland, the Liberal MP who championed the co-operative cause in the Commons, played an important role here. As Minister of Education, Acland tried to persuade School Boards to adopt textbooks which discussed the history and development of working-class association, particularly co-operation. In 1893 he drew up an Evening School Code and co-operation figured prominently in the proposed syllabus; the recommended text was Arnold Forster's *Laws of Everyday Life*.[52] Although co-operators welcomed these initiatives with enthusiasm, private traders were furious and in November a deputation from the Federation of Grocers' Associations waited upon Acland at the Education Department to make a formal complaint. The code was vigorously attacked in the pages of the private traders' journal, *The Grocer*.[53]

At the Co-operative Congress the following year W. R. Rae moved a resolution thanking Acland for his efforts. The leader of the Huddersfield Secularists, Owen Balmforth, seconded the motion and observed that:

Mr Acland was the first Minister who had introduced into our schools
some knowledge of the working class movements of this country – co-
operation, trades unionism and friendly societies. What would have
been our fate if these great movements had been blotted out? There
was now a prospect that the children would be trained in a knowledge
of the best history of our country. There had been too much history
taught about wars and kings and court life.[54]

The issue was debated in the Commons soon after: John Burns as
well as Acland vigorously supported the code. Temple's motion,
which would have erased the controversial clause, was eventually
defeated.[55]

No outright victory was achieved though, as private traders were
a powerful lobby on many School Boards. In Brighton the Board
decided to cut the offending chapters of Forster's book, but this decision was contested by the local co-operative society, represented
by Holyoake, who eventually won the case.[56] In Bolton the decision
went the other way. Undaunted the society launched a propaganda
campaign: the Educational Committee reprinted the chapters on co-
operation in Forster's text and distributed them throughout the bor-
ough under the title of 'The Prohibited Book'. Despite this the
School Board withdrew the heretical sections.[57] In their report for
1896 the Central Board of the Co-operative Union noted that private traders in Scotland had managed to delete all reference to the
Evening School Code and remarked that: 'This, to our mind, shows
the importance of co-operators having representatives in Parliament
to watch their interests without regard for creed or party.'[58]
Acland's elder brother Thomas achieved limited success in 1907
when he persuaded the Devonshire Education Committee to recommend the teaching of the history and principles of co-operation in all
council elementary schools in the country. No special text-book was
produced, however, and teachers could ignore the advice if they
wished as instruction was left to their own discretion.[59]

As the local and national state proved largely hostile, co-operators were left with no choice but to provide a more formal teaching
of history themselves, in order to try and counter the dominant history of 'wars and kings and court life'. Consequently classes were
organised by the Co-operative Union from about this time and more
text-books appeared to serve a growing market. The following were
the most important: Beatrice Potter, *The Co-operative Movement in*

Great Britain (1891); G. J. Holyoake, *The Co-operative Movement Today* (1891); Ben Jones, *Co-operative Production* (1894); and Catherine Webb (ed.), *Industrial Co-operation: The Story of a Peaceful Revolution* (1904). The works by Potter and Holyoake were polemical interventions in the internal debate over profit-sharing; they had little substantive to say about the history of the movement. Jones's work was a monumental study, too specialised for general class-work. Webb's text was designed specifically to fill this niche and, as the title suggested, the work articulated the highest aspirations for the movement. Webb's definition of the co-operative ideal was decidedly neo-Owenite in tone: 'By means of mutual association to eliminate the present industrial system, and to substitute mutual Co-operation for the common good as the basis of all human society.'[60]

Special classes in 'industrial history' were commenced in 1897 but their appeal was fairly limited; only 211 members took this class in the 1913–14 session. This figure probably underestimates the interest as history also figured prominently on courses in general co-operation; in the same session 1,200 members took the intermediate and adult classes in this subject.[61] Some joint work was also undertaken with the Workers' Educational Association; R. H. Tawney, for example, taught a WEA course on 'Economic History' to Rochdale co-operators in 1907.[62] However, classes for children proved most popular. Meeting once a week for a few hours, boys and girls aged between ten and thirteen read and discussed the history of the movement presented in Isa Nicholson's *Our Story*. This specially-written text, first published in 1903, had sold 61,000 copies by 1911. It was republished for the ninth time that year in a penny illustrated edition which ran to 250,000 copies.[63] *Our Story* described in simple prose the 'horrors' of industrialisation, Owen's role, the 'revolution' effected by the Pioneers and the development of the modern movement. Fred Abbotts, a Walsall co-operator who attended these classes before the First World War and later went on to be a class-teacher himself, recalled that;

> There (in the class) we were given a book to read. It was a sort of text-book for junior classes called *Our Story* by Nicholson. You read the childish version of the Rochdale Pioneers, and of course I used to know the thing off by heart almost, and I became very interested in the educational side.[64]

We can only speculate about how many other working-class boys and girls were inspired in this way but the continuing expansion of the movement in the early twentieth century may have been due in part to this initiative. At the turn of the century 1,967 children attended classes in junior co-operation. Fourteen years later the figure had reached 16,777.[65]

IV

Besides these initiatives many societies celebrated their 'jubilees' or fiftieth anniversaries in grand style during the twenty years preceding the First World War. The programme of the Hyde Society in Lancashire may be taken as representative. It commenced with an exhibition of CWS goods in May 1912 which occupied all three floors of the local Mechanics' Institute and was visited by over 20,000 people. A Jubilee Gala and sports day held in June attracted nearly 4,000 children and 1,500 adults. The following month the employees made a trip to Southport and the society closed for the day. An 'old folks' party took place at the end of September when 600 over-sixties were treated to a tea and concert. During October five free concerts were held in the district and in November every member (in total over 3,200) was presented with a souvenir crockery tray and a copy of the society's jubilee history. This text marked the culmination of a wide repertoire of social events designed to remind members and their families of both past achievements and future prospects.[66]

This pattern was repeated elsewhere and the jubilee histories constitute an important and largely forgotten genre of 'people's history'; they will be explored in some detail in the rest of this chapter. Between 1897 and the end of the First World War at least seventy-five were produced in England. They were distributed free of charge and, as many societies in the industrial North counted their members in tens of thousands, the expense was considerable. The Bolton Society, for example, had over 36,000 members in 1909, its jubilee year, and the cost of providing each with a history which was almost 700 pages long must have accounted for a large proportion of the £3,000 the Society allocated for celebrations that year.[67] Ten thousand copies of the Accrington Society's history were distributed at a cost of £450.[68] A conservative estimate would put the total number of texts produced at about half a million.

Before proceeding a few caveats are in order. Although an analysis of the thematics of these texts is a legitimate exercise we must be mindful of their limitations as a source. Apart from their uneven quality (in terms of composition, historical methodology, argument and imagination) it is very difficult to ascertain the purchase these texts had on the movement. It is unlikely that they merely reflected widely-held attitudes toward the past and we have no way of knowing how many rank-and-file co-operators read these works or shared their authors' opinions. There is also, as one would expect given the spatial development of the movement, a geographical imbalance; nearly two-thirds of my sample originated from the mill towns of Lancashire and the West Riding of Yorkshire. Of the rest, most were produced by societies dependent on mining communities in the North-East with a scattering of societies in the Midlands and South-West. Such specificities make any generalisations concerning the historical consciousness of the movement based on this body of evidence highly problematic; political traditions were often deeply rooted within local cultures, as Snell has recently underlined.[69]

It is also difficult to discover much about the authors of these texts. Holyoake was commissioned to write some of the earliest, including the histories of the Leeds and Derby Societies.[70] A few were written by talented labour movement journalists like James Haslam or Montague Blatchford, well-known figures with a national profile. Both were New Life socialists. Haslam was born into a handloom weaving family in Bolton in 1869 and started work as a little piecer in a cotton mill at the age of eight. Trade union activity led to victimisation and he worked on various papers (including the *Cotton Factory Times*) before joining the staff of the *Co-operative News* full-time in 1915. Haslam wrote histories of two Lancashire societies: Eccles in 1907 and Accrington in 1910.[71] Montague Blatchford was the elder brother of Robert, editor of the *Clarion*. Born in Aberdeen in 1848, the family moved to Halifax in 1862 and Montagu was apprenticed in a lithographic printing company. He helped launch the *Clarion* in 1891 and contributed numerous articles, political cartoons and verse under the name of 'Mont Blong'. Unlike Haslam he knew little about co-operation before the jubilee committee of the Halifax Society asked him to write their history in 1900. In the preface to the volume he admitted that he had 'commenced the task with a feeling of indifference', but after studying the origins and principles of the movement had come to feel 'sympathy and respect for the men who have, by patience and industry, achieved so much . . . .'[72]

Most of these histories, however, were written by members of local societies, usually by the secretary or an activist in the educational department. We know even less about these individuals. Some referred to their parentage and upbringing in their work: Thomas Boydell, who wrote the history of the Leigh Society in 1907, for example, was born into a family of silk handloom weavers and could remember his own father complaining about unfair methods of abating.[73] Others were occasionally mentioned in the local co-operative press. The Bolton historian, F. W. Peaples, was also assistant secretary and librarian. A great lover of books, he ran the large library (which issued between 500 and 1,000 books daily by 1905) for over twenty years.[74] More is known about the Oldham historian, J. T. Taylor. Born in Chadderton just outside Oldham in 1851 into a family of silk handloom weavers like Boydell, Taylor started work at the age of eight, first in a brickyard, then in the iron trade. He was employed at Platt's shop until at least the mid-1890s, eventually becoming a foreman. Taylor picked up his education at the local Unitarian Sunday School and the Co-op library and newsroom and remained a fervent Unitarian and co-operator all his life, taking a keen interest in the educational side of the movement.[75] As I noted in chapter two, the nonconformist influence was common – even Holyoake had been taught by Unitarians in Birmingham in the 1830s.[76]

It seems not unlikely that many of the writers of these texts came from similar backgrounds. In fine, they were probably skilled working men with strong religious and social convictions who had struggled hard to raise themselves in life. A few had probably secured part-time or full-time employment in the movement in clerical or managerial positions. These autodidacts were not financially better off than most skilled artisans but may have experienced their own careers in terms of an improvement in status. This would help to explain the haughty and impatient tone adopted by a small minority when speaking about what Peaples referred to as the 'idle, thriftless, roving section of poor people' who could not be helped by co-operation because they would not help themselves.[77] Most authors did not differentiate in this way, however, and described themselves as 'workers' who had to fit in the role of 'historian' or 'compiler' in their spare time.[78] Moreover, these texts were often addressed directly to a working-class audience for, as Redshaw asserted: 'The Co-operative Movement is inherently and distinctively a working-class movement.'[79]

It is possible to piece together some idea of the varieties of written history that had influenced these authors. Most important was the work of J. R. Green whose *Short History of the English People* (1877) could be found in most co-operative libraries. Green had shifted the emphasis away from the 'drum and trumpet' history of the State towards English society and civilisation; Samuel has discussed the influence of Green's liberal-radical version of 'people's history' on early British Marxists but his work had a much wider purchase.[80] The Fabian co-operator Harry Snell wrote in *Comradeship* in 1900 that, 'Before the time of J. R. Green, English history was but the record of triumphant scoundrelism.'[81] An article entitled 'A Hero of Literature' in the *Wheatsheaf* in 1907 described the *Short History* as 'the first book to replace dry collections of dates by a living chronicle of a people's life.' Green's contact with the London working class bore fruit in a work which was to 'become a classic in many a workman's home, which is the highest place of all.'[82]

Other important texts included Thorold Rogers, *Six Centuries of Work and Wages* (1884); Arnold Toynbee, *The Industrial Revolution* (1884); and H. de B. Gibbins, *Industrial History* (1892). Many jubilee historians were indebted to this corpus of work and used it to buttress a pessimistic reading of the industrial revolution. Thomas Jones and Joseph Rhodes quoted Toynbee on the dehumanising nature of the cash nexus and factory production and also commended Rogers for his harsh, succinct judgement of early industrial capitalism: 'the 25 years beginning in 1796 were the worst years in the whole history of English labour', Rogers had written in *Six Centuries*.[83] The historians of the Bishop Auckland, Stocksbridge, Bingley and Great Horton Societies all made use of Gibbins' work in a similar way. His vivid description of child exploitation in the early factories was rehearsed in detail.[84]

Such familiarity testifies to the narrowing gap between 'high' and 'low' histories in this period; as Joyce has argued, working-class autodidacts stood at the juncture between printed accounts of the past and the shifting narratives which informed custom and oral culture.[85] This allowed the jubilee historians to make an important methodological breakthrough, for although their accounts were

based on a wide range of written and printed sources, unlike professional academics they also had direct access to the experiences and
memories of working people. Many drew attention to this aspect: in
his history of the Keighley Society published in 1911 Joseph Rhodes
explained that

> no written record – unless the scribe has been guided by the historical
> rather than the business instinct – can give as vividly as the living
> witness a picture of the surroundings of an epoch-making event.[86]

Individuals were frequently interviewed as part of the jubilee celebrations in order to honour the early pioneers and recover the
shadowy origins of co-operation in each locality. Rhodes, for example, included in his text the reminiscences of Mrs Ben Wild, the
84–year-old widow of one of the founders, who recalled the bread
and porridge diet of her youth and the invaluable support local
women had given to the first store.[87]

These links with a predominantly oral culture in which memory
and story-telling played such a vital part made it possible for some
jubilee historians to grasp the political significance of 'history from
below'. Blatchford, for example, criticised professional historians
who ignored 'the everyday doings and quiet lives' of the majority
and focused instead on 'the folly or extravagance of a monarch, or
the bloody and devastating victory of a famous general . . . '.[88] 'The
genuine history of a nation', according to Bramwell Hudson, the
historian of the Cainscross Society, was the story of 'those who live
amid the realities of everyday life, and by their labours in peaceful
industry contribute to make a country what it is.'[89] Scholastic 'objectivity' was also rejected. The jubilee committee of the Bedlington
Society apologised to members for the shortcomings of their history
but trusted that it 'will interest you, your children, and your children's children, and stir them up to effort for their own emancipation from the thraldom of capitalism.'[90]

This emphasis on 'history from below' helps explain the struc-
tural importance of visual images in these narratives. Co-operators
recognised the democratic potential of photography early on; for
Holyoake it was 'a source of revelation greater than the telescope.'[91]
Photographs of co-operative buildings documented the rise of the
association and marked out 'public' territory for working-class people. Images of the society's pioneers and officials provided a link
between past and present and helped preserve the efforts of work-

ing-class men and women in memory. As John Berger has argued, photographs, unlike paintings, are more akin to memory because they are 'traces' of a person or event (like a footprint) rather than reconstitutions. They furnish a set of instant appearances, like the eye: memory and photography hold the single event.[92] These texts were densely peopled and carried a personal, 'humanistic' tone, reinforced by the inclusion of biographical detail in the text.[93]

Berger has also pointed out that photographs have public and private functions, are either of friends, family or 'events'. Private photographs do not lend themselves to *any* use because 'the use reconstitutes the continuity from which it was taken.' Public photographs on the other hand usually isolate the image, 'like the memory of a total stranger'. The 'objectivity' of the camera leads to a suspension of judgement: 'It is an eye which records in order to forget'. Berger maintains that a progressive photographic practice would have to bridge this public/private divide and argues for a proper contextualisation which integrates image and written narrative. He further suggests that photographs cannot be replaced in original time, that they are represented in narrated time and 'Narrated time becomes historic time when it is assumed by social memory and social action' – that is it becomes a story which helps certain groups of people to understand and change the world.[94] Co-operative photography attempted to dissolve this public/private antinomy. Activists wore their best suits and dresses but this was more a case of unabashed and public class-pride than 'incorporation'. Images were for 'private' consumption, within the co-operative 'family', were placed within the narrated time of the society's progress and helped constitute the historic time which was predicated on the movement's expansion. In short, the inclusion of images of working-class faces and buildings constructed with their own capital within the written narrative made historic time, in Berger's sense, desirable and possible.

Apart from their focus on 'the everyday doings and quiet lives' of working people, the jubilee historians also rooted their narratives firmly within the specific locality. There was a pre-existing tradition to work with and modify here: urban history had been a common preoccupation for local ruling elites for much of the nineteenth century. This interest can be discerned in the proliferation of archaeological, antiquarian and natural history societies established throughout the country from the 1840s as well as in a spate of texts which celebrated middle-class hegemony and 'progress' at the local level.[95] The jubilee historians were probably influenced to a certain degree by the latter. Some prefaced their texts with a discussion of the changing local landscape.[96] Others described the operations of medieval guilds which were regarded as forerunners of the modern co-operative society.[97] A number based their accounts on a sophisticated range of sources including Court Rolls, ecclesiastical records and parish registers as well as local histories.[98]

Again we may note the traffic between classes and cultures here, facilitated by the increase in literacy. However, for the majority of these writers the most appropriate framework for their narratives was the early industrial revolution and its impact on the lives of the common people in the area. Half of these historians portrayed the transition to industrial capitalism as a cultural disaster for the working class; as we noted above, a liberal-radical academic tradition was employed to strengthen their case. The disruption of the local economy caused by the shift from domestic to factory production and the distress which had accompanied this change was a ubiquitous theme. Peaples described the 'great suffering' produced by a transformation which had reduced the condition of the workers 'from comparative freedom to one of slavery . . . .'[99] All trades had been affected but the plight of none, perhaps, had made such a deep impression on the popular historical consciousness as that of the hand-loom weavers.

Boydell's work, which described in some detail the destitution of the local silk-weavers in the early nineteenth century, provides an excellent example here. The 1820s saw the disruption of the local economy through the introduction of cotton goods, the truck system and the power loom. Boydell used the local press – the *Leigh Advertiser* – and an enquiry by a specially-convened silk weavers' committee consisting of local philanthropists, to construct a sophisticated case-study of capitalist development. Boydell quoted the weavers' evidence to the committee and recorded their attempted resistance through the County Court. The weavers' Protection Society, which later developed into the co-operative society, was shown to be a collective defence against the tyranny of industrial capitalism.[100] The early establishment and success of co-operation had often depended on the efforts of similar groups of workers: flannel handloom weavers in Eccles, hand wool-combers in Bingley, stuff weavers in Brighouse, stockingers in Leicester, ribbon weavers in Coventry.[101] It is not surprising that many of these texts strike a nostalgic and elegiac chord: by the late nineteenth century only a few traces of these vanished forms of labour and community life still remained and for the jubilee historians the co-op store was a symbolic as well as an eminently practical survival.

Some writers went further than this and firmly situated co-operation within the context of local radical politics in the early nineteenth century. The Chartist legacy had been almost totally expunged from the majority of written accounts of the recent past and many working-class autobiographers in the latter part of the century hoped specifically to remedy this absence.[102] The jubilee histories also provided some fascinating, albeit fragmentary, glimpses from this earlier phase. The historian of the Bridge End Society maintained that Chartist leaders like Ernest Jones and Feargus O'Connor had encouraged co-operative experiments in the 1840s. James Haslam's history of the Accrington Society contained a detailed account of the 1842 general strike. Boydell noted that workers in Leigh had learnt co-operation from the *Northern Star*.[103] The historian of the Great Horton Society also pointed to the popularity of this paper and, drawing on local oral traditions, described O'Connor's visit to the village:

> We are told that no royal personage could have been received with greater honour than was the leader of democracy in England on that day. All the village was astir before the dawn broke, and when O'Connor appeared, the horses were taken from his carriage and he was drawn through the streets amidst the wildest enthusiasm.[104]

Blatchford highlighted the role played by Halifax Chartists, particularly Ben Wilson, in the establishment of the first co-operative store. Rigby pursued a similar theme in his history, noting that in some districts 'the Chartist Club became the Chartist Shop'; in others co-operation arose out of industrial conflict and the general loathing for truck and forced tenancy.[105]

Many more historians drew attention to the influence of Robert Owen, the Owenites and the early Union Stores. The authors of the Coventry Society history described how Owenites had started the first store in the city in 1840. Simpson referred to the Owenite stores as 'co-operative communities' in his history of the Cramlington Society. Rhodes based his account on the recollections of John Bland, one of the original members of the Keighley Society, and stressed the formative influence of both Chartism and Owenism in the district.[106]

The historian of the Huddersfield Society described the local Hall of Science opened in 1838 with obvious relish:

> An old friend of mine, long since dead, often told me about his visits to this hall; how he revelled in the social and dancing parties held there; and how he heard from time to time lectures eloquently depicting in glowing language 'the good time coming', when people would live in 'Communities', where everybody would do their share of work, and hours of labour would, consequently, be reduced to about four per day! The rich people left outside, with no one to work for them, would then come and plead to be allowed to come in and join! 'Joyful news', he said, 'eagerly listened to and welcomed by the poor working people of those days'.[107]

Owen Balmforth, a leading local Secularist and co-operative leader, went on to note Holyoake's activity in the Rational Society and quoted from one of the Owenites' Social Hymns. These prefigurative moments had been orally transmitted through the second half of the nineteenth century. Owenism in particular did not just vanish without trace after its collapse but continued to influence co-operative practice: Owenism persisted as a set of cherished images within popular memory. For the historians of the Compstall Society, the significance of the Rochdale Pioneers lay precisely in the fact that they had 'put new life into the dry bones of Owenian Co-operation'.[108]

V

It is now time to recapitulate the argument of this chapter and pull together some of the most important threads. Written forms of history – which were becoming increasingly powerful in shaping popular conceptions of the past – were a central component of co-operative culture throughout our period. Many co-operators realised that written history was a contested terrain and that it was therefore imperative that the early history of one of the most successful working-class associations was properly articulated and bequeathed to future generations. Texts were important here but largely unsuccessful attempts were also made to communicate a sense of the past via the state schools and co-operative classes. The early historians of co-operation, particularly Holyoake, read the development of the movement as evidence of 'progress'; although even Holyoake often tempered his teleological narratives with a sense of the contradictions and tensions which could not easily be abolished by the incantation of this magic word. The jubilee historians plotted their narratives in a similar fashion but, for various reasons, the limits to 'progress' were becoming more and more apparent to these writers. We need to explore this ideological and political shift in a little more depth.

In order to do this it is necessary to recall that Holyoake's vision of the past, as well as his hope for co-operative advance in the present, was predicated on the separation of the political from the economic, a division underpinned and symbolised in the second half of the nineteenth century by free trade finance. As long as the state remained neutral, so the argument ran, then co-operators could continue to expand their interests and influence indefinitely by reorganising and moralising the sphere of consumption. Although the majority movement remained hostile to protection before the First World War, this compromise was beginning to break down from the turn of the century. A later chapter will elaborate this important theme more fully; here it is necessary to trace how the crisis precipitated by this shift – the crisis of Liberalism itself – marked the productions of the jubilee historians.

Let us now turn briefly to the history of the Barnsley Society published in 1903. Local miners were locked-out for four months in 1893 and the text included a detailed treatment of the violent conflict which ensued. Collieries were attacked during the dispute and police and dragoons were drafted into the district to maintain 'public order'. Miners' funds of £167,000 were soon exhausted and members of the society withdrew £67,000 to tide them over; the society proved a vital material resource, paying out over £4,000 in relief grants alone. 'So keen a struggle between capital and labour was probably never known in the history of this country . . . ', observed the authors. This episode was deliberately foregrounded because it clearly demonstrated the conditional nature of co-operative advance. Other hostile forces constrained and threatened to undermine co-operative practice; the Barnsley historians also pointed to the boycotts organised by private traders and, more importantly, the rapidly-changing nature of the economic system itself. They argued that the present age was 'an age of Trusts', and that although the Co-operative movement was also a 'Trust', it was 'as widely different as the Poles from others which seek to enrich but a few capitalists'.[109] The survival of the society, let alone its success, could not simply be assumed in the future.

Within this context reassuring narratives of progress became increasingly difficult to sustain. We must not overestimate the speed of this transformation – co-operators did not formally enter the political arena until 1917 – but the direction and tone is clear enough. Many co-operators were coming to accept that political action was necessary to defend the movement against the antagonistic economic forms which had mushroomed since the 1880s. Hand-in-hand with this went a heightened sense of the movement's potential, particularly apparent during the labour unrest which preceded the First World War. A disproportionate number of the histories deployed here were published between 1910 and 1914, and although this was due to the fact that the early 1860s had witnessed the fastest expansion of distributive societies, especially in Lancashire and Yorkshire,[110] the combative and sometimes utopian stance adopted by these texts cannot easily be explained away by this coincidence. The sense of crisis and hope comes through again and again.

It led some to reflect on the original, revolutionary meanings of 'jubilee' for example. The historians of the Bradford Society highlighted the speech made by John Baldwin, one of the society's directors, at a concert arranged as part of the jubilee celebrations in October 1910. Baldwin had declared that

> it was particularly appropriate that a Co-operative Society should celebrate its Jubilee, and quoted Biblical authority that Moses first instituted a jubilee (Leviticus xxv.10) which was a time of great rejoicing and liberty. According to the law of Moses a jubilee represented three things, viz, freedom from slavery, freedom from debt, and freedom in land. In the last-named respect, land went back at a jubilee to its original owners.[111]

Baldwin believed that co-operation embodied the modern realisation of this emancipatory vision. Malcolm Chase has traced the employment of 'jubilee' in religious, radical-political and patriotic discourses in an earlier period. By the late nineteenth century the dominant meaning of jubilee was far removed from the revolutionary Biblical sense: private companies like the Stockton and Darlington Railway and nonconformist religious organisations, particularly the Methodists, also produced their own jubilee histories in this period. Chase argues that the radical impulse had been largely smothered from above and the term was now used as a loose description for any celebration commemorating a fiftieth anniversary and was linked particularly to displays of monarchical stability and grandeur.[112] This appropriation was not total however; other jubilee historians were well aware of the subversive meanings, which emerged explicitly once more in the tense social and political atmosphere of the late Edwardian climacteric.[113]

It required more than the rediscovery of a lost Biblical tradition and the sound of trumpets to make a new world; as I noted in chapter two, the agency for such a transformation was the will of the common people directed through the Wholesale Societies. In 1912 Simpson, the historian of the Cramlington Society, referred to 'those stately erections of Wholesale Societies' which had been designed specifically to realise 'the dream of Robert Owen and of the Rochdale Pioneers, the dream of the people possessing the sources and means of production whereby each man is to receive his due.'[114] At the Co-operative Congress at Portsmouth that year, William Rae, chairman of the Education Department of the Co-operative Union, made the connection between the movement's more overtly oppositional, anti-capitalist stance and history-teaching. The Union, he observed, 'had been fanning the flame of industrial unrest. They had been teaching Industrial History, and no thoughtful man could read industrial history and be at rest.'[115]

We can only speculate about the impact the texts and initiatives discussed in this chapter had on the rank-and-file members of the movement and it would be too easy to get carried away by this efflorescence of passionate, engaged rhetoric. However, we can say that for many of the movement's local and national leaders the utopian imagination was strengthened by, indeed depended on, a particular reading of working-class endeavour since the early nineteenth century; from this angle historical and political consciousness was intimately connected.[116] Percy Redfern, editor of the *Wheatsheaf* at this time, was very enthusiastic about the growing interest in what he termed 'economic' history and believed that a sense of the past made it easier for co-operators

> to remember that the present co-operative system is only the means to an end, and that the emancipation of the proletariat is of more consequence than an extra penny in the pound at the present time.[117]

The label 'progress' does not adequately capture the movement's historical sensibility in the years which immediately preceded the First World War, for now the goal was increasingly defined in terms of *emancipation*.

Part two

Appropriation

6

The middle-class embrace

Plausible noblemen, philanthropic middle-class spouters, and even keen political economists, have all at once turned nauseously complimentary to the very co-operative labour system they had vainly tried to nip in the bud by deriding it as the Utopia of the dreamer, or stigmatising it as the sacrilege of the Socialist.

> Karl Marx, *Inaugural Address of the Working Men's International Association*, 1864

I

The contributor to the 1877 edition of the *Encyclopedia Britannica* provided the following succinct, no-nonsense definition of co-operation:

Co-operation, as technically understood, occupies a middle position between the doctrines of the communists and socialists (see COMMUNISM) on the one hand, and the private property and freedom of individual labour on the other. It takes its departure from communism at a very definite and significant point. While the latter would extinguish the motive of individual gain and possession in the sentiment of a universal happiness or good, and remodel all the existing rights, laws, and arrangements of society on a basis deemed consonant to this end, co-operation seeks, in consistency with the fundamental institutes of society as hitherto developed, to ameliorate the social condition by a concurrence of increasing numbers of associates in a common interest.[1]

Many social historians would acknowledge that the ability to name and define conveys power on certain groups in society; we pattern and make sense of the world discursively and particular words/concepts can make available, or help exclude, certain possibilities. The contributor to the *Encyclopedia Britannica* wanted to contain the meaning of co-operation and simultaneously assuage the fears of a largely middle-class audience: 'Co-operation, as technically understood' (that is within the discourse of political economy), was a world removed from 'communism' and intended merely to 'ameliorate' rather than 'remodel' the 'social condition'. Nevertheless, one can detect a certain unease beneath the confident surface of this text. The boundaries are too rigid, too clear-cut: 'It takes its departure from communism at a very definite and significant point.' Aware of the potential threat, the writer fell back on comforting assertion.

The unease was understandable. Only thirty years earlier such a definition would have been impossible, for within Owenism the term had been defined in a specifically anti-capitalist manner. In the *Economist* in 1821 for example, Owen proclaimed: 'The secret is out; it is unrestrained Co-operation on the part of all the members, for every purpose of social life.' The encroaching and immoral system of 'Individual Competition' was contrasted with the ideal civilisation of the future, based on the principle of 'Mutual Co-operation'. During this phase 'co-operation', 'socialism' and 'communism' were synonymous.[2] These connections were broken after the collapse of organised socialism and working-class radicalism more generally in the late 1840s and early 1850s. It was now possible for those concerned with the 'betterment' of the working classes to isolate, contain and support co-operation, a term which spun off as a relatively free-floating signifier. Thus in 1863 the *Quarterly Review* admonished earlier utopian socialists for their muddleheadedness: 'Most of these thinkers had a glimpse, more or less clear, of the principle of co-operation . . . but unfortunately they were unable to distinguish this principle from that of community of goods.'[3]

It was the rapid expansion and popularity of the Co-operative movement during the second half of the nineteenth century which forced the debate on co-operation (as concept and movement) onto the bourgeois agenda; it is the purpose of this chapter to explore middle-class definitions and representations in some detail. I argue that the keyword 'co-operation' was a site of intense conflict throughout this period and that many prominent middle-class liberals 'policed' this concept and the related movement: they attempted to appropriate the meaning and direction of co-operation and render it a harmless palliative which would not fundamentally challenge the foundations of bourgeois society. It will be necessary therefore to pay close attention to the written and spoken 'language of co-operation' as it was utilised and developed by various middle-class reformers and suggest how that language was both shared and contested by many working-class co-operators.

The complexity (sometimes even the usefulness) of 'class' as an analytical category has generated much debate amongst historians in recent years and a brief word on the employment of the concept is appropriate. In their excellent, layered accounts of middle-class formation at the local level, both John Seed and R. J. Morris have demonstrated the importance of divisions and conflicts within the middle class in the first half of the nineteenth century and the role of voluntary associations in forging class identity. Davidoff and Hall have also shown how new patterns and forms of consumption – organised and represented in terms of gender as well as class – were crucial to the making of the middle class before 1850.[4] As this work suggests, the 'middle class' was in a continual process of decomposition and recomposition during this period and it required a great deal of associational and ideological effort to create unity out of difference. The same holds true for the later period, although existing accounts have tended to focus, somewhat unhelpfully, on the purported 'failure' of the middle class – its lack of entrepreneurial drive and preference for the 'gentlemanly ideal'.[5]

In terms of the concerns of this chapter, it is not possible easily to distinguish between the attitudes of different fractions of the middle class towards co-operation; hence the term must be employed as a broad, heuristic category to refer to those whose economic, cultural and symbolic capital simultaneously conferred power within the social field and separated their interests (potentially) from those of workers who owned very little capital in whatever form. This loose (but not, therefore, simply meaningless) definition can encompass big industrialists and national political leaders at one end of the spectrum and vicars, doctors and university professors – that is, professional men – at the other. However, we can refine this a little. Firstly, although middle-class enthusiasts for co-operation often spoke from different social positions they can all be regarded as intellectuals in the Gramscian sense: that is they performed an 'organisational' function for the middle class and helped to communicate the *Weltanschauung* of that social group in a wide range of social domains. Secondly, it is legitimate to exclude lower middle-class shopkeepers from our discussion. Threatened by economic extinction, this group were invariably hostile, sometimes hysterically so, and as we shall see in chapter eight, campaigned against the movement from its inception.

The relationship between class and language has also generated heated debate recently. In this chapter it is argued that 'languages of co-operation' did not merely 'reflect' prior and objective class interests and it would be seriously misleading to suggest that alternative and competing languages were specific to particular classes. One has only to think of J. S. Mill's advocacy of a co-operative utopia in the second edition of his *Principles of Political Economy* (1849) to register the limitations of such a position.[6] Language, as Williams argued, is best understood as a *constitutive activity*: it is not prior to, or a result of, a 'given' material reality but rather intimately bound up with the very possibility of existence of that reality. In this materialist account language plays a profoundly important role in the production and transformation of social relationships and contests over particular words and concepts actually help constitute social groups as certain definitions and understandings seek to impose a distinctive vision of the social world.[7] Bourdieu's recent observations are most helpful here:

> The social world is the locus of particular struggles over words which owe their seriousness – and sometimes their violence – to the fact that words to a great extent make things, and that changing words, and more generally representations . . . is already a way of changing things. Politics is, essentially, a matter of words.[8]

Besides the more particular meanings which developed from the early nineteenth century the term 'co-operation' also implied, in its generic sense, the action of working together for the same end. This meaning could appeal to capitalists as much as anti-capitalists; after all, workers had to co-operate with their 'masters' to produce wealth.[9] Thus the concept was and still is a rich, positive signifier, an 'essentially contested concept'.[10]

Many middle-class reformers identified closely with the Co-operative movement from mid-century and indeed some devoted their lives to this cause. The Christian Socialist involvement is well

known and I do not intend to go over this ground again.[11] There was
a more general middle-class presence within the movement and it is
with this that I am most concerned. Some middle-class individuals
actually played a part in the formation of co-operative stores after
mid-century; it has been claimed, for example, that Joseph Cowen
Jr, the radical Liberal proprietor of the *Newcastle Daily Chronicle*,
helped rejuvenate the movement in the North East during the late
1850s, though his influence is easily over-estimated.[12] The movement itself was not innocent in the attempted re-definition of the co-
operative project and deliberately projected a 'respectable' image,
inviting middle-class figures to preside over the annual Co-operative
Congresses, from the first in 1869. Bishops, Lords, bourgeois intellectuals and politicians all appeared over the years until the practice
was curtailed in the early 1890s when co-operators honoured individuals from their own ranks. The Presidential Addresses during this
period therefore provide much pertinent material.

The annual congresses of the Social Science Association (SSA)
held between 1857 and 1883 furnish another major site of bourgeois discourse. Thousands of members and their guests attended
these events which were dominated by Liberal politicians, businessmen and professionals; the annual subscription of one guinea (£1 1s)
precluded wider participation. The association conducted lengthy
discussions on working-class problems, or rather the working class
as problem, and their proposed solutions can be viewed as attempts
to quantify this problem and facilitate middle-class 'order or control'.[13] Topics covered included law and jurisprudence, education,
public health, economy and trade, art and literature. The most recent historian of the SSA has described it as 'a type of research institute attached to the emergent Liberal Party' and has argued that
'social science' – a phrase that the Owenites had used between the
1820s and 1840s to designate their utopian methodology and practice – was 'captured' from above and drained of its radical meanings
during the 1850s by bodies like the SSA.[14] Goldman links this phenomenon to the degeneration of the communitarian impulse within
the Co-operative movement, though it is not clear that this was a
necessary precondition or that it had in fact happened. In 1877 Dr
Henry Travis – an old Owenite and regular contributor to the *Co-
operative News* – pointed out that the SSA 'does not even know
what Social Science is . . . There is no Social Science in endeavours to
patch up or to improve in any way the present system.'[15] Regardless

of the wider significance of this body, co-operation was frequently debated by the SSA and its transactions consequently furnish an excellent source for this chapter.

In order to illuminate the major theme, the discussion which follows considers three specific areas: middle-class support for co-operatives, and especially co-partnerships as alternatives to trade unions; co-operation as a vehicle for the inculcation of a new morality within the working class, a notion shared to a certain extent by both middle-class supporters and working-class activists and one which made communication between these groups possible; and the repeated, unsuccessful attempts to represent co-operation as an antidote to socialism. These themes are tracked back and forth across time and significant shifts in attitudes and language are explored. One reason why the Co-operative movement has been so grossly misunderstood by historians is that they have taken the definitions and representations of middle-class reformers as the truth rather than as specific and intentional interventions in a continuing debate. What follows is a preliminary reconstruction of that debate.

II

Co-operation, profit-sharing and co-partnership schemes (which gestured toward worker participation in the capitalist enterprise) appealed to middle-class opinion as peaceful alternatives to trade unions and industrial militancy. In his presidential address to the SSA in 1861 Lord Brougham argued that the recent strikes in Colne could 'be ascribed to the want of co-operative unions in the district'.[16] Five years later Eckroyd recommended industrial partnerships as a way of ending 'the chronic strife between capital and labour . . . .'[17] In 1874 Lord Rosebery asked: 'So long as capital and labour continue distinct and opposing interests, is it likely that strikes will be rare? Co-operation indeed is the obvious remedy for all these troubles . . . .'[18] Many members of the SSA shared this concern about the deleterious effects of the capital/labour antinomy. From the 1860s, within the context of rising labour unrest and the fear that Britain's industrial hegemony was being rapidly undermined by overseas competition, co-partnership was increasingly regarded as a form which would heal this breach. Co-partnership was seen as part of the wider Co-operative movement but was singled out for special attention; the differences between co-partnership and co-operation were frequently blurred and an attempt was made to elide the two terms, as related components of a project which promised to defuse 'social' antagonism.

Profit-sharing, of course, was an old Christian Socialist panacea: Ludlow, Neale, Hughes and Maurice had espoused the 'workshop idea' as an alternative to the regenerated Chartism of 1848. Their cause was joined in the late 1860s and early 1870s by co-operators like G. J. Holyoake, Lloyd Jones and E. O. Greening who were worried about the increasing power of the Wholesale societies. Some of the latter colluded in the reading sketched above. In Ludlow and Jones' key text of 1867 trade unions were described as 'at best one-sided and one-eyed. Existing simply to protect or further a single class-interest, they appear to us far inferior to Co-operation, which seeks to harmonise warring interests . . . .'[19] Co-operative production and co-partnership were especially beneficial because such forms 'create(s) new ties between man and man, suggest(s) new forms of fellowship, till there grows up a sort of family feeling . . . .'[20]

The English CWS abandoned profit-sharing in its works in the mid-1880s, and preferred instead to return profits to consumers via the stores. A vigorous debate on this issue ensued.[21] Holyoake and a phalanx of younger middle-class reformers like Greening, Aneurin Williams, Thomas Blandford and Henry Vivian, argued that the prioritisation of consumption would do nothing to transform the present alienated state of the worker and established a pressure group in 1884 to press their case – 'The Labour Association for Promoting Co-operative Production, based on the Co-partnership of Workers'. They lost the battle within the movement, launching their last unsuccessful attack on the CWS at the 1890 Co-operative Congress. In 1902 the Labour Association changed its name to the Labour Co-partnership Association in order to make itself more appealing to employers and rapidly degenerated into a small, *petit bourgeois* body. Profit-sharing firms had a limited success: in 1893 the Association counted 77 and this figure had risen to 132 by 1906.[22] Most of these were short lived and it was very difficult to define precisely what were the differences between profit-sharing, co-operative and co-partnership schemes. Some of these ventures, as we shall see, were little more than employer initiatives designed to undermine working-class independence and solidarity. Others were built from below, especially by workers in sectors of the economy affected by rapid mechanisation: the Leicester Manufacturing Boot and Shoe Society, which entered into production in 1887, hoped eventually to establish a 'brotherhood of workers'. The CWS supported yet another form of co-operative production, one regarded as illegitimate by the Labour Association. It was precisely this confusion of forms and definitions that facilitated inter-class communication.

These confusions also led certain co-operators to occasionally rub shoulders with some of the most virulently anti-working-class individuals. One of these was Archibald Briggs, secretary of the Briggs Colliery which instituted a profit-sharing scheme in the mid-1860s, an initiative praised by Holyoake before the SSA in 1865.[23] The following year Briggs detailed the scheme which gave half of the company's profits, when in excess of 10 per cent per annum, to the workers. According to Briggs the initial employee response was impressive but unrest was later fomented by the trade union. Typically, blame was apportioned to outside 'agitators' who had stirred up the 'ignorant mass of colliers'.[24] The most important reason for failure, however, was that the miners believed that the scheme had been set up to undermine the union, as indeed it had. Briggs was deliberately reticent on this issue, and merely stated that membership of the union was not disallowed, though he himself looked forward to the time when it would die 'a natural death.'[25]

This is not the place for a detailed history of the co-partnership movement, whose fortunes rose and fell with the tempo of industrial militancy; the largest expansion of profit-sharing ventures coincided uncannily with periods of unrest, the mid-1860s, the late 1880s, 1908–9 and 1912–14.[26] The attempt made on the platforms of the SSA to blur the distinctions between co-operation and co-partnership helps contextualise the movements' reception by the bourgeoisie, a confusion aided by the well-intentioned activities of individuals like Holyoake. But even he could be pushed too far. Holyoake scathingly attacked the practice of using profit-sharing as a stick with which to beat trade unions in a paper to the SSA in 1872. The Briggs colliery, which had threatened workers with the loss of their percentage of the profits if they attended union meetings, and Fox, Head and Co., a Middlesborough firm which had banned unions outright, were singled out and roundly condemned: 'This is the insolence of mastership – the abuse of industrial partnership'.[27] Although Holyoake fraternised with and promulgated his co-operative ideology to members of the SSA (he attended the annual congress six times between 1862 and 1884), their ambitions were rather dissimilar. For, as Holyoake continued, profit-sharing was for him a way of transcending competitive society and implanting the 'social idea', a way of encouraging everyone to treat one's neighbour as 'a person not an instrument'.[28]

The major stumbling block for middle-class supporters of co-operation and co-partnership was the principle of authority: middle-class advocates of profit-sharing were careful to maintain existing divisions between mental and manual labour, heads and hands. Workers could be given a share of the profits but they were to have no say in the management of the firm. Lending qualified support in 1867, John Ruskin reminded his working-class readers that whereas 'co-operation is better than unjust or tyrannous mastership, there is very great room for doubt whether it be better than a just and benignant mastership.'[29] In his presidential address to the SSA the following year the Earl of Caernarvon argued that trade unions were a temporary phenomenon which would eventually be replaced by Boards of Arbitration (Mundella gave a paper at this meeting) and co-operation, which he called 'the sister principle of arbitration'. He defined co-operation as 'both the union of workmen amongst themselves, primarily and principally for the sale and purchase of articles of consumption, and the union of workmen and capitalists for the purpose of industrial partnerships.'[30] Note how forms of co-operative production which involved working-class ownership and control were deliberately excluded from this definition. Co-partnership was regarded as a higher form and co-operators warned not to meddle too much in the complex sphere of production.[31]

The problem was one of containment. As the Liberal MP and railway magnate Thomas Brassey pointed out to the SSA in 1873, strikes were destructive and workers would obtain a proper appreciation of the pressures of business through co-operative production. The snag was that many of these enterprises were too democratic.[32] At the same meeting, T. Y. Strachan alluded to the democratising influence of co-operation:

> It has seemed to be a belief in co-operative stores, and not altogether avoided in co-operative works, that anyone, without previous training or knowledge, might be a manager. It would be strange if a man whose life had been spent in manual labour could successfully and instantaneously become a buyer and trader in commodities of which

he has hitherto been only a customer, and much more strange to find one totally unaccustomed to mercantile life who could successfully carry on a large manufacturing concern.[33]

The threat, of course, was that working-class co-operators were doing just that. Co-operation, particularly in the sphere of consumption, as Strachan observed, furnished an education in democratic association and this practice stood in direct opposition to modes employed by private capitalism, instilling the subversive notion that 'anyone . . . might be a manager.'

During the next wave of co-partnership expansion in 1890, General Booth of the Salvation Army singled out the Co-operative movement for special praise. In fact Booth went so far as to state that co-operation was '*the* key to the solution of the social problem . . . .' He was an enthusiastic supporter of co-operative farming and wished to renew E. T. Craig's Ralahine experiment. Booth noted the comparative success of distributive ventures and then asked why initiatives in co-operative production had so often come to grief. His answer is illuminating:

> Management signifies government, and government implies authority, and authority is the last thing which co-operators of the utopian order are willing to recognise as an essential element to the success of their schemes. The co-operative institution which is governed on parliamentary principles, with unlimited right of debate and right of obstruction, will never be able to compete successfully with institutions which are directed by a single brain wielding the united resources of a disciplined and obedient army of workers. Hence, to make co-operation a success, you must super-add to the principle of consent the principle of authority . . . [34]

For many middle-class commentators, co-partnership was attractive precisely because the 'principle of authority' could easily be 'super-added' to this form.

Co-operators contested the sacrosanct principle of authority. J. T. W. Mitchell preferred to talk of 'servants' rather than 'an army of workers'. For Mitchell, the Congregationalist, every employee and member of the movement was a 'servant', responsible to the larger body. He employed this Biblical term (all were God's servants) as a way of overcoming (and sometimes obscuring) dominant divisions of labour; all were servants helping to build the Co-operative Commonwealth, and made contributions of equal value, from the work-ing-class housewife to the CWS employee and the Wholesale's board of directors. He was badgered before the Royal Commission on Labour in 1892 on the question of profit-sharing by Livesey (the Commission was very keen on this innovation) who argued that profit-sharing would give employees a greater 'interest' in their work. Mitchell replied emphatically:

> I have been a servant all my life. I worked for 1s 6d a week at the beginning of my days, and whatever profit might have been handed to me in the work I do not see that I could have done more than I did. I should not like to think that the selfish instinct would give increased energy to the work of any man.[35]

Pressed again by Tait he exclaimed that such schemes would only create 'a new order of capitalists.'[36] He was fond of referring to him-self and the Committee of the CWS as 'obedient servants', who car-ried out the wishes of the democratically-elected delegates of the stores.[37] Schatz has argued that the hegemony of the CWS from the early 1890s facilitated a closer relationship between trade unionists, who had been generally antagonistic towards profit-sharing, and co-operators.[38] Further research is needed to substantiate this claim, though its plausibility is appealing. We can say, however, that the success of the CWS and the 'purging' of the champions of co-part-nership over the subsequent decade signalled the increasingly stri-dent plebeian image of the movement and the alienation of much middle-class opinion.

Many bourgeois reformers found the CWS threatening precisely because this huge, democratically-owned and -controlled organisa-tion demonstrated in a most blatant and concrete way that large-scale production was possible without the intervention of a capitalist class. Little wonder then that it was often singled out for criticism. At the National Co-operative Festival in 1900 Earl Grey, then president of the Labour Association, launched a vehement at-tack on the CWS for its refusal to introduce profit-sharing into its productive works. He drove a wedge between this form of co-opera-tive production, where profits were redistributed to the membership via the retail societies, and profit-sharing enterprises. Grey argued that the latter were to be approved because they 'do not aim at being workshops entirely owned and run by workers. They seek rather to establish a partnership between the interests of Capital, Labour and

Custom, on lines which are fair to all.'[39] Grey's strictures were criticised in The *Wheatsheaf* which asserted that the organisation followed the 'fundamental ideals of Robert Owen . . . ', was
democratic and aimed to abolish the capitalist system. It went on to
remind readers that Grey 'does not want the workers to be independent of private capitalists; he recognises the competitive state as
permanent and desirable . . . .'[40]

Over the following decade co-partnership and co-operation were
wrenched further and further apart. By the time the next wave of co-
partnership enthusiasm broke during the labour unrest of 1908–9,
its chief spokesmen were scathingly attacked in the co-operative
press. One of these was the big capitalist W. H. Lever, one of the Co-
operative movement's most active antagonists. He had been interested in co-partnership since the late 1880s and sketched out his
scheme of 'despotic benevolence' in an interview in 1903. Lever
frankly admitted that his object was to discourage workers from
spending their spare cash on 'bottles of whiskey, bags of sweets, or
fat geese for Christmas'. Better by far if they left it with their employer who would provide 'nice houses, comfortable homes, and
healthy recreation'.[41] Lever insisted that the scheme must be left
completely in the hands of the capitalist – 'I am disposed to allow
profit-sharing under no other than that form' he concluded – and
the importance of authoritarian control was a favourite theme.

In a pamphlet in 1909, the year a profit-sharing scheme was finally introduced at his soap factory at Port Sunlight, Lever asserted
that 'in all well-organised industries some must work with their
heads and others with their hands . . . there must be a head prepared
to control.'[42] Lever was the beneficent master *par excellence*. He
argued that co-partnership would teach workers the 'facts' of competition and would reduce the cost of supervision, thereby reducing
overall production costs. Moreover, it served a psychological function and encouraged workers to discipline themselves. Lever expressed this in a most revealing manner: 'Just as a slave worked
better than a man-eating savage, and a wage-drawer worked better
than a slave, I am convinced that copartners will do better work and
more of it . . . .'[43] Co-partnership was the natural partner of 'efficiency' – an important term used to mask relations of dominance
and subordination and sweeten the pill of increased labour exploitation.

If 'improvement' was a key term for the reforming bourgeoisie of the nineteenth century, as Corrigan and Sayer have argued[44], then 'efficiency' provided a similar ideological nexus in the early twentieth century. Britain's relative economic decline could be halted through greater 'efficiency', that is more effective management and control of the work force. Co-partnership was one employer strategy amongst a much wider repertoire; J. R. Hay has pointed to the wages system, state welfare, moderate unions, ideological modes (especially the press) as well as co-partnership itself as various 'social control' strategies employed during this period.[45] Attempted redefinitions of co-operation could be added as an important strategy in the construction and maintenance of what is better understood as hegemony rather than social control because of the formers' dynamic and conflictual emphases. Lever entitled a later publication *Co-partnership and Efficiency* and argued that co-operative production failed because it 'lowers management to the position of a fixed wage drawer.'[46] With the language of co-partnership thus articulated it was hardly surprising that co-operators treated it, in the main, with hostility and repugnance.

When co-partnership schemes made a resurgence during the industrial unrest of 1911–12, T. W. Mercer, the Plymouth co-operator, stated that the only real solution was the establishment of a Co-operative Commonwealth. He observed that the House of Commons had set up a special committee to study co-partnership, but paid no attention to the Co-operative movement. Mercer shrewdly reflected: 'I expect the idea is, however, to save individualism by co-partnership.'[47] He believed that this strategy had been chosen by the middle class because co-operation was now too dangerous, as the working class became controllers of industry by this method, and not merely subordinate 'partners'. D. H. MacGregor, Professor of Political Economy at the University of Leeds, admitted at the time that

> as things are now the Co-operative Movement is too large to take liberties with . . . Co-operation shows that the people have the ability to construct and govern industry, to devolve responsibility, and to choose and trust leaders of their own.[48]

The majority movement distanced itself from co-partnership initiatives and had a strong sense of its own potential. The success of co-operation, especially the remarkable growth of the Wholesales, lent a self-confidence and assurance which characterised the movement in the years before the First World War.

III

Earl Grey, W. H. Lever and a host of liberal philanthropists, continued to be enamoured by profit-sharing during the late nineteenth
and early twentieth centuries but the hegemony of the CWS and the
ideology of consumption from the early 1890s made it more and
more difficult to build lasting alliances on the basis of this panacea.
There was also a linguistic barrier by the turn of the century, which
was considered in chapter two; with the ultimate goal described and
celebrated within the movement as the 'Co-operative Commonwealth' it was indeed a difficult task to represent co-operation as
'the best friend of capital'. Nevertheless, alternative languages (often, though not mechanistically, related to 'class' interest) could and
did overlap and this issue deserves closer attention. As Collini has
shown, middle-class opinion concerning the condition of the working class was saturated with moral terminology before the First
World War. Mill and Spencer, Gladstone and Bright utilised a cluster of key-terms: 'sobriety', 'self-reliance', 'independence', 'self-improvement'. This moral discourse provided a strong defence against
state intervention and continued to inform the debate between 'individualists' and 'collectivists' from the 1880s to 1914.[49] Like
'collectivists', co-operators did not simply oppose this language but
employed moral arguments in their own characteristic ways.
Though their intentions often differed, both middle- and working-
class reformers hoped that co-operation would transform and 'improve' working-class manners and morals and this shared
assumption made communication easier.

Let us listen first to some middle-class voices. That archetypal
moral reformer, the Reverend Henry Solly, delivered a paper to the
SSA in 1862 on the educational and moral improvement co-operation effected within the working class and recommended that the
middle class should not interfere directly in this area but should encourage working-class 'independence'; important lessons had been
learnt from the failure of bodies like the Mechanics' Institutes.[50]
Three years later he observed that:

> It is very remarkable to watch the moral influence produced on work-
> ing men by the Co-operative movement. Taking it in the lowest case, I

have known men whom nothing on earth would have induced to give up their earnings in the public house, who have gone on for years spending their time and their money in the taproom, who have been induced to leave that place, and to become saving men and moral men, by joining the co-operative society; nothing else would have drawn them from the public house fireside . . . [51]

In his autobiography Solly recalled how he had helped establish a co-operative society in Lancaster in the early 1860s and again sang co-operation's praises.[52] In 1868 the Reverend James Fraser, one of the Assistant Commissioners responsible for the *First Report of the Royal Commission on the Employment of Children, Young Persons and Women in Agriculture*, recommended co-partnership farms and co-operative stores for their 'educational' effect on the morals and habits of agricultural labourers. According to Fraser, co-operation 'put an end to strikes' by harmonising the relations between capital and labour, encouraged 'independence and self-respect', provided a valuable lesson in thrift and helped curtail 'self-indulgence at the beerhouse'.[53]

Consumer co-operation appealed to middle-class reformers like Solly and Fraser because it encouraged thrift, temperance, and 'moral relations' among and between the classes. It exerted a disciplining and 'civilising' influence on workers whose profligacy was notorious, whose way of life or culture was a cause for concern and fear. Most importantly co-operation promised to stabilise and re-produce patriarchal structures of consciousness and action within the working-class family, ensuring responsible, home-loving and sober male breadwinners ('saving men and moral men' as Solly put it) and rational female consumers. This is a vital key to understanding why so many middle-class intellectuals warmly embraced the consumer movement; the beauty of this form of association lay precisely in its presumed effects on the working-class family as a whole.

In short, and perhaps not surprisingly, languages of co-operation were invariably gendered. Introducing the Representation of the People Bill in the Commons in March 1866, Gladstone pointed to Rochdale as a place

which has probably done more than any other town in making good to practical minds a case for some enfranchisement of the working classes; because it is the town where that remarkable system, and at first sight I do not hesitate to say that most critical and even perilous system, obtained, under which the working class ousted the retail dealer from his accustomed province, and took into its own hands the business of supply; and where, through the extraordinary intelligence and self-governing power of these men, that system has been brought to a successful issue, and has become a source of the greatest comfort and profit to themselves.[54]

Gladstone admitted the calculated risk involved in supporting 'that most critical and even perilous system' which condemned competition and directly squeezed the *petit bourgeoisie*, but considered it worth taking in the interests of social peace. From this angle, Rochdale co-operation had produced hard-headed, working-class capitalists, men who could themselves support a home and a dependent wife and children; their *manliness* now entitled them to the vote. The irony, of course, was that the remarkable success of co-operative stores in Lancashire from the 1840s had been made possible, in large measure, by the ardent efforts of working-class women.[55]

Occasionally middle-class commentators lamented the fact that their own class had failed to draw appropriate lessons from the efforts of their social inferiors. In a paper to the SSA in 1872 Jeremiah Head recommended co-operation to the better-off in the hope that it would result in less waste, greater efficiency and cheaper prices. But according to Head – and this was his key point – it would also abolish 'false sentimentality' and lead to the adoption of a more systematic, methodical approach to shopping by middle-class women:

> Many ladies seem to me scarcely to look at the commercial business of buying from a sufficiently serious point of view. They appear rather to regard streets of shops as their natural promenades – places for air, exercise and amusement. They delight in seeing what that is pretty or attractive is displayed in the windows; and the result not unfrequently corresponds with that recorded in the fable of the spider and the fly.[56]

Head believed that the boundless and irrational desires stimulated by the developing fantasy world of consumption could only be contained by the masculinisation of consumption practices; working-class co-operation furnished an available model. For many the appeal of co-operation lay precisely in the idea that it fostered 'manly' virtues and a rational, calculating mentality.

Issues of gender and class were clearly intertwined within this ubiquitous moral discourse. Commentators, whose background and social position differed in so many ways, all praised co-operation for its presumed effects on working-class morality and personal behaviour. In his address to the SSA in 1870, William Armstrong linked co-operation to the middle-class reforming project, because of the inculcation of values like frugality and temperance. At the same meeting R. Kettle remarked that in order to accumulate capital working men must practice 'industry, self-denial and frugality' as capitalists had done in the past. There was a catch of course: even then 'they could only hope to compass the small undertakings of co-operative work.' The following year Frederick Hill discussed the moral benefits conferred by industrial co-partnership and argued that this form caused 'both parties to promote, by diligence, punctuality, thrift and intention, the success of their joint undertaking . . . .'[57] This moral arena was imaged in a supra-class way, a sphere 'above' the sordid world of class-conflict and trade unions, where contradictions could be peacefully resolved and inter-class relations harmonised unproblematically. This specifically moral reading of co-operation, which informed many of the debates discussed in this chapter, enjoyed a long popularity. At the Co-operative Congress in 1890 Lord Rosebery opined that co-operators acted as 'missionaries for certain moral qualities', which he later listed as 'thrift, temperance and independence.'[58]

Old Owenites like G. J. Holyoake always insisted that co-operation was a 'moral art' as well as a new form of economy and in his tendentious work *The Co-operative Movement Today* (1891) he lamented the fact that in the main 'society does not recognise that morality has material conditions.' Co-operation's moral mission was also advocated by a younger generation of co-operative ideologues including the Bristol co-operator Edward Jackson who reckoned co-operation effected 'a great moral awakening among the shareholders'.[59] Jackson believed that this was the crucial difference between the capitalist joint-stock form of collective ownership, where shares meant individual power, and the democratic co-operative form, where power resided in the membership. The former bred selfishness and greed; the latter mutuality and fellowship. The rub of course – and this problem has been raised in earlier chapters – was that not everyone could afford to participate in this 'great moral awakening'. Before the First World War the movement drew most of its support (not to mention its national and local leadership) from what George Hines once referred to as 'the cream of the working class'.[60] Many had struggled hard to achieve a certain measure of 'respectability' and values like 'thrift', 'independence' and 'self-denial' had proved invaluable. Sometimes, as we noted in chapters two and three, co-operators blamed the partiality of their reforming project on the cupidity of the 'masses' who failed to live by these precepts and it was not surprising that middle-class supporters were also keen to emphasise the importance of these qualities.

But even if we admit that the movement's leaders often donned the mantle of 'respectability' and utilised moral terminology, we should bear in mind Bailey's contention that 'respectability' cannot simply be read as evidence of 'embourgeoisement'. He has argued persuasively that this concept of respectabilty should be seen not as an overall social code or ideology, but as the performance of a particular role in a specific situation. Importantly, the middle-class observer was eager to discover evidence of its adoption as 'the myth of substantial working-class respectability was a necessary prop to the self-esteem of his own class, proof of the middle-class capacity to remake society in its own image . . . .'[61]

G. J. Holyoake embodied the 'respectable' side of co-operation better than most and projected this image in his speech, manner and dress. But as we have seen, this persona was in many ways a resource which conferred confidence and neither silenced his voice nor rendered it harmless. At the Co-operative Congress in 1892 he supported a motion calling for legislative action to deal with the problem of sweated labour in the following manner:

> As to remedies for sweating, he was in favour of self-help, but he sometimes heard people make a brutal use of that doctrine [Samuel Smiles' latter-day disciples, perhaps?] in order to excuse their own cupidity and selfishness towards the helpless. How could we preach thrift to those who had nothing to save? or temperance in eating to those who had nothing to eat? He had pleasure in supporting the motion, because it was neither unpracticable nor Utopian. It proposed a practical way of dealing with the unscrupulous conscienceless capitalists who used their power merely to subjugate the most helpless of workers.[62]

Holyoake and most other national and local co-operative activists understood the material realities of working-class life far better than the movement's bourgeois supporters. Like Holyoake, the Bolton co-operator William Yates also refused to simply celebrate 'thrift' and pointed out: 'A man who simply saved to have money was a miser.'[63] Moral terminology formed a constellation around the keyword 'co-operation' and provided points of contact but also, simultaneously, moments of struggle; the precise mix depended on context and intention. Although it is possible to discern a shared commitment to 'independence', 'self-help', 'temperance', 'thrift' and so on, working-class co-operators knew only too well that 'moral' advance and the collective abolition of scarcity went hand-in-hand.

IV

We must now draw out a final thread in the analysis and consider the way in which co-operation often figured as an alternative to, even a check on, socialism, in middle-class representations of the movement throughout the second half of the nineteenth century. Not surprisingly perhaps, given its earlier location within radical discourse, attempts were made to separate co-operation from socialism or communism, from the earliest meetings of the SSA. At Glasgow in 1860 the Recorder of Birmingham, M. D. Hill, gave a paper which distinguished between the 'co-operative principle and the socialistic'. According to Hill, co-operation was a form of individualism which conferred individual benefits for individual merit and was essentially voluntary, as opposed to socialism which was 'a slavish principle. The actions of the Socialist must be under rule'.[64] Such rigid oppositions were a common topos.

An obstacle that made Hill's distinction problematic was, of course, the movement's own historical links with Owenite Socialism. These had to be severed to make co-operation palatable to members of the SSA. In 1863 J. Plummer explained that earlier co-operative initiatives had failed because they 'were tainted too deeply with the crude socialistic theories of Robert Owen . . . .'[65] In the discussion which followed, Professor Fawcett reinforced this opinion and maintained that it was incorrect to suppose that there was any conflict between co-operation and competition, as there was between socialism and capitalism:

> The new era which had been commenced in co-operation was this, and he believed that it was first commenced by the Rochdale Pioneers. They clearly saw that there was no antagonism between co-operation

and competition, and that if a co-operative society succeeded, it must compete with other trading establishments, and unless the co-operative societies could succeed in doing business as well as institutions carried on by individual capitalists, whether these societies were philanthropic or not, they would inevitably fail, as the other co-operative societies had failed.[66]

Different class actors often used the 'myth' of the Rochdale Pioneers in different ways. Co-operatives and even the 'divi' long predated 1844 but the 'myth' served a symbolic function for the movement's own sense of historical identity: from this date co-operative success was guaranteed. Middle-class commentators commonly perceived this as an altogether more profound caesura, evidence of the deradicalisation of a once-threatening project. It was all a matter of perspective and intention. In 1864, for example, Richard Cobden praised the Pioneers for simultaneously alleviating working-class suffering and easing the social tension which accompanied the trade disruption caused by the American Civil War:

> The members of Co-operative Stores cannot expect to escape from a share of the loss and suffering which must be a common fate of all classes in Lancashire, and I thank the salutary influence of your movement in the calm and reasonable demeanour of the population during these trying seasons of adversity, which may be largely attributable to the fact that members of the working classes have, by Co-operation, been added to the ranks of capitalists, and have thus become participators in both the benefits and reverses to which possessors of property are liable.[67]

Once again the attempted appropriation of the meaning and direction of co-operation by members of the liberal bourgeoisie was partially facilitated by certain leading co-operators who colluded in this reading, or something quite similar. Three years later Ludlow and Jones also drew a clear distinction between Owenism and co-operation. The Owenites, readers were assured, were never more than a 'sect' and their views on common ownership were 'matters for private experiment rather than general acceptance.'[68]

This appropriation did not go uncontested, even by those who cultured sympathetic relations with members of the middle class. G. J. Holyoake was present at the 1863 SSA meeting at which Fawcett spoke, and he satirised this mis-reading of the historical record:

Mr Fawcett sought to account for old failures by referring them to an antagonism of co-operators against competition. That was the voice of theory speaking. The co-operators of Rochdale were world-workers. They intended to recast society, and for this purpose they saved up their capital. It was this fortunate 'delusion' which was the secret of their accumulation. Had they not been Communistic there had never been co-operative success in Rochdale.[69]

Holyoake's supposed 'incorporation' was not simply achieved; as we have already seen, he frequently scorched middle-class audiences with unpleasant truths. The radical lineage of post-1844 co-operation was one of these.

The effort to narrow the definition of co-operation recurred. In 1880 the Bishop of Durham, President of the Co-operative Congress, confided to his audience that he had received a letter warning him to have nothing to do with the Congress as it was linked to Communism. He asserted that they were poles apart, hence his presence, but added this cautionary note:

Co-operators would do well to beware of indulging too sanguine expectations. Exaggerated hope leads by an inevitable reaction to exaggerated disappointment. It is the child of impatience, and it is the mother of despair. Do not set out with the idea that co-operation will regenerate society.[70]

The fear of 'regeneration' or revolution was never far off the bourgeois horizon in the 1880s; the rediscovery of poverty in the early 1880s, as Stedman Jones has demonstrated, prompted fear rather than guilt.[71] An attempt was made to separate co-operation, the preserve of the 'moral' and 'respectable' portion of the working class, from the infant socialist movement.

In 1881, the year of the foundation of the Social Democratic Federation, the President of the SSA, Goldwin Smith, recommended profit-sharing in the following manner:

Everything which tended to improve the relations between employer and employed, and to purify and sweeten the atmosphere of industry, must help to avert from society the great storm which seemed to be gathering over it in the shape of the various forms of socialism.[72]

In the discussion which turned to the question of co-operative endeavour in general, Standish O'Grady was puzzled. He had believed that co-operation was indeed a form of socialism, 'when pushed to its final conclusion', and asked for someone to explain where socialism 'began and ended'.[73] Professor Shaw of Trinity College Dublin obliged with a sketch of state socialism: abolition of private property and the compulsory division of the products of industry from above. He believed that a crisis was fast approaching which would 'not be between party and party but between class and class. A social revolution must be looked for if a state of things was continued which caused the "employee" to look on the capitalist as his tyrant and natural enemy.' Shaw was convinced that the only hope for the future was the gradual working out of a new industrial system and that co-operation had a vital role to play here. In the present context it was very important to distinguish between alternative projects and Shaw asserted reassuringly that 'Co-operation and socialism were entirely distinct, because, if socialism involved co-operation, co-operation did not involve socialism.'[74]

The following year, at the Co-operative Congress, the president, Lord Reay, argued that the movement exerted a conservative influence and defused potential conflict. His words echoed the Bishop of Durham:

> English co-operators never have boasted that they were going to renovate English society, and the consequence is, undoubtedly, that by their aid English society has been spared a good deal of the friction which we see elsewhere . . . Co-operation has been the best friend of capital and is therefore the strongest ally of the middle class.[75]

Lord Reay clearly considered – and wanted to make the audience *believe* – that co-operation was a bulwark against revolution. Such beliefs were comforting to the middle class but also made class alliances possible. If co-operation was to be rendered harmless, it had to be constantly represented as harmless; bourgeois hegemony depended on this kind of ideological work. He closed by arguing that co-operation was not a panacea, these were 'absurd utterances' and totally misguided.[76]

In his Presidential Address to the Glasgow Congress in 1890 Lord Rosebery was well aware of the relationship between socialism and co-operation but made sense of the connection in this way:

> Fourier, St Simon and Owen were words of ill-omen and ill-savour in the eyes and in the nostrils of the country. But now the case is widely

altered. Society sees that it can pull down what it sees objectionable in these experiments to a reducible minimum [*sic*], and that it can welcome all the rest. It sees also that it has included in the word 'socialistic' that which is not merely unobjectionable but desirable, and if there still survives a little confusion of mind on this question, you must expect confusion of mind long to outlive the causes which it maintains.[77]

Some 'individualists' like Rosebery believed that an extensive range of state activities, including the protection of children, fair trading and the prevention of disease, were compatible with Individualism; and they rejected the extreme *laissez-faire* doctrines advocated most famously by Herbert Spencer – later himself a convert to co-partnership – in *The Man Versus the State* in 1884.[78] The problem was how to redefine and contain 'socialistic' or 'collectivist' projects in acceptable ways, or as Rosebery delicately put it, 'pull down . . . to a reducible minimum.' The 'little confusion of mind' that persisted testified to the fact that co-operation was still a dynamic signifier.

By the 1890s the profit-sharers were getting desperate. Another of these, Lord Beauchamp, opened an exhibition of co-operative productions organised by the Worcester Society in 1896 and declared in his address that co-operation helped cement and harmonise employer-worker relations – indeed that was the symbolic meaning of the exhibition. He expressed heartfelt relief that the Society 'had outlived the bugbear of being called bad names like Communism and Socialism and things of that kind . . . .' Unfortunately soon after Beauchamp's speech, Mr Clay of the Gloucester Society who shared the platform argued that the exhibition symbolised the coming co-operative utopia in which 'working men would work for themselves and reap the fruits of their own labour, and not only receive the best wages for themselves, but the profits as well, and take the responsibility *(Applause)*.'[79] The clash between Beauchamp and Clay is emblematic of the contests over meaning that have been traced in this chapter.

These contests were played out in other national contexts, and although this is not the place for a detailed treatment, we may note that the early history of the International Co-operative Alliance also reveals how international co-operation was similarly regarded by some as an antidote to international socialism from the mid-1880s to the late 1890s. Recovering from their defeat in the domestic movement, Christian Socialists like E. V. Neale and middle-class advocates of profit-sharing, including E. O. Greening and Earl Grey, sought to regroup with allies across Europe like Edouard de Boyve, the founder of the French Co-operative Union who had delivered a speech in support of an international co-operative organisation at the Plymouth Congress in 1886. In the debate which followed, Arthur Acland, the Liberal MP, strongly backed the idea and compared the proposed body with another 'International' which indulged in 'folly or selfishness'.[80] At Rochdale in 1892 de Boyve made his fears explicit:

> The apostles of co-operation hold, as seems to me, principles directly opposed to the principles of the apostles of revolution. The first teach the union of all classes, the second the hatred of one class of society. Both would attain the same end – a better distribution of wealth, which would produce among men more thorough solidarity.[81]

The ultimate objective shared by socialism and co-operation was left conveniently vague. (They both desired more than a better distribution of wealth.) For de Boyve, and some of the other middle-class instigators of the International Co-operative Alliance, international co-operation would head-off the possibility of violent, revolutionary change.[82]

Under the original constitution of 1895, individual profit-sharing companies, whether they were linked to Co-operative movements or not, could be affiliated to the Alliance.[83] This rule was abandoned in 1900; two years later both the English and Scottish CWS joined and the leadership of the ICA quickly came to regard co-operation and socialism as not only compatible but inextricably bound together. Dr Hans Muller, the Swiss delegate at Middlesborough in 1901, noted that when co-operation had first been introduced into Germany, Austria and Switzerland, it was seen as entirely pragmatic, a protection for artisans and small traders against large capital. Whereas middle-class support was immediately forthcoming, socialists and Marxists were critical and suspicious of co-operation and looked to the state as the only means of radically transforming society. Muller accepted this view until he read a book by a German clerk, Ernest Busch, entitled, *The Social Question and its Solution*, which explained the potential power of the consumer, and advised workers to start distributive and eventually productive co-operatives, making capitalists redundant. Most Marxists considered this a utopian scheme, but Muller declared that he had been convinced of its soundness. He went on to describe how after reading the German translation of Beatrice Potter's book, *The Co-operative Movement in Great Britain*, which seemed to indicate the practicality of Busch's doctrines, he threw in his lot whole-heartedly with co-operation. At the 1901 Congress he related the British movement, via his reading of Busch, directly back to the Owenite heritage: 'Accustomed to meet only with co-operators who had a horror of socialists we were surprised to find here [in Britain] a new type of co-operator, whose ideas were those of Robert Owen.'[84]

On the eve of the First World War at a Congress Concert in Dublin, an Irish supporter and profit-sharing enthusiast, Sir Henry Grattan-Bellew, paid a fulsome tribute to the movement. Grattan-Bellew asserted that co-operation did not seek to destroy either capital or capitalists and that the movement was destined to co-exist peacefully with capitalism. The editor of the *News* violently disagreed with this lame attempt to patch-up a long-standing quarrel:

> To run concurrently with the capitalistic system would be co-operation of the wrong kind. Co-operation means in its ultimate object the transformation of the present capitalistic system. That, at any rate, is what the advanced minds who did most to start the Rochdale Pioneers meant . . . we want people to comprehend clearly that co-operation, above all other movements in the world, stands for an entire capitalistic change. Co-operation means the ownership and control of capital investment in production and distribution, broadly speaking, on a co-operative basis. Private capitalism does not mean that.[85]

This impatient, optimistic response underlines the fact that middle-class attempts to redefine and appropriate co-operation had failed by 1914, though this failure was neither total nor fixed; bourgeois hegemony required constant negotiation in post-mid nineteenth century Britain.

The debate over the meaning and representation of co-operative forms and practices brings into focus the potential instability of hegemonic social relations. Middle-class moral and intellectual leadership in civil society, their ability to dominate the production of 'common sense', was challenged by the growth of working-class association. This challenge found articulate expression within the Co-operative movement. As I have argued, the keyword 'co-operation' could easily be bent to a unified, harmonious vision of the social order, but from the turn of the century especially it was commonly construed in an explicitly oppositional manner within the movement and regarded as a complete alternative to capitalist competition. Co-operators sought to impose their own 'vision of divisions' and maintained that a separate capitalist class was now historically redundant.[86] As we saw in chapter two, in theory their rhetorical appeal was not limited to a single class (co-operation would transcend class society) but neither were co-operators blind to the fact that it was working-class association which had made it possible to change the world as well as to speak about it with confidence and hope. In an important and neglected sense the growth of consumer consciousness and class consciousness in this period were intimately bound up with each other.[87]

7

Socialists, co-operators and the state

Co-operation, and every other bastard form of socialism, will be forgotten as the clumsy efforts of a generation which had failed to understand even the problem that was set for it to solve . . .

Frederic Harrison in the *Fortnightly Review*, September 1872

I

When organised socialism re-emerged in the early 1880s there were already well over a thousand distributive co-operative societies with almost three-quarters of a million members in Britain. A superficial (or paranoid) observer may have supposed that there were strong affinities between the two movements: after all, they both tended to recruit their leaders from the more 'respectable' strata of the working-class and they also shared utopian aspirations to some extent. Aware of these apparent similarities, socialists themselves were from the start both fascinated and infuriated by a movement which had successfully harnessed so much valuable working-class energy and talent. Thus from the 1880s through to the First World War socialists and co-operators engaged in a heated debate on the function and meaning of their respective movements on the platform and in the press. This debate was never completely resolved before 1914 though by this time both groups agreed that a 'Co-operative Commonwealth' should be substituted for competitive capitalism. Why then did they not join forces and work together to achieve this goal as socialists and co-operators did in France?[1]

Marx's comments in his *Inaugural Address of the Working Men's International Association* (1864) suggest some preliminary answers.

In this text Marx argued that two important victories of what he called 'the political economy of labour over the political economy of property' had occurred in England since 1848: these were the Ten Hours Bill and, more importantly, the Co-operative movement. But this praise was highly qualified. Marx stressed that the experiments in co-operative production were of more lasting import as they demonstrated that production could be carried out without the intervention of a capitalist class. Moreover, without direct state intervention ('fostered by national means' was Marx's preferred euphemism), co-operation would remain confined 'within the narrow circle of the casual efforts of private workmen' and would never be able 'to free the masses, nor even to perceptibly lighten the burden of their miseries.'[2] There was little chance that such a contradictory assessment would win favour amongst co-operators themselves; Marx's English disciple Ernest Jones had launched a similar attack in the early 1850s which had merely polarised opinion.[3]

Marxian socialists in the late nineteenth century frequently took a similar line: even when they admitted that co-operation had achieved much, they tended to treat any wider ambitions with extreme scepticism if not outright hostility. Caution is needed, however, as not all socialists shared the Marxist critique and regional differences also complicate the picture considerably; studies of the interaction between socialists and co-operators at the local level are needed to provide a properly-nuanced account. Bill Lancaster, for example, has demonstrated how in late nineteenth-century Leicester, co-operators and ILP activists worked together and shared a similar anti-capitalist vision, at least until 1895 when, according to Lancaster, the issue of 'poverty' replaced that of 'worker autonomy' as the dominant strand in Leicester socialism.[4] Such local studies are invaluable, and a focus on co-operative response at this level would shed new light on the 'rise of Labour' debate, as most late nineteenth-century co-operators were Liberals who often found the transition to Labour highly problematic.[5] While it illuminates this issue, the present chapter adopts a general approach: I explore the lack of understanding and common action between socialists and co-operators at the national level in this period. The focus is on the ideological contradictions which tended to pull socialists and co-operators apart, at least theoretically, and the discussion which follows therefore considers four key themes which structured controversy: conflicting emphases on production and exchange; the role of class conflict in society; the role of the state in effecting the transition to a 'Co-operative Commonwealth' and remedying social ills; and finally, the problematic but growing appeal of 'socialism' and 'collectivism' within the Co-operative movement before 1914.

II

Late nineteenth-century socialists, especially though not exclusively those who defined themselves as Marxists, tended to prioritise relations of production over those of consumption. This emphasis can of course be traced to Marx's own writings; I noted above how he regarded co-operative factories, *a priori*, as a superior form and in volume one of *Capital*, published in England in 1867, Marx virtually ignored the sphere of consumption. As many commentators have noted, production carried an ontological significance for Marx – labour defined man's 'species being' – and it was within the sphere of production that both 'exploitation' and 'alienation' occurred.[6] Consumption on the other hand enjoyed an inferior status and was functionally tied to the production and reproduction of capital. It took two forms: 'productive consumption' happened when the worker consumed the means of production with his labour and converted them into products whose value was higher than that of the capital advanced; 'individual consumption' referred to the worker's need to purchase the means of subsistence to live and reproduce. Marx wrote that 'The worker's productive consumption and his individual consumption are therefore totally distinct'.[7] The point here is not that this discourse was theoretically incorrect in any absolute sense but that it made no mention of strategy. J. T. W. Mitchell, perhaps, would have retorted with the observation that these two forms of consumption were united in the Co-operative movement, which, it could be argued, was organising 'individual consumption' in a collective or 'class' way, and was building an institution which could, once successful in this sphere, move on to the more difficult terrain of production.

   The 'ideology of consumption', as I argued in chapter two, completely dominated the Co-operative movement after the defeat of the Christian Socialists and profit-sharers in the 1880s. Henceforth the interests of working-class consumers and the present immoral workings of the capitalist system of exchange were the common reference points. Thomas Tweddell of the CWS articulated the dominant position explicitly at the 1894 Congress:

> Profit upon cost I look upon as one of the many devices which human
> ingenuity has contrived to enable one section of the community to
> appropriate the wealth produced by another, and it should have no
> place in a well-ordered co-operative community. Unfortunately that
> ideal society still lies in the realm of the future, and in the absence of a
> perfect system of exchange, that would give to each the value of his
> labour, and make available to all the multiform gifts and forces of
> nature, we have to adapt ourselves to existing conditions, to conform
> to existing methods, in which profit upon cost unfortunately plays an
> important part.[8]

For Tweddell, relations of production were of secondary importance; the ultimate aim was to abolish profit, the method, a just
system of 'fair exchange' which would enable everyone to receive
the value of their labour. The similarities between this position and
Owenite arguments about the centrality of exchange are striking. In
his meticulous study Noel Thompson has argued that the Owenites
failed to develop a theory of 'exploitation' before mid-century and
that this damaging absence can be explained by their emphasis on
exchange rather than productive relations.[9] Thompson's plausible
argument could easily be transposed to the late nineteenth- and
early twentieth-century Co-operative movement but this would be a
little too easy. Co-operation, like Owenism, was not Marxism assuredly and was certainly marked by internal 'flaws' or contradictions but so too are all ideologies and social forms, including
Marxism in the past and the present. In fine, there were strengths as
well as silences on both sides of the debate.

   Not surprisingly socialists at the time took the movement to task
over this issue; this lacuna made co-operators an easy target for possible antagonists. Writing in the SDF journal *Justice* in 1898, A. P.
Hazell read co-operators a long lesson (it was not the first or last) in
basic Marxist theory:

> So long as co-operators claim exchange to be the basis of their eco-
> nomic creed, they will be confronted with the same social evils which
> afflict a capitalist society founded on the same principle. Exchange
> presupposes private property, and leads to the money form of com-
> modity, which in its turn, gives rise to capital, and enables its owner to
> purchase and exploit labour, thus fulfilling the conditions necessary

for the supremacy of the capitalist system.[10]

According to Hazell, co-operative attempts to remodel the economy by reconstructing exchange relations were doomed from the start. This emphasis was not only misguided; it also encouraged co-operators to close their eyes to the position of workers within the movement, who were necessarily exploited themselves. Even socialists who did not share Hazell's pessimism or circular logic, like Robert Suthers, who wrote regularly on co-operative matters in the *Clarion* (under the pseudonym 'The Whatnot'), reminded co-operators that 'It is a principle of Socialism that in any industry the welfare of the producer is of the first importance' and that the treatment of workers employed in co-operative enterprises often left a lot to be desired.[11] This charge was frequently made. A front page article in *Justice* in 1890 declared that co-operative societies were 'mere profit-mongering institutions, which resort even to the sweating of women to increase their profits.'[12]

What made matters more difficult was that there was more than a grain of truth in these accusations; the language of 'community' tended to conceal difference within as well as outside the movement and many co-operators were thoroughly insensitive to the status of 'labour'. Co-operative employees in the distributive stores were treated little better than employees in the private sector and their union, the Amalgamated Union of Co-operative Employees (the AUCE was formed in 1895) met resistance from many local societies. By 1900 there were nearly 80,000 co-operative employees and this had risen to 150,000 by 1914; about 50 per cent of these were employed in distributive stores. Wages were hardly generous. In 1891 a manager or head counterman in the Manchester area could expect to earn between 18s and 40s per week; other countermen received between 7s and 25s The WCG, critical of the existence of 'sweated labour' in the movement since the early 1890s, joined forces with the AUCE in 1905 to campaign for a minimum wage. The Newcastle Congress in 1909 eventually recommended 24s per week for males over 21 and 17s for females over 20, but local societies and the CWS were slow to implement these rates.[13] The movement's critics often raised this issue. In *Shop Slavery and Emancipation* (1912) the Fabian socialist William Paine observed that many societies paid managers only 28s a week and, as for the salesman, 'His hours under the co-operative system are a little better, and his wages a little worse. The difference to him is merely the difference of the hand that holds the pincers.'[14]

Perhaps the clearest illustration of this insensitivity is provided by the series of strikes which occurred in CWS productive works. For all the bias and anti-working-classism of many profit-sharing 'individualists', there is some truth in their criticisms of CWS 'federalists'. Noting that the CWS treated its 2,000 employees with 'exceptional consideration' Mitchell declared at the 1886 Congress that 'there was no higher form of co-operative production in the world than that carried on by the Wholesale Society.'[15] Ironically, trouble was brewing at the Leicester Shoe Works over the issue of low wages and the alleged practice of putting work out to cheaper shops. After a strike which lasted two weeks, discontent simmered throughout the year. Mitchell himself resented the action and showed no sympathy for the men's grievances.[16] The question of labour relations within the CWS deserves systematic study but we may note that demands for wage increases and strikes persisted. The 1890s was clearly a key decade: the CWS had major investments in the footwear industry which was revolutionised by the introduction of American machinery at this time and the pressure to adopt this new technology in order to compete successfully with capitalist manufacturers generated heated conflicts over democratic form. Percy Redfern presented a sanitised version of these conflicts in his histories but recent research has suggested just how ruthless the CWS could be toward alternative co-operative organisations. After the 1886 dispute, for example, a group of workers from the CWS footwear factory left to found the Leicester Manufacturing Boot and Shoe Society, known as the 'Equity'. Taking full advantage of economies of scale and the new technology the CWS attempted to drive the 'Equity' out of business.[17]

An uncritical acceptance, even celebration, of the existing division of labour was characteristic of the Wholesale's apologists by this time. In his major study, *Co-operative Production* (1894) Ben Jones asserted that co-operators must be educated in the

> inevitable necessity for division of labour . . . The division and specialisation of labour are the only means of procuring the wherewithal for living civilised lives; and even under despotic industrial systems, give such enormously increased power to those who use them, that any primitive democracy, which preferred less elaborate methods,

would be swept away by the despotic competitor or rival, whenever he chose to do so.[18]

Anticipating the Webbs' attack on 'primitive democracy', Jones came to believe that the triumph of large-scale industry, organised and directed by a bureaucratic elite (albeit one recruited from the working class and democratically-controlled), was historically inevitable. This view, which was widely shared, led some of the Wholesale's ideologists to drift away from 'association' towards 'collectivism' before 1914, a tendency which will be discussed in more detail later in this chapter. Note also that CWS spokesmen like Jones and Percy Redfern and before them J. T. W. Mitchell (who all considered the division of labour to be a civilising force), came from clerical rather than artisan backgrounds unlike, say, G. J. Holyoake or Robert Halstead who had a much keener sense of the rights of labour. The point that needs to be stressed is that for many socialists, especially Marxists in the SDF and ILP-ers with roots in the trade union movement, Jones' position was highly problematic.

Notwithstanding their misgivings about organising around the sphere of consumption and their often justified criticisms of the treatment of labour within Co-operative works, socialists themselves, particularly SDF members, experimented with various co-operative forms before the First World War. The Ghent Society in Belgium furnished the most attractive model: even James Blackwell, who often described English co-operators as 'mere profit-mongers', praised their Belgium namesakes – 'all avowed socialists' – in the pages of *Justice* in the spring of 1888. There were already some socialist stores in the London area at this time, co-ordinated by the Socialist Co-operative Federation whose supporters included William Morris. By the summer of that year the SDF was running stores in Battersea, Chelsea and Tottenham as well as Salford and Edinburgh. Most sold basic goods like tea on a very small scale, but the Tottenham branch also opened hosiery and drapery departments. Profits were used mainly for propaganda purposes and to augment branch funds. The main London store collapsed after four years; anarchists who used the premises as a 'discussion forum' were made the unconvincing scapegoats. It seems unlikely that the other stores lasted this long.[19]

The SDF also established a co-operative bakery in London under the auspices of the Workers' Co-operative Productive Federation or

WCPF. Started at the end of 1890 to employ foreign bakers excluded from the trade, by the autumn of the following year this body had extended its operations to include boot and shoe making, cigar and hat making, milling, printing and tailoring. Numerous public meetings were held in an effort to drum up support but the WCPF quickly collapsed and a reaction set in. A front page article in *Justice* in 1896 underlined the notion that despite the views of some anarchists, co-operation would never revolutionise society. One correspondent caught the mood soon after when he opined that 'this talk about Socialist trading is all bunkum.' Bunkum or not, co-operative forms continued to fascinate socialists in the SDF and the ILP right up until the First World War. Following a conference of London ILP branches in the spring of 1898 a Socialist Co-operative Trading Society was founded in Fleet Street; an article in the *Labour Leader* which announced its formation asked whether socialists ought to further the success of Lewis's, Whiteley's or 'the ubiquitous Lipton'. The SDF and later the British Socialist Party supplied 'Liberty' tea, coffee, cocoa and tobacco to members throughout the next decade; 'Strike capitalism with a bit of its own machinery' read the caption on an advertisement for the Trading Committee of the BSP in 1913.[20] This ambivalent attitude toward co-operation, whether practised by themselves or others, continued to characterise the socialist position. Many socialists undoubtedly grasped the advantages and potential of co-operation, but unfortunately socialists and co-operators were separated by far more than different understandings of the meaning and significance of production and consumption.

III

Another important area of contention in the late nineteenth and early twentieth centuries focused around what SDF-ers referred to as the 'class war'. Both Marxists and 'ethical' socialists often viewed moments of confrontation between employers, workers and the state in a positive light; and though 'ethical' socialists may have regretted the need for violence, the catalytic effect produced by the Manningham Mills strike in 1890–91 for example, which helped pave the way for the foundation of the ILP in Bradford in 1893, was fully appreciated.[21] Co-operative ideologists were much less sanguine about such episodes. For them social transformation depended on the gradual and peaceful expansion of the movement, facilitated by an educational strategy, until capitalism was 'unmade'. The saliency given to particular forms of class struggle within this schema was seriously curtailed. Indeed co-operators, like earlier utopian socialists, tended to regard class-struggle negatively and, as I argued in chapter two, usually emphasised class-collaboration rather than the leading role of the working-class.[22] 'Co-operators were not hot-headed revolutionists' – declared William Maxwell at the 1899 Congress – 'they had no personal quarrel with the rich, but they had a standing quarrel with the methods that made some men rich.'[23]

For socialists, particularly members of the SDF, overt forms of conflict were in themselves educational. Marxist discourse emphasised the downtrodden and desperate condition of 'wage slaves' who had nothing to lose but their chains; an advocate of Lassalle's 'iron law of wages', H. M. Hyndman regularly underlined the reality and usefulness of the 'class war' in changing circumstances and selves. The SDF invested a great deal of energy into mobilising and publicising the condition of unemployed workers, especially in London during the 1880s: *Justice* employed a language which combined melodrama with the promise of apocalyptic change.[24] The worst forms of capitalist exploitation were regularly exposed – especially 'sweating' and 'shop slavery' – and obituaries of paupers who had died of starvation frequently appeared on the front page. Not only did this constituency best fit the SDF's analysis of social breakdown but the unemployed, the poor and the insecure were most likely to be excluded from the network of voluntary associations, including co-operative societies, which had done much to improve the lives of many working-class people. Support for the latter from a correspondent in 1894 provoked 'Tattler' to spell out why such agencies were no more than a diversion. The 'conditions of today', he argued, 'condemn us to a fratricidal struggle' and socialists must direct their energies to changing these conditions rather than 'giving mocking exhortations to our fellow combatants to practice virtues which the rules of the fight make impossible.' When Peter Glasse, a socialist director of the SCWS, was interviewed a few years later, he was asked whether he 'believed in the class war.' Glasse replied in the affirmative but noted that his was a minority voice within the Co-operative movement.[25]

The major virtue 'Tattler' had in mind when he denounced co-operative practice was of course 'thrift'. The editor of *Justice*, Harry Quelch, shared this critique which keyed into the SDF's obsession with the unorganised, dispossessed working class. Quelch described thrift as a 'mischievous doctrine' which had been 'crammed down the throat of the working classes by bourgeois economists.' Well aware of the dangers of the middle-class embrace, Quelch believed that 'thrift' was an ideological weapon which enabled employers to shirk their responsibilities and make workers responsible for their own poverty and distress. In short, it helped 'make the present evil system of society bearable' and deflected workers' attention from 'the real cause of, and remedy for, the evils they have to suffer.' Working-class associations based on this principle, notably co-operative societies, did more harm than good as they made open conflict less likely.[26]

Quelch's condemnation of 'thrift' makes sense when we remember his own formation. Born into extreme poverty in London, he believed initially in the power of the individual to transform society: 'Industry, frugality, abstinence and thrift were the cardinals of my ethical code', he later recalled. He even joined a co-operative society in Southwark in the late 1870s but a series of low-paid, exploitative jobs left his ethical code in ruins. London at this time was a 'co-operative desert' and the shifting, casual nature of the labour force was notoriously difficult to organise; Quelch's critique of thrift and his emphasis on the role of the poor and the unorganised grew directly out of this context. He had little direct knowledge of the communities or lives of those workers in the North of England who had built a remarkable movement by means of 'thrift' and who were suspicious of an ideology which placed a premium on direct action and promised a sudden transformation rather than gradual though inexorable advance.[27]

It would be misleading to portray this particular dichotomy as either rigid or unchanging. Until the early twentieth century, industrial conflicts received slight coverage in the co-operative press, but by the time of the labour unrest which preceded the First World War attitudes had shifted; before we leave this theme it would be worth tracing the contradictory reactions provoked within the Co-operative movement by industrial crises at this time. The *Co-operative News*, for example, reported the South Wales miners' strike of 1910 in detail. The paper explained that the dispute had real material causes and was not simply due to the influence of inflammatory orators, as the capitalist press maintained. The correspondent regretted, however, the violence that had been occasioned:

> We lament the scenes which have occurred in South Wales this week, because there are much better ways by which the working classes may secure full justice. It is not to be found in strikes, but in organisation prompted and controlled in accordance with sound co-operative effort.[28]

The condescending tone must have alienated many trades unionists, especially those engaged in struggle. As the labour unrest intensified the paper merely reiterated this advice. The miners' strike of 1912 proved that individualism had 'had its day and broken down' and proved the efficacy of co-operation. On the ground, in the affected localities, the response was rather different: the *News* also carried details of relief afforded to the striking miners by co-operatives during the dispute,[29] as did the *Wheatsheaf* which published selections from the many hundreds of local pages to illustrate this support, in its national format. Nevertheless, the over-riding lesson to be drawn was still the desirability of co-operation, though strikes were not disparaged.[30]

The *Millgate Monthly* covered the unrest more sensitively than any other national co-operative organ. The journal supported the idea of sympathetic strikes used by dockers in Hull, Manchester and Liverpool in the summer of 1911 and argued for industrial solidarity. The unrest was considered integral to capitalism, though co-operation – 'when labour and capital become one' – was seen as the only long-term solution.[31] The magazine also noted the 'unofficial', rank-and-file nature of many of the labour disputes of this period and observed that it was 'questionable . . . whether many trade union leaders have been sufficiently alive to the desires of the men they represent.' Referring to the Railway Strike, the editor opined that recent events had proved the power of the strike weapon at a time when many believed it to be obsolete, though he hoped that arbitration would prevail.[32] In 1912 the paper lent support to London dockers over the issue of 'free-labour' and the language of class-war made a rare appearance: 'It is no use mincing words, or trying to disguise the fact that we are living through a period of bitter class war – a determined struggle between labour and capital.'[33] Once again though, the message insistently communicated was the necessity of co-operation, particularly in the field of production.[34] Co-

operators were being perfectly consistent when they advocated co-
operation over trades unionism and strikes but their critique of
strike action, logical in terms of co-operative ideology, was an obstacle to understanding and an opportunity for socialists of various
kinds who had identified closely (albeit not uncritically), since
Frederic Harrison's days, with the unions. For many workers, particularly those whose employment was irregular and whose wages
were low, the appeal of any theory of class and class struggle, however crude, must have been very strong indeed.

IV

Despite these major differences, if they so wished co-operators and
socialists could find a lot of common ground: they often agreed on
the moral and economic bankruptcy of the capitalist system and the
important role that education must play in bringing about any lasting transformation. However, alternative conceptions of the form
and function of the state remained the major obstacle to sympathetic dialogue throughout this period. G. J. Holyoake's rejection of
statist social reform was predictable perhaps – 'The State is ponder-
ous, unsympathetic and slow to move, except on behalf of property'
he once declared – but such fears were widely shared, as we have
already seen.[35] No matter the particular variety of 'modern' socialism, this sticking place remained.

In the late 1880s and early 1890s, for example, co-operators and
leaders of the SDF publicly debated the merits of their respective
associations. First in the field were Ben Jones and Henry Champion,
the 'Tory socialist' secretary of the SDF, who argued their case in
London in January 1887. Champion maintained that at present
'mere Co-operation' only benefited 'the highest class of workmen'
and equated generalised co-operation with state socialism. In order
to bring about the great change, what Champion delicately referred
to as 'a certain amount of paternal legislation' would be necessary,
because many workers were too 'degraded' and 'brutalised' at
present to respond to persuasion alone. Jones humorously countered
with the suggestion that the word 'Despotic' ought to be substituted
for 'Democratic' in the SDF's title if they intended to abolish freedom of election and replace it with a benevolent autocracy. Whilst
he did not reject forms of municipal socialism, Jones contested the
notion that 'State action [was] the highest form of co-operative ac-

tion' and instead asserted that 'State control was like a rod of iron; voluntary co-operation was like a fluid.'[36] These oppositions recurred. At Burnley five years later William Simpson made Harry Quelch admit that state socialism was not the only form of socialism that could or did exist and that co-operation was a viable alternative. Like Jones, Simpson doggedly pursued the question of democratic control and prophesied that instead of empowering the worker, 'State Socialism . . . would organise a great system of State Slavery'.[37] In response Quelch merely underlined the limits to co-operative success.

Whether this complacent attitude to the state represented the majority position within the SDF cannot be pursued here, although it seems likely that critical voices were heard at the local level; this would help explain the supportive links which existed between co-operators and SDF-ers in areas like Reading, and detailed local research might clarify these connections.[38] But at the national level there was general hostility towards the movement (a feeling reciprocated in the co-operative press) and the state was commonly idealised: it was not until 1905 that H. M. Hyndman, president of the party, openly rejected the term 'State Socialists' for 'Social Democrats' in *Justice*. He now warned of the dangers of bureaucracy and admitted that state socialism could leave wage slavery and competition intact. Social democracy, on the other hand, promised the abolition of the state and its replacement with a 'co-operative Social Democracy'. However, the state would still have to be wielded against landlords and capitalists in the transition period.[39] There was a growing awareness of the 'state' as a problem from this time and, more specifically, the SDF came to adopt an overtly critical stance toward social reform undertaken by the capitalist state, as Pat Thane has shown.[40] Nevertheless, attempts to obscure the SDF's statist orientation by yoking the term 'co-operative' to social democracy only raised further suspicions amongst co-operators themselves.

Fabian Socialists, who showed more interest in the Co-operative movement, openly embraced a neo-Hegelian conception of the state as a benign motor of social progress. Sidney and Beatrice Webb's important connections with co-operators are well-known; I noted in chapter one how Beatrice Webb 'discovered' the world of working-class association through her contact with the movement in the late 1880s. Sidney Webb was often seen at co-operative gatherings and both he and Beatrice disparaged attempts at co-operative production, arguing that production would be better organised by the state under the direction of an expert elite.[41] Their paternalistic, condescending attitude typified the Fabian approach generally; it marks Harry Snell's pamphlet, *Socialism and Co-operation: their fundamental unity* (1908). As the title made plain, Snell wanted to yoke Fabian socialism and co-operation together and he consequently stressed that both movements were committed to gradual, peaceful change and shared a common ancestor – Robert Owen. Snell's text circled round the issue of the state and he observed disarmingly that the older type of co-operator 'is terrified by the word "State", as if it represented a clique of merciless capitalists, instead of the whole of the people working co-operatively for their own common good.'[42] The problem with this formulation was that the state was hardly democratic at this time; less than a third of the population of the United Kingdom aged over twenty were registered electors until the Representation of the People Act in 1918.[43] The conspiratorial view dismissed so easily by Snell contained more than a grain of truth and was regularly articulated by co-operators before the First World War, a point which will be discussed in more detail later. Finally, tired with his effort to reassure, Snell chillingly declared that under socialism 'the State would, as now, be the supreme authority to which all other forces would bow.'[44] Thus Fabian attempts at conciliation.

The attitude of members of the so-called junta which dominated the ILP was no better: Philip Snowden, Ramsay MacDonald and Keir Hardie all tended to damn the movement with faint praise. In his presidential address to the ILP Annual Conference in 1905 Snowden contended that the social problems which called the Co-operative movement into existence 'are too great to be solved except by the power of an united democracy, working through the State.'[45] *Socialism and Society*, MacDonald's classic formulation of state socialism published the same year was very popular, running to eight editions by 1908.[46] Indebted more to Compte than Marx it contained an organic, evolutionist view of social development and was hardly likely to find favour in co-operative circles. MacDonald pushed Snowden's critique further for he was convinced that the Co-operative movement had had its day and now acted as a brake on progress: belief in 'individual self-help' retarded the spread of 'collectivist economics' and thus strengthened the present industrial system. Co-operation also undermined class unity, according to MacDonald, because it reinforced divisions within the proletariat and inculcated the 'capitalist frame of mind.'[47]

Keir Hardie's *From Serfdom to Socialism*, which rehearsed many of MacDonald's views, was published two years later in 1907. In this text Hardie deployed a number of arguments designed to placate co-operators' fears and reassure them that socialists were their natural allies. First he scorned the anti-statism of anarchists like Kropotkin who hoped that co-operative organisations would one day entirely replace the state. Hardie lamented the fact that many co-operators as well as anarchists shared the 'individualistic conception of the State as some external authority exercising a malign influence upon the community'. This notion was hopelessly outmoded, according to Hardie, for now the state embodied 'the aptitude for freedom and self-government to which any people has attained.'[48] Having brushed aside this issue Hardie then tried to unite socialists and co-operators around a shared goal: although their strategies differed they had a common ambition – the collective ownership of the means of production. Thus the central message was to ignore the means and concentrate on the ends 'upon which all are agreed'. As to the role of voluntary co-operation in the future, Hardie preferred not to speculate: 'To dogmatise about the form which the Socialist State shall take is to play the fool.'[49] In effect, 'Trust to luck' seemed to be Hardie's advice and he assured his readers that 'communism' would follow naturally and easily from the transition phase inaugurated by state socialism. What worried co-operators was the thought that state socialism might eventually drive out other forms and represent itself as the final phase of social development to the profound detriment of their own project.

In a skilful analysis of the early history of the ILP, Carl Levy has demonstrated how the party appealed mostly to skilled workers and lower-middle-class individuals who shared a desire for education and 'respectability', but we ought to note that socialists from a wide variety of backgrounds all uncritically embraced the state: Quelch, Snell and Hardie had roots in the manual working class, MacDonald and Snowdon were white-collar workers for most of their lives, Champion was upper-class.[50] I argued in chapter two that co-operation drew most of its active membership from the skilled artisan stratum within the working class and also provided 'improvement' for some through white-collar employment in the movement. These individuals could also be regarded as 'respectable' but this label should not obscure the ideological differences which made common understanding with socialists difficult if not impossible. Most leading socialists would have accepted the description offered by the Positivist Frederic Harrison which was quoted at the beginning of this chapter: they regarded co-operation as a 'bastard form' – an illegitimate hybrid – because it held out the 'false' promise that everyone could be a master. The exception which proves the rule here was the idiosyncratic Tom Mann.

Mann was the only leading socialist of his generation who supported co-operation wholeheartedly over a long period. He recommended co-operative forms of organisation during the Great Dock Strike in 1889 (rather naïvely as it happened – comrades in the SDF were quick to pounce) and regularly appeared on Co-operative platforms over the next decade. To give just one example of his approach, at a meeting of the Worcester Society in 1895, Mann sketched the following socialist utopia:

> Applied Co-operation, as advocated by Owen, meant nothing else but the ultimate elimination of ownership in land, the elimination of the individual owner and controller of machinery, and the elimination of the individual ownership and control of the capital. *(Applause)* It was a big order, but that was Co-operation. Were they afraid of it? Did they know they were harbouring such a revolutionary force? *(Laughter)* . . . Co-operation was the superseding of the capitalist system . . . Co-operation meant also the establishment of a brotherhood and a sisterhood. *(Applause)*[51]

Two years later Mann was looking forward, over-optimistically, to the foundation of a 'Socialist Co-operative movement' which would amalgamate and concentrate the forces of labour.[52] Mann continued this advocacy during his syndicalist phase before the First World War and beyond. In his election address to the ASE in 1919 he declared that 'I am not afraid of the terms Socialist, Spartacist, Bolshevist or Syndicalist. I know that in essence these all mean the thorough application of the principle and practice of *true co-operation*, and I unmistakably stand for co-operation and the wiping-out of the capitalist system.'[53] Patrick Joyce's unsupported assertion that 'a marked anti-statism continued in [late nineteenth-century] socialism' is very misleading: Mann's grasp of both the achievements and the potential of the Co-operative movement, which went hand-in-hand with his distrust for the capitalist state and statist modes of social transformation, was highly unusual, amongst leading socialists at any rate.[54]

Co-operators on the other hand continued to regard the state with suspicion before the First World War and their reaction to the Liberal welfare legislation passed between 1908 and 1911 bears this out well. By the turn of the century the movement was experiencing a crisis of conscience: the 'discovery' of poverty and continued pressure from the WCG, which established a number of 'settlements' in poor districts, made the limitations of co-operative practice all too clear.[55] Many working-class families could simply not afford to associate and co-operation had signally failed to lay the ghosts of unemployment, sickness and old age, as socialists and trade unionists were fond of pointing out. Increasingly, both the responsibility and the remedy seemed to lie with the state, though co-operators found this solution problematic.

After a great deal of national and regional debate the movement eventually backed the idea of state pensions in 1901. Some of the oppositional voices heard in the debate were smug and complacent: the editor of the local record of the Manchester and Salford Society, for example, observed that many members already drew pensions saved through trading at the stores, a practice preferable to state action and which could be easily generalised so long as working men cut their beer intake.[56] But Frank Hardern's caution furnishes a better guide to the opinion of the majority: 'We have built up a State without State help, but if we are not careful the State will mar our building', Hardern remarked in his Presidential Address to the 1899 Congress. Co-operators later supported the Old Age Pensions Act of 1908, though they made no effort to conceal the partial and unsatisfactory nature of this measure.[57]

Rather more complex reactions were provoked by the National Insurance legislation of 1911. Whilst the editor of the *Co-operative News* referred to 'Mr Lloyd George's well-constructed measure', the WCG had misgivings from the start. The exclusion of married women who were not wage-earners from the Act provoked a great deal of anger; and as the workings of the scheme became clearer, criticism mounted. The fact that the Act might undermine the friendly societies which were under democratic control became increasingly apparent.[58]. Drawing attention to the great concentrations of wealth in British society, the editor of the *Millgate Monthly* grudgingly admitted that 'the Insurance Act is a tardy recognition by the State of the justness of the workers' claim to a share of this surplus'. However, the anti-democratic bias of the Act and the tendency for employers to intimidate their employees into joining private insurance companies – thereby diverting funds away from working-class association – was thoroughly berated.[59]

Two major arguments informed the co-operative critique of statist social reform. Firstly the class composition of the state was seen as a bar to effective change from above, a theme which became increasingly common as war approached. Early in 1914, for example, the editor of the *Millgate Monthly* sympathised with those 'advanced thinkers' in England who questioned nationalisation as a panacea because 'While the State is run in the interests of the capitalist class the benefits of nationalisation would go to the middle and upper classes instead of to the workers.'[60] Secondly and more insistently, many co-operators anticipated Poulantzas' understanding of the capitalist state by arguing that the state attempted, through competition and coercion, actively to disorganise working-class association and to render workers passive and dependent.[61] Social reform could be seen, from this angle, as part of a political or class *strategy*.

In his inaugural speech at the Bradford Congress in 1911, George Thorpe argued that the expansion and success of the Co-operative movement had had an important influence on the 'humane legislation' introduced in recent years. He instanced the Old Age Pensions Act and the Insurance Bill, welcomed the changes in attitude towards the poor from those above, but reminded his audience that:

> a crisis arrives at stated times in the history of all progressive nations, when politicians have recourse to expedients, and generally these expedients are very partially remedial in their effects, and greatly palliative in their nature, which for the time being tide politicians and statesmen over their difficulties by raising false hopes and lulling the great mass of the people into a sense of false security.[62]

The dominant 'idea of the state', as a number of historical sociologists have suggested, was challenged between 1911 and 1914 by an increasingly militant working-class movement.[63] The crisis referred to by Thorpe concerned the nature of Liberalism itself and necessitated the sensitive political handling of the relationship between 'individualism' and 'collectivism', a subject which will be explored in more detail in the final section of this chapter.

V

As we have seen, the meaning of 'socialism' and the emergent social-ist movement provoked considerable debate within co-operative cir-cles throughout this period. From the early 1880s a new term appeared – 'collectivism' – and henceforward the key polarity that structured political debate in England, as Stefan Collini has persua-sively argued, was between 'individualism' and 'collectivism'; the concept of 'co-operation' was pulled back and forth within the field of force constituted by these poles. The question of the state again intrudes here, for as Collini also points out, arguments about these 'essentially contestable' concepts involved an assessment of the role of the state.[64] None of these keywords had a fixed or rigid meaning before the First World War but we may note once again that many leading socialists came to elide their own project with that of 'collec-tivism'; the Fabian take-up was examined some years ago.[65] This trend increased after the New Life phase in the history of socialism and the increasing routinisation of politics which characterised the ILP especially after the mid-1890s.[66] Parliamentary power rather than 'making socialists' was increasingly prioritised, especially after the formation of the LRC. Socialist collectivists idealised state ac-tion; this clashed with co-operators' anti-statist orientation and en-couraged many of them to stress the 'individualist' nature of the co-operative project.

I shall return to this 'individualist' reading of co-operation in a moment but first it is worth noting that when the 'collectivist' shell was peeled off and rejected, 'socialism' usually got a much more sympathetic reception from co-operators. One possible reconcilia-tion insistently offered by both co-operators and sympathetic out-siders was that co-operation represented 'practical socialism', a transition phase or bridge between competition and the 'Co-opera-tive Commonwealth'. Unlike 'theoretical socialism' co-operation was actually helping to create an alternative, qualitatively superior economy and society in the womb of the present, or so the argument ran. Thomas Kirkup, whose *History of Socialism* first appeared in 1887, believed that the movement was a 'partial realisation of the socialistic ideal . . . well-founded, solid and most promising.'[67] We may note in parenthesis that the movement's critics also tried to

force a similar identification for rather different ends: the Bishop of
Manchester, for example, condemned co-operation as 'Selfish Socialism' in 1886.[68] Not that 'socialism' itself was always anathematised, even by die-hard 'individualists'; faced with a renewed threat
from below in the 1880s, various middle-class reformers started to
advocate their own varieties of 'socialism' or 'collectivism'. Canon
Barnett recommended 'Practicable Socialism' – piecemeal social reform – in 1888; Charles Booth considered 'limited Socialism' to be
the best prop for 'individualism' and free-market competition the
following year.[69]

The contests and complexities were manifest but the range of
positive couplings which appeared over the subsequent decades can
be briefly surveyed: 'the most practical Socialism' (Mr H. Smith at a
meeting of the Leeds Society in 1892); 'Reasonable Socialism' (the
Reading co-operator, Walter Carter, in a pamphlet in 1894); 'ex-
perimental socialism' (Ben Tillett, the Dockers' leader and ILP-er,
interviewed in 1895); 'practical socialism' (*Reynold's News*, 1897);
'Practical Socialism' (*Comradeship*, 1906); 'voluntary Socialism'
(the editor of the *Record* of the Leeds Society in 1907); 'a socialism
by itself, without state interference' (William Maxwell, chairman of
the SCWS, interviewed in 1908).[70] One thing these proposed definitions had in common, apart from the stress on the utility of co-operative practice, was that they reached back (often explicitly) to the
voluntaristic, pacific form of socialism which had existed before
mid-century. Sometimes, however, co-operators became exasperated with all this semantic wrangling. As the debate on these keywords raged in the *Co-operative News* in 1903 one correspondent
whose patience was exhausted declared that 'it is very childish to
quarrel about mere names when the thing is the same. The point is
to promote the extension of collective ownership in every possible
way, both socially and politically.'[71] This reaction was understandable but the phrase 'collective ownership' concealed a multitude of
meanings which could not easily be reconciled. It was, after all, a
small step from 'collective ownership' to 'collectivism'.

This was precisely the fear which haunted G. J. Holyoake who
believed that the Co-operative movement would literally be swallowed up by the triumph of 'collectivism', whether inaugurated by
capitalists or modern socialists. Worried by the hegemony of the
Wholesales, which he read as a symptom of creeping 'collectivism',
and alarmed by the Fabian promise to reduce the movement to a sub-

department of the socialist state, Holyoake regularly articulated a more openly 'individualist' position during the last years of his life. He referred favourably to the *Liberty Review*, journal of the right-wing Liberty and Property Defence League, in 1904 and in the revised version of his *History of Co-operation* published in the year of his death he described co-operation as 'self-defensive Individualism'.[72] As I argued in chapter five, the majority of local and national co-operative leaders, including Holyoake himself, were Liberals who broadly accepted the separation of politics and economics underpinned by free trade finance; for the majority 'collectivism' was anathema because it conjured up a vision of a future society in which the economy was totally subordinated to a bureaucratic state led by an elite of experts. What would become of working-class 'independence', that touchstone of radicalism and popular liberalism, within this schema, they wondered.[73] The widely-shared belief was that voluntary association (particularly co-operation) and not the state offered the best solution to the 'social question' and that the main concern of 'politics' was merely to ensure and protect the rights of individual citizens, especially the right to associate.

This position came under increasing attack from both right and left in the late nineteenth and early twentieth centuries. Joseph Chamberlain's Tariff Reform League proposed to reunite the political and economic systems in 1903 and Marxists shared a similar ambition – Harry Quelch once referred to free trade ideology as 'one of the most impudent humbugs that was ever foisted on long-suffering humanity'.[74] Large sections of the working class, as Ross McKibbin has trenchantly argued, rejected this strategy before the First World War; free trade finance held a lasting appeal because it seemed to work, for many at any rate.[75] But there were important exceptions within the ranks of co-operators, especially amongst a younger generation of activists who reckoned that it was becoming increasingly unrealistic to keep economic and political domains apart, and that *laissez-faire* had had its day. This takes us to the heart of the 'crisis of liberalism' and what this actually meant to co-operators. A number of factors which intermeshed and helped to precipitate this crisis can be identified: as the discussion above suggested, the limitations of co-operative practice were harder to deny from the turn of the century and state intervention to remedy the problem of poverty, if not celebrated uncritically, was at least tolerated within the movement. Further than this there was also a grow-

ing awareness – and this is a major theme in the next chapter – that
the reorganisation of the economy along monopoly capitalist lines
had made any neat separation of politics and economics impossible
to sustain, for the boundaries could not easily be distinguished any
more. Consequently a number of prominent co-operators came to
the conclusion that some form of 'collectivism' was not only inevitable but also desirable if these multiple challenges were to be defeated.

One of these was the Bolton co-operator and director of the CWS,
William Lander. At a meeting organised by the Beswick Society in
1908, Lander gave an address in which he embraced 'collectivism' in
a way which would have shocked many anti-statists in the movement and his remarks nicely condense the tensions and linkages in
this area:

> Collectivism must govern the England of the future. Some people
> might think that that sounded like socialism. He was not frightened
> by the word socialism, but he wanted their socialism to be of the prac-
> tical kind. Co-operation was the embodiment of the collective system
> for the development of the industry, trade and the commerce of the
> country. The business was done by the people themselves, and he
> thought he might say that co-operation was socialism of the very best
> type.[76]

Opening an exhibition for the Bradford Society two years later,
Lander declared that:

> He was a Socialist, and he believed in the money of the world going to
> the masses, so that there would be less poverty, less vice and less deg-
> radation. He contended that Co-operation was the highest form of
> Socialism; it aimed not at making its main men rich, but in making the
> masses feel that the movement was theirs.[77]

It was Lander's belief in the 'ideology of consumption' and the efficacy of the Wholesale societies which enabled him to openly affirm
both 'socialism' and 'collectivism', after he had cut a path through
the morass of meanings. His language, however, was revealing: the
distancing concept of 'the masses' partially exposed the anti-
associationist tendencies of the 'collectivist' project. For neither 'collectivism' nor the CWS, as I argued above, promised the democratic
re-ordering of 'heads' and 'hands'; both would leave the productive
relations of capitalist industry intact and could indeed generate new

forms of labour oppression and exploitation.

One of the CWS's most ardent apologists, Percy Redfern, recognised this danger before the First World War. Redfern had described himself as a 'collectivist' in an article in the *C.W.S. Annual* in 1910.[78] Reflecting on the earlier debate between 'individualists' and 'federalists', advocates of profit-sharing and the CWS, in the official history of the CWS three years later he admitted that the arguments had not all been on one side and that something had been lost by the resultant alienation of opinion. Redfern then added a prophetic caution:

> With all its appeal of unity to the idealist, and of economy to the man of business, the collective method has its dangers. Institutions too confidently founded upon it may end in neglecting individuality and fostering bureaucracy, the stream of their vital force running dry in deserts of officialism and enslavement to routine. Hence the not unreasonable criticism which collectivism meets in our own day from individualists at one extreme to syndicalists at the other.[79]

The prospect was too much for Redfern to contemplate for long and he quickly moved on; elsewhere in the text he sidestepped this issue by defining co-operation as 'voluntary collectivism'.[80] In the subsequent history of the movement, however, this intractable problem could not be disposed of quite so easily.

The linguistic and theoretical contradictions and overlaps which have been traced above provoke a number of reflections. On the one hand they help us to understand the tenacity of popular liberalism within the movement and how working-class hostility toward modern forms of socialism could be motivated by more than just reactionary self-interest. On the other hand they suggest an increasing demand before the First World War for a *rapprochement* with socialists, voiced by those who admitted that co-operation, even when aided by sympathetic Liberals like Maddison in the House of Commons, could not provide all the answers on its own. Although the timing of this shift has been the subject of some debate – the Co-operative movement did not formally 'enter' politics until 1917 (and even then affiliation to the Labour Party was not countenanced) and the appeal of Liberalism remained strong after the war – a good deal of evidence points to a growing socialist presence within the movement from the turn of the century at least.[81] Once again local studies would help us grasp this development in its full complexity because

relations depended so much on the varieties and histories of socialism and co-operation within particular regions.

In the mid-1890s, for example, two members of the SDF sat on
the educational committee of the Burnley Co-operative Society. The
upshot was that the central library was stocked with socialist texts,
and socialist periodicals like *Clarion* and *Justice* were taken by thirteen district newsrooms. Socialist lecturers (including Quelch) also
regularly addressed the society.[82] From the late 1890s many commentators in the socialist press generally were recommending a
policy of 'permeation'.[83] The debates on direct political action at the
Co-operative Congresses were often reported sympathetically and
after the General Election in 1906 the editor of the *Wheatsheaf*
noted 'the connection of one or other of the new Labour MPs with
particular Co-operative Societies.'[84]

On the eve of the First World War these links were becoming
more and more visible. This was especially true in Scotland where,
according to the socialist co-operator, James Maclean, by 1913 the
ILP had 'systematically saturated all committees and associations
within the Co-operative movement.'[85] We might question Maclean's
objectivity but even hostile Marxists like H. W. Lee admitted at this
time that 'there is no doubt that the principles of Socialism have
been making steady headway in the co-operative societies of this
country. This has been noticeable during the last few years.'[86] At the
ILP's coming-of-age conference in Bradford in 1914 Mr Foulger of
the Co-op Union supported this notion – 'there never had been a
period when more members of the ILP and co-operators had been
seen on the same platform', he remarked – and concluded, reassuringly, that 'they were travelling to the same goal, although by different roads.'[87] The qualifying clause was both important and ominous
for many co-operators continued to believe, for the reasons explored in this chapter, that their own road was not only better built
but was more likely to get them to their utopian destination.

Part three

Containment

8

The politics of working-class consumption

I look upon the Co-operative movement, through its very strength and universality, to be the bedrock of the future democracy; because the nearer we approach the end of the present competitive system all industries, productive and otherwise, will become trustified, and the final struggle will result in a fight to the death between co-operation and trustification . . .

James Sim in *Justice*, 27 September 1902

I

The forms and relations of consumption were revolutionised in the last decades of the nineteenth century. As the incomes of many working-class households gradually increased, innovative entrepreneurs began to recognise the potential profits to be made from the 'mass market'. Thus capitalist modes of retailing, marketing and wholesaling were transformed during this period to create what we now recognise as particularly 'modern' forms of mass consumption – department stores, multiples, standardised and branded commodities, advertising and so on. The persistence of the small trader should not be underestimated, but the future lay with men like W. H. Lever, Lord Vesty and Thomas Lipton who made spectacular fortunes from the sphere of consumption. Between 1858 and 1879, for example, only 3.3 per cent of all millionaires and 2 per cent of all half-millionaires in Britain had made their money from the manufacture and sale of food, drink and tobacco; between 1880 and 1899 the figures had risen to 23.7 per cent and 14.6 per cent respectively. By 1914 there were 16 multiples with over 200 branches each and 7 with over 500 branches. The tendency was not hard to discern.[1]

This profound transformation did not take place in a social and political vacuum. The 'capitalist production of the mode of consumption' was a contradictory, uneven process but it was also contested; there was after all a huge and growing working-class movement constructed around consumption which pre-dated large-scale capitalist investment.[2] It is important to note here how transformations in the sphere of consumption lagged behind those which occurred in the sphere of production. E. P. Thompson once suggested that in the 1830s 'many English people felt that the structure of industrial capitalism had been only partly built, and the roof not yet set upon the structure.'[3] Non-capitalist forms and relations of production became increasingly marginalised after the collapse of Owenism and Chartism – that is, the roof was eventually erected – but it took almost another hundred years for capitalist domination of the sphere of consumption to be finally assured; and this depended, to a large extent, on the defeat of the co-operative alternative. The politics of this confrontation provide the focus for this chapter.

It is possible to mark out some of the major issues which were at stake via a brief consideration of the growth and role of advertising in this period, a practice once described by J. T. W. Mitchell as 'the Barnum wickedness of the competitive world'.[4] Advertising clearly exposed the clash between what I have called the moral economy of co-operation, disseminated by the movement culture and dependent on an active membership, and a capitalist culture of consumption which was intended to produce passive consumers. Co-operators' critique of, and response to, the new commodity culture which developed during this period was severely limited: they underestimated the attractions of the phantasmogorical commodity form, and their understanding of consumption as concept and activity revolved around notions of thrift, restraint and utility. Although the allure of abundance and excess had fascinated working people from the Great Exhibition onwards, co-operators were often content to wag a disapproving finger rather than wrestle with this problem head-on.[5]

Some acknowledged that the commodity culture represented a serious challenge, wondered how Equity boots or CWS flour could compete against powerful counter-attractions but were loathe to take up the weapons of their adversaries. In a pamphlet published in

1903 James Cheyne noted that the movement seriously lagged behind in the field of advertising and argued that co-operators needed to organise a vigorous propaganda campaign in order to check the advance of 'combines'. He insisted, however, that 'co-operative advertising must have tone' and that 'We ought to avoid the common puff and bluster about the quality of our goods.'[6] Cheyne's advice went largely unnoticed though by the First World War it was clear that something had to be done. The CWS did not finally establish a publicity department until 1916 and although this department was expanded after the war the main emphasis was still on co-operative literature and trade exhibitions. This negative attitude continued in the inter-war years, W. H. Watkins chiding co-operators who were 'hypnotised' by advertisements for proprietary articles at the Congress in 1920.[7]

Consumer capitalists were not constrained by such scruples and for them consumption implied excess and was limited only by the desires of the 'masses' which were waiting to be stimulated; the figure of the modern 'consumer' emerged, reduced to the (repulsive) image of the stomach and the gaping mouth, to complement the 'hands' of the factory system.[8] Advertising endowed commodities with qualities and significances which connected (in theory) with consumers' anxieties, dreams and inchoate beliefs. The major tropes employed included sex, the Empire and notions of racial superiority, as well as the body and individual health and hygiene.[9] Drawing on the American experience, big capitalists like W. H. Lever intuited that the success of the new consumer culture was bound up with the progress of advertising; high advertising costs were an effective means of excluding the entry of smaller capitals (which could not afford to match this expenditure) into particular markets. But it was more than that. Lever for instance believed that advertising could invest the commodity with a mystical, religious aura: he once explained that the real purpose of advertising was 'to create a halo round the article.' Lever spent around £2 million during the last two decades of the nineteenth century trying to create a halo around Sunlight Soap.[10]

Other big capitalists fully realised the potential power of this new medium. Thomas Lipton, 'the archetypal figure of multiple retailing', opened his first grocery store in Glasgow in 1871 and by the time shares were offered to the public in 1898 – total capital issued was £2.5 million – Lipton claimed to own over 400 shops employing

10,000 people around the world. During this decade expenditure on advertising had been running at about £40,000 per annum and Lipton himself did not doubt that this investment had been amply rewarded.[11] From the earliest days Lipton thought up wonderfully inventive promotional gimmicks which appealed directly to those 'low' elements within working-class culture that were celebrated on the stage of the Victorian music hall. Coarse humour, vulgarity and bad taste were regularly utilised in order to drum up custom. He installed trick mirrors at shop entrances marked 'Going to Lipton's' and 'Coming from Lipton's'; the former made customers look thin, the latter puffed them out to look well-fed! In fine, he is best understood as a clever populist, a man who cultivated friendly relations with royalty (including Edward VII and Queen Alexandra) and music hall stars like Harry Lauder, connections which served to keep him and his business before the public.[12]

The contrast with the culture of co-operation, which as we have seen was shaped by a commitment to internationalism and the ethic of 'improvement', need not be laboured. The oppositions sketched above help contextualise the huge material and ideological problems that co-operators confronted from the late nineteenth century. As the multiples steadily increased their hold on the working-class consumer before the First World War and as accumulations of capital increased apace, a series of crises occurred. Although some excellent work on the politics of consumption in France and America in the late nineteenth and early twentieth centuries has recently appeared, we know very little about the British experience.[13] Adopting a broadly chronological framework this chapter first explores the conflicts with *petit bourgeois* interests, then considers co-operators' attitudes toward monopoly capitalist intervention in the sphere of consumption and the impact of a particular *cause célèbre* – the struggle with Lever. I then detail the catalytic effect the First World War had on the movement and argue that activists faced an impossible dilemma: deeply suspicious of the capitalist state, many recognised that unless the state was recruited as an ally which could be used to check 'monopolies' and 'profiteers', the future of co-operation was, to say the least, uncertain. Finally, I examine how this dilemma played out from the end of the war through to the Report of the Royal Commission on Food Prices in 1925, a humiliation and defeat which heightened the sense of isolation and exclusion within the movement.

II

Many private capitalist traders were highly disconcerted by the remarkable success of Co-operative stores, particularly in the industrial North after mid-century, and began to organise against the movement. 'Trade wars', as they were called by co-operators, were a regular feature of working-class community life in the second half of the nineteenth century. Jubilee histories are replete with such conflicts – highlighted of course in order to demonstrate the inevitable triumph of co-operative praxis – yet despite Crossick's useful essay these episodes have not received the scholarly attention they undoubtedly deserve.[14] Faced with growing competition for custom, traders banded together to produce anti-co-operative literature; endeavoured to victimise the stores and their supporters by encouraging employers to sack co-operators and local councils to thwart co-operative ambition; and attempted to cut off supplies of goods from manufacturers and merchants. From the mid-1860s through the early 1870s this antagonism was focused in the pages of the *Grocer*.[15] These attacks, though often vicious, were sporadic, largely uncoordinated and tended to do the traders' cause more harm than good as they helped root co-operation more firmly in the public imagination. The CWS already had a turnover of well over £1 million per annum by the early 1870s and it was becoming more and more difficult to check co-operative advance.

The stakes were raised in the 1890s. From 1896 the Glasgow Society faced determined opposition from private traders and wholesalers in the meat trade who denounced them in the local press and urged employers (especially railway owners) to sack known co-operators. The rapid expansion of the movement from the late 1880s, particularly the establishment of productive works at Shieldhall, Paisley, Selkirk and Edinburgh by the SCWS, had caused much consternation amongst the local bourgeoisie and *petit bourgeoisie* and a protracted battle was fought, which spread throughout the industrial regions of Scotland. This direct assault galvanised Scottish co-operators and, according to the most recent historian of the Glasgow Society, strengthened their anti-capitalist ambitions. Early in 1896, for example, the *Scottish Co-operator* reminded its readers that they

> must not be content with dividends, or even with improved production and distribution. They must use the means at their disposal, and

the influence which they can exercise, as instruments for revolutionising the economic and social conditions of the world.[16]

Co-operators rose to the challenge and organised public meetings, debates and huge demonstrations: the cavalcade of vehicles and brass bands which wound through the streets of Glasgow when new premises were opened on Morrison Street in January 1897 was two miles (3km) long. The boycott was eventually defeated and James Deans correctly described it as an 'ignominious failure' in 1899.[17]

Over the border in England the situation became more tense: traders in Lancashire commenced a series of local boycotts which were nationally co-ordinated in 1902 by the newly-formed Traders' Defence Association (TDA). Initially the campaign was spearheaded by grocers in St Helens but soon spread to Wigan, Burnley and Hull, old heartlands of co-operation. The usual repertoire of tactics were employed and a new journal, the *Tradesman and Shopkeeper*, helped sustain momentum. Importantly the TDA also clamoured for the taxation of co-operative 'profits' (a demand heard over twenty years before) which would have undermined the dividend and hence the movement. Under the provisions of the Industrial and Provident Societies Act of 1893 societies were exempted from income tax under Schedules C and D as long as they placed no limitation on the entry of new members and made sure that non-members did not receive a share of the trading surplus. Societies were liable under Schedules A and B, however, which meant that they still had to pay tax on income from land ownership and that individual members whose incomes exceeded the exemption limit had to pay tax on interest from share or loan capital.[18] But at least the state recognised the difference between co-operative 'surplus' and capitalist 'profit' and this was regarded both as a fundamental point of principle and a necessary desideratum for continued success. The TDA refused to accept this distinction and argued for the removal of what appeared to them to be nothing less than an unfair advantage. Co-operators reacted to this threat by setting up a Co-operative Defence Committee in September 1902 which organised demonstrations in affected areas, produced anti-boycott literature and took subscriptions for a defence fund for victimised co-operators: societies immediately guaranteed over £100,000.[19]

The attack spread from Plymouth to Scotland over the next few years; as co-operatives continued to expand their membership and turnover, more and more private traders became publicly hostile. An anti-co-operative campaign was begun in Preston in the spring of 1905, for example, in a town which had only recently witnessed co-operative success. The local society had fewer than 3,000 members in 1885, but on the eve of the boycott it had nearly 16,000, sales of £100,000 a quarter and 54 branch stores. What most worried private traders was that the co-op was rapidly monopolising the trade of the better-off customers: skilled textile workers were often the most active members. The regular custom of this group had allowed private traders to take credit risks occasionally with the less well-off sections of the working-class. Thus the loss of the more 'respectable' elements seriously undermined their financial stability.[20] Moreover, the Co-op aimed to eliminate private profit and the competitive principle and thus by implication (and sometimes more directly) also promised the extinction of the private trader. The manifesto issued by the Preston traders made these fears explicit:

> It is much to be regretted that the defensive measures are forced upon us, but when it is remembered that the avowed object of Co-operation is the entire 'elimination of all private traders' and that as a means of bringing about that policy of elimination they never cease telling their members that 'behind every counter there probably stands a knave'.[21]

The campaign in Preston collapsed by the end of July due to the fact that private traders were themselves divided over this issue – many recognised the futility of attacks on such a stable movement – and because supplies could not be effectively restricted owing to the operations of the CWS.

Nationally 1905 proved to be a turning point. The Plymouth Society won an action for libel against the Argus Printing Company Limited in the High Court and was awarded a total of £5,000 in damages.[22] This meant that printers were now unwilling to print anti-co-operative literature and boycotts quickly ceased. The private traders active in the TDA were in the main the owners of small-to medium-sized concerns, pinched between the Co-operative movement and the multiples. Their fears were much exaggerated – they survived and prospered well into the twentieth century – though they could not halt co-operation. At the Co-operative Congress the following year Duncan McInnes, chair of the Co-operative Defence Committee, expressed relief that this particular contest had been won but warned delegates of the dangers of complacency:

His view was that, as we produce for the wants of our members in an
ever-increasing degree, we shall be attacked by a different grade of
people to retail traders. We shall touch their interests, and possibly we
may have a more considerable competition to meet in the immediate
future than in the past.[23]

The 'different grade of people' McInnes referred to were big capitalists like W. H. Lever who was soon to engage directly with the
movement.

III

From the late nineteenth century, the structure of the British and
indeed the world economy was undergoing a profound transformation, as J. A. Hobson clearly perceived in *The Evolution of Modern
Capitalism* (1894). Individual capitalists began to co-ordinate their
production targets and price strategies to a much greater extent, either formally or informally. Big capitalists began to swallow up
their weaker competitors in greater numbers than ever before. By
the turn of the century many commentators, from a variety of ideological positions, were describing the new century as an age of
trusts, syndicates and combines (the terms were commonly employed in a deliberately vague, interchangeable fashion). This phenomenon was particularly visible in the American context but what
David Landes memorably described as a 'new, commercial version
of the enclosure movement', was also apparent on this side of the
Atlantic.[24] One measure of the change is provided in a recent study:

> Between 1888 and 1914 an average of at least sixty-seven firms disap-
> peared in mergers each year, and in the three peak years of high share
> prices and intense merger activity between 1898 and 1900 as many as
> 650 firms valued at a total of £42m were absorbed in 198 separate
> mergers.[25]

Conceding that developments in this country may have been less
spectacular (and public) than in the United States, Bill Schwarz has
nevertheless concluded: 'It is hard to accept that the formation of
monopoly capitalism in Britain was massively "retarded" ....'[26]

For their part, co-operators were well aware of these changes; the
international restructuring of the mode of production/consumption
along monopoly capitalist lines was commonly discussed from the

1890s. Some responses were briefly noted in chapter four but this theme merits closer investigation. Many co-operators had long recognised that 'monopolists', who desired to dominate the market for particular commodities, represented a very serious threat to their own project. Writing in the *CWS Annual* in 1890 W. E. Snell, drawing mainly on American examples (Cotton Oil Trust; Sugar Refineries Company and so on), argued that trusts had re-introduced the old fraudulent practices of regrating, engrossing and forestalling and concluded that 'the moral influence of rings and trusts cannot fail to be injurious throughout the world of commerce.' This appeal to the 'moral economy' of co-operation was sure to strike a chord. Snell recommended immediate government intervention to control these practices.[27] Similar warnings were regularly sounded in the years which followed but an appropriate remedy, agreeable to all sections of the movement, was very hard to find. In 1901 the *Wheatsheaf* reviewed Macrosty's important work, *Trusts and the State*. The reviewer affirmed Macrosty's belief that the 'age of trusts' imposed increased burdens on the working class but pointed out that the major problem with the book was that Macrosty expected 'too much from the State, proverbially hard to move.'[28]

Although internal differences should not be underestimated, the 1903 Co-operative Congress unanimously passed a resolution which condemned combines as 'a menace to the well-being of the community.' Moving the motion, W. H. Berry had presciently observed that

> Socially and commercially, the trust movement was opposed to the co-operative movement. Trusts were organised in the interests of the few, whilst the co-operative movement was organised in the interests of the many. He thought that in the future we should see a large extension of this trust movement, and it seemed to him that, as co-operators, we must see to it that we maintain and extend the people's trust, – organised by the people, for the people, and under the control of the people.

The motion was seconded by J. T. Brownlie of Woolwich who asserted that trusts would inevitably force co-operators to 'capture the administrative and legislative machine'.[29] The necessity for political action made slow headway, as we have noted, but Berry's notion of a 'people's trust' was enthusiastically taken up and frequently reiterated before the First World War. What the economic historian Charles Wilson referred to as 'the war in the soap trade' was soon to strengthen this belief.[30]

Before this set-piece conflict is considered, it would be worth glancing at socialist understandings of this transformation; despite the obvious dangers it is possible to offer some broad generalisations here. *Justice* was positively sanguine from the late 1880s, for example: 'The growth of syndicates points to the gradual growth and incorporation of capitalism under one head' noted a front page article in 1889. This necessary stage of economic and social evolution, the author concluded, 'will culminate in the socialisation of all the means and instruments of production . . . probably decapitation will not even be necessary.'[31] Thus the growth of monopolies was regarded as an inexorable process and a hopeful sign of the socialist society of the future, views which were repeated *ad nauseam*, not only by members of the SDF, but also by a wide variety of state socialists during subsequent years. There were some dissentient voices, like those of James Sim quoted at the beginning of this chapter and James Maclean, but their opinions were marginalised.[32]

H. W. Lee's pamphlet, *The Triumph of the Trust Under Free Trade* (1908), which demonstrated how 'the trust clears the way for Socialism', articulated a widely-held belief.[33] The ILP leader Philip Snowden put the case very clearly just before the First World War:

> It is no more possible to prevent the formation of the Trust than it was possible for the Luddites to succeed in preventing the adoption of machinery by the drawing of boiler plugs. The Trust is a great step forward in economic advance . . . The Trust is concentrating industry, and is evolving Capitalism to that stage where the public ownership and control of the great industries will be possible. Competition – the Trust – and then Socialism.[34]

The implicit comparison with the Luddites was hardly flattering and Snowden's neat, simplistic formula ('Competition – the Trust – and then Socialism') cut no ice with co-operators. Many state socialists and Marxists simply misread the signs of the times in this period (in continental Europe as well as in Britain) and held wildly optimistic views concerning what Landes referred to as 'the growing pains of a system in process of germination.'[35]

To return to the slippery subject which brought these issues into the open, the Co-operative movement had entered soap production in a small way in the mid-1870s but a real opportunity opened up when Lever attempted to corner the production of this commodity in 1906. Ironically this initiative was blocked by the energetic opposition of a fellow mass-market capitalist, Lord Northcliffe: the *Daily Mail* ran a vigorous campaign against the 'soap trust' and the 'Earl of Sunlight' and the popularity of Lever's brands plummeted. The CWS response was prompt. The Irlam plant near Manchester, which was opened in 1894, produced 265 tons of soap weekly in 1905. The following year Irlam worked around the clock to increase output to 660 tons a week. Extensive new plants were quickly erected in the Newcastle and London areas over the next few years.[36] It became clear to many leading co-operators that this covert struggle would inevitably become overt. At the annual meeting of the Coventry Society in the winter of 1906, for example, William Lander declared that 'The "soap combine" was only an indication of "combines" yet to come. It was only the beginning of the fight.' The appropriate lesson to be drawn, according to Lander, was that it was now imperative for the movement to enter industry and take their share in 'controlling the raw materials, the markets of the world'.[37]

This inroad into the soap market represented an important gain for co-operators as Lever had been in the forefront of the capitalist drive to produce a new mode of mass consumption. He desired to generalise and universalise the commodity culture of Victorian England and, as I noted earlier, helped to create a new identity for the subject as consumer via advertising. Lever revolutionised the commodity form; shaped, packaged and transformed the humble bar of soap into the tablet, a major aesthetic icon of modernity; and developed branding and 'consumer loyalty' in order to endow this commodity with a personality and a life of its own.[38] Soap was no longer merely useful and necessary in order to clean one's body and clothes (as it was for co-operators), it was vital in order to ensure personal and social success, ease anxiety and help provide what Jackson Lears has termed a 'therapeutic ethos'.[39] Lever lived for the commodity and spent his whole life trying to make the world conform to the neat regularity of a bar of Sunlight soap.

Other factors helped draw attention to the threat from 'monopolists' (co-operators' preferred term for men like Lever) at this time. In particular, links were made between the rise of the 'trust' and new, 'scientific' methods of adulteration. The critique of adulteration as an integral feature of competition had always been important within the movement, but from the early years of this century a new emphasis was apparent. An editorial in the *Co-operative News* in 1906 noted the sophisticated techniques adopted by the adulterator – 'the latest researches of science are at his disposal' – and concluded that the movement had to be vigilant as never before if these abuses were to be kept in check. The existing government legislation was regarded as hopelessly outdated and inadequate.[40] The *News* reviewed Upton Sinclair's socialist novel *The Jungle* in the same year and argued that the real importance of the book lay in its 'revelations of trust methods'. Sinclair had shown how monopoly, political corruption and adulteration were inextricably intertwined in modern Chicago though his model, it was maintained, had a general application. The review closed on an ominous, prophetic note: 'The trust means gross immorality now, but it is determined to own the country, and what will be its standard of morality then?'[41]

Lever may not have produced adulterated soap but he was portrayed as an archetypal big capitalist, a man whose wallet matched his voracious appetite for personal power. A Liberal bigwig in the North-West, his paternalistic vision of industrial relations (described by Wilson as 'despotic benevolence' though despotic malevolence would be nearer the mark) clashed directly with co-operative ambition.[42] It was little wonder then that the movement drew Lever's ire. His patience finally ran out when 400 co-operative societies resolved to stock only CWS soaps and in the summer of 1910 a number of 'trap orders' were arranged and 38 actions taken against individual societies. It was claimed that societies were committing fraud by passing-off their own goods for Lever's brands ('CWS Flakes' for 'Lux', 'Parrot Brand' for 'Monkey Brand') which they refused to stock. Although the movement sought a compromise and promised to make the distinction explicit, Lever was emboldened by his pyrrhic victory over the *Daily Mail* and would not be satisfied out of court.

The first case came before Mr Justice Joyce in the Chancery Court in October 1911 and lasted nine days. Lever lost and the judge shrewdly noted that 'the real ground of offence . . . [was] that the co-operative societies will make and sell their own soap and other goods without dealing with the plaintiffs or private makers.'[43] Early the following year the case came before the Master of the Rolls who intimated that Lever was wasting the court's time and was even more emphatic in his rejection of the claim, saying that he regarded this action as an attempt by the plaintiffs to compel the defendants to stock their soaps, or abstain from selling their own goods. Sir William Lever had said that in the hurry of business it was impossible to avoid supplying their own soaps without warning customers. This was, in his lordship's opinion, a somewhat audacious claim to a monopoly without warrant in law. [44]

Though the remaining cases fell with the appeal, the euphoria this victory generated in the movement was to be relatively short-lived.

Before the First World War many leading co-operators, whilst recognising the dangers that threatened, continued to believe that if the sources of supply were open (that is if free trade stayed in place), the movement allowed to compete equally and not unfairly taxed, then not even the burgeoning trust movement could halt co-operative expansion. As the Liberal-Labour MP Fred Maddison remarked during the debate on trusts at the 1903 Congress: 'So long as they could draw upon the markets of the world for their supplies, the whip hand of the trusts would always remain in their hands.'[45] Unfortunately for Maddison and his supporters this scenario was rapidly becoming a fiction, as capitalists like Lever expanded their operations, integrated both horizontally and vertically and stitched-up raw material markets. The battle over soap brought out the limitations of the traditional position in full relief. In the spring of 1911, just before his assault on the movement, Lever signed a treaty with the Belgian Government – 'almost like a sovereign prince' as Wilson tellingly observes – and secured unlimited commercial control over the Congo, one of the world's largest sources of palm oil. The town established as a co-ordinating base for the operation was named, appropriately enough, Leverville.[46]

Co-operators responded in kind: as noted in chapter four, William Lander secured a concession for the CWS in Sierra Leone in 1913. The following summer the editor of the *News* drew attention to the fact that the British Government had recently purchased a dominating influence in the Persian oilfields in order to check the power of oil combines and protect the security of the Royal Navy. There followed a devastating critique of the theory of perfect competition and the notion of the open market which is worth quoting in full:

The old economic theory that the competition of sellers in the open market keeps prices down to a reasonable point, is proved in practice to be a fallacy. The reason is that the open market has, with regard to many commodities, ceased to exist. Wherever the trusts hold sway there is no open market. The very purpose of a trust is to destroy the competition of the open market in order to be in a position to dictate prices. The power of the trusts grows every day. Amalgamations succeed amalgamations; the ring fence is being drawn more tightly around the general consumer, who everyday finds himself at the mercy of a comparatively small number of men, who govern the policy of the world trusts which threaten to become the most awful tyranny the world has ever known. As co-operators we are doing what we can to get such control of raw materials as will limit that tyranny.[47]

As far as the editor was concerned the only long-term solution to these anti-democratic tendencies was the national ownership, or better still, the co-operative ownership and control of all basic commodities. This belief was soon to gain a much wider currency in the context of total war.

IV

During the war, state intervention and regulation of the economy were rapidly introduced to meet the exigencies of the immediate crisis, first by the Liberal, then by the coalition government under Lloyd George. The railways were taken over at the outbreak of war and under the Defence of the Realm Act in March 1915 the government acquired the right to take over factories if necessary; wage controls were imposed and conditions in factories regulated by the Ministry of Munitions (later the Ministry of Labour) from this time.[48] Like many in the wider labour movement, co-operators frequently read these developments as evidence that 'individualism' had irreparably broken down and from the start of the war they called for joint state and co-operative control of the price and supply of foodstuffs in order to check 'profiteering'. Attempting to preserve some vestige of *laissez-faire*, the government ignored this demand until no other option was left.

Pressured by food shortages (exacerbated by the success of the German submarine campaign) and the related increase in labour unrest, early in 1917 the coalition government finally established a Ministry of Food under the direction of a Food Controller, to ensure that the civilian population was properly fed. To their surprise and chagrin co-operators found they were left out in the cold, as G. D. H. Cole noted 'The Government, so far from showing any appreciation of the potential value of the Movement as an instrument of war-time control, treated it right up to 1918 with studied neglect.'[49] This exclusion was particularly galling because the number of co-operators rapidly expanded during the war – from 3,054,000 in 1914 to 4,131,000 by 1919. This represented an average annual percentage increase of 6.2 per cent compared to a rate of 3.6 per cent during the six years preceding the war. Over 10 per cent of the total retail sales of food and household goods were sold by Co-operative societies by 1918.[50] Activists reasoned that if any organisation had the right to speak for the consumer it was the Co-operative movement yet they had been deliberately denied a voice.

This sense of isolation and exclusion had profound repercussions on the trajectory of the movement. In the first two years of the war, co-operators' often critical and suspicious attitude toward the state hardened into outright hostility. The Munitions of War Bill, which seriously curtailed the right to strike amongst other things, was attacked for its unfairness in the *News* in the summer of 1915. If the working-class had to surrender hard won privileges, then it was only right that 'ordinary methods of profit-making and usury' should be 'strictly supervised by the State.'[51] Symptomatic of the increasing militarisation of British society, the idea of conscription simultaneously provoked a torrent of criticism, the *Millgate Monthly* arguing that this measure 'would be a new weapon in the hands of the employing classes'.[52] Conscripts, it was feared, might soon be used as strike-breakers. Old 'individualists' like E. O. Greening, who was opposed to direct political action, and 'socialist' co-operators like T. W. Mercer, found common ground here. The following year Mercer sketched a terrifying, prophetic vision:

> The State, it seems, has no need of those who are not directly, or indirectly, engaged in the work of destruction. Like a great, soulless, inhuman machine, the State, speaking by the mouths of its trusted officials, – who are themselves slaves of the machine – declares that, since the war must be won, nothing else must be thought of until victory is secured.[53]

Discussing the future of social reform, the editor of the *News* picked up this theme and pointed out that 'the workers' had to wrest control of the state from 'the capitalist and landlord classes' as soon as possible. This would enable them to reverse the present tendency and establish 'not the "Servile State" but the Co-operative Commonwealth.'[54]

If the critique of the state sharpened during the early years of the war, so too did the critique of monopoly capitalism. Alternative paths of economic and social development were increasingly polarised in terms of a choice between the capitalist or the people's trust. The *Bolton Co-operative Record*, for example, published a series of articles by H. C. Gray in 1915 which argued that price increases since 1900 were due to the 'corrupt' practices of trusts and combines, specifically the formation of price associations and the cost of advertising. Gray stressed that the only hope lay in the organisation of 'a trust not for the few but for the many – a trust of and for the people.'[55] In the spring of 1916 T. W. Mercer likened the officials of the 'multiple-shopkeeping capitalists' to those of the 'German General staff', equally efficient and just as dangerous. He concluded that it was 'idle to suppose that the growth of our movement will not be challenged by these embattled Trusts.'[56]

The issue of taxation forced these antagonisms into the centre of debate and added a new twist. In an effort to quieten mounting public concern over 'profiteering' the coalition government introduced the Excess Profits Duty which made co-operative 'surplus' subject to taxation in the same way as any private capitalist concern. The imposition of EPD was deeply resented by co-operators, not only for its adverse financial effects, but also because it implied that the state was no longer even nominally neutral: direct links were perceived between the domain of the state and the interests of capital. Mercer recognised that EPD satisfied the wishes of the small shopkeeper but regarded this group as merely a 'stalking-horse'. The real threat lay elsewhere: 'Behind the present agitation to cripple us by unjust taxation stand the monopolists, who realise that the time has come to determine who shall be the masters of industry' he wrote.[57] According to Mercer, this attack would have much the same effect as the Osborne Judgement had had on the trade unions; others compared it to Taff Vale.[58] However, this pessimistic response was somewhat premature and a loophole was soon discovered. The CWS had to pay nearly £1 million pounds in excess profits duty in 1916 and 1917, but in 1918 reduced its prices in order to ensure a trading loss; this enabled it to reclaim the whole of the tax that it had paid under the averaging system. Cole noted that many other societies followed suit 'and thus both defeated the attempt to tax them and successfully demonstrated the vital difference between Co-operative and private trade.'[59]

Various commentators since Cole have emphasised the catalytic effect of the Excess Profits Duty and how important this factor was in determining the movement's entry into politics in 1917: the proposal for the formation of a Co-operative Party was carried at the Congress in Swansea that year by 1,979 to 201 votes.[60] It is not necessary to retell this story and in terms of the concerns of this chapter the events which occurred later in the year were just as significant. For the Co-operative movement directly encouraged the overt politicisation of consumption which took place within working-class communities that year, and it helped to shape and articulate the grievances of countless numbers of working-class consumers who took to the streets to protest about the economic and social inequalities that the war had thrown into vivid relief. The only in-depth study of the politics of food that we have for this period refers to the Co-operative movement merely in passing; the seriousness of this omission is easily demonstrated.[61]

As I noted above, co-operators had been calling for greater food control – including rationing – since the start of the war: 166 societies sent delegates to a national conference held at the Central Hall, Westminster in December 1916 which called for urgent government intervention to halt the rise in food prices.[62] By the spring of the following year the editor of the *Co-operative News* was upbraiding the Food Controller, Lord Devonport, for his failure to protect consumers from 'the unashamed practices of profiteers'. The York Society had passed a resolution calling for Devonport's resignation; the editor also wished to see the back of this ineffectual man, whom he later described as an 'erstwhile grocer'.[63] The Ministry of Food had done little to keep prices down and had repeatedly disregarded the views of co-operators; the vast majority of local food committees set up by the Ministry in an effort to regulate prices and supplies excluded Co-operative representatives. The sense of injustice ran deep and the local and national press conducted a vigorous campaign on this issue.

Matters came to a head in the summer and autumn of 1917. An editorial in the *News* in June complained that the government had packed these committees with 'representatives of the very classes from whom the masses had to be saved', that is, local capitalists and private traders. This anomaly was compounded by the daily increase in the movement's membership.[64] Societies contested their exclusion at the local level and the *News* featured reports of demonstrations and protests organised in towns and cities throughout the country including London, Coventry, Pendleton, York, Macclesfield, Bradford, Huddersfield and Plymouth.[65] It seems likely that this was just the tip of the iceberg. The War Cabinet fully recognised the seriousness of the situation and the centrality of the politics of food, and had set up eight regional commissions at the end of May to investigate the causes of the industrial unrest which was spreading fast. All reported that the price and scarcity of food were root causes. The commissioners for the North-West were very worried indeed and opined that unless the government intervened soon there would 'not only be unrest before the winter but something much worse.'[66] The recent example of the Russian Revolution, in which food had played such an important role, also inflamed the imaginations of leading politicians during these troubled months. The new Food Controller appointed in June, Lord Rhondda, shared these fears and took urgent action. He expanded the Ministry's staff tremendously, from 400 when he took over to about 3,400 by the end of the year. Simultaneously he tried to appease organised labour: Rhondda publicly conceded that co-operators ought to be represented on food committees but refused to intervene directly to right the situation. As one would expect, this only made things worse.[67]

Bernard Waites has recently suggested that the keyword 'profiteering', which entered the language of class in the latter stages of the war, helped to encourage a 'them/us' view of the social world. This term made it possible to expose dominant and inequitable social relations of consumption; whilst the rich and powerful could still enjoy smoked salmon at the Ritz, paid for out of excess profits made during the war, the majority working class had to endure high food prices and scarcity. The moral indignation focused by the critique of 'profiteering' helped undermine the 'reciprocal' view of class relationships which, according to Waites, was part of the 'subordinate value system'.[68] In the context of working-class self-sacrifice the 'unfairness' of all this was intolerable and rapidly generated an oppositional class-consciousness. This argument is appealing and plenty of supporting evidence can be found within the Co-operative movement. Attacks on 'profiteering' abounded in the Co-operative press, especially from the summer of 1917. In September, for example, the editor of the *News* linked the political campaign against the movement with its unstoppable growth and remarked that the 'blasts of war had blown the sheep's clothing off the profiteering wolves'. The president of the Bolton Society later delivered a lecture on 'Co-operation and Profiteering' in which he passionately denounced growing inequalities and concluded that co-operators were left with no alternative but independent political action.[69] Such sentiments were voiced time and again and considerably raised the temperature of the debate.

Although some local food committees began to modify their line, the fight continued as co-operative representation was at best minimal and the movement continued to be boycotted throughout London (except in Woolwich where the Royal Arsenal Society was able to exert pressure successfully) and other large cities like Sheffield, Plymouth and Norwich. At the beginning of September a deputation to Lord Rhondda from the War Emergency Workers' National Committee (WEC), which included prominent co-operators, raised the issue once again but still the Food Controller refused to make the appointment of co-operators compulsory.[70] Reaction was swift and the movement organised an Emergency Conference, made up of more than nine hundred co-operators from all over the country. Held once again in Westminster so that the government could not fail to notice their presence, the conference took place on 17 October. In his opening speech the usually moderate T. W. Allen warned the government not to underestimate the militancy of working-class 'shopkeepers' nor mistake old images for present realities:

> Their methods might have led them to believe that co-operators were a subservient, peace-loving people of no political importance – a people content to play at revolutionising society and creating a new social order by shopkeeping for each other. If that was their reading they had misread the Co-operative movement badly.[71]

Allen related how co-operators had sought an interview with the Prime Minister, but Lloyd George had refused. This was hardly surprising as 'the "first Commoner" was the last to consider the Co-operative Commonwealth as they understood it.' The conference strongly condemned exclusion from food committees, profiteering, and the Excess Profits Duty. Another deeply resented grievance was the unfair treatment by military tribunals – packed with private traders – which often refused to excuse Co-operative employees from military service, out of spite, they believed. After the meeting the entire conference proceeded to the lobby of the House of Commons where delegates interviewed individual members. The message was clear and unequivocal: co-operators' patience had been exhausted.[72]

Lloyd George eventually received a deputation of fourteen leading co-operators (including W. H. Watkins, William Lander, T. W. Allen and Willie Gallacher) at 10 Downing Street on 31 October 1917. They were in angry mood and the premier had to use all his guile to placate them. Lloyd George tried to worm his way out of the accusation that he had refused to meet co-operators in the past and, predictably, attempted to win them over with fulsome praise for a movement which he described as 'the solid, sound, most sensible, and most practical side of the great industrial movement in the kingdom.' It is difficult to gauge how worried Lloyd George actually was but some insight can be gained from his tone:

> We have a strong sympathy with them, deep appreciation of the work accomplished, and full knowledge of the significance of the movement in the organisation of society in the future. Therefore, to treat the Government as though they are engaged in some sort of sinister conspiracy through agents and spies to destroy co-operative societies, believe me, is ludicrous . . . [73]

Reassuring urbanity was a favourite tactic but Lloyd George's final remarks, simultaneously imploring and impatient, reveal far more. Perhaps he reckoned that co-operators were aware that the government was in fact keeping them under surveillance at this time; the Home Office drew the Cabinet's attention to the movement's progress in its weekly intelligence summary, otherwise known as the 'Reports on Revolutionary Organisations'.[74] The not unreasonable fear was that the impressive resources of the movement would be utilised by workers in the event of a general strike, which seemed more and more likely. There is no direct evidence that co-operators knew that they were being watched but many surely would have guessed and Lloyd George probably sensed this. He carefully evaded discussion of particular grievances and passed responsibility to Lord Rhondda, who was also present. The latter promised that the movement would be fully utilised in the future.

Over the next few months working-class unrest continued una-
bated. The queues outside provision stores grew longer and could
quickly turn into angry crowds. In late November women in Sheffield threatened to raid stores unless they received tea and sugar; in
the middle of December over 3,000 people were reported queuing
for margarine in south-east London; 'rowdy demonstrations' were
held in the West Riding of Yorkshire.[75] The War Cabinet was concerned about the effects on the morale of both the civilian population and the armed forces; reports of shortages and hardship were
filtering back to troops at the front.[76] Industrial workers also took
action throughout January and February 1918: munitions workers
came out on short protest strikes and Woolwich shop stewards demanded that food supplies be distributed at cost price through the
local co-operative society. At the beginning of February the Cabinet
was informed that: 'The number of workers involved in short strikes
which are occurring all over the country as protests against the food
situation is becoming a matter of serious national importance.'[77]
The government took two steps to head off this crisis: rationing of
basic foodstuffs was made compulsory (many local co-operatives
had introduced rationing months before), and working-class representatives were co-opted onto a new body, the Consumers' Council.

The strategy worked, at least in the short run, and unrest subsided. Looking back a few years later the editor of the *Co-operative
News* remarked that it was not unreasonable to believe 'that [food]
control had almost averted revolution at that period.'[78] The rationing scheme quietened criticism of profiteering and the Consumer
Council acted as a bridge between the Ministry of Food and organised labour. An editorial in the *News* in January welcomed the establishment of this body which was to be composed of six
representatives from the WEC and the Parliamentary Committee of
the TUC combined; six from the Co-operative movement; three
from the Women's National Industrial Organisation; four from the
Ministry of Food; and three individuals appointed by the ministry to
represent the 'unorganised consumer'.[79] The moderate union leader
and ILP member J. R. Clynes was appointed as chairman; T. W.
Allen led the Co-operative group and acted as Clynes' deputy; and,
though cynical from the start, the old Marxist H. M. Hyndman
joined the Council as a representative of the WEC. The most significant aspect of this purely advisory body was its symbolic value: the
Council acted as a kind of safety valve for the antagonism of work-

ing-class consumers and incorporated key co-operators like Allen
and William Dudley into the state apparatus. Allen, who took over
as acting chairman when Clynes replaced Lord Rhondda after the
latter's death in July 1918, was knighted the following year.
Hyndman ironically remarked at the time that 'honours were an
abomination, but that if anyone deserved that particular type of
abomination it was Sir Thomas Allen.'[80]

The process of 'incorporation', however, was only one strand in a
complex and continuing story. The radical sense of identity and purpose stimulated within the movement during the war became more
explicit after hostilities ceased. The danger of a 'return to 1914' was
a common theme. Speaking at a meeting held at the Didsbury Liberal Club in March 1919 W. H. Brown, who had stood (and lost) as
a Co-operative candidate for Mossley in Manchester in the General
Election in December 1918, declared that:

> At the beginning of the war individualism went by the board. They
> now had collective ownership of the railways and other great indus-
> tries, and if the people were wise they would see to it that never again
> were those industries run for the profit of a few.[81]

On his return from France the young Walsall co-operator Fred
Abbotts immediately set up a branch of the Co-operative Party. Interviewed in the mid-1980s, he remembered that until the war he
had only a vague conception of co-operation as a total alternative to
capitalism. Life at the front and the events back home changed him
and, reaching for a copy of Arnold Bonner's textbook, *British Co-
operation*, Abbotts explained:

> It was the period of course for one thing. There was that ferment . . .
> At the end of [t]his book is a chapter on the Co-operative Common-
> wealth. Now all that sounds ridiculous today, but it wasn't ridiculous
> then . . . . There was that kind of looking forward, something better . . . [82]

By the end of the war it seemed to many co-operators as if the capitalist social order had been unmade: 'individualism' had finally broken down and the state was demystified; and, if 'collectivism'
offered a problematic solution, it had helped finally bury *laissez-
faire*. To many the Co-operative Commonwealth seemed possible,
even imminent.

V

The 'bonfire of controls' which occurred at the end of the war partially closed the lid not only on the 'doctrineless collectivism' which had evolved during the conflict but also on the more radical ambitions of co-operators.[83] Simultaneously, co-operators had now to confront directly the many challenges that had caused concern for so long: and the most general threat came from the increasing power and influence of monopoly capitalist forms within the sphere of consumption. The Committee on Trusts which reported to the Ministry of Reconstruction in April 1919 detailed the progress of trade associations and combinations during the war and concluded that they 'may within no distant period exercise a paramount control over all important branches of the British trade.' The committee recommended that the Board of Trade set up a body to monitor developments in order to safeguard the public interest. In an addendum to the report four members of the committee, Ernest Bevin, J. A. Hobson, Sidney Webb and the Plymouth co-operator, W. H. Watkins, argued that this recommendation did not go nearly far enough. For them 'profiteering' was the inevitable corollary of combination and therefore the Government had a duty to intervene to protect the consumer. The control of prices and a mixture of state and co-operative ownership was therefore the only real solution to the problem of the trust.[84]

Co-operators regarded the multiple shop companies, which had expanded enormously from the turn of the century, as yet another form of 'monopoly': the project of individuals like Lever, Lipton and Vesty, it was believed, was related and equally inimical to the formation of a democratic 'people's trust'. Warning voices had been heard before the war: the *Co-operative News* drew attention to the progress of the 'combine' store in 1910 and two years later members were alerted to the 'multiple shop menace'.[85] But after 1918 the situation became more acute: multiples already outstripped Co-operative societies in the sale of many types of goods and were fast approaching a similar percentage share of the market for food and household stores, the mainstay of Co-operative trade. Lipton's fortunes, for example, received a major fillip during the war; dividends on ordinary shares rose from 6 per cent in 1912–14 to 12.5 per cent annually from 1917 to 1923. There were 500 branches of Liptons in 1919, rising to 600 by 1925.[86] Moreover, the owners of multiple

shop companies now threw their weight behind a renewed campaign for the taxation of Co-operative 'profits'. In 1920 imposition
of a corporation tax briefly satisfied the demands of this group until
it was removed the following year.[87] Thereafter they intensified their
campaign. Not surprisingly the records of local societies are littered
with denunciations of multiple shops in the early 1920s.[88]

The movement also faced a resurrected Traders' Defence League
which launched a new propaganda campaign in the early 1920s and
attempted to discredit Co-operative candidates in local and general
elections.[89] Far more damaging were the activities of the Proprietary
Articles Traders' Association, a price-fixing organisation originally
formed in 1896. The PATA represented the producers of branded
and highly-advertised products like patent medicines, toilet prepara-
tions and baby foods; goods which were in the vanguard of the new
commodity culture. In 1906 the PATA ruled that co-operators could
only sell these goods at the minimum price plus dividend, which in
effect meant a boycott as consumers could obtain these articles
much more cheaply through non-Co-operative outlets. The conflict
sharpened during the First World War owing to the fact that if societies charged the higher price they were brought up before local
profiteering tribunals.[90] By the end of the 1920s this organisation
was supported by 437 manufacturing firms, 63 wholesalers and
8,700 retail firms and claimed to control the price of some 8,000
commodities. According to one study, by the end of the 1930s about
30 per cent of all consumer spending went on price-fixed goods.[91]

These were long-term threats; the more immediate crisis was precipitated by trade union demands for nationalisation. As many historians have emphasised, labour relations in the immediate
post-war period were extremely volatile; even C. L. Mowat, who
was not prone to hyperbole, reckoned that there existed 'the mak-
ings of a civil war' at this time.[92] Inspired by syndicalist ideas and the
success of the Russian Revolution, and emboldened by the formation of the Triple Alliance with railwaymen and dockworkers in
1914, the miners demanded the nationalisation of the mines. Lloyd
George initiated the Sankey Commission to stall for time and on the
eve of publication of the Commission's Interim Report in March
1919 he sketched the worst possible outcome in a letter to Bonar
Law:

The miners I happen to know, are relying upon the Co-operative stores to feed them. The great co-operative supplies are outside the mining areas. They ought not to be removed. Once the strike begins it is imperative that the state should win. Failure to do so would inevitably lead to a soviet Republic.[93]

It would be too easy to dismiss such fears out of hand; Lloyd George correctly intuited the central role that the politics of food was to play during this crisis. He must surely have remembered how angry and confrontational 'moderate' co-operators had been less than eighteen months before. And the drift of events within the movement (which was still under government surveillance) since that time, especially the demand for political action – formalised in the summer of 1919 by the establishment of the Co-operative Party – tended to confirm this 'alarmist' view. Lloyd George was not alone either; the Home Office was convinced that the Bolshevik regime had 'practically been kept alive' by the Russian Co-operative movement at this time.[94]

There were other examples of 'revolutionary co-operation' closer to home. During the civil war in Ireland co-operatives (creameries and stores) were deliberately targeted and burnt to the ground by the Black and Tans. At least 55 were damaged or destroyed at an estimated cost of £600,000. In one attack, at Ballymacelligot, two co-operators were shot dead by troops. Many co-operatives had close links with Sinn Fein and there is some evidence to suggest that leading co-operators like Patrick Gallagher acted as gun-runners for the Volunteers during the troubles. The Royal Navy blockaded Londonderry in order to cut off Co-operative supplies coming from the SCWS in Glasgow. Gallagher successfully evaded the blockade and later recalled that managers in Scotland believed that 'if the average Englishman or Scotchman knew how the bloody bastards of politicians are treating the Irish there would be a revolution, and the sooner the better.'[95] The Co-operative Congress in 1921 passed a resolution which condemned these attacks and called for immediate government protection and compensation.[96] In a changed context – and this is the important point – co-operatives could be regarded by the state as subversive, even revolutionary organisations, and thus legitimate targets. Lloyd George understood this only too well.

In the event, the delaying tactics successfully wrong-footed the miners. Faced with determined opposition and weakened by the onset of post-war depression, the Triple Alliance collapsed on 'Black

Friday' in April 1921 and the threat of a General Strike was temporarily averted. Before this débâcle *The Times* propagated the idea of a conspiracy between co-operators and hot-headed trade unionists. Although the CWS denied the existence of such a plot there was some evidence for those who cared to look. At a conference organised by the Communist Party in Manchester on 23 April 1921 Sally Wilkinson, an official of the National Union of Distributive and Allied Workers, stated that her union had 'organised the whole of the co-operative workers of the country, and we were prepared to put that organisation at the service of the Triple Alliance.' The object was to prevent 'the strikers and their families from being starved during the crisis.'[97] Of course there was a good deal of bluff in all this and Wilkinson's claim was suitably vague. But in a sense the lack of a co-ordinated plan made little difference. During the subsequent strike local Co-operative societies, particularly those in mining districts, supported striking miners up to the hilt, sometimes to the point of bankruptcy; in 1926 it was estimated that 571 societies alone had given £526,322 in credit to their members, £82,395 in loans and goods to the value of £639,962 during the dispute in 1921.[98]

For co-operators the overriding lesson of the immediate post-war years was the necessity for political action; the previously widespread belief, that politics and economics were domains which could and should be separated withered during this phase. It was widely acknowledged that co-operators would not be able adequately to safeguard their interests unless they worked independently with and through the state. The Co-operative Party put up eleven candidates in the General Election of 1922 and four were elected; A. V. Alexander, Alfred Barnes, R. C. Morrison and T. Henderson.[99] Supporting a Congress resolution against combines the following year, T. H. Gill argued:

> It is purely hypocritical if we are going to condemn the combines and trusts and not work to abolish the present economic system which is responsible for combines and trusts . . . the resolution suggests we should go to the Government. What is the use of going to the Government on a question of this kind? Who is behind the present Government? And to whom are the present Government responsible? The answer in each case is: to the trusts and combines that you are suggesting that you ask the Government to kill.[100]

In similar vein Alf Barnes wrote that year that it is 'impossible to separate business from politics'. According to Barnes the war had been the real turning point because it had 'burned down the painted transformation scenery of the pre-war political stage' which had obscured the real nature of economic and social relationships.[101]

Headed by A. V. Alexander, the Co-operative group in the Commons pressed, in the first instance, for government regulation of the price and supply of food. They maintained that 'profiteering' was symptomatic of the rise of trusts and price-fixing associations; co-operation acted as a brake on the progress of these forms but would ultimately fail unless aided by the state. Alexander was made parliamentary secretary to the Board of Trade in the Labour Government of 1924 but the fall of the minority government in October scotched hopes of immediate intervention. Though more often remembered for the 'Zinoviev letter' episode, the price of food and the 'profiteering' issue played a vital role in the General Election which followed. In a campaign designed to appeal particularly to those women and unorganised working-class voters enfranchised only six years before, Stanley Baldwin repeatedly drew attention to the rise in prices since the end of the war, blamed Labour for failing to deal with the problem and promised an expert investigation. At the Queen's Hall in London on 15 October 1924 he announced that 'there is no subject I am more eager to attack', a commitment reiterated at Southend a few days later.[102] After the Conservatives won the election Baldwin made good his promise and set up a Royal Commission on Food Prices. The victory speech at the Albert Hall on 4 December was a typical example of Baldwin's political rhetoric – themes of classlessness and patriotism were to the fore – and the Commission was singled out as evidence of the party's desire to 'force a way through the jungle of interests' and the Conservative preference for practical action over idealistic panaceas.[103]

As Ross McKibbin has observed, the big business 'profiteer' was one of a number of stereotypes – including the insurgent working-class activist – which informed the discourse of the Conservative Party in the 1920s. Speaking for the 'public', Baldwin and the Tory press demonised not only class-conscious workers who threatened the *status quo*, but also those individuals who had made huge fortunes, particularly out of the nation's food, during the war and the post-war inflation. This was a rhetorical strategy which helped unify contending interests and class fractions and thus contributed, in no small measure, to the formation and maintenance of Conservative hegemony in the 1920s and 1930s, but it was never only that. The deflationary economic policies pursued by the Conservatives benefited those on fixed incomes much more than big capitalists like Lipton, Vesty or Alfred Mond; thus the country was governed, essentially, in the interests of the professional and commercial middle classes rather than in the interests of big business for most of the inter-war years.[104] Further than this, however, the attack on 'profiteering' was little more than a useful political ploy as the proceedings of the Royal Commission on Food Prices made abundantly clear.

The commission sat for four months from December 1924 and examined ninety witnesses, mainly representatives from the food trades. Only three of the fifteen commissioners were labour people: W. E. Dudley of the CWS, Walter Smith the trade union leader and Mrs Philip Snowden. Sir Auckland Geddes, who had introduced conscription when director of recruiting in 1916, was appointed chairman. A number of leading co-operators were interviewed in January 1925, including Alexander himself who was badgered and bullied by Geddes for nearly a whole day. Geddes refused to recognise the difference between 'profit' and 'surplus', 'consumer' and 'member', and openly belittled the Co-operative movement. Alexander stood up well to this barrage but Geddes was bent on publicly humiliating both the man and what he stood for, insisting that 'you are really indistinguishable, so far as your trading operations are concerned, from any big capitalist trust'.[105] Alexander patiently attempted to explain why the movement should not be confused with a trust, but Geddes would not listen and became increasingly rude and hostile. He was thoroughly incensed when Alexander later teased him with the suggestion that the analogy had been an attempt to lead him 'up the garden a little.' 'I was leading you where?' Geddes barked, then accused co-operators (unfairly) of rigging the market for tea and curtly dismissed the Co-operative MP.[106]

A few days later Lord Vesty and Sir Edmund Vesty appeared before the commission. Archetypal 'profiteers', the Vesty brothers controlled the Union Cold Storage Company Ltd and had made huge fortunes out of the refrigerated meat trade. By 1925 they owned over 2,300 shops; cattle ranches and meat works in South America, Australia and New Zealand; cold stores throughout the United Kingdom; and the fleet of Blue Star refrigerated steamers.

The evidence they submitted maintained that the company made less than half a penny profit per pound of meat sold. Geddes was almost sycophantic in the interview and accepted their claims without question. Seizing this opportunity Lord Vesty argued that he was really a misunderstood philanthropist and that his company performed nothing less than a public service, since 'we devote our whole time and thought', he remarked pathetically, 'to providing the public with the meat they require on the most economical basis.'[107] As if this was not enough, Vesty larded his evidence with an appeal to patriotism: even if the UCSC was a trust, it was rather an English than an American trust. When Sir Henry Rew, a commissioner from a Civil Service background, got fed up with this and started to ask more searching questions about profit rates, Vesty was understandably evasive. At once Geddes closed the discussion and forced the commission to take the rest of the evidence in private.[108]

Not surprisingly, co-operators and the wider labour movement were very critical of what promised from the outset to be little more than a cover-up. In the *Clarion*, for example, R. B. Suthers ridiculed the philanthropic pose of big capitalists like Lord Vesty: 'It seems that, far from profiteering, they work for nothing, and even lose money in their efforts to provide the people with cheap food!'[109] Early in March George Lansbury moved a motion condemning the commission in the Commons. In an eloquent and passionate speech Lansbury drew attention to Sir Auckland Geddes' business interests (he was, amongst other things, a director of the Rio Tinto Company) and concluded: 'It is like appointing a wolf to find out why a lamb should complain about being eaten.'[110] Lansbury argued that evidence of profiteering abounded: multiples like Home and Colonial and the Maypole Dairy Company had declared dividends of 25 per cent and 100 per cent respectively in recent years and food companies like the Union Cold Storage Company, Lyons, Spillers and so on had prospered enormously from the prolonged crisis. Supporting the motion A. V. Alexander also underlined the commission's cosmetic purpose: Baldwin knew full well that the facts of the case had already been revealed by the Linlithgow Committee in 1923. Secure in their majority, Conservative MPs ignored these serious charges and merely proclaimed the sanctity of the laws of supply and demand.[111]

A number of Labour Party leaders, including J. R. MacDonald

and Ellen Wilkinson, joined in the attack outside Parliament; at a public meeting in Wallasey, Fred Jowitt maintained that the commission was 'not only hopeless, but dangerous. Sir Auckland Geddes's conduct in the chair had been scandalous.'[112] Although this episode made it possible to construct closer links between the two movements for a while, the relationship between co-operators and socialists remained highly problematic, a point emphasised by Alexander at the first conference of the Co-operative Party in early February. Admitting that they shared much common ground, he said that conflicting views of the role of the state continued to undermine unity. Alexander sounded this warning:

> Last year, at a Labour conference, a definite programme was laid down which, carried into effect, meant the state monopoly of food. Were we prepared to say that, as a movement that for eighty years has been changing the face of this country we would surrender our position of economic freedom . . . ?[113]

Condescendingly described by some Labour members as a 'Liberal impossibilist' because of his attachment to free trade, Alexander's fears were well founded: the ILP member E. F. Wise put the case for state rather than co-operative control before the Royal Commission at this time.[114]

The commission's report, published at the beginning of May 1925, came as no surprise to its critics. The fall in the price of gold was blamed for the rise in food prices; this technical (and spurious) lecture on the neo-classical theory of money served to deflect charges of profiteering. The commission completely exonerated big capitalists like the Vesty brothers and declared in the preamble to the report that 'we do not bring any accusation of dishonest trading or of profiteering against dealers in wheat, flour, bread or meat.'[115] The only concrete proposal was for the establishment of a Food Council (along the lines of the old Consumers' Council) which would have a purely advisory function. There were two non-signatories and two minority reports: one by T. H. Rylands (President of the National Farmers' Union) who objected to the proposed Food Council as a form of state socialism; the other by the union leader W. R. Smith who argued for government intervention against capitalist combinations – including the UCSC – which made the so-called laws of supply and demand nothing more than a convenient ideological smoke-screen.[116]

The idea of a Food Council was coolly received by those on the right and the left. *The Times* supported Ryland's minority report and agreed that such a body would aid the drift toward state socialism. The editor quite properly questioned the need for a Food Council when the commission had, to its own satisfaction, dispelled all charges of profiteering.[117] The *Co-operative News* argued that only state regulation of monopolies would protect the working-class consumer from the machinations of men like Lord Vesty. As Alexander's Trust and Combines Bill had been blocked in the Commons in February, there now seemed very little hope that any effective legislation would be seriously considered by Parliament.[118] When the members of the Food Council were announced in the summer the story degenerated into farce: Lord Bradbury, who was appointed chairman, openly admitted that 'his main qualification for the post was that he knew nothing about the subject'.[119] Co-operators now realised that they had to face the many challenges generated by economic changes in the structure of society alone; at best the state would not actively persecute the movement, and only lukewarm support for the rights and interests of the consumer could be expected from the Labour Party in the future. The prospects were not encouraging.

9

The experience of defeat

It is the genius of modern capitalism that producers must also be consumers, and in precisely this way the fetters of production have been replaced by those of consumption. Most members of modern society, like Gulliver awakening in Lilliput, have been tied to the consumer society by a thousand tiny chains.

David Levine, 'Recombinant family formation strategies', *Journal of Historical Sociology*, June 1989

I

The politics of consumption and production moved to a syncopated rhythm during the early 1920s: for in many ways the General Strike was an anti-climax as far as the Co-operative movement was concerned. As I argued in the previous chapter, the crisis came in 1925, a year which witnessed not only the ignominy of the Royal Commission but also a prolonged and damaging confrontation between the movement and its own employees. Relations between trade unions and co-operators steadily degenerated after the miners' strike in 1921; although many societies provided invaluable financial and material support to miners and their families, unpaid loans were a continuing source of friction. The Co-op Union attempted to estimate the outstanding debt in 1925 and found that 271 societies alone were still owed about £200,000.[1] For various reasons internal relations with trade unionists also became much more strained. As the economy suffered a downturn in the early 1920s, local societies made economies and cut wage rates. Tensions were also heightened by a 'Red scare': a minority of societies feared that communists were attempting to infiltrate boards of management and branches of the Women's Guild in order to enlist co-ops in the industrial 'class war'.[2] The militant leadership of NUDAW – the main union for Co-operative shop workers after 1921 – could quite easily be portrayed as part of this threat; remember Sally Wilkinson's remarks at the Communist Party conference in Manchester in the spring of 1921 quoted above. Matters reached a head early in 1925 when NUDAW demanded wage increases – or rather attempted to restore rates which many societies had paid at the end of the war – and an improvement in conditions for all grades employed in distributive stores. The bitter struggle which ensued exposed some of the inherent contradictions of the co-operative project very clearly.

The dispute centered on the North-West area. NUDAW refused to negotiate their claims through the Joint Committee of Trade Unionists and Co-operators – they had no representation on this body which had in any case been condemned by the TUC – and threatened a number of societies with strike action. Liverpool and Chester conceded NUDAW's demands but the Preston Society, backed by the Co-op Union, dug in its heels. Co-operators then went on the offensive and locked-out their employees at the end of March; at least 110 societies in the North-West issued lock-out notices. The Co-operative press condemned the union in no uncertain terms: NUDAW was 'attacking' the movement and if successful would pass all the advantages of consumers' co-operation 'to a privileged class of workers.' The union was also vehemently denounced at the local level: 'Better give them the shops', declaimed a member at a meeting of the Accrington Society. In an effort to maintain supplies a number of societies even employed blackleg labour for a time. Within a fortnight a compromise was reached; negotiations were resumed but the Joint Committee was soon replaced by a Court of Arbitration constituted according to NUDAW's wishes.[3] The overriding lesson of the conflict was clear: the interests of workers as producers and consumers were not easily reconciled, especially in a hostile economic climate, and the 'fusion of forces' – the unification of different wings of the labour movement – which had worried Lloyd George so much at the end of the First World War, was no longer a serious proposition.

The General Strike exacerbated these divisions. Despite monies owed, there was a great deal of sympathy for the miners' cause within the Co-operative movement and a resolution in favour of the nationalisation of the mines was passed unanimously at the 1926 Congress, held just before the General Strike was declared.[4] Many societies were adversely affected by the stoppage: trade unions called out members who worked for the Co-op, and local strike committees frequently refused to grant societies permits to enable them to transport supplies. The situation soon became ridiculous; Ernest Bevin ignored repeated deputations and stubbornly insisted that Co-operative employees, like their fellow workers employed in capitalist concerns, stop work for the duration of the strike. He told the CWS that they 'should go to the Government for assistance' over transport problems, though Co-operative supplies were needed to feed striking communities.[5] Many co-operators would have agreed with the editor of the Derby *Record* who later wrote that 'it required more courage . . . to call off' the strike than it did to keep it going.[6] At Congress the following year it was revealed that out of 771 societies which had replied to a questionnaire sent out by the Central Board, 100 societies were interfered with by strike committees and had had trouble with permits. A resolution was passed which deplored this lack of unity and underlined the fact that 'in some towns trade union organisations appeared to treat co-operative societies more harshly than they treated capitalistic undertakings trading for private profit.'[7] Financial support for the miners was not negligible but was less than that given five years before; the Central Board had recommended societies not to advance money without security and this advice had been heeded, even in mining districts. Nevertheless a total of £465,697 in credit had been granted.[8]

II

Demoralised and isolated, co-operators continued to seek parliamentary protection in the late 1920s. It became increasingly apparent, however, that this strategy stemmed more from the growing sense of desperation within the movement than from any utopian vision or optimism. Co-operative politicians like A. V. Alexander adjusted to this new situation and began to take the marginalisation of their movement and themselves almost for granted. Describing a recent encounter between co-operators and a leading state servant at the 1928 Congress, Alexander made the following ironic revelation:

the Parliamentary Secretary to the Board of Trade said it was the first deputation he had received since being elected to office, and he would remind us that until he went to the office he was himself the secretary of a trade association.[9]

Alexander's tone was that of a man who had seen it all before. Not that the anger had dissipated; such brusque treatment, coupled with the increasing threat from capitalist combines, prompted T. W. Mercer to move a resolution which advised members to vote for the Labour Party at Congress the following year. Mercer reminded delegates that 'the whole policy of Mr Baldwin's administration from first to last has been an anti-co-operative policy' and the resolution was passed by a large majority.[10]

The movement continued to face boycotts, from the PATA and the manufacturers of new consumer durables such as gramophones, cameras, vacuum cleaners and radios; commodities that simultaneously promised new forms of pleasure and signified a future in which the drudgery of the past would be replaced by democratised and individualised forms of leisure and repose. The Co-operative response to these pressures was two-fold. Firstly, the CWS attempted to produce these commodities. The drug factory at Drolysden was expanded from the late 1920s and in 1933 a Co-operative radio was marketed, aptly named 'Defiant'.[11] As this did little to stem the tide, Congress passed repeated resolutions against the activities of the PATA and other trade associations and demanded protective legislation for consumers.

Expectations were raised after the Labour victory in 1929. The Joint Parliamentary Committee of the Co-operative Union quickly drafted a Consumers' Bill (modelled on the earlier Bill and on the Canadian Combines Act, which had made a similar organisation to the PATA illegal in that country) designed to empower the Board of Trade to inquire into trade associations. Once again progress was slow; a Government Committee on Restraint of Trade was set up to investigate the matter but this was little more than a sop. Fred Longden, Co-operative and Labour MP for Deritend in the period of the second Labour Government, raised this subject with William Graham, Labour President of the Board of Trade, in 1930. Longden later recalled the meeting between Graham and a deputation of co-operators and furnished a fascinating explanation for this inaction.

What did decide the position was what the President told us: that he

had been advised that if the Labour Government attempted to introduce legislation to protect the movement against the given trade
monopolists and Co-op-strangling Proprietary Trade Association, the
numerically stronger Opposition in the House would throw out the
Government. So nothing was done.

According to Longden he was the last to leave Graham's office that
day. On his way out Graham held his arm familiarly and confided:
'After all, Fred, your opponents have some sort of case against you
in the sense that they may call it "undercutting" when you pay a
dividend on purchases.'[12] Whether this account is entirely accurate
we cannot be sure, but what it does point to is a serious failure even
to communicate with each other let alone co-ordinate a strategy
which satisfied the whole of the labour movement. With friends like
Graham, wondered Longden, who needed enemies?

Thus Labour proved just as adept at prevarication and inaction as
the Conservatives; as we have already seen, many leading state socialists simply did not share the negative assessment of 'trusts'. The
report – which concluded that the PATA had been acting illegally –
did not finally appear until the National Government was in office
and no statutory regulations were laid down. According to the Central Board of the Co-operative Union its recommendations were
'quite useless'.[13] This defeat had profound repercussions. The development of a capitalist mode of mass consumption received a major
fillip as consumer capitalists were able freely to re-invent the old
'immoral' practices of regrating, engrossing and forestalling.[14] Co-
operators hoped that the state would at least not directly attack the
movement but in 1933 their worst fears were partially realised when
co-operative reserves were taxed, an intervention encouraged by a
fierce campaign waged by businessmen and large sections of the
press.[15]

Supported by a defensive trade union movement, the Parliamentary Labour Party increasingly regarded Parliament as the key arena
of struggle and concentrated on capturing the state machine and
reforming the system from above. The Co-operative movement was
pushed to the side-lines by its 'natural' allies and by the mid-1930s
many leading co-operators had come grudgingly to accept this subordinate role. In 1934 William Mellor wrote:

Let co-operators think to-day less in terms of the movement they up-
hold being either a permanent irritant in a Capitalist economy or the

gradual supplanter of that economy, and more in terms of its becoming now an integral part of the forces which are combating Capitalism and, in the future, a functioning authority under the general control and direction of a Socialist State.[16]

As I have argued, this narrowing of ambition was neither inevitable nor was it due solely to the movement's internal dynamics. Nevertheless, Percy Redfern's useful caution went largely unheeded after the débâcles of the 1920s: 'We need to live in the movement, but not to bury ourselves in it', he had warned in 1914.[17] Co-operators understandably were more introspective after these defeats; the culture of co-operation lost much of its oppositional edge and became more of a refuge than a resource.

III

In the rest of this chapter I wish to offer some final reflections on this process of containment or 'defeat' and raise a number of themes which deserve more systematic enquiry. The attempt to generalise the moral economy of co-operation via the Co-operative movement culture was ultimately unsuccessful and I have stressed how this ambition was actively constrained by antagonistic capitalist interests and the state, particularly after the First World War. This perspective however, though useful in itself given the developing historiographical consensus which tends to ignore questions of agency and power, is too one-sided and conspiratorial and does not fully explain why the 'retailing counter-revolution' won through. The increased tax burden was hardly crippling after all – the movement continued to expand throughout the 1930s – and if working people had boycotted the emergent mode of mass consumption the outcome could have been very different. Any critical historical assessment of the movement therefore must necessarily confront the fact that the co-operative project was deeply marked by theoretical and ideological silences and tensions, and contributed in significant measure to its own defeat. This book has explored these contradictions in detail in the belief that such an approach can help us understand why working-class associations failed to become hegemonic in the early twentieth century.

In an attempt to handle internal contradictions and contextual pressures the movement's leadership embarked on a policy of centralisation. Some co-operators had been arguing along these lines for years, believing that unless the movement was strengthened through co-ordinated effort 'combines' would soon triumph. In 1903 James Deans had condemned competition between individual societies and urged them to amalgamate: this was necessary because 'the trend of events at the present time is for the distribution of the commodities of life to be carried on by large syndicates, trusts and combines . . . .'[18] The burgeoning number of retail outlets owned by the multiples seemed to bear this out. By the First World War the Co-operative movement and the multiples each controlled about 7 per cent of total retail trade, but thereafter the multiples drew ahead, until by the end of the 1930s market share stood at 11 per cent and 18 per cent respectively.[19] Although the importance of amalgamation – regarded by many as the inevitable corollary of capitalist 'rationalisation' – was insistently underlined[20], progress was faltering as many societies fiercely guarded their independence and refused to be swallowed-up into larger units. But the trend was definitely in this direction: in 1918 there were 1,364 societies in Britain and this number had fallen to 1,077 by 1939.[21]

These centralising tendencies also affected the organisational development of the Women's Co-operative Guild – arguably the most radical voice within the movement. Under the leadership of the middle-class, ethical socialist Margaret Llewelyn Davies, the Guild had matured into an active, campaigning body by the First World War which was not afraid to speak out on controversial issues like female suffrage, divorce law reform, maternity care and so on. It also had a federal, highly democratic structure. Llewelyn Davies was succeeded by Eleanor Barton, a working-class 'collectivist' who was General Secretary between 1925 and 1937. Barton helped undermine the Guild's federal democratic structure and replace it with a strong centralised government, a transformation which was symptomatic of the wider changes sketched above. The Central Committee became a ruling caste within the guild, consolidated its own power and suppressed dissent; communists were proscribed in 1936, though this was not Congress policy. Specifically feminist politics, geared to the needs of working-class women, were also simultaneously abandoned. The earlier commitment to women's autonomy gave way to a particular version of the domestic ideology which placed women firmly and unproblematically within the confines of the home.[22]

Perhaps the process of bureaucratic centralisation would have been difficult to resist but the movement was also handicapped by its own conceptions of consumption. It has been emphasised above how co-operators underestimated the allure of the new commodity culture; and they also failed to think seriously about fantasy more generally. Some of the most outstanding recent work on consumption has rightly drawn attention to the vital role fantasy played in the new palaces of consumption, the department stores like the Bon Marché in Paris, which according to Miller helped define bourgeois culture in France in the second half of the nineteenth century.[23] Within these 'dream worlds' middle-class consumers, particularly women, were encouraged to give their imaginations free rein, to wander within an opulent and exotic material environment, indulging their daydreams and utopian desires.[24] Such dream worlds began to be democratised in England in the late nineteenth century; David Lewis opened his own Bon Marché in Liverpool in 1878 after a visit to Paris but, unlike the Paris store, Lewis targeted (and helped create) a specifically 'mass market'. The intention was to combine high quality, small profit margins and high volume turnover, and Lewis explicitly compared this system to the one utilised by Co-operative societies.[25]

Unlike the Co-operative movement, however, Lewis eagerly exploited modern forms of advertising which increasingly depended on spectacle and display. During the International Exhibition opened by Queen Victoria in Liverpool in 1885, for example, he chartered the steamship *Great Eastern* and used this to advertise his business, a stunt praised at the time by none other than the master of spectacle himself, P. T. Barnum.[26] Elaborate displays of goods were staged within the stores; seasonal sales and a Christmas Fairyland became regular features. By the end of our period Lewis's stores had been established in Manchester, Sheffield, Birmingham, Glasgow, Leeds and Hanley. They gave access to a luxurious and glamorous world, a world in which working-class people, especially women, could forget their worries and feel, however transiently, like film stars. The store which opened in Leeds (a city with one of the largest Co-operative societies in the country) in 1932 was a specifically modernist creation. It had five floors above street level and stood 40 feet (12 m) higher than any other retail business in the area. It had four escalators, the first to be installed in any shop in Leeds, five passenger lifts and dozens of 'Ask Me' girls who gave directions to the 157 different departments 'in which everything can be had from a theatre ticket to a permanent wave, a pound of sausages to a suite of furniture'. Over 120,000 people invaded the store on the opening day.[27]

It seems not unreasonable to assume that many of these excited consumers would have also shopped regularly at the local Co-op. Less puritanical than the numerically fairly small activist strata, most working-class co-operators enjoyed the experience of shopping at department stores like these and adapted their consumption practices according to taste and income. The stress on utility meant that co-operative stores did not usually stock the latest fashionable designs and this led many younger consumers to look elsewhere in the inter-war years. In their unpublished study of the Bolton Society in 1937, Mass Observation noted that:

> The general impression in regard to the drapery department seems to be that it deals in good solid quality goods but is unable to supply the demand for 'fashion goods'. As one retailer put it – 'if a girl wants a new blouse for Blackpool, she doesn't go to the Co-op. She gets it at a new gown or blouse shop.'[28]

Fantasy and pleasure took myriad forms of course, but the Co-op was often found to be sadly lacking. Roy Garrett, the late librarian of the Co-operative Union, once told me about his own childhood in Manchester in the 1930s. Many stores, including the Co-op, had their own Father Christmas by this time but Roy liked his mother to take him to see the 'real' Father Christmas. And the 'real' Father Christmas only went to Lewis's!

The vital role played by the growth of 'consumerism' and popular department stores like Lewis's and Marks and Spencer in the re-structured British capitalism of the inter-war period has been widely acknowledged, and the Co-operative movement was ill-prepared to meet this challenge.[29] Although in some medium-sized towns like Whitehaven modern department stores were opened by local societies during the 1930s, in the large urban conurbations like Leeds, Liverpool, Manchester and Birmingham, private stores really set the pace.[30] Many co-operators regarded the showy extravagance of these palaces of consumption as both wasteful and immoral; and in the hostile inter-war climate the puritanical voice of the local leadership became shriller as the more 'reactionary', complacent tendencies came to the fore. W. H. Oliver, editor of the *Coventry*

Wheatsheaf, is a good example here. Oliver was a lay preacher and member of the Christian Social Union who had the highest aspirations for the movement. He despaired of the young men and women on whom the future of co-operation depended though and regularly attacked 'the tendency of the masses towards materialism' during the 1920s in the local *Record*.[31] Young men, Oliver contended, now displayed an 'apish spirit', but far more dangerous were young women affected by the 'boy complex', for they had dispensed with 'sheer femininity' and 'emulated men in every way'.[32] The worst type was represented by 'the cigarette girl' whose appearance heralded social catastrophe: 'cigarette smoking by young women is likely to lead to physical and moral degeneracy, and if so the race will be doomed', Oliver wrote.[33] This attitude, which was neither peculiar nor uncommon, helped to alienate an increasingly important section of consumers and drive them toward the more seductive delights of consumer capitalism.[34]

Puritanism seeped in everywhere. During the debate over the purchase of *Reynold's News*, which was bought by the movement in 1929, one delegate hoped that co-operators would produce a 'cleaner paper' and exclaimed that 'if I want horrors I can always go to the "Pictures"'.[35] *Reynold's* had attempted, with considerable success, to hold together 'high' and 'low' elements within working-class culture since the mid-nineteenth century. After the movement took it over, the 'low' was expunged and the popularity of the paper plummeted. A valuable window onto the movement culture that had developed by the late 1930s is furnished by the Mass Observation study quoted earlier. One observer attended a cinema lecture arranged by the Bolton Society and noted that:

> There were two introductory speeches about the films to be shown. The audience was very bored, the President himself asleep in his chair for at least four minutes . . . . The audience was not much interested in the parts of the films which told them about the production of Co-op goods, but commented on the everyday things that appeared in the films – household scenes, animals, children etc . . . . The comments on leaving made no reference to the lecture or the purpose of the show . . . .[36]

The films were short documentaries about the manufacture of goods by the CWS; there was little to differentiate them from the so-called 'industrials' which had been made to demonstrate the modern production processes of capitalist concerns since before the First World War. The observer emphasised that the audience was over-whelmingly composed of middle-aged women; women over forty made up 75 per cent of an audience of 280. Admittedly the lecture may have been held on a weekday (the observer failed to make this clear) which would have accounted for the absence of men and young women. But the M.O. report generally found that young Boltonians showed little active interest in the society.[37] No wonder that the audience was bored; a CWS soap factory could hardly compete with Gracie Fields, let alone Clark Gable. Again we are back in the realms of fantasy.

How did these developments affect membership? Numbers increased as co-operation spread to the relatively buoyant South and South-East of England during the depression; by 1939 the movement could boast a paper membership of well over 8.5 million.[38] However, formal participation was another matter. It had been low enough in the late nineteenth century, when less than 5 per cent of members regularly attended quarterly meetings. It seems likely that if anything the situation worsened after 1918, as the movement's local and national leadership became more and more isolated from the class. The few detailed case studies we have of local societies in the inter-war years support this contention;[39] and in the longer term things were undoubtedly getting worse. In his diagnosis of the 'crisis' facing the movement published in 1951 (the movement had been in 'crisis' for at least thirty years by this time), G. D. H. Cole made the following pertinent observation:

> The system of 'lay' control which dominates Co-operative organisation is in form highly democratic; but, in face of the apathy of most Co-operative members and of the usually small attendance at members' meetings, it has produced the result of the emergence of a class of 'professional laymen' . . . On this body of some thousands of active 'laymen' Co-operative democracy really rests.[40]

Increasingly, democracy and commercial success were seen as incompatible goals. Pressured from inside and from without, the bureaucratic leadership and the 'professional laymen' plumped for the latter: the Co-operative Independent Commission Report of 1958 which investigated the stagnation of co-operative trade symbolised this preference. Chaired by Gaitskell with Crosland as secretary, the Commission treated the movement as a capitalist business and produced a report and a set of recommendations intended to maximise its efficiency as a capitalist concern. No account was taken of the membership or the movement culture. Economic questions, now posed within a separate domain, were simply and absolutely prioritised.[41] Thereafter the process of amalgamation and centralisation continued apace.

It would be inappropriate to end on such a gloomy note. Things could have turned out differently. Just as there were historical alternatives to mass production, so too were there alternatives to mass consumption.[42] Co-operation in the late nineteenth and early twentieth centuries opened up a specific range of historical possibilities, some of which were decidedly utopian in reach. This period saw the 'interpenetration' of modes of production and consumption and the triumph of a particular capitalist mode of mass consumption and the degeneration and ossification of other, more democratic and egalitarian forms, but this was neither given nor inevitable.[43] No irresistible, inevitable logic secured the victory of the commodity culture, though there was a systemic tendency which worked in its favour: mass production, as Henry Ford was fond of pointing out, depended for its success on mass consumption. The precise outcome was the result of complex social and political struggles which we have only just begun to investigate. The contest was not just between capitalist and co-operative forms either; capitalists also fought bitterly amongst themselves, especially in the early decades of the twentieth century. Capitalist forms were relatively fragile, were often in danger of melting into air. Lever and Lipton insisted on autocratic control and the result was weak and ineffective management. Both businesses were over-capitalised before and after the First World War and suffered a number of financial crises; Lever was forced to relinquish sole command in the early 1920s in order to avoid bankruptcy. Vicious and protracted price-cutting campaigns depleted profits and almost resulted in ruin. The solution was amalgamation, the formation of the huge 'combines' which now dominate the sphere of consumption: Lipton's merged with the Dutch giants Van den Burghs in 1927 and then Jurgens in 1931; and Lever Brothers merged with the Margarine Union (which included Jurgens and Van den Burghs) in 1929 to become Unilever.[44] These developments have to be placed within the appropriate field of force; the success and stability of co-operation helped make mergers such as these imperative.

Counterfactual arguments are notoriously misleading but it is tempting to wonder what would have happened if the mainstream Labour Party had not been stuck in a statist rut from the 1920s, had not nailed itself to nationalisation but had built instead an alliance with the Co-operative movement which effectively tapped the latter's mutualistic potential.[45] Perhaps then the dreams of individuals like J. T. W. Mitchell and Margaret Llewellyn Davies could have been at least partially realised after the Second World War. But if the experience of defeat was real enough, the mode of consumption which had emerged by the 1930s was somewhat different to that envisaged by Lever or Lipton. On the simple quantitative level the movement still controlled a substantial share of the distributive trade, but even the moral economy no doubt lingered on, especially amongst the older generation within some communities. At a moment when it is becoming increasingly clear to many in the West that excess is likely to bring catastrophe, earlier attempts to moralise the market and invent a more humane language of 'need' deserve serious attention and respect.

Appendices

Appendix 1

The growth of consumers' co-operation in Britain, 1873–1940

Year	No. of distributive societies	Total membership (thousands)	Annual increase of membership (%)	Average number members per society
1873	—	350	—	—
1874	—	375	7.2	—
1875	—	440	17.4	—
1876	—	468	6.8	—
1877	—	483	3.2	—
1878	—	510	5.6	—
1879	—	525	3.0	—
1880	—	554	5.5	—
1881	971	547	—	564
1882	1,043	599	9.6	574
1883	1,051	628	4.9	597
1884	1,128	696	10.8	617
1885	1,148	747	7.4	650
1886	1,148	774	3.6	675
1887	1,153	828	7.0	718
1888	1,204	867	4.7	720
1889	1,297	932	7.5	719
1890	1,240	962	3.2	775
1891	1,307	1,045	8.6	799
1892	1,420	1,127	7.9	794
1893	1,421	1,169	3.7	823
1894	1,421	1,213	3.8	854
1895	1,417	1,275	5.1	899
1896	1,428	1,356	6.8	950
1897	1,442	1,466	8.1	1,016
1898	1,436	1,536	4.8	1,069
1899	1,446	1,613	5.0	1,116
1900	1,439	1,707	5.9	1,186
1901	1,438	1,793	5.0	1,247
1902	1,454	1,893	5.6	1,302
1903	1,455	1,987	5.0	1,366
1904	1,454	2,078	4.6	1,429
1905	1,452	2,153	3.6	1,483
1906	1,441	2,222	3.2	1,542
1907	1,432	2,323	4.6	1,622
1908	1,418	2,414	4.0	1,696
1909	1,430	2,469	2.2	1,727
1910	1,421	2,542	3.0	1,789
1911	1,403	2,640	3.9	1,882
1912	1,392	2,751	4.3	1,976

Appendix 1 continued

Year	No. of distributive societies	Total membership (thousands)	Annual increase of membership (%)	Average number members per society
1913	1,382	2,878	4.6	2,083
1914	1,385	3,054	6.1	2,205
1915	1,375	3,265	6.9	2,374
1916	1,362	3,520	7.8	2,585
1917	1,366	3,788	7.7	2,773
1918	1,364	3,847	1.5	2,820
1919	1,357	4,131	7.4	3,045
1920	1,379	4,505	9.1	3,267
1921	1,352	4,549	1.0	3,364
1922	1,321	4,519	—	3,421
1923	1,314	4,569	1.1	3,477
1924	1,314	4,703	3.0	3,579
1925	1,289	4,911	4.4	3,810
1926	1,280	5,187	5.6	4,052
1927	1,267	5,579	7.6	4,403
1928	1,245	5,885	5.5	4,727
1929	1,234	6,169	4.9	4,999
1930	1,210	6,403	3.8	5,292
1931	1,188	6,590	2.9	5,547
1932	1,171	6,760	2.6	5,773
1933	1,150	6,917	2.3	6,015
1934	1,135	7,203	4.2	6,346
1935	1,118	7,484	3.9	6,694
1936	1,107	7,808	4.4	7,053
1937	1,094	8,085	3.6	7,390
1938	1,085	8,405	4.0	7,746
1939	1,077	8,643	2.8	8,025
1940	1,065	8,717	0.8	8,185

[A dash means that data are missing or incomplete. This table is derived from G. D. H. Cole, *A Century of Co-operation* (Manchester 1945) pp. 371–2. My thanks to the Co-operative Union for copyright permission.]

Appendix 2

The cost of living in Victorian and Edwardian Britain

Year	Bowley index	Year	Bowley index
1886	97	1901	97
1887	95	1902	98
1888	96	1903	100
1889	97	1904	99
1890	97	1905	100
1891	98	1906	102
1892	98	1907	104
1893	97	1908	102
1894	92	1909	103
1895	90	1910	105
1896	91	1911	106
1897	93	1912	109
1898	95		
1899	94		
1900	100		

[Taken from Ian Gazeley, 'The cost of living for urban workers in late Victorian and Edwardian Britain', *Economic History Review*, 42/2, 1989.]

Appendix 3

Regional distribution of consumers' co-operative societies

3A Societies in the East and West Midlands, founded up to 1875 and still existing in 1912

Date of foundation	East Midlands	West Midlands	Totals
Before 1844	0	1	1
1845–50	1	0	1
1851–55	1	0	1
1856–60	14	2	16
1861–65	24	5	29
1866–70	19	7	26
1871–75	27	11	38
Totals	86	26	112

3B Co-operative Societies in Lancashire and Yorkshire founded up to 1884 and still existing in 1912

Date of foundation	Lancashire	Yorkshire	Totals
1825–29	0	1	1
1830–34	0	2	2
1835–39	0	1	1
1840–44	1	2	3
1845–49	4	4	8
1850–54	17	5	22
1855–59	22	18	40
1860–64	45	44	89
1865–69	17	36	53
1870–74	19	26	45
1875–79	13	13	26
1880–84	8	7	15
Totals	146	159	305

[These tables are derived from G. D. H. Cole, *A Century of Co-operation* (Manchester 1945) pp. 155, 177. My thanks to the Co-operative Union for copyright permission.]

Appendix 4

Competition from large-scale retailers, 1876–1920

4A   Rate of net increase in the number of branches of
multiple shop firms in the UK, 1876-1920

i)   Branches of firms with 10–24 branches

Year	Net increase in no. of brances	Percentage net increase	Average yearly net increase in numbers
1876–1880	586	60	117
1881–1885	1,223	78	245
1886–1890	1,884	68	377
1891–1895	3,136	67	627
1896–1900	3,838	49	768
1901–1905	3,597	31	719
1906–1910	4,610	30	922
1911–1915	2,903	15	580
1916–1920	1,958	9	392

ii)   Branches of firms with 25 or more branches

Year	Net increase in no. of brances	Percentage net increase	Average yearly net increase in numbers
1876–1880	368	51	74
1881–1885	833	76	167
1886–1890	1,542	80	308
1891–1895	2,549	74	510
1896–1900	3,239	54	648
1901–1905	3,130	34	626
1906–1910	4,076	33	815
1911–1915	2,523	15	505
1916–1920	1,617	9	323

4B Estimated share of multiple shop firms in the total retail sales
by main commodity groups, 1900–1920

Commodity group	Percentage of total retail sales taken by multiple shop firms				
	1900	*1905*	*1910*	*1915*	*1920*
Food & household stores	3.5–4.5	4.0–7.0	6.5–9.0	8.0–10.5	8.5–11.0
Confectionery, reading/writing materials & tobacco goods	1.5–3.0	2.0–3.5	2.5–4.0	3.0–4.5	3.5–5.0
Clothing & footwear	3.5–5.5	4.5–6.5	6.0–8.0	6.0–8.0	7.0–10.0
Other goods	2.0–3.5	3.0–5.0	3.5–5.0	4.5–6.0	5.0–6.5
All commodities	3.0–4.5	4.5–5.5	6.0–7.5	7.0–8.5	7.0–10.0

4C Estimated share of large–scale retailers in the total retail sales
by main commodity groups, 1900–1920

Commodity group	Percentage of total retail sales taken by multiple shop firms				
	1900	*1905*	*1910*	*1915*	*1920*
Food & household stores	11.5–13.5	13.5–16.0	17.0–19.0	19.5–22.0	22.0–24.0
Confectionery, reading/writing materials & tobacco goods	3.0–4.5	4.0–5.0	4.5–5.5	5.0–6.0	6.0–7.0
Clothing & footwear	14.0–16.0	17.0–18.5	20.0–21.5	21.0–24.5	23.0–25.5
Other goods	6.0–7.5	8.0–9.5	9.0–11.0	12.0–14.0	14.0–16.0
All commodities	11.0–12.5	13.0–14.5	15.5–17.5	17.0–20.0	19.0–21.5

4D Estimated share of the different economic types of retailer
in the total retail trade

Type of retail organisation	*Percentage of total sales taken by different types of retailer*				
	1900	*1905*	*1910*	*1915*	*1920*
Co-op Societies	6.0–7.0	6.0–7.5	7.0–8.0	7.5–9.0	7.5–9.0
Department stores	1.0–2.0	1.0–2.5	1.5–3.0	2.0–3.0	3.0–4.0
Multiple shop retailers	3.0–4.5	4.5–5.5	6.0–7.5	7.0–8.5	7.0–10.0
Other retailers (by difference)	86.5–90.0	84.5–88.5	81.5–85.5	79.5–83.5	77.0–82.5

[These tables are taken from J. B. Jefferys, *Retail Trading in Britain 1850-1950*
(Cambridge 1954) pp. 24–30. My thanks to the trustees of Cambridge University
Press for copyright permission.]

Appendix 5

The expansion of the English CWS, 1864–1937

Year ended	Individual membership of federated societies	Total capital (£)	Net sales (£)	Total returned in dividend (£)
1864 (30 weeks)	18,337	2,455	51,857	236
1865	24,005	7,182	120,754	—
1866	31,030	11,050	175,489	—
1868 (65 weeks)	59,349	26,313	331,744	—
1869	74,737	32,062	412,240	4,447
1870	79,245	40,658	507,217	—
1871 (53 weeks)	89,880	44,164	677,734	—
1872	114,588	52,088	758,764	—
1873	134,276	146,857	1,153,132	—
1874	168,985	200,044	1,636,950	12,733
1875	198,608	263,282	1,964,829	—
1876	249,516	379,607	2,247,395	—
1877 (53 weeks)	276,522	417,985	2,697,366	—
1878	274,649	418,525	2,827,052	—
1879 (50 weeks)	331,625	494,330	2,645,331	—
1880	361,523	565,854	3,339,681	—
1881	367,973	580,046	3,574,095	—
1882	404,006	632,203	4,038,238	—
1883	433,151	691,181	4,546,889	44,359
1884 (53 weeks)	459,734	761,358	4,675,371	—
1885	507,772	841,175	4,793,151	—
1886	558,104	944,379	5,223,179	—
1887	604,800	1,017,042	5,713,235	—
1888	634,196	1,116,035	6,200,074	—
1889 (53 weeks)	679,336	1,251,635	7,028,944	—
1890	721,316	1,474,466	7,429,073	—
1891	751,269	1,636,397	8,766,430	—
1892	824,159	1,741,645	9,300,904	—
1893	873,698	1,779,301	9,526,167	88,016
1894	910,104	1,891,102	9,443,938	—
1895 (53 weeks)	930,985	2,093,578	10,141,917	—
1896	993,564	2,316,042	11,115,056	—
1897	1,053,564	2,472,321	11,920,143	—
1898	1,118,158	2,632,000	12,574,748	—
1899	1,179,609	2,829,501	14,212,375	—
1900	1,249,091	3,187,945	16,043,889	—
1901 (53 weeks)	1,315,235	3,416,049	17,642,082	—
1902	1,392,399	3,502,650	18,397,559	—
1903	1,445,099	3,737,548	19,333,142	285,297

Appendix 5 continued

Year ended	Individual membership of federated societies	Total capital (£)	Net sales (£)	Total returned in dividend (£)
1904	1,594,145	3,929,176	19,809,196	—
1905	1,635,527	4,398,933	20,785,469	—
1906	1,703,564	4,955,943	22,510,035	—
1907 (53 weeks)	1,768,935	5,407,120	24,786,568	—
1908	1,845,415	5,758,750	24,902,842	—
1909	1,925,517	6,161,316	25,675,938	—
1910	1,991,576	6,566,641	26,567,833	—
1911	2,067,776	7,397,430	27,892,990	—
1912 (53 weeks)	2,160,191	8,055,473	29,732,154	—
1913	2,272,496	9,027,371	31,371,976	467,457
1914	2,336,460	9,902,447	34,910,813	652,818
1915	2,535,972	11,075,199	43,101,747	977,909
1916	2,653,227	13,575,587	52,230,074	984,635
1917	2,748,277	15,218,107	57,710,132	662,956
1918 (53 weeks)	2,854,584	18,683,169	65,167,960	248,670
1919	3,088,136	23,640,717	89,349,318	—
1920	3,341,411	27,844,322	105,439,628	210,712
1921	3,457,556	30,403,592	80,884,661	—
1922	3,494,335	34,448,177	65,904,812	—
1923	3,567,410	38,765,354	66,205,566	264,513
1924 (53 weeks)	3,662,765	43,462,294	72,888,064	551,666
1925	3,778,659	45,369,050	76,585,764	725,820
1926	3,876,695	45,552,080	75,292,233	866,157
1928 (55 weeks)	4,020,332	47,890,633	86,894,379	1,001,495
1929	4,454,793	53,431,067	87,294,025	1,006,036
1930	4,565,372	59,229,542	89,288,125	1,021,415
1931	4,884,090	66,517,146	85,313,018	981,006
1932	5,138,124	72,366,833	81,498,234	1,249,816
1933 (53 weeks)	5,352,310	76,467,379	82,769,119	1,271,883
1934	5,488,364	84,060,875	82,120,864	1,411,922
1935	5,983,810	93,660,021	90,177,672	1,755,908
1936	6,155,964	104,098,125	98,283,975	1,979,463
1937	6,379,274	112,785,492	107,691,527	2,168,956

[A dash means that data are missing or incomplete. This table is derived from P. Redfern, *The Story of the C.W.S.* (Manchester 1913) pp. 418–9 and P. Redfern, *The New History of the C.W.S.* (Manchester 1938) pp. 532–3. My thanks to the Co-operative Wholesale Society for copyright permission.]

Appendix 6

The ideology of consumption: J. T. W. Mitchell's Presidential Address at the Co-operative Congress, Rochdale 1892

Mr J. T. W. Mitchell, on ascending the pulpit, was loudly cheered. He said: Ladies and gentlemen, – You who compose this audience are met in a sacred place to consider a sacred question. In the name of the Equitable Pioneers and all other co-operators in Rochdale I give you a hearty welcome, and I trust that the cause under whose auspices we are met to-day, will take a new stride forward towards the completion of that great work, the successful part of which was begun in 1844 in Rochdale.

Co-operation did not begin in 1844, it began many years before. The struggle of the industrious classes of this country is not one of a score of years, but of centuries; and in its growth it has had to overcome selfishness which controlled the legislative and other forces of the nation, and which used the under classes to sustain and strengthen that selfishness. You had a Bill of Rights, and you had before that the appropriation of what I call the property of the nation, which ought to have been kept in the nation's hands, but it was appropriated for services rendered; it retained the property, but the charges of the services were thrown upon the nation. *(No, no.)* There may be a difference of opinion about that. I know I shall say many things to which people will say 'No, no' this morning, but I intend to say them none the less. It is time that namby-pambyism is crushed in these Congresses. We have had selfishness in centuries past, there is selfishness in our own day, and there is selfishness even amongst us. Pure as we profess ourselves to be, there are manifestations of that most unholy quality even amongst ourselves: and it will take co-operation all its time to prevent the growth of selfishness, and of selfishness controlling all its financial forces. But I trust that there will be in this movement of ours that measure of unselfishness which will control its forces.

In 1692, there were established the Bank of England and the Stock Exchange. I give you these facts at the beginning, and I shall apply them presently. These institutions were established 200 years ago; Rochdale today is worth 200 times as much as it was in 1692; but where has the increment of value gone? Has it gone to the multitude of the population? *(No.)* No, it has gone to a limited section. The township of Manchester, in which our Wholesale Society is situated, has increased nearly ten times in value. Where has that value gone? To a section of the community. The early co-operators made up their minds that there should be a change in that direction. At the beginning of the reign of George III the struggle began, and it continued until his death. The National Debt was increased many hundreds of millions, the mass of the people were without employment, living in starvation, while the others lived in luxury. In 1815 the war was closed, but the struggle kept on. In 1828 Sir R. Peel [who was then Home Secretary of the Duke of Wellington's administration] said, 'I wish the working classes would take their own affairs into their own hands.' They took him at his word. In 1832 we had the Reform Bill.

Between 1828 and 1832 there had been a great struggle going on by co-operators, and some of the co-operators said of the trading classes of that day that they were corrupt, dishonourable, and practically dishonest. A person named Thomas Hirst spoke to thousands of his countrymen in as good speeches and as earnest words as any I ever heard, and he laid the foundation of this struggle for co-operation. The first Co-operative Congress was held in 1831, not 1832, as some have stated. There was a Congress held in Birmingham in 1831. The last of that series was held in Liverpool in October, 1832, at which a Wholesale Society was represented. There is an honourable name connected with those days – Robert Owen – but, so far as I can gather, he did not believe so much in co-operation; he thought the tribe of merchants could do business for them as well as they could do it for themselves. The rank and file did not believe in co-operation as we understand and practice it.

In 1844, when the Rochdale Pioneers began, there were great struggles both in Parliament and out. There have been many misconceptions about our society, therefore I want to show what were the real intentions of the Pioneers at the commencement. Their intentions were not altogether what some people have said, and I want to correct the error. This book I hold in my hand is one of the first copies of the rules. The name on the book is 'Samuel Ogden, No. 1', but I do not know whether he was the first member. At that time the committee worked for nothing. There was no bother in those days about fees and fares. At the end of the rules it says: – 'If the auditor does not attend to his duties he is to be fined 2s. 6d.' And the cashier was to pay 1s. Now, you committeemen, remember this, if the president was late, he was fined threepence, and if he did not come at all he had to pay sixpence. And so with the other committeemen. Some people have said the we co-operators have forsaken our first faith, and that we are nothing now but dividend hunters. The trade journals charge us with this; others say that the charm of dividend has passed away. Has it? You know it has not. I may say many things you have heard before, but it is necessary to repeat them over and over again. The old truth cannot be told too often.

I should not have made these remarks but for the sermon I heard last night from my own spiritual adviser, who is a capital adviser on spiritual matters, but not altogether reliable on co-operation. He was disparaging the store. Now the very first thing the Pioneers did was to arrange for the establishment of a store. They saw that wealth was made by keeping a store, and they knew by bitter experience that the wealth thus created was used by its possessors to tyrannise over working people. A vast number of the wealthy people in Rochdale and other places have arisen from families who were very poor sixty or seventy years ago. They can run their carriages today, but they started from the poorest of the poor. Some of their ancestors baked bread in cellars. It is no discredit to earn a livelihood by honest industry. They rose from the slums of poverty, and we also want to use our powers to obtain a competency for the time allotted to us in this vale of tears. Let us gather as much honey as we can, and leave some little for those who are left behind. The store was the beginning of money making, and I say to all, never despise the store. Make as much dividend as you can make honestly, but don't make it for the sake of making it; appropriate it when you have made it.

When the Pioneers had made money they proposed to deal with it in this way – first in building houses. Among co-operators the idea largely prevails that they would like to build their own houses and live in them. I prefer the Pioneers' plan. I gather from the rules that the houses were to be built by the society, and that the members were to live in them. Then they were to commence manufacturing. They were to produce, distribute and educate. Now another principle comes in. It was adopted in 1832. I will read the clause: – 'That as soon as practicable the society shall proceed to arrange the powers of production, distribution, education, and government, or in other words to establish a self-supporting home colony of united interests for the common good of all.' Remember that: not one interest, not individual, but united interests. The clause proceeds: – 'That the causes of the difficulties and embarrassments under which society is now labouring in commercial affairs is attributable to individuals interested in the production of and distribution of wealth, and that in order to remove these difficulties it is necessary for society to be based on the principle of united interests.' The Pioneers of 1844 adopted the principle laid down in 1832 of a common interest.

Now, you teetotalers, look out for the next clause. The last work the Pioneers put down in their programme was – 'That for the promotion of sobriety a temperance hotel be opened in one of the society's houses as soon as convenient.' Thus we find that the early co-operators were in the forefront of all good causes. If there are any co-operators here who have not signed the temperance pledge, I hope after hearing this they will do so. These were the principles laid down by the early co-operators. Their method of co-operation did not start with either capital or labour, but with consumption. Mark that. According to my conviction consumption ought to be the basis of the growth of wealth in this country. *(Hear, hear,* and *No.)* So far as I am concerned all my labour and my efforts and the power of my voice will be in favour of making consumption the basis of the growth of all co-operative organisation. If you do not do that, I know what will be the result. In a hundred years' time there will be, I trust, a still more intelligent population, the ages will move on, and all good causes will move on with the ages, so that the generations to come will have greater opportunities of enjoying life than those of the past or the present.

Now, why do I say that consumption ought to be the basis of all the accumulation of wealth? For this reason – that consumption bears all the charges. That is true from the highest to the lowest, from the richest man to the poorest peasant; and the humblest contribute most largely in proportion to their means to the luxury of the rich. All the charges come from consumption. If co-operators take that principle as their standpoint every working man will be better off. If you do not establish that principle what will be the result? The plan of some capitalists is to get labour united in order to crush the poor consumer. I want as much as anyone to see the elevation of labour. I think labour ought to be elevated. But how? That is the question. How? Simply by making the interests of our common humanity equal all round. I don't believe in the selection of a few to receive the contributions of the many, and watch them enjoy the luxuries I ought to have a share of. Ministers have got power, if they would use it, in this direction; and they know a text in the Old Testament which is very applicable to the case. The people wanted a god, and they brought their trinkets and made them into a god and fell down and worshipped it. It is very much like that in the present day. Poor people subscribe to make others rich, and then they fall down and worship them.

I don't believe in the present distribution of wealth. It is said that the United Kingdom has a capital of something like ten thousand millions sterling, equal to about £300 per head of the population. Now I say, that instead of one man having £200,000 or £300,000 and others having nothing, it would be better if they had £300 apiece. I am not opposed to capital; I am not opposed to wealth; I like it, and I want to accumulate it, but I don't want wealth to stand to the credit of the 'upper ten', but to those who are sometimes called the 'lower five'. I want wealth to stand to the credit of the whole population. The joint-stock companies of this nation own a thousand millions of money. The National Debt is about nine hundred millions, and the capital of railways as much. Between two and three thousand millions of money are engaged in those three enterprises. Now, what I would like would be for co-operators to allow their profits to be so massed together, that instead of a few persons owning this money, it would belong to the whole people of the United Kingdom. That is the burden of my remarks.

My desire is that the profits of all trade, all industry, all distribution, all commerce, all importation, all banking and money dealing, should fall back again into the hands of the whole people. If co-operators will manage their enterprises in such a way as to concentrate all their trade into one channel, I am certain that this can be accomplished. I made a calculation the other day, that if the world would conduct its business on co-operative lines, the population of the world could have amongst them between three and four hundred thousand millions of money; and if the fifteen hundred millions of population divided it amongst them at so much each, it would be much better for the world at large. I am not one of those who would divide other people's property. I am nothing of the kind. I want no laws to be passed to divide anybody's property. What I want is for co-operators, trade unionists, and all the industrious classes of this and every other country to combine in keeping their own shop, making a good dividend, producing, distributing, and financing, and let all the profits come to those who consume the goods, because they have made them.

Another great power in the country is the newspaper press. It is said that there are about 5,000 periodicals and newspapers in the United Kingdom, and something like 40,000 in all the world. I have made an estimate that gives this rather curious conclusion, that all the advertisements in those papers were equal to about five hundred millions a year, or about equal to a lawyer's fee for each person. The power of the press is great in this and every country, but I do not think it is wisely used so far as co-operators are concerned. Why? Because a great political gathering has a five or six columns report in the newspapers, but for a great gathering of co-operators – except at Congress time, when we are better treated – we get only a three or four inch paragraph. Co-operators and trade unionists have very few papers, and have very little influence upon the press. The trade unionists started a paper the other day, and I am told that it has already collapsed. If co-operators are to have greater influence in the nation and in the world they will have to control the press more largely, and it must be of our own colour. The writers in newspapers fill many columns about how desirable it is that the working classes should have their condition improved; and then there is a line at the bottom saying that they cannot tell how to do it. This is the very thing we want the people to know. If any plan can be devised to renovate and bless mankind, by all means let us know it. But we don't get the information.

The three great forces for the improvement of mankind, are religion, temperance, and co-operation; and as a commercial force, supported and sustained by the other two, co-operation is the grandest, the noblest, and the most likely to be successful in the redemption of the industrious classes. Some are for Positivism, and others want an industrial republic; why don't they come into co-operation, which will do everything they want? What do I find? If people want to start a new organisation they desire to get associated with existing organisations in order to give them character and position. Now we, as co-operators, have been sought in that direction many times, but what I tell them is this – if you want the benefit of our organisation you must come and be one of us. We have spent our thousands and thousands of pounds in getting up an organisation of this magnitude, and we cannot appropriate its benefits to some struggling person who has some particular fad of his own. If you want your plan to succeed, come with us and we will do you good. I want co-operators to be all for co-operation. If others will help you, you can help them; but if you do not get them to help you, they will weaken your own forces.

I referred to the Stock Exchange and the Bank of England. In 1694 the national debt was about £684,000. In the days of William and Mary the rulers of the nation wanted some money, and they went to the merchants of London, and borrowed twelve or thirteen hundred thousand pounds. The merchants of London were wise in their day and generation, as I want you co-operators to be, and they were quite willing to lend this money if they got 8 per cent. for it. In the second place the rulers were to grant the merchants a privilege, and they did grant it, and so far as I know that privilege lasts till to-day, and it is a great financial force in this country, but not always used for the benefit of the people. At that time there grew up in connection with that privilege persons who were disposed to deal in securities, of course, private persons are always ready with their kind consideration to confer a benefit on those who have a privilege, and they dealt in those securities; they bought and sold them, and I do not say that they always exercised that due regard to integrity of dealing which is desirable in all financial transactions. If history tells true, there was a good deal of stock-jobbing in those days; and I don't think, from what I am told outside, that it is altogether abolished to-day. Those privileges given in the past are possessed now. The Bank of England has the privilege which was given to those rich merchants of London who lent money to the State. It is said that a very considerable portion of the national debt was lent in those days by people who paid down £60 sterling for £100 of stock. That was the way our national debt has accumulated. When we find that there has been so much privilege and evil in the past, does it not prove, ladies and gentlemen, that you have undertaken a most arduous task? But you can accomplish it. The task is no greater than your power. Provided you can bring all your trade within yourselves you will very soon shut up some of the other people's shops. Those privileged persons who have been fed and fattened at the public expense don't want to give up their privileges. We will let them alone if they are content with what they have got; but from this time henceforth let us make up our minds that all our trade shall come within our own channels, and let these men of privilege fight their own battle amongst themselves.

My time is gone, but there is another thing I must mention. I want to speak to you about the Wholesale Society and its productive departments. Some people write in the papers that co-operative production has been a failure. It has been nothing of the kind. It has been a grand success, and will be more so in the future than it has been in the past. Our Wholesale friends in Scotland and ourselves are doing a grand and noble work. Some of you will say, 'Yes, they are doing better than you are.' Well, about that we are not going to fall out this morning, but I think we are the best. My friend Mr Maxwell is here, and he can speak for himself. So far as we are concerned, there is nobody in the world pays better wages than we do. The two Wholesale Societies have something like £500,000 invested in co-operative production. Sometimes we have profits and sometimes we have losses. We are like matrimony – it is for better or worse. Everything in this world is for better or worse. The profits of both Wholesale Societies far exceed any losses we have sustained. We have made about £80,000 in addition to interest, depreciation, and wiping out losses; therefore let no man say that Wholesale co-operation has not been a success. It has been, and will be, an eminent success.

Some people think we shall injure others. Neither Wholesale Society will ever take and steps whatever to cause unnecessary injury to any existing society. We shall have to take steps forward. I have tried to show you, from the history of the Stock Exchange and the Bank of England, that when privileges were granted 200 years ago, individuals sought to gain an advantage from the State; and wherever there is a corporate institution the monied classes will cluster round it, and try to suck its honey. Therefore, if you want your great work to proceed it will have to proceed on corporate and not on individual lines, it will have to proceed in the interest of the entire body politic and not in the interest of a section of the community. While I live I shall work for these principles and try to persuade others to adopt them and work for them with all the force and energy of will that I can; because if individual forces grow up and cluster around this movement of ours you may depend upon it the cause of co-operation will be weakened.

Now, friends, I have done. There are other things I should like to say, but I have been persuaded not to say them. *(Go on.)* There are things that relate to persons outside. There is one thing I will tell you, the Pioneers started on honourable lines to do themselves good, not advertising themselves to do other people an injury. They never put misleading tickets in their window like the shopkeepers do to-day in towns where they are trying to hunt down a few working men who have joined together for their own benefit. This is done by many persons who ought to know better, and the trade journals gloat over their success in putting out the Wholesale Society. When you find the trade journals nearly every week publishing scandalous things about co-operation, ought you not to rise *en masse* and determine to bind yourselves together as one united force in order to do your own business in your own way, and let the outside people look after themselves?

I am bound to tell you another thing. In these trade journals you have read something about bribing managers. I was at a store not long ago, and the manager told me that some time previously he had received from a private firm two halves of a £5 note in separate letters. Let me remark parenthetically that these private firms tempt not only managers but committeemen. But this manager in question submitted the matter to his committee, and the committee told him to keep the money. Shortly after the representative of the firm visited the store, and very politely requested to know whether the manager had received the £5 note, at the same time placing another in his hands. The manager submitted this also to the committee, and again they told him to keep the note. And I am told that even the branch shopkeepers receive visits from the same firm, and the shopmen have half-sovereigns placed in their hands.

But, as I said, this applies not only to the servants but to the committee themselves. I know a committee that was taken some miles into the country and entertained to a good dinner at a public house by a tea dealer. That I know because one of those who were going told the gentleman who told me – *(laughter)* – he couldn't go to a co-operative meeting because he was going to that dinner. Don't imagine that private firms are free themselves. I have known in my time as much – if not more – bribery with private firms as ever I have known with co-operative societies, and therefore if the trade journal to which I have referred replies to my remarks, let the writer find out those who have been guilty of bribery with private firms in times past. There is a gentleman in this room who for several years has received a cheque and has passed it through his cash account. Seeing that this is my one opportunity of speaking to the largest and most representative assembly possible within the limits of a year, I would urge you all to be true and faithful to the great cause with which you are associated, and tell those people who want to throw £5 notes or half-sovereigns into your midst to keep them to themselves, and their business to themselves.

If you will rally round the Wholesale Societies of England and Scotland you will find these two great organisations, with all their forces of distribution, production, banking, importing, and exporting – you will find they will do the best for you. The two Wholesale Societies have received money, and have also paid it away. I wanted to tell you that, because the facts of to-day show that these societies themselves have in their funds nearly £200,000 more than the societies ever put into them. That is to say the societies in connection with the Wholesale Societies have drawn out every penny they ever put into them, and yet there is now nearly £200,000 more than they ever put in. These two great institutions are therefore creating their own capital, which capital will be useful for the redemption of the industrial classes.

I trust that this Congress in Rochdale will mark a new era of progress in the great cause which bands us together, and I also hope that Britain, yea, the United Kingdom of England, Ireland and Scotland, bound together in one common bond, will raise itself higher than it has ever been thought capable of being raised.

[From the *Co-operative Congress Report* (Manchester 1892), pp. 6-8.]

Notes

(The place of publication is London unless otherwise specified)

Chapter one: Co-operation and the historians

1 Beatrice Webb, *My Apprenticeship* (Cambridge 1926, 1979), p. 357. The text in question, published under her maiden name of Potter, was *The Co-operative Movement in Great Britain* (1891).

2 Leonard Woolf, *Beginning Again: An Autobiography of the years 1911–1918* (1964), p. 104. His major writings on the movement were *Co-operation and the Future of Industry* (1918) and *Co-operation and Socialism* (1921).

3 On strategies of condescension see Pierre Bourdieu, *Language and Symbolic Power* (Cambridge 1991), pp. 66–71.

4 The most important works in the inter-war period included Catherine Webb, *The Woman With the Basket* (Manchester 1927); Fred Hall and W. H. Watkins, *Co-operation: A Survey of the History, Principles and Organisation of the Co-operative Movement in Great Britain and Ireland* (Manchester 1937); T. W. Mercer, *Towards the Co-operative Commonwealth* (Manchester 1937); Percy Redfern, *The New History of the C.W.S.* (1938). An uncritical approach marks the post-war literature including Arnold Bonner, *British Co-operation* (Manchester 1961); J. Gaffin and D. Thoms, *Caring and Sharing: The Centenary History of the Co-operative Women's Guild* (Manchester 1983); Johnston Birchall, *Co-op: The people's business* (Manchester 1994).

5 G. D. H. Cole, *The World of Labour* (1913, Brighton 1973), p. 340. See also Margaret Cole's remarks in *The Life of G. D. H. Cole* (1972) p. 55.

6 Margaret Cole, *Life of G. D. H. Cole*, pp. 78, 256; L. P. Carpenter,

G. D. H. Cole. *An Intellectual Biography* (Cambridge 1973), p. 65.

7 G. D. H. Cole, *Self-Government in Industry* (1917, 1972), pp. 227–30; *The World of Labour* (1919), p. xxiii. See also his *Guild Socialism Re-stated* (1920) and Carpenter, *G. D. H. Cole*, pp. 65–8.

8 G. D. H. Cole, *A Century of Co-operation* (Manchester 1945), pp. 292, 378, 398–9. Note also the later, highly-critical analysis presented in *The British Co-operative Movement in a Socialist Society* (1951).

9 G. D. H. Cole, *A Century*, p. 89.

10 Sidney Pollard, 'Nineteenth-Century Co-operation: From Community Building to Shopkeeping', in Asa Briggs and John Saville (eds), *Essays in Labour History* (1960), p. 95.

11 On this theme see Richard Johnson, 'Culture and the Historians', in Jon Clarke, Chas Critcher and Richard Johnson, *Working Class Culture: Studies in History and Theory* (1979); and Harvey J. Kaye, *The British Marxist Historians: An Introductory Analysis* (Cambridge 1984).

12 See Pierre Bourdieu, *Homo academicus* (Cambridge 1988).

13 Eric Hobsbawm, 'The Labour Aristocracy in Nineteenth Century Britain', in *Labouring Men: Studies in the History of Labour* (1964); John Foster, *Class Struggle and the Industrial Revolution* (1974), pp. 221–2.

14 This approach had also been favoured by others including Robbie Gray, *The Labour Aristocracy in Victorian Edinburgh* (Oxford 1976) and Trygve Tholfsen, *Working-Class Radicalism in Mid-Victorian England* (1976).

15 Geoffrey Crossick, *An Artisan Elite in Victorian Society* (1978), chapter 8. For an earlier emphasis on ideology see Harold Perkin, *The Origins of Modern English Society* (1969), pp. 384–7.

16 The debate can be tracked in H. F. Moorhouse, 'The Marxist Theory of the Labour Aristocracy', *Social History*, 3, 1978; Patrick Joyce, *Work, Society and Politics* (Brighton 1980); Robbie Gray, *The Aristocracy of Labour in Nineteenth-century Britain, 1850–1914* (1981); John Breuilly, 'The Labour Aristocracy in Britain and Germany 1850–1914: A Review Article', in K. Tenfelde (ed.), *Arbeiter und Arbeiterbewegung im Vergleich* (Munich 1986). Note also Hobsbawm's careful re-assessment of the controversy, 'Artisans and Labour Aristocrats', in *Worlds of Labour* (1984).

17 Neville Kirk, *The Growth of Working-Class Reformism in Mid-Victorian England* (1985), pp. 166–7.

18 *Ibid.*, p. 25. In a famous passage, quoted selectively by Kirk, Edward Thompson suggested that having failed to overthrow capitalist society the working class proceeded to 'warren it from end to end' with their own institutions, including co-operatives. Although Thompson employed the term 'reformism' in this essay he was not entirely happy with the ideological baggage it carried and emphasised that although a particular *kind* of revolutionary movement (his emphasis) was no longer possible in this later phase, this did not mean that the working class was no longer 'revolutionary' in any fixed or absolute sense. See E. P. Thompson, 'The Peculiarities of the English' in Ralph Miliband and John Saville, *The Socialist Register*, 2, 1965, p. 343. The burrowing metaphor (repeated a few paragraphs later) underlined the continuing instability of capitalist social relations.

19 Standish Meacham, *A Life Apart: the English Working Class, 1880–1914* (1977); Richard Hoggart, *The Uses of Literacy* (1957), pp. 318–23.

20 George Orwell, *The Road to Wigan Pier* (1937); Hoggart, *Uses of Literacy*; Perry Anderson, 'Origins of the Present Crisis', *New Left Review*, 23, 1964; Tom Nairn, 'The English Working Class?', *New Left Review*, 24, 1964.

21 Gareth Stedman Jones, 'Working-Class Culture and Working-Class Politics in London, 1870–1900: Notes on the remaking of a working class', *Journal of Social History*, 7, 1974, p. 237.

22 See for example Joyce, *Work, Society and Politics*; Jay Winter (ed.), *The Working Class in Modern British History* (Cambridge 1983); Gareth Stedman Jones, *Languages of Class: Studies in English Working-Class History 1832–1982* (Cambridge 1983); Ross McKibbin, *The Ideologies of Class: Social Relations in Britain, 1880–1950* (Oxford 1990); Alastair Reid, *Social Classes and Social Relations in Britain, 1850–1914* (1992). Although they share certain similarities, these texts cannot be squeezed together unproblematically. McKibbin's work, for example, contains a sensitive exploration of the independent, 'political' nature of working-class culture which thoroughly subverts Stedman Jones's notion of a 'culture of consolation'. See especially McKibbin's essays on gambling and hobbies included in the collection cited above, chapters 4 and 5.

23 Winter, *Working Class*, pp. vii-viii, x.

24 The fictive persona of the 'objective' and distanced historian has been subjected to some rigorous criticism in recent years. Texts which pull 'literature' and 'history' together as forms of 'writing' include Dominick LaCapra, *History & Criticism* (Ithaca 1985); Hayden White, *The Content of the Form* (Baltimore 1987); Keith Jenkins, *Re-Thinking History* (1991).

25 For a brief but stimulating account of the reception of *The Making* within American universities and its initial marginality see Peter

Linebaugh, 'From the Upper West Side to Wick Episcopi', *New Left Review*, 201, 1993, pp. 18–25.

26 This is a huge theme which deserves detailed study. Useful insights can be found in the article by David Mayfield and Susan Thorne, 'Social History and its Discontents: Gareth Stedman Jones and the Politics of Language', *Social History* 17/2, 1992, p. 173, fn.22.

27 Paul Johnson, *Saving and Spending: The Working-class Economy in Britain, 1870–1939* (Oxford 1985), pp. 127, 143. See also the comments by Neville Kirk in his article, '"Traditional" Working-class Culture and the "Rise of Labour": some preliminary questions and observations', *Social History* 16/2, 1991, pp. 205–6.

28 David Beetham, 'Reformism and the "Bourgeoisification" of the Labour Movement', in Carl Levy (ed.), *Socialism and the Intelligentsia, 1880–1914* (1987), p. 131.

29 See P. Backstrom, *Christian Socialism and Co-operation in Victorian England* (1974); Thomas Cooper, *The Life of Thomas Cooper* (1872, Leicester 1971), p. 393; Theodore Rothstein, *From Chartism to Labourism* (1929), p. 184.

30 James Deans, *Co-operation versus Private Trading: A Public Discussion held in the Waterloo Rooms, Glasgow Feb. 5th 1889, between Mr J. Deans of Kilmarnock (Central Co-op Board) and Mr R. Walker of Glasgow (Scottish Traders' Defence Association)* (Manchester 1889), p. 9.

31 Pierre Bourdieu, 'Doxa and Common Life', *New Left Review*, 191, 1992, p. 118.

32 Backstrom, *Christian Socialism*, p. 6. This line also informs Malcolm Hornsby's otherwise useful unpublished MPhil thesis, 'The Consumers' Co-operative Movement in the Twentieth Century', University of York, 1989.

33 See Mike Savage, *The Dynamics of Working-class Politics: The Labour Movement in Preston, 1880–1940* (Cambridge 1987); Bill Lancaster, *Radicalism, Co-operation and Socialism: Leicester working-class politics, 1860–1906* (Leicester 1987); Stephen Yeo (ed.), *New Views of Co-operation* (1988).

34 Reid, *Social Classes*, pp. 49–59.

35 Redfern, *New History*, p. 6; Jennifer Tann, 'Co-operative Corn Milling: Self-help During the Grain Crisis of the Napoleonic Wars', *Agricultural History Review*, 28, 1980, pp. 46–51.

36 Maxine Berg, *The Age of Manufactures: Industry, innovation and work in Britain, 1700–1820* (1985), p. 87; Charles Sabel and Jonathan Zeitlin, 'Historical Alternatives to Mass Production', *Past and Present*,

108, 1985.

37 Ben Jones, *Co-operative Production* (Oxford 1894), pp. 170–4.

38 Tann, 'Corn Milling', pp. 53–5.

39 Roy Church, *Economic and Social Change in a Midland Town. Victorian Nottingham 1815–1900* (1966), p. 47.

40 See for example the work of J. F. C. Harrison, *Robert Owen and the Owenites in Britain and America* (1969) and Barbara Taylor, *Eve and the New Jerusalem: Socialism and Feminism in the Nineteenth Century* (1983).

41 The *Co-operator*, 1 February 1829.

42 See R. C. N. Thornes, 'The Early Development of the Co-operative Movement in West Yorkshire, 1827–1863' (Unpublished DPhil thesis, University of Sussex 1984), pp. 1–12.

43 For the persistence of truck see Redfern, *New History*, pp. 10–11; John Burnett, *Plenty and Want: A social history of diet in England from 1815 to the present day* (1966), pp. 55, 157.

44 Thornes 'Early Development' (thesis), pp. 94–5. The 'ulterior measures' await their historian but see the documents in Dorothy Thompson, *The Early Chartists* (1971), pp. 190–5.

45 F. W. Leeman, *Co-operation in Nottingham: A History of 100 Years of Nottingham Co-operative Society Limited* (Nottingham 1963), pp. 13–14. Sweet, secretary of the Nottingham Chartists, was quoting directly from Robert Lowery's *Address to the Fathers and Mothers, Sons and Daughters of the Working Classes, on the System of Exclusive Dealing, and the Formation of Joint Stock Provision Companies* (Newcastle-upon-Tyne 1839). There is a useful treatment of Chartist co-operation in Thornes 'Early Development' (thesis), chapter 6.

46 For women and exclusive dealing see *Northern Star*, 8 December 1838; 22 December 1838; 1 June 1839; 27 July 1839; 5 October 1839.

47 For the significance of the 1842 strike see Mick Jenkins, *The General Strike of 1842* (1980).

48 Kate Tiller, 'Late Chartism: Halifax 1847–1858', in Dorothy Thompson and James Epstein (eds), *The Chartist Experience: Studies in Working-Class Radicalism and Culture, 1830–1860* (1982), pp. 328–33; Kirk, '"Traditional" culture', p. 143.

49 G. J. Holyoake's early propagandist work, *Self-Help by the People: History of Co-operation in Rochdale* (1858) traced the origins of the 'modern' movement to Rochdale though Holyoake recognised that the 'divi' did not originate there. See his general text, *The History of Co-operation in England,* (1875, complete edition 1906), pp. 278–9; and (below)

chapter 5.

50   For the distinction between 'short' and 'long', 'political' and 'cultural' revolutions see Raymond Williams, *Politics and Letters: Interviews with New Left Review* (1979), pp. 420–5.

51   Nicos Poulantzas, *Political Power and Social Classes* (1972); and also Poulantzas' succinct notes in Robin Blackburn (ed.), *Ideology in Social Science* (Glasgow 1972), p. 246, where he observed that 'it can be said that the capitalist State best serves the interests of the capitalist class only when the members of this class do not participate directly in the State apparatus, that is to say when the *ruling class* is not the *politically governing class*.'

52   R. K. Webb, *Modern England: From the Eighteenth Century to the Present* (1969), pp. 261–72; Michael Barratt Brown, 'Away With All the Great Arches: Anderson's History of British Capitalism', *New Left Review*, 167, 1988, pp. 22–51.

53   N. C. Masterman, *J. M. Ludlow: The Builder of Christian Socialism* (1963); Backstrom, *Christian Socialism*, and (below) chapter 6.

54   For the changing legal status of co-operation see Holyoake, *Co-operation in England* pp. 289–93; Jones, *Co-operative Production*, pp. 11–15; Cole, *A Century*, pp. 114–26.

55   For Ernest Jones' views see *Notes to the People*, I, 1851, pp. 27–31, 407–11, 470–6, 543–46 and 561–66 (cited in Backstrom, *Christian Socialism*, p. 49); and for Marx see (below) chapter 7.

56   Karl Marx, *Capital*, vol I (1867, Penguin 1976) pp. 1019–38. See also Gareth Stedman Jones, 'Class Struggle and the Industrial Revolution', *New Left Review*, 90, 1975, pp. 49–50.

57   As Raphael Samuel demonstrated in 'Workshop of the World: Steam Power and Hand Technology in Mid-Victorian Britain', *History Workshop Journal*, 3, 1977.

58   Peter Kropotkin, *Fields, Factories and Workshops* (1899, London 1974, ed. C.Ward) p. 150.

59   See Appendix 1.

60   See Appendix 2; W. H. Fraser, *The Coming of the Mass Market, 1850–1914* (1981), pp. 15–16.

61   For the regional dynamics see Appendix 3; Martin Purvis, 'The development of co-operative retailing in England and Wales, 1851–1901: a geographical study', *Journal of Historical Geography*, 16, 3, 1990, pp. 314–31; Martin Purvis, 'Co-operative Retailing in Britain', in John Benson and Gareth Shaw (eds), *The Evolution of Retail Systems, c. 1800–1914* (Leicester 1992); John K. Walton, 'Co-operation in Lancashire, 1844–1914', *North West Labour History*, 19, 1994/5, pp. 115–25.

62 Appendix 4; J. B. Jefferys, *Retail Trading in Britain 1850–1950* (Cambridge 1954), pp. 24–7.

63 Appendix 5; Percy Redfern, *The Story of the CWS*. (Manchester 1913), pp. 418–19; Redfern, *New History*, pp. 532–3; P. L. Payne, 'The Emergence of the Large-Scale Company in Britain 1870–1914', *Economic History Review*, 3, 1967, pp. 519–42.

64 This line informs the work of Thomas Cooper, Theodore Rothstein, Orwell and Hoggart (referred to above) and can be found in a populist contemporary form in the writings of Jeremy Seabrook, especially *Working-Class Childhood* (1982).

65 See the literature review by Mike Featherstone, 'Perspectives on Consumer Culture', *Sociology*, 24/1, 1990.

66 Michel Aglietta, *A Theory of Capitalist Regulation. The US Experience* (1979), p. 79. See also Ernest Mandel, *Late Capitalism* (1975), pp. 387–407.

67 Thomas Richards, *The Commodity Culture of Victorian England: Advertising and Spectacle, 1851–1914* (1991), p. 15.

68 Daniel Miller, *Material Culture and Mass Consumption* (1987), pp. 167–77.

69 Mary Douglas and Baron Isherwood, *The World of Goods: Towards an Anthropology of Consumption* (1979) p. 4.

70 Savage, *Dynamics*, pp. 20–28, discusses co-operation as a form of working-class 'mutualism' made possible by particular configurations of skill, gender and neighbourhood. He usefully distinguishes this strategy from that of 'economism' (pursued by trades unions) and 'statism' (advocated by the Labour Party).

71 G. J. Holyoake, *The Co-operative Movement Today* (1891, 4th edn. 1905), p. 74; Edward Jackson, *A Study in Democracy; being an account of the rise and progress of Industrial Co-operation in Bristol* (Bristol 1911), p. 5.

72 There has been some excellent work by American scholars on the politics of consumption, particularly T. H. Breen, '"Baubles of Britain": The American and Consumer Revolutions of the 18th Century', *Past and Present*, 119, 1988; Dana Frank, '"Food Wins All Struggles": Seattle Labor and the Politicization of Consumption', *Radical History Review*, 51, 1991; Ellen Furlough, *The Politics of Consumption: The Consumer Co-operative Movement in France, 1834–1930* (Ithaca 1992).

73 Fraser, *Mass Market*; John Benson, *The Rise of Consumer Society in Britain, 1880–1980* (1994).

74 Barry Supple, 'A Framework for British Business History', in B.

Supple (ed.), *Essays in British Business History* (Oxford 1977); Asa Briggs, 'The Language of "Mass" and "Masses" in Nineteenth-Century England', in David Martin and David Rubinstein (eds), *Ideology and the Labour Movement* (1979).

75 Raymond Williams, *Culture* (Glasgow 1981), p. 13.

76 See Richard Johnson, '3 Problematics: Elements of a Theory of Working-class Culture', in Clarke, Critcher and Johnson (eds), *Working-Class Culture*, p. 235.

77 C. Offe and H. Wissenthal, 'Two Logics of Collective Action: Theoretical Notes on Social Class and Organisational Form', in *Political Power and Social Theory* (Greenwich 1980), quoted in Scott Lash and John Urry, 'The New Marxism of Collective Action: A Critical Analysis', *Sociology*, I, 1984, p. 40.

Chapter two: Education and social transformation

1 Trygve Tholfsen, *Working-Class Radicalism in Mid-Victorian England* (1976); Neville Kirk, *The Growth of Working-Class Reformism in Mid-Victorian England* (1985).

2 Richard Johnson, '"Really Useful Knowledge": Radical Education and Working-Class Culture, 1790–1848', in John Clarke, Chas Critcher and Richard Johnson (eds), *Working-Class Culture* (1979), pp. 75–102. See also Brian Simon, *Studies in the History of Education, 1780–1870* (1960); J. F. C. Harrison, *Learning and Living 1790–1960: A Study of the History of the English Adult Education Movement* (1961) and the same author's *Robert Owen and the Owenites in Britain and America* (1969); Harold Silver, *The Concept of Popular Education* (1965).

3 Brian Simon, *Education and the Labour Movement,1870–1920* (1965), p. 46. For a detailed study of the educational activities of the Royal Arsenal Co-operative Society see John Attfield, *With Light of Knowledge* (1981).

4 *Co-operative News*, 7 March 1874, p. 114.

5 *Ibid.*, 13 July 1878, p. 449.

6 *Ibid.*, 12 May 1888, p. 442.

7 H. J. Twigg, *An Outline History of Co-operative Education* (Manchester 1924), p. 25.

8 Philip Gardiner, *The Lost Elementary Schools of Victorian England* (1986).

9 *Co-operative News*, 17 November 1900, pp. 1294–5.

10 W. P. McCann, 'Trade Unionist, Co-operative and Socialist Or-

ganisations in Relation to Popular Education, 1870–1902' (Unpublished PhD thesis, University of Manchester 1960), p. 407.

11   This can be found in McCann 'Trade Unionist'; Simon, *Education and the Labour Movement*, pp. 212–14 (though Simon relies almost exclusively on McCann). See also Kevin Brehony, 'Popular Control or Control by Experts? Schooling between 1880 and 1902', in Mary Langan and Bill Schwarz (eds), *Crises in the British State 1880–1930* (1985), pp. 256–73.

12   *Co-operative News*, 5 May 1906, p. 506. For more on resistance to this system in the classroom see Stephen Humphries, *Hooligans or Rebels? An Oral History of Working-Class Childhood and Youth 1889–1939* (1981).

13   *Manchester and Salford Co-operative Herald*, July 1911, p. 142.

14   Barbara Taylor, *Eve and the New Jerusalem: Socialism and Feminism in the Nineteenth Century* (1983), p. 231.

15   See the pamphlet by Abraham Greenwood, *The Educational Department of the Rochdale Equitable Pioneers' Society Limited* (Manchester 1877).

16   *Co-operative News*, 11 October 1879, p. 661.

17   *Ibid.*, 12 June 1897, p. 654.

18   See Mike Savage, *The Dynamics of Working-Class Politics: The Labour Movement in Preston, 1880–1940* (Cambridge 1987), pp. 127–9.

19   *Co-operative News*, 27 February 1875, p. 103; 3 March 1900, p. 217; *Co-operative Congress Report*, 1919, p. 137. For the background to the establishment of the *News* see Lloyd Jones's paper in the *Co-operative Congress Reports*, 1870; W. M. Bamford, *Our Fifty Years, 1871–1921* (Manchester 1921); F. Hall, *The History of the Co-operative Printing Society, 1869–1919* (Manchester 1919).

20   *Co-operative News*, 9 June 1900, p. 618; *Co-operative Congress Reports*, 1916 p. 100; *Leeds Co-operative Record*, September 1917, p. 15.

21   *Wheatsheaf*, February 1903, p. 128; *Co-operative Congress Reports*, 1919, p. 137.

22   For some strong denunciations of the capitalist press see *Co-operative News*, 21 May 1904, p. 594; *ibid.*, 5 January 1907, p. 15. The latter editorial was a review of H. W. Massingham's article on 'The Modern Daily Press' which appeared in the *C.W.S. Annual* that year.

23   Margaret Llewelyn-Davies (ed.), *Life As We Have Known It* (1930, 1977 edn), p. 66. For more on women and co-operative education see Jane Purvis, 'Working-class Women and Adult Education in Nineteenth Century Britain', *History of Education*, 3, September 1980, pp. 206–11.

24   *Oldham Co-operative Record*, April 1895, p. 11.

25 Co-operative News, 19 May 1883, pp. 420–21.

26 Co-operative News, 12 June 1897, pp. 654–6; pamphlet by Fred Hall, The Co-ordination and Extension of Co-operative Education and the Part of the Co-operative College Therein (Manchester 1914), p. 21.

27 Some societies did heed this proscription. See, for example, J. H. Ogden, Failsworth Industrial Co-operative Society Ltd: jubilee history, 1859–1909 (Manchester 1909), p. 53; George Briggs, Jubilee history of the York Equitable Industrial Society Ltd., established August 26th 1858 (Manchester 1909), p. 237.

28 On this theme see Eileen and Stephen Yeo, 'Perceived Patterns: Competition and Licence vs. Class and Struggle', in their Popular Culture and Class Conflict (Brighton 1981), especially pp. 283, 302.

29 For the school, which ran between 1872 and 1875 until forced out of business by the new Board School, see P. A. Darvill, 'The Contribution of Co-operative Retail Societies to Welfare within the framework of the North East Coast area' (Unpublished MLitt thesis, University of Durham, 1954), pp. 200–201. The strategy of substitution is discussed in Johnson, '"Really Useful Knowledge" . . . ', pp. 94–5.

30 Philip Backstrom, Christian Socialism and Co-operation in Victorian England (1974), p. 211.

31 Co-operative News, 22 January 1876, p. 44.

32 Logie Barrow, Independent Spirits: Spiritualism and English Plebeians 1850–1910 (1986), pp. 146–9.

33 Quoted in the Co-operative News, 10 September 1887, p. 906.

34 Acland and Jones, Working Men Co-operators (1884; 1898 edn), p. 150.

35 Co-operative News, 16 July 1887, p. 714.

36 H. D. Lloyd, Labour Co-partnership (New York 1898), p. 148. According to Eileen Yeo the late 1840s and early 1850s saw the expansion of a new 'Public' territory, engineered by the middle class, in order to defuse initiatives from below; a civic ideology was used to bolster this effort. See her chapter 'Culture and Constraint in Working-Class Movements, 1830–55', in Yeo, Popular Culture, pp. 177–81.

37 P. Corrigan and V. Gillespie, Class-struggle, Social Literacy and Idle Time (Brighton 1977) pp. 16–17. As the authors note, the keyword 'public' carries its own exclusions and omissions which have changed over time.

38 Hugh Cunningham, Leisure in the Industrial Revolution 1780–1880 (1980), p. 153.

39 For examples see Montague Blatchford, The history of Halifax In-

dustrial Society for the first fifty years, to commemorate the celebration of its Jubilee in January 1901: 1851–1901 (Halifax 1901), pp. 122, 174; Francis Purnell and Henry Williams, *Jubilee History of the Gloucester Co-operative Industrial Society, 1860–1910, established 10th July 1860* (Gloucester 1910), p. 197.

40 *Co-operative News,* 27 September 1902, p. 1161.

41 *Co-operative Congress Report,* 1904, pp. 376–86.

42 *Comradeship,* 32, November 1901, pp. 6–7.

43 *Co-operative Congress Report,* 1904, p. 390.

44 *Co-operative News,* 10 December 1904, p. 1493.

45 *Ibid.,* 17 December 1904, pp. 1144–5.

46 *Plymouth Co-operative Record,* January 1912, p. 12.

47 See the March and September editions of the *Leeds Co-operative Record* between these years. There is a survey of the position of Co-op libraries after the war in the *Bolton Co-operative Record,* February 1925, pp. 5–7.

48 Pamphlet by G. J. Holyoake, *Essentials of Co-operative Education* (Manchester 1898), p. 7. For a useful discussion of the contest over the term 'social' see Raymond Williams, *Keywords* (Glasgow 1976), pp. 238–9.

49 *Co-operative News,* 7 April 1877, p. 162.

50 *Comradeship,* October 1900, p. 99.

51 *Co-operative News,* 10 June 1882, p. 383.

52 *Ibid.,* 4 November 1882, p. 745. Sympathetic outsiders like the editor of the *Progressive Review,* shared this opinion. See *Progressive Review,* 4 January 1897, p. 301.

53 See Jones's remarks at the Cardiff Congress in 1900 quoted in the *Co-operative News,* 16 June 1900, p. 684.

54 *Ibid.,* 7 August 1886, p. 810.

55 Arnold Toynbee, the Oxford historian and University Extension lecturer, is a good example here. See his advocacy of an education in individual citizenship at the Oxford Congress in 1882, reported in *Co-operative News,* 10 June 1882, p. 382.

56 *Co-operative News,* 4 November 1882, p. 745. The comment is an oblique swipe at Toynbee.

57 Johnson, '"Really Useful Knowledge" . . . ', p. 97.

58 On the problem of patronage within the Owenite movement, see B. Taylor, *Eve,* pp. 258–9.

59 *Co-operative News,* 22 May 1880, p. 337.

60 *Co-operative Congress Report,* 1887 p. 7. See also his comments in

the Co-operative News, 22 January 1876 p. 44.

61   Ben Jones, Co-operative Production (Oxford 1894), p. 737. See also his description of 'complete co-operation' on p. 143.

62   Stefan Collini, Liberalism and Sociology: L. T. Hobhouse and political argument in England 1880–1914 (Cambridge 1979), p. 33.

63   Labour Co-partnership, September 1907, p. 137.

64   Reported in the Co-operative News, 17 August 1907, p. 1002. The complete paper appeared in the C.W.S. Annual (Manchester 1908), pp. 135–45.

65   It is difficult to pinpoint exactly when the term 'Co-operative Commonwealth' entered co-operative discourse. Writing in the late 1930s, W. H. Brown noted the general purchase it now had within the movement and stated that he had been able to trace the term to an address given by Dr Garth Wilkinson, the spiritualist homeopath, to members of the St John's Wood Co-operative Society in London in 1866. See Brown, The Co-operative Manager: Being the Silver Jubilee History, 1912–1937, of the National Co-operative Manager's Association (Manchester 1937), p. 60. The American Marxist, Laurence Gronlund, entitled his description of a post-revolution society The Co-operative Commonwealth (1886) and this usage is better known. Ironically Gronlund was an anti-co-operator who saw no role for co-operatives in the making of the socialist state.

66   Co-operative News, 3 July 1909, p. 877.

67   Burnley Co-operative Record, August 1912, pp. 5–6.

68   Middlesbrough Co-operative Record, August 1914, p. 11.

69   Peter Kropotkin, Mutual Aid; A Factor of Evolution (1902, 1910), pp. 271–2.

70   E. P. Thompson, Witness Against the Beast: William Blake and the Moral Law (Cambridge 1993), p. xiv.

71   See David Vincent, Literacy and Popular Culture: England 1750–1914 (Cambridge 1989).

72   For further details consult the first two volumes of John Saville and Joyce Bellamy, Dictionary of Labour Biography (1972 & 1974).

73   See Mitchell in the Co-operative News, 21 March 1891, p. 271.

74   T. W. Mercer, 'Some of My Books and Their Former Owners', Millgate Monthly, May 1925, p. 500.

75   I have excluded the earlier generation of Owenites as well as middle-class supporters from this group. The breakdown is as follows: Methodists (21%); Primitive Methodists (6%); Wesleyan Methodists (8%); Congregationalists (15%); Unitarians (12%); and Baptists (8%).

76   See Robert Colls, The Collier's Rant: Song and Culture in the In-

dustrial Village (1977); and his later *The pitmen of the northern coalfield. Work, culture, and protest, 1790–1850* (1987).

77 *Burnley Co-operative Record*, September 1914, p. 14. See also *ibid.*, February 1912, pp. 2–3; and for a historical investigation of this concept Stephen Yeo, 'On the uses of "Apathy"', *Archives Européenes de Sociologie*, 15, 1974.

78 Barrow, *Independent Spirits*, p. 274.

79 For a good example see the serial by the Ipswich co-operator, George Hines, entitled 'Co-operation did it: Or a Strike and What Came of it', which commenced in the *News* in December 1899. The co-operative press provided an important platform for working-class novelists and poets in this period (including Edwin Waugh, Mathew Tate, Patrick MacGill, and Ethel Carnie among others) and my criticisms are not intended to detract from this considerable achievement. This area can be explored via Martha Vicinus, *The Industrial Muse* (1974); and H. Gustav Klaus (ed.), *The Rise of Socialist Fiction 1880–1914* (1987).

80 See the pamphlet produced by the Co-op Union, *250 Good Books for Co-operative Libraries* (Manchester 1894). No novels were recommended, only works of history and social theory.

81 G. Ritter argues similarly in relation to the workers' libraries in Imperial Germany in the late nineteenth century. See his 'Workers' Culture in Imperial Germany', *Journal of Contemporary History*, 13/2, 1978, p. 176.

82 *Co-operative News*, 9 May 1874, pp. 254–5.

83 *Ibid.*, 6 June 1885, p. 524.

84 *Ibid.*, 16 July 1910, p. 938. Local activists did not tire in their admonitions to members to increase circulation. The Manchester and Salford Society, for example, could only dispose of 1,000 copies a week though it had a membership of 16,000 in the early 1900s and the editor of the *Record* frequently voiced his chagrin. See *Manchester and Salford Co-operative Herald*, March 1905.

85 Linda McCullough Thew, *The Pit Village and the Store* (1985), p. 106.

86 Pamphlet by F. Garnett, *Co-operative Classes; How to Make Them More Attractive and Successful* (Manchester 1892) p. 7.

87 There is a useful discussion of this development in Raymond Williams, *The Long Revolution* (1961), pp. 225–6.

88 Pamphlet by Hall, *The Co-ordination and Extension of Co-op. Education . . .* (1914), p. 21.

89 Saville and Bellamy, *Dictionary of Labour Biography*, vol. 1,

p. 198.

90   Michels developed the mischievous notion of the 'iron law of oligarcy' in *Political Parties* (1915). For an excellent analysis see David Beetham, 'From socialism to fascism: the relation between theory and practice in the work of Robert Michels', *Political Studies*, 25, 1977, pp. 3–24.

91   On the failure to reach the poor see R. D. Sutton, 'Co-operation and the Poor, 1890–1908' (MA thesis, University of York 1985), who notes (on p. 42) the 'strong assumptions of cultural condescension' in Women's Co-op Guild pamphlets which addressed this issue.

92   J. Smith and J. K. Walton, 'Property, Employment and the Co-operative Movement: The Social Structure of Co-operation in Sabden, 1923', *The Historic Society of Lancashire and Cheshire*, vol. 134, 1985.

93   Jack Lawton, *A Man's Life* (1932), p. 54.

94   *Ibid.*, p. 55.

95   *Co-operative News*, 20 August 1892, p. 920.

96   For Cowen see Nigel Todd's engaging biography, *The Militant Democracy: Joseph Cowen and Victorian Radicalism* (Tyne and Wear 1991). Greening's variety of Christian Socialism can be picked up from his *Co-operative Life* (1889); though Tom Crime's study, *E. O. Greening: A Maker of Modern Co-operation* (Manchester 1923) is useful, there is no adequate modern biography.

97   For Mitchell's view of the social structure see the *Co-operative News*, 16 January 1875, pp. 29–30; 22 January 1876, p. 44; 22 May 1880, p. 337; 20 September 1884, p. 832; 19 June 1886, p. 581; 26 May 1888, p. 492; *Co-operative Congress Report*, 1887, p. 7. Mitchell was not consistent and sometimes declared that 'the working classes should possess, not a share, but all the profit from their labour . . . .' *Co-operative News*, 13 June 1891, p. 610. See also Stephen Yeo, 'Who was J. T. W. Mitchell?', unpublished paper, University of Sussex, 1987. Mitchell's 'ideology of consumption' is encapsulated (below) in Appendix 6.

98   Patrick Joyce, *Visions of the People: Industrial England and the question of class 1848–1914* (Cambridge 1991), pp. 64–5; *Co-operative Congress Report*, 1889, p. 19.

99   *Co-operative News*, 20 September 1884, p. 834.

100   *Co-operative Congress Report*, 1887, p. 6.

101   *Ibid.*, 1909, p. 476.

102   *Ibid.*, 1910, p. 34.

103   For a contrasting view see Eugenio Biagini, *Liberty, Retrenchment and Reform: Popular Liberalism in the Age of Gladstone, 1860–1880* (Cambridge 1992), pp. 139–44, who argues that 'independence' helped

seal the compact between the working-class and Victorian Liberalism.
104 See Trygve Tholfsen, *Working-Class Radicalism,* especially chapter 1; Joyce, *Visions* p. 65.
105 In Harison, *Learning and Living,* p. 238, J. F. C. Harrison gives two causes for the failure of this movement – financial problems and the middle-class composition of the local Extension Committees which largely failed to attract working-class audiences.
106 For the origins and development of the WEA see Mansbridge's sugary account, *An Adventure in Working-Class Education* (1920); Harrison, *Learning and Living,* pp. 261–75 *passim*; and Simon, *Education and the Labour Movement,* pp. 305–11 *passim*. For the more combative approach of the labour colleges see W. W. Craik, *The Central Labour College 1909–29* (1964); and A. Phillips and T. Putnam, 'Education for Emancipation: The Movement for Independent Working Class Education', *Capital and Class,* 10, 1980.
107 Simon, *Education and the Labour Movement,* p. 305.
108 *Co-operative News,* 13 August 1910, p. 1044.
109 *Ibid.,* 10 September 1910, p. 1191. This was one of a number of letters condemning Mansbridge. Sims was secretary of the Oxford Society.
110 *Co-operative News,* 17 October 1910, p. 1220. The author was James Haslem who concluded that the working-class 'must build and maintain an Oxford of their own'. A National Co-operative Scholarship was founded in 1911 to send a student to Ruskin College. The movement had sponsored scholarships to Oxford for a number of years (the Blandford and Neale Scholarships) and this move underlined the growing recognition that students should 'remain faithful to their own class'. *Ibid.,* 13 January 1912, p. 44. See also *ibid.,* 27 April 1912, pp. 510–11.
111 *Ibid.,* 20 August 1910, p. 1081.
112 *Co-operative Congress Report,* 1910, p. 447.
113 *Co-operative Congress Report,* 1914, p. 474.
114 See Harrison, *Learning and Living,* pp. 275–89.

Chapter three: The means of social life

1 Gary Cross, *A quest for time: the reduction of work in Britain and France, 1840–1940* (Berkeley, Cal. 1989); Ian Gazeley, 'The Cost of Living for Urban Workers in Late Victorian and Edwardian Britain', *Economic History Review,* 42/2 (1989), pp. 207–21.
2 On the commercialisation of leisure see Peter Bailey (ed.), *Music Hall: The Business of Pleasure* (Milton Keynes 1986); Tony Mason, *Asso-*

ciation Football and English Society, 1863–1915 (Hassocks 1980); Asa
Briggs, *Mass Entertainment: the Origins of a Modern Industry* (Adelaide
1960). Two useful overviews discuss these changes: John Lowerson and
John Myerscough, *Time to Spare in Victorian England* (Brighton 1977);
Hugh Cunningham, *Leisure in the Industrial Revolution c. 1780–c. 1880*
(1980). Later developments are covered in Stephen G. Jones, *Workers at
Play: A Social and Economic History of Leisure 1918–1939* (1986). A use-
ful theoretical treatment can be found in John Clarke and Chas Critcher,
The Devil Makes Work: Leisure in Capitalist Britain (1985).

3   Peter Bailey, *Leisure and Class in Victorian England: Rational Recreation and the Contest for Control, 1830–1885* (1978). See also Helen
Meller, *Leisure and the changing city, 1870–1918* (1976).

4   Stephen Yeo, 'A New Life: The Religion of Socialism in Britain,
1883–1896', *History Workshop Journal*, 4, 1977, p. 38.

5   Chris Waters, *British Socialists and the Politics of Popular Culture,
1884–1914* (Manchester 1990).

6   Ross McKibbin, 'Why was there no Marxism in Britain?', *English
Historical Review*, 99, 1984, reprinted in *The Ideologies of Class: Social
Relations in Britain 1880–1950* (Oxford 1990), p. 38 and *passim*.

7   For the cultural politics of the SPD see Vernon Lidtke, *The Alternative Culture* (Oxford 1985); P. Nettl, 'The German Social Democratic Party
1890–1914 as a Political Model', *Past and Present*, 30, 1965. In his influential work, *The Social Democrats in Imperial Germany: A Study in Working Class Isolation and National Integration* (1963), Günther Roth argued
that the culture of the SPD helped integrate the working class 'negatively'
into the Wilhelmine polity. For an assessment and critique of this view see
the special edition of the *Journal of Contemporary History*, 13, 1978, especially the contributions by Dieter Dowe and Gerhard Ritter.

8   For the distinction between alternative and oppositional culture see
Raymond Williams, 'Base and Superstructure in Marxist Cultural Theory'
in *Problems in Materialism and Culture* (1980), p. 42.

9   Q. Hoare & G. Nowell-Smith (eds), *Selections from the Prison Notebooks of Antonio Gramsci* (1971), p. 133.

10   Mary Douglas and Baron Isherwood, *The World of Goods: Towards an Anthropology of Consumption* (1979), pp. 65–6.

11   M. Weir, *Shoes were for Sunday* (1970), p. 74. More generally see
Ellen Ross, 'Women's Survival Networks: Neighbourhood Sharing Before
World War One', *History Workshop Journal*, 5, 1983.

12   Weir, *Shoes*, p. 54. See also M. Llewelyn Thew, *The Pit Village and
The Store* (1985), pp. 84, 109; and P. Johnson, *Saving and Spending: The*

Working-class Economy in Britain 1870–1939 (Oxford 1985), who notes (on pp. 133–7) that over 80% of Co-ops extended credit in 1911 and that credit trading grew in the inter-war years.

13   Weir, *Shoes*, p. 56.

14   Interview with Miss Haigh, Golcar, Huddersfield, 2 March 1994.

15   See Michael Winstanley, *The Shopkeeper's World 1830–1914* (Manchester 1983).

16   *Wheatsheaf*, July 1900, p. 1.

17   There is a useful report of one of these events organised by the Bolton Society in the late 1930s in an unpublished MS, 'The Co-operative Movement in Worktown', *Worktown Collection*, Box 32 D, Mass Observation Archive, University of Sussex. This source is discussed in chapter nine, below.

18   From 'Th' Store An' Th' Store Picnic', by Eawr Sally's Husband, published in the *Oldham Industrial Co-operative Society Record*, July 1894.

19   Weir, *Shoes* p. 56.

20   *Failsworth Co-operative Messenger*, June 1913, p. 150. For another excellent example of the uses of the 'divi' see Fred Pickles, *Jubilee History of the Bridge End Co-operative Society Limited: From 1847 to 1901* (Manchester 1902) p. 115.

21   Details can be found in Thew, *Pit Village and Store*, pp. 109–12. For the notion of rational forecasting see Pierre Bourdieu, *In Other Words: Essays Towards a Reflexive Sociology* (Oxford 1990), p. 7.

22   Interview with Mrs Scrimshaw, Leeds, 16 February 1994. Mrs Scrimshaw's father was a labourer at a sewage works in Leeds and earned no more than 30 shillings a week.

23   See McKibbin's useful comments on this theme in *McKibbin, Ideologies of Class*, pp. 115–6; 175–7.

24   W. H. Oliver (ed.), *Coventry Society's Jubilee History* (Coventry 1917) p. 310.

25   *Co-operative News*, 11 December 1880, p. 809.

26   Raymond Williams, 'Advertising the Magic System', in *Problems in Materialism and Culture* (1980), p. 179. For the cultural impact of advertising see Thomas Richards, *The Commodity Culture of Victorian England: Advertising and Spectacle, 1851–1914* (1991).

27   See Eileen Yeo, 'Culture and Constraint in Working-Class Movements, 1830–55' in Eileen & Stephen Yeo (eds), *Popular Culture and Class Conflict 1590–1914: Explorations in the History of Labour and Leisure* (Brighton 1981) p. 168.

28 G. J. Holyoake, *Leeds Industrial Co-operative Society Ltd., 1847–1897: traced year by year* (Manchester 1897), p. 77.

29 Montague Blatchford, *The history of Halifax Industrial Society for the first fifty years, to commemorate the celebration of its Jubilee in January 1901: 1851–1901* (Halifax 1901), p. 7.

30 *Co-operative News*, 11 January 1873 p. 6.

31 Blatchford, *Halifax Society*, p. 215.

32 *Leeds Co-operative Record*, October 1900, p. 13.

33 *Manchester and Salford Co-operative Herald*, February 1899 p. 24.

34 T. Redshaw, *Jubilee History of Bishop Auckland Industrial Co-operative Flour and Provision Society Ltd. from 1860–1910* (Manchester 1910), p. 70. On Co-operative cinemas see Ralph Bond, 'Cinema in the Thirties: Documentary Film and the Labour Movement', in Jon Clark *et al.*(eds), *Culture and Crisis in Britain in the 30s* (1979), pp. 253–4; Alan Burton, *The People's Cinema: Film and the Co-operative Movement* (BFI 1994).

35 Toshio Kusamitsu, 'Great Exhibitions before 1851', *History Workshop Journal*, 9, 1980.

36 Edward Jackson, *A Study in Democracy; being an account of the rise and progress of Industrial Co-operation in Bristol* (Bristol 1911), p. 108.

37 *Labour Co-partnership*, October 1897, p. 174.

38 G. J. Holyoake, *The History of Co-operation in England* (complete edn 1906), pp. 656–7.

39 *Co-operative News*, 3 August 1889, p. 830; 17 August 1889, pp. 877–9.

40 *Norwood News*, 25 August 1894.

41 *Labour Co-partnership*, August 1895, p. 164.

42 *Ibid.*, September 1897, pp. 152–3. This journal, the official organ of the Labour Association, carried extensive reports of these festivals from 1894. For this body see chapter six, below.

43 G. D. H. Cole, *A Century of Co-operation* (Manchester 1945), p. 225. In 1904 only 30 women sat on the management committees of 20 minor societies.

44 *Co-operative Record of the Birmingham District*, April 1894, p. 7.

45 *Co-operative News*, 10 August 1907, pp. 978–9.

46 *Our Circle*, August 1911, p. 533.

47 *Ibid.*, January 1908, p. 89; May 1908, pp. 180–1.

48 *Ibid.*, November 1909, p. 31; *Co-operative News*, 25 February 1911, pp. 235–6; Raphael Samuel, 'Theatre and Socialism in Britain

1880–1935', in R. Samuel, E. MacColl and S. Cosgrove (eds), *Theatres of the Left 1880–1935* (1985), pp. 26–30.

49   *Co-operative News*, 28 June 1884, pp. 594–5. For the place of music in working-class life generally see Dave Russell, *Popular Music in England, 1840–1914* (Manchester 1987); and for music and socialist culture see Waters, *British Socialists*, ch.4.

50   *Co-operative News*, 18 March 1905, p. 313; Duncan McInnes, *Co-operative Education and the Sectional Choral Association* (Manchester 1914).

51   *Co-operative News*, 16 October 1909, p. 1364.

52   *Songs and Readings for Co-operators* (Manchester 1896), preface.

53   *Failsworth Co-operative Messenger*, December 1910, p. 289.

54   *Co-operative News*, 27 May 1905, p. 606.

55   *Co-operative Record of the Birmingham District*, November 1902, p. 117; June 1904, p. 84.

56   *Wheatsheaf*, September 1900, p. 39.

57   *Co-operative News*, 1 September 1900, pp. 974–6; *Manchester and Salford Co-operative Herald*, October 1900 pp. 165–6.

58   *Wheatsheaf*, September 1900, p. 42; *Manchester and Salford Co-operative Herald*, October 1900, pp. 159–60.

59   For the changing meanings of 'social' see Raymond Williams, *Keywords* (Glasgow 1976), pp. 238–9.

60   *Co-operative News*, 26 February 1910, p. 252.

61   *Ibid.*, 28 February 1914, p. 276.

62   See Cunningham, *Leisure in the Industrial Revolution*, pp. 157–9; John Walton, 'The demand for working-class seaside holidays in Victorian England', *Economic History Review, 34*, 1981, pp. 249–65.

63   *Co-operative News*, 6 June 1874 p. 307; *Comradeship*, July 1898 pp. 37–8; August 1900, p. 80.

64   Mary Bentley, *Born 1896: Childhood in Clayton and Working in Manchester and Cheshire* (Manchester 1985), p. 26.

65   *Wheatsheaf*, November 1907, p. 66.

66   Waters, *British Socialists*, pp. 100–101.

67   *TNAPSS*, 1875, p. 717. Cited in Corrigan & Sayer, *The Great Arch: English State Formation as Cultural Revolution* (1985), p. 177.

68   *Co-operative News*, 31 October 1874, pp. 218–9.

69   *Ibid.*, 4 November 1882, p. 748. See also *ibid.*, 12 July 1884, p. 639. Ironically music halls achieved 'respectability' before the First World War. For this transformation see Bailey, *Music Hall* and Sara Maitland's engaging biography of *Vesta Tilley* (1986).

70   *Co-operative News*, 4 April 1905, p. 22.

71   *Ibid.*, 12 September 1903, p. 1112; 18 March 1905, p. 313; 17 April 1909, p. 472.

72   See Bailey, *Leisure and Class, passim.*

73   As Waters demonstrates in *British Socialists*, pp. 21–32 and 36–44, *passim.*

74   *Labour Co-partnership*, September 1896, p. 171.

75   *Co-operative News*, 10 August 1912, p. 995. See also *ibid.*, 1 August 1914, pp. 998–9.

76   See Raymond Williams, *Culture and Society 1780–1950* (1958), p. 289; Williams, *Keywords*, pp. 158–63.

77   *Manchester and Salford Co-operative Herald*, August 1917, p. 156.

78   *Bolton Co-operative Record*, April 1918, pp. 9–10.

79   *Failsworth Co-operative Messenger*, December 1917, p. 244.

80   *Co-operative News*, 3 August 1907, p. 957. Co-operative pageants became a major feature in the inter-war years.

81   Bramwell Hudson, *History of Co-operation in Cainscross & District: a souvenir in commemoration of the Jubilee of Cainscross and Ebley Co-operative Society, 1863–1913* (Manchester 1913), p. 106.

82   *Oldham Co-operative Record*, May 1894, p. 9.

83   Patrick Joyce, *Visions of the People: Industrial England and the Question of Class, 1848–1914* (Cambridge 1991), pp. 151–6; Bernice Martin, *A Sociology of Contemporary Cultural Change* (Oxford 1981).

84   Joyce, *Visions*, pp. 223–9; Peter Stallybrass and Allon White, *The Politics and Poetics of Transgression* (1986), pp. 179–80.

85   A brief history of the festival can be found in E. O. Greening's article in the *Economic Review*, January 1902, pp. 87–90.

86   *Co-operative Congress Report*, 1900, pp. 157–8.

87   *Ibid.*, 1901, pp. 38, 185.

88   *Labour Co-partnership*, September 1901, p. 134.

89   *Ibid.*, September 1904, p. 139.

90   For an example of an earlier railway boycott see C. J. Beckitt, *Darwen Industrial Co-operative Society, 1860–1910; Souvenir in commemoration of its jubilee* (Manchester 1910), pp. 109–11.

91   *Co-operative Congress Report*, 1901, p. 190. A similar resolution was passed at the Plymouth Congress nine years later. Strong anti-trust arguments informed the latter; see *Co-operative Congress Report*, 1910, p. 498 and chapter eight (below).

92   *Co-operative News*, 25 February 1911, p. 216.

93   Waters, *British Socialists*, pp. 145–6.

94   *Co-operative News*, 12 June 1909, pp. 750, 762; 19 June 1909, pp. 796, 798–9, 803.

95   *Ibid.*, 3 July 1909, pp. 864–5.

96   *Ibid.*, 19 June 1909, p. 803; 7 August 1909, p. 1029; 9 October 1909, p. 1328; 16 October 1909, p. 1351.

97   *Ibid.*, 7 May 1910, p. 563.

98   *Ibid.*, 4 June 1910, pp. 728–9; 30 July 1910, p. 988.

99   *Ibid.*, 19 July 1913, p. 900; 6 September 1913, p. 1150. The decision was made by a vote of 62 to 27 which made the importance of local political control clear. The Manchester Traders' Defence League had a good deal of support on the council. For the political lessons and John Burn's involvement see *ibid.*, 20 September 1913, p. 1216; 17 January 1914, p. 70; 7 March 1914.

100   *Ibid.*, 6 June 1919, p. 4.

101   *Ibid.*, 12 July 1919, p. 5.

102   Andrew Davies, *Leisure, gender and poverty: Working-class culture in Salford and Manchester, 1900–1939* (Buckingham 1992), p. 169.

103   McKibbin, *Ideologies of Class*, p. 15.

Chapter four: Internationalism

1   See, for example, Fred Hall and W. P. Watkins, *Co-operation* (Manchester 1937); G. D. H. Cole, *A Century of Co-operation* (Manchester 1945); Arnold Bonner, *British Co-operation* (Manchester 1961); W. P. Watkins, *The International Co-operative Alliance, 1895–1970* (Manchester 1970).

2   See J. F. C. Harrison, *Robert Owen and the Owenites in Britain and America* (1968); Barbara Taylor, *Eve and the New Jerusalem: Socialism and Feminism in the Nineteenth Century* (1983).

3   See T. Christensen, *Origin and History of Christian Socialism 1848–54* (1962); N. C. Masterman, *J. M. Ludlow. The Builder of Christian Socialism* (1963); A. D. Murray (ed.), *J. M. Ludlow. The Autobiography of a Christian Socialist* (1981).

4   See the *Co-operative Congress Report*, Newcastle-upon-Tyne, 1880, p. 42.

5   *Co-operative Congress Report*, 1869, pp. 17–28.

6   *Co-operative Congress Report*, 1871, pp. 74–81.

7   *Co-operative Congress Report*, 1872, p. 85.

8   *Co-operative Congress Report*, 1885, p. 8.

9   *Co-operative Congress Report*, 1908, pp. 40–41.

10 *Co-operative Congress Report*, 1910, pp. 459–60.

11 See Bonner, *British Co-operation*, pp. 466–7. An excellent film of the International Co-operative Day Pageant held at the Wembley Stadium in 1938, with the title 'Towards Tomorrow', is held by the Co-op Retail Services London Region film archives.

12 *Report of the Proceedings at the 41st Annual TUC held in . . . Nottingham . . . 1908* (1908), pp. 26, 54–5, 156–7.

13 *Co-operative Congress Report*, 1880, p. 42.

14 Holyoake's *Self-Help* was reprinted thirteen times between 1858 and 1907, and was translated into Spanish, French, Italian, German and Hungarian. According to Holyoake's biographer *Self-Help* took 'co-operative inspiration all over the civilised world'. See Joseph McCabe, *Life and Letters of George Jacob Holyoake* (1908), vol. I, p. 292.

15 *Co-operative Congress Report*, 1891, p. 12.

16 *Co-operative Congress Report*, 1908, pp. 373–4.

17 *Co-operative News*, 11 August 1909, p. 1184. See also Clayton's remarks at a Northern Sectional Conference in Sunderland in *ibid.*, 25 December 1909, p. 1673. Three years before Mr Van der Veer, the Dutch journalist, had declared before the RACS that Robert Owen had taken the idea of association from Fourier. See *Comradeship*, April 1906, p. 34.

18 *Co-operative News*, 26 January 1907, pp. 94–5.

19 See *Co-operative Congress Report*, 1906, pp. 72–3, 76; and for the ICA pp. 233–5.

20 *Co-operative News*, 22 August 1908, p. 1012; 29 August 1908, p. 1043; 5 September 1908, p. 1077.

21 *Ibid.*, 3 September 1910, pp. 1148–9; 9 April 1910, p. 463; 20 August 1910, p. 1089.

22 *Leeds Co-operative Record*, October 1910, p. 154.

23 *Co-operative News*, 23 February 1907, pp. 205–6; 6 April 1907, pp. 409–10; 13 April 1907, pp. 437–8; 21 March 1908, pp. 330–31 for various articles on co-operation overseas. See *ibid.*, 24 August 1912, pp. 1040–41 for a report on a British delegation to Belgium. This was the fourth annual trip to the continent organised by the Co-op Union. Thirty-five went, ten were women. See also the description and photograph of the famous Maison du Peuple in *ibid.*, 31 August 1912, pp. 1068–9. The *News* detailed the Co-operative Housing Settlements in Hamburg in 18 January 1913, p. 66; 25 January 1913, pp. 102–3.

24 *Wheatsheaf*, November 1904, pp. 75–6; March 1905, pp. 139–40; June 1905, pp. 186–7; May 1906, pp. 163–5. Muller wrote all these articles.

25   See Ben Jones on 'Possibilities of International Co-operative Trade' in the *C.W.S. Annual* (1898); Jones again on the 'Position of Co-operation in Other Lands' in *ibid.*, 1901; H. W. Woolf on the same topic in *ibid.*, 1903; and W. H. Brown on the effects of the First World War One in *ibid.*, 1918.

26   *Our Circle*, January 1908, p. 98.

27   *Ibid.*, September 1911, p. 567.

28   *Ibid.*, September 1914 p. 269; October 1914, p. 300 (an enthusiastic review of Margaret Pease's anti-war book *True Patriotism*); April 1916, p. 153.

29   *Co-operative News*, 14 September 1907, pp. 1121–2; 21 September 1907, pp. 1166–7; 28 September 1907, pp. 1185–6, 1198–1201; 5 October 1907, pp. 1226–33. *Millgate Monthly*, November 1907, pp. 72–3; October 1910, pp. 10–14.

30   *Leeds Co-operative Record*, November 1907, p. 187; December 1907, pp. 198–201; *Failsworth Co-operative Messenger*, November 1910, pp. 252–3. For other examples of local enthusiasm for the ICA see the *Oldham Co-operative Record*, October 1895, pp. 8–9; *Comradeship*, August 1903, p. 5; June 1906, p. 60.

31   *Co-operative News*, 23 August 1913; 30 August 1913. See also the *Millgate Monthly*, October 1913, p. 7; *Failsworth Co-operative Messenger*, October 1913, pp. 237–8.

32   Percy Redfern, *The Story of the C.W.S.* (Manchester 1913), pp. 41–3.

33   *Co-operative Congress Report*, 1889, p. 97.

34   *Co-operative Congress Report*, 1898, p. 126. See also the *Wheatsheaf*, May 1909, p. 162.

35   *Co-operative Congress Report*, 1901, p. 190.

36   *Co-operative Congress Report*, 1903, p. 103.

37   See the *Co-operative Congress Reports* for 1908, pp. 366, 368 and 1914, p. 498. In 1913 the German movement sent over 100 delegates to the ICA Congress in Glasgow who visited the CWS factories and workshops.

38   *Co-operative Congress Report*, 1908, pp. 443–5.

39   *Report of the Proceedings of the 7th. Congress of the I.C.A. held at Cremona, 1907* (1908), p. 132. See also Maxwell's pamphlet, *The I.C.A.: its claims* (Glasgow 1909).

40   *Co-operative Congress Report*, 1911 p. 446.

41   *Co-operative Congress Report*, 1914 p. 496.

42   See J.A.Hobson, *The Evolution of Modern Capitalism* (1894; 1917), p. 215: 'While . . . the greater part of our industrial system still

continues to be competitive, the area of the power of capitalist combination is growing and the effective protection furnished by competition to the consumer is diminished.'

43   *Co-operative Congress Report*, 1897 p. 112.
44   *Co-operative Congress Report*, 1901, p. 15.
45   *Co-operative Congress Report*, 1902, p. 148.
46   *Co-operative News*, 7 September 1907, p. 1095.
47   *Ibid.*, 23 August 1913, p. 1067.
48   *Millgate Monthly*, August 1917, p. 569.
49   *Russian Co-operator*, I, 1 December 1916.
50   See *Co-operative News*, 24 March 1917, pp. 278–9, 282; *Co-operative Congress Report*, 1917, pp. 79, 82. The Report of the Central Board submitted to this Congress emphasised the centrality of co-operation in the making and future progress of the revolution: 'The revolution of the Russian people, which the democracies of the world have hailed with delight as a great stride towards freedom and universal brotherhood, owes much to co-operation.' *Ibid.*, p. 251. By 1917 there were about 46,000 societies with over thirteen million members throughout Russia. The report pointed out that co-op societies shared, to the extent of as much as two-thirds, in the representation on the provisional authorities set up by the revolutionaries in the towns, and were practically the sole authorities in the country districts and villages. See also M. Llewelyn-Davies' sympathetic response published in the *Russian Co-operator*, I, 7 June 1917; and the editorial in the *Co-operative News*, 17 November 1917, p. 1087.
51   *Russian Co-operator*, II, 7 June 1918, p. 98. A resolution in support of Anglo-Russian trade links passed by the Bradford Congress of the WCG appeared in the *Russian Co-operator*, II, 7 June 1918, p. 98. The WCG also published a pamphlet by A. H. Enfield, *International Co-operative Trade* (Manchester n.d. but early 1920s) which put the case forcefully for Anglo-Russian trade links. See also the comments of the Russian delegate, Mr Asantcheef, who praised the British CWS for their 'splendid help' during the revolution, in *Co-operative Congress Report*, 1919, p. 106. British co-operators continued to be sympathetic towards their Russian comrades, though they did not share the uncritical exuberance of Fabians like the Webbs for Soviet society, especially after events in the 1920s made voluntary co-operation in the USSR impossible. For the British movement, the degeneration of the revolution, the increasing hegemony of the bureaucratic Party and State, served to reaffirm the vitality of co-operative strategies and solutions. The fluctuating fortunes of Russian co-operation post-1917 are discussed in E. H. Carr, *The Bolshevik Revolution,*

1917–23, vol. II (1952), and *Socialism in One Country, 1924–26, vol. I* (1958); Charles Bettelheim, *Class Struggles in the USSR* (Brighton 1976); and Bonner, *British Co-operation*, p. 443

52 *Co-operative Congress Report*, 1919, pp. 104–5.

53 See Cole, *A Century*, p. 359, and Bonner, *British Co-operation*, pp. 458–60.

54 *Co-operative Congress Report*, 1889, p. 97.

55 *Co-operative Congress Report*, 1899, p. 12.

56 *Co-operative Congress Report*, 1905, p. 28.

57 W. F. Cottrell, *The Jubilee Record of the Pendleton Co-operative Industrial Society Limited 1860–1910* (Manchester 1910), pp. 195–6; *Co-operative News*, 14 September 1912, p. 1142; *Pendleton Co-operative Record*, February 1914, p. 24; Ernest Poisson, *The Co-operative Republic* (1925), p. 216.

58 *Co-operative Congress Report*, 1901, p. 191.

59 *Co-operative Congress Report*, 1908, pp. 359–60.

60 Hugh Cunningham, 'The Language of Patriotism', *History Workshop Journal*, 12, Autumn 1981.

61 *Co-operative Congress Report*, 1909, p. 410.

62 *Ibid.*

63 *Co-operative Congress Report*, 1910, p. 474.

64 *Co-operative Congress Report*, 1915, p. 54.

65 Douse's speech was attacked, for the offence given to German co-operators, by H. J. May of the ICA at a meeting in Brighton soon afterwards. Mr H. Lorenz of the Central Committee of the ICA criticised the attitude of the British Co-operative press generally in the *International Co-operative Bulletin* in August 1915. For this debate see the *Co-operative News*, 24 July 1915, p. 1002; 4 September 1915, pp. 1184–5.

66 *Co-operative Congress Report*, 1915, p. 59. The editor of the *Plymouth Co-operative Record* (T. W. Mercer) made the same connection the following year: 'We are proud of our comrades in khaki and blue. Each victory they win fills our hearts with splendid pride and they in turn boast the victories we are winning at home in *the same democratic cause*. [My emphasis] For the great fight for freedom and democratic government is being fought on two fronts – the battle-front abroad and the industrial front at home.' January 1916, p. 4. This combination of right-wing patriotism, pride in the nation and a radical associational project was common during the war. For another example see W. H. Oliver (ed.), *Coventry Perseverance Co-operative Society Limited, Jubilee History, 1867–1917* (Coventry 1917), pp. 376, 406–7.

67   *Co-operative Congress Report*, 1915, p. 59.

68   *Manchester and Salford Co-operative Herald*, January 1917, p. 20.

69   Sidney Pollard, 'The Foundation of the Co-operative Party', in Briggs and Saville (eds), *Essays in Labour History, 1886–1923* (1971). See also (below) chapter 8.

70   *Co-operative Congress Report*, 1915, p. 559.

71   *Co-operative News*, 8 August 1914, pp. 1034–5.

72   These articles were written by J. F. Mills the paper's correspondent in Germany, and were dissected by the socialist co-operator, E. C. Pratt; see *ibid.*, 19 September 1914, p. 1196. The editor later sided with Mills. The paper was more concerned with the issue of international co-operative trade by 1917 and sympathetic reviews of anti-war novels by Patrick MacGill – *The Great Push* – and Romain Rolland – *Above the Battle* – were featured. *Ibid.*, 11 August 1917, pp. 762–3; August 1916, p. 710; August 1917, pp. 610–13.

73   *Pendleton Co-operative Record*, October 1914, pp. 137–8.

74   *Ibid.*, February 1915, pp. 15–16.

75   *Ibid.*, August 1916, p. 102.

76   *Bolton Co-operative Record*, August 1916, p. 19.

77   *Co-operative Congress Report*, 1883, p. 66.

78   *Wheatsheaf*, October 1902, p. 53.

79   *Millgate Monthly*, June 1911, p. 606. See also the editorial praising King George's tour of northern industrial districts which aroused the loyalty of all sections of workers 'whatever their politics'; August 1913, p. 657.

80   Phillip Corrigan and Derek Sayer, *The Great Arch: English State Formation as Cultural Revolution* (1985), p. 78.

81   *Pendleton Co-operative Record*, January 1915, p. 1. The editor stressed the inadequacy of the competitive system in the same leader. For more nationalistic pronouncements see *ibid.*, March 1915, p. 1; September 1915, p. 1.

82   *The Manchester and Salford Co-operative Herald* published letters from members describing life in the Transvaal. No criticisms were made, but neither was the war openly supported in the record's pages. Victoria, of course, continued to be regularly lauded. See May 1900 pp. 73, 74–5, 80; June 1900 p. 96. For the lack of enthusiasm generally amongst English workers for the Boer War see Richard Price, *An Imperial War and the British Working Class: Working-Class Attitudes and Reactions to the Boer War, 1899–1902* (1972). Price's work has not gone unchallenged. See M. D. Blanch, 'British Society and the War', in P. Warwick (ed.), *The South*

African War (1980); J. M. Mackenzie, *Propaganda and Empire: The ma-nipulation of British Public Opinion* (Manchester 1984); J. M. Mackenzie (ed.), *Imperialism and Empire* (Manchester 1986).
83 *Co-operative News*, 26 October 1907 p. 1313.
84 *Ibid.*, 3 October 1914, p. 1259.
85 *Ibid.*, 21 November 1914, p. 1433.
86 *Ibid.*, 6 May 1916, p. 480. The News had paid no real attention to Larkin and his connection with co-operation, but the editorial ended by recommending transformation through peaceful co-operation as a solution to the Irish 'problem'; a policy, it was argued, advocated by James Connolly before he had thrown in his lot with 'this mad moloch of rebellion'. For an analysis of Larkin's co-operative ideology see Keith Harding, 'The "Co-operative Commonwealth": Ireland, Larkin, and the *Daily Herald*', in Stephen Yeo (ed.), *New Views of Co-operation* (1988).
87 *Bolton Co-operative Record*, November 1914, pp. 3–4.
88 *Ibid.*, May 1915, p. 3.
89 Burnley Co-operative Record, September 1914, p. 4.
90 *Millgate Monthly*, February 1917, p. 263.

Chapter five: The sense of the past

1 G. J. Holyoake, *The History of Co-operation*, vol. 2 (1879; complete edn referred to here published 1906), p. 422.
2 *Co-operative News*, 21 August 1875, pp. 438–9. The week before, the *News* had carried a favourable review of Holyoake's history: 14 August 1875 pp. 426–7.
3 David Vincent, *Bread, Knowledge and Freedom* (1981), pp. 14–38.
4 David Vincent, *Literacy and Popular Culture: England 1750–1914* (Cambridge 1989).
5 Patrick Joyce, *Visions of the People: Industrial England and the Question of Class* (Cambridge 1991), pp. 172–192. See also pp. 287–88.
6 See Raphael Samuel's introduction to the collection, *People's History and Socialist Theory* (1981) pp. xiv–xl.
7 *Review of Reviews*, September 1901, pp. 249–61. For Stead see Judith Walkowitz, *City of Dreadful Delight: Narratives of Sexual Danger in Late-Victorian London* (1992). There is a discussion of the Macerone pike in Holyoake's *History of Co-operation*, vol. 2, pp. 513–15. Holyoake also acquired John Frost's sword in 1876 though it is not mentioned in the Stead interview.
8 The best biography remains Joseph McCabe's *Life and Letters of*

George Jacob Holyoake, 2 vols. (1908). See also Lee Grugel, *George Jacob Holyoake: A Study in the Evolution of a Victorian Radical* (Philadelphia 1976).

9 See Edward Royle's remarks in his entry in John Saville and Joyce Bellamy (eds), *Dictionary of Labour Biography*, vol. 1 (1972), p. 184; and Grugel, *G. J. Holyoake*, p. 141. On the 'collector', Walter Benjamin's essay, 'Edward Fuchs: The Collector as Historian', in *One Way Street* (1979) is a marvellous *tour de force*.

10 Pamphlet by G. J. Holyoake, *The Liberal Situation: necessity for a Qualified Franchise* (1865), p. 35.

11 For the notion of a selective tradition see Raymond Williams, *Marxism and Literature* (Oxford 1977), p. 115. Stimulating historical treatments of this theme can be found in Eric Hobsbawm and Terence Ranger (eds), *The Invention of Tradition* (Cambridge 1983).

12 Pamphlet by G. J. Holyoake, *The Life and Character of Henry Hetherington* (1849), p. 9.

13 Pamphlet by G. J. Holyoake, *Public Speaking and Debate* (1849), p. 4.

14 *Ibid.*, p. 48. See also his pamphlet *Practical Grammar* (1846).

15 Marx referred to 'the thin-voice, intrusive, consequential Holyoake' in a letter to Engels, 27 July 1866, quoted in Royden Harrison, *Before the Socialists: Studies in Labour and Politics, 1861–1881* (1965), p. 170

16 Trygve Tholfsen, *Working-Class Radicalism in Mid-Victorian England* (1976), p. 264. This line is adopted by Grugel, *G. J. Holyoake.*

17 See Mick Jenkins, *The General Strike of 1842* (1980); John Saville, *1848: The British state and the Chartist movement* (Cambridge, 1987).

18 Quoting from John Vincent, *The Formation of the Liberal Party 1857–68* (1966), Patrick Joyce in *Visions*, p. 52, notes Holyoake's employment of a 'populist' discourse in the 1860s. However, the original source is ambiguous. In this text, as well as elsewhere, Holyoake used the term 'the people' and 'the working class' synonymously: 'it only needs that the people be taught to imitate their new "superiors". Let the working class show as much pluck, as much sense, and as much resolution as the middle have done, and they may become as influential and as much respected by those who rule, as the middle class now are" he wrote in *The Liberal Situation*, p. 7. This pamphlet, as I noted above, also contained a rather illiberal recommendation of direct action!

19 Pierre Bourdieu, *In Other Words: Essays Towards a Reflexive Sociology* (Oxford 1990), p. 155.

20   See above pp. 91-92. Holyoake's interest in co-operation long pre-
dated the publication of *Self-Help*. For an early, enthusiastic reaction see
his pamphlet *Rationalism: A Treatise for the Times* (1845), p. 34.

21   Nigel Todd, *The Militant Democracy: Joseph Cowen and Victorian
Radicalism* (Tyne and Wear 1991), p. 106, quoting P. A. Darvill, 'The Contribution of Co-operative Retail Societies to Welfare within the framework
of the North East Coast area', unpublished MLitt thesis, University of Durham (1954), p. 6.

22   For example, Martin Purvis, 'Co-operative Retailing in England,
1835–1850: Developments beyond Rochdale', *Northern History*, 22,
1986; and Robin Thornes, 'Change and Continuity in the Development of
Co-operation, 1827–1844' in Stephen Yeo (ed.), *New Views of Co-operation* (1988).

23   For a later, influential example of this narrative strategy see *The
Progress of the Working Classes* (1867), a text written jointly by the ex-
Owenite, Lloyd Jones and the Christian Socialist, J.M.Ludlow. See also
chapter six (below).

24   Vincent, *Bread, Knowledge and Freedom*, p. 36.

25   G. J. Holyoake, *The History of Co-operation in Halifax* (1867),
p. 6.

26   See Holyoake, *History of Co-operation*, p. xvii; Grugel, *G. J.
Holyoake*, pp. 140–41.

27   These texts included a Christian Socialist defence of profit-sharing
by Thomas Hughes and E. V. Neale, *A Manual for Co-operators* (1881);
and Arthur Acland and Ben Jones's *Working Men Co-operators* (1884), a
work which adopted a less biased stance. For an analysis see my 'Heads,
Hands and the Co-operative Utopia: An Essay in Historiography', *North
West Labour History*, 1994.

28   Holyoake, *History of Co-operation*, vol. 1, pp. 14, 88, 197.

29   *Ibid.*, vol. 2, pp. 583–4.

30   G. J. Holyoake, *Life of Joseph Rayner Stephens* (1881), p. 60. Local
middle-class historians also mythologised the role of free trade at this time.
See Frank Peel, *The Risings of the Luddites, Chartists and Plug-Drawers*
(1880; fourth edn 1968), p. 349. This passage was added to the second
edition of 1888.

31   For the notion of 'fair play' and its importance in radical politics see
Rohan McWilliam, 'Radicalism and Popular Culture: The Tichborne Case
and the Politics of "Fair Play", 1867–1886', in Eugenio Biagini and Alistair
Reid (eds), *Currents of Radicalism: Popular Radicalism, Organised Labour
and Party Politics in Britain, 1850–1914* (Cambridge 1991), pp. 57–9.

32 Holyoake, *Life of J. R. Stephens*, p. 198.

33 *Ibid.*, p. 235.

34 Eugenio Biagini, *Liberty, Retrenchment and Reform: Popular Liberalism in the Age of Gladstone, 1860–1880* (Cambridge 1992), pp. 141, 380. For an excellent critique of this harmonious account of popular Liberalism see Robert Gray, 'Class, Politics and Historical "Revisionism"', *Social History*, 19/2, 1994, pp. 209–20.

35 This concept, coined by Milan Kundera, is employed by Phillip Corrigan and Derek Sayer in *The Great Arch: English State Formation as Cultural Revolution* (1985), pp. 195, 230 fn.11.

36 Pare to Holyoake, Holyoake Collection, Co-operative Union Archive, Manchester. Letter dated 16 August 1867 (no. 1739). As registrar for Birmingham, Pare had officiated at Holyoake's wedding in 1840.

37 G. J. Holyoake, *The Logic of Co-operation* (1873), p. 7.

38 Quoted in J. McCabe, *George Jacob Holyoake* (1922), p. 115. This was an abridged, reworked treatment of the subject.

39 On the centrality of the notion of 'independence' to co-operators see Biagini, *Liberty, Entrenchment and Reform*, pp. 139–44 and my discussion in chapter two above.

40 *Subjects of the Day*, August 1890, p. 96.

41 *Justice*, 21 May 1898, p. 2.

42 For more detail see my chapter, 'George Jacob Holyoake: Socialism, Association and Co-operation in Nineteenth-Century England', in Yeo, *New Views*, pp. 65–9.

43 *Millgate Monthly*, October 1905, pp. 5–6.

44 See Holyoake's review of Mill's book in the *Birmingham Weekly Post*, 5 June 1869 in *Holyoake Papers*, reel 9, 6a.

45 G. J. Holyoake, *Sixty Years of an Agitator's Life*, 2 vols. (1892, complete edn referred to here published 1906), p. 275.

46 Biagini, *Liberty, Retrenchment and Reform*, p. 142.

47 Pamphlet by G. J. Holyoake, *The Opportunity of Ireland* (1886), p. 4. This passage appears in a slightly re-written form in his *Sixty Years*, pp. 83–4. Holyoake often 're-cycled' his writing in this way, not surprising given his busy public life and his limited financial means.

48 Ross McKibbin, *The Ideologies of Class: Social Relations in Britain, 1880–1950* (Oxford 1990), pp. 31–2, 296; Joyce, *Visions*, pp. 89–90, 114, 141, 189, 287; Biagini, *Liberty, Retrenchment and Reform*, pp. 93–102, 134, 142.

49 See *Co-operative Congress Report*, 1892, p. 125.

50 An excellent example can be found in the chapter by Holyoake

entitled 'In the Days of Protection' in H. W. Massingham (ed.), *Labour and Protection* (1903), pp. 93–117. A review in *Justice* 12 December 1903, p. 3, referred to Holyoake's contribution as '25 pages of senile irrelevancies.' For more on Holyoake's attitude to free trade and his praise for the Anti-Corn Law League see *Sixty Years*, pp. 219–31

51 See Valerie Chancellor, *History for their Masters* (1970) for a useful study of the history-texts used in these schools. How far working-class children passively accepted this view of history is very difficult to assess. For evidence of resistance see Stephen Humphries, *Hooligans or Rebels? An Oral History of Working-Class Childhood and Youth 1889–1939* (1981).

52 The code was intended for use in the rapidly-proliferating continuation schools which received government grants. These schools were for young people aged over 15 and were therefore especially important to the working-class. See Brian Simon, *Education and the Labour Movement 1870–1920* (1965) pp. 184–6.

53 *Co-operative News*, 8 July 1893, pp. 733–4; 18 November 1893, p. 1236.

54 *Co-operative Congress Report*, 1894, p. 125.

55 *Co-operative News*, 2 June 1894, pp. 626–7.

56 *Ibid.*, 30 December 1893, p. 1412; 20 January 1894, p. 71.

57 F. W. Peaples, *History of the Educational Department of the Bolton Co-operative Society Limited, 1861–1914* (Manchester 1915), pp. 46–8

58 *Co-operative Congress Report*, 1896, p. 25.

59 *Co-operative News*, 16 February 1907, p. 180.

60 Catherine Webb (ed.), *Industrial Co-operation: The Story of a Peaceful Revolution* (Manchester 1904; third edn 1907), p. 2.

61 Fred Hall, *The Co-ordination and Extension of Co-operative Education and the Part of the Co-operative College Therein* (Manchester 1914), p. 21.

62 Arnold Bonner, *British Co-operation: The History, Principles, and Organisation of the British Co-operative Movement* (1961), p. 122; Simon, *Education and the Labour Movement*, pp. 309–10.

63 *Co-operative News*, 8 April 1911, p. 437.

64 Interviewed by the author at Roe Green, 22 April 1986

65 Hall, *Co-ordination*.

66 Thomas Jones and Joseph Rhodes, *Jubilee history of the Hyde Equitable Co-operative Society Ltd., 1862–1912* (Manchester 1912), pp. 143–6.

67 F. W. Peaples, *History of the Great and Little Bolton Co-operative*

Society; showing fifty years of progress, 1859–1909: A souvenir in com-memoration of the Society's Jubilee (Manchester 1909) p. 520.

68 James Haslam, *A History of fifty years of progress of Accrington and Church Industrial Co-operative Society Ltd., a souvenir of the Society's Jubilee: 1860–1910* (Manchester 1910), p. 181.

69 Keith Snell, *Annals of the Labouring Poor: Social Change and Agrarian England, 1660–1900* (Cambridge 1985), pp. 336–43.

70 G. J. Holyoake, *Leeds Industrial Co-operative Society Ltd., 1847–1897: traced year by year* (Manchester 1897); G. J. Holyoake and Amos Scotton, *The Jubilee history of Derby Co-operative Provident Society 1850–1900* (Manchester 1900). Holyoake also updated his history of the Rochdale Society in 1878 and 1893.

71 See James Haslam, *A History of fifty years progress of Eccles Provident Industrial Co-operative Society Ltd: Jubilee souvenir, 1857–1907* (Manchester 1907); and Haslam, *Accrington.* Biographical details can be found in Saville and Bellamy, *Dictionary of Labour Biography*, vol. I, pp. 155–6.

72 Montague Blatchford, *The history of Halifax Industrial Society for the first fifty years, to commemorate the celebration of its Jubilee in January 1901: 1851–1901* (Halifax 1901), p. 6. Biographical details in Saville and Bellamy, *Dictionary of Labour Biography*, vol. 4 (1979), pp. 31–3.

73 Thomas Boydell, *The Jubilee history of the Leigh Friendly Co-operative Society Ltd., 1857–1907* (Manchester 1907), p. 58.

74 *Bolton Co-operative Record*, February 1905, p. 1.

75 *Oldham Co-operative Record*, September 1894, pp. 1–2.

76 For the impact of Unitarianism on Holyoake see his letter to Toulmin Smith dated 25 March 1867, Holyoake Collection, no. 1728. On the links between Congregationalism and co-operation see Alistair Reid, 'Old Unionism reconsidered: the radicalism of Robert Knight, 1870–1900', in Biagini and Reid, *Currents of Radicalism*, p. 222, who erroneously states that Holyoake came from a Congregationalist family.

77 Peaples, *Bolton*, p. 23. For the alienating effects of autodidact culture see Vincent, *Literacy and Popular Culture*, pp. 265–6; Logie Barrow, *Independent Spirits. Spiritualism and English Plebeians 1850–1910* (1986), p. 274.

78 W. H. Childe, *Batley Co-operative Society Ltd.: a brief history of the Society, 1867–1917* (Manchester 1919), p. 7.

79 T. Redshaw, *Jubilee History of Bishop Auckland Industrial Co-operative Flour and Provision Society Ltd. from 1860–1910* (Manchester 1910). Redshaw included an occupational breakdown of the original mem-

bers on p. 61 to support this claim. For similar statements see Haslam, *Accrington*, pp. 14–15; W. H. Oliver (ed.), *Jubilee History of Coventry Perseverance Society, 1867–1917* (Coventry 1917), pp. 366–7; Joseph Rhodes, *Half a century of Co-operation in Keighley, 1860–1910: Jubilee history* (Manchester 1911), pp. 155, 220; and even Peaples, *Bolton*, p. 21.

80 See J. R. Green's preface to his *Short History of the English People* (1877); Samuel's comments in his *People's History* pp. xvii–xviii; and his article 'British Marxist Historians, 1880–1980: Part I', *New Left Review*, 120, 1980, pp. 40–41.

81 *Comradeship*, February 1900, p. 23.

82 *Wheatsheaf*, November 1907, p. 75. According to the writer, Green, an East London clergyman, had come to understand what life for the majority was like through his contact with churchwardens, schoolmasters, the courts and Boards of Guardians and through observation of the daily lives of local working people. Mrs Green's invaluable support was noted in the press and she was interviewed at length by the *Millgate Monthly* at this time. See also *Bolton Co-operative Record*, April 1918, pp. 9–10.

83 Jones and Rhodes, *Hyde*, p. 6.

84 W. Hartley, *Fifty Years of Co-operation in Bingley; a Jubilee record of Bingley Industrial Co-operative Society Ltd.* (Bingley 1900), pp. 20–21; H. Hodgson, *Fifty Years of Co-operation in Great Horton and District, being the Jubilee history of the Great Horton Industrial Society, 1859–1909* (Manchester 1909), p. 24; Joseph Kenworthy, *History of the Stocksbridge Band of Hope Industrial Co-operative Society Ltd., 1860–1910* (Manchester 1910), p. 16; Redshaw, *Bishop Auckland*, pp. 16–17.

85 Joyce, *Visions*, pp. 177–8; Vincent, *Literacy and popular culture*, pp. 187–8.

86 Rhodes, *Keighley*, p. 20.

87 *Ibid.*, pp. 22–3. 67% of my sample used oral evidence. For further examples see Haslam, *Eccles*, p. 29; Haslam, *Accrington*, p. 20; Oliver, *Coventry*, pp. 376–92. Note, however, that Frank Peel had also made extensive use of oral tradition in *Risings of the Luddites*.

88 Blatchford, *Halifax*, p. 183.

89 Bramwell Hudson, *History of Co-operation in Cainscross & District: a souvenir in commemoration of the Jubilee of Cainscross and Ebley Co-operative Society, 1863–1913* (Manchester 1913), p. 1. See also John Oxberry, *Windy Nook village, its inhabitants and their Co-operative store: a jubilee tribute and historical sketch* (Pelaw-on-Tyne 1924), p. 13.

90 *Jubilee history of Bedlington Equitable and Industrial Co-operative Society Ltd., 1861–1911* (signed by the 'Book Committee', Manchester 1911). See also Haslam, *Eccles*, p. 7.

91 Holyoake, *Leeds*, p. 173. See also Hartley, *Bingley*, p. vi. The co-operative press made extensive use of photography, especially the *Millgate Monthly* which established a photography club before the First World War. Local records frequently carried biographies of individual members, and these invariably featured a photographic portrait.

92 John Berger, 'Ways of Remembering', in *Camerawork*, no. 10, 1978, p. 1; See also Susan Sontag, *On Photography* (1978).

93 This is also a feature of recent community publications and working-class autobiographies. See Popular Memory Group, 'Popular Memory: Theory, Politics, Method', in R. Johnson et al., *Making Histories: Studies in History-writing and Politics* (1982), pp. 244–5.

94 Berger, 'Ways of Remembering'.

95 Charles Dellheim, *The Face of the Past: The Preservation of the Medieval Inheritance in Victorian England* (Cambridge 1982), pp. 33–75. See also E. P. Thompson's sensitive introduction to Peel, *Risings of the Luddites*, pp. vii-xv.

96 William Cottrell, *Jubilee history of the Pendleton Co-operative & Industrial Society, 1860–1910* (Manchester 1910), pp. 261–9; Anon, *Bedlington*, p. 11; Oxberry, *Windy Nook*, p. 13.

97 Hudson, *Cainscross*, p. 15; Duncan McInnes, *History of Co-operation in Lincon, 1861–1911* (Manchester 1911), pp. 21–6.

98 John Caldwell, *History of Brighouse and its Co-operative Society* (Brighouse 1899), pp. 10–11; Oxberry, *Windy Nook*, pp. 25–6.

99 Peaples, *Bolton*, p. 26.

100 Boydell, *Leigh*, pp. 60–61, 63, 70–71.

101 Haslam, *Eccles*, p. 29; Hartley, *Bingley*, p. 23; Caldwell, *Brighouse*, p. 90; T. Blandford & G. Newell, *History of the Leicester Co-operative Hosiery Manufacturing Society Limited* (Leicester 1898), pp. 10–11; Oliver, *Coventry*, pp. 6–11. Note that the latter account is based on a working class autobiography, that of Joseph Gutteridge, *Lights and Shadows in the Life of an Artisan*, published in serialised form, in the *Coventry Herald and Free Press* (1891). Haslam also wrote a novel which dramatised this phase, *The Hand-Loom Weaver's Daughter* (Manchester 1904), and contributed a series of articles on the skills and traditions of this craft to the *Millgate Monthly* in 1912.

102 Vincent, *Bread, Knowledge and Freedom*, pp. 27–9.

103 Fred Pickles, *Jubilee History of Bridge End (Todmorden) Co-op-*

erative Society Ltd., 1847–1901 (Manchester 1902), p. 1; Haslam, *Accrington*, pp. 194–208; Boydell, *Leigh*, p. 91.

104 Hodgson, *Great Horton*, p. 30.

105 Blatchford, *Halifax*, p. 38; Thomas Rigby, *The origin and history of Co-operation in Bury; written in commemoration of the Jubilee of the Bury District Co-operative Society Ltd., 1855–1905* (Bury 1905), p. 7.

106 Oliver, *Coventry*, pp. 22–3; W. Simpson, *Jubilee Souvenir; a short history of Cramlington District Co-operative Society, 1861–1911* (Manchester 1912), p. 5; Rhodes, *Keighley*, pp. 12–19.

107 Owen Balmforth, *A history of fifty years progress, 1860–1910, of Huddersfield Industrial Society Ltd.* (Manchester 1910), p. 27. Balmforth also wrote the *Jubilee History of the Corporation of Huddersfield, 1868–1918* (Huddersfield 1918). For his secularist connections see Edward Royle, *Radicals, Secularists and Republicans: Popular Freethought in Britain, 1866–1915* (Manchester 1980), pp. 15, 120, 217, 326.

108 J. McClean and A. Hewitt, *Fifty Years' history of the Compstall Co-operative Industrial Society Ltd., 1851–1901: A Souvenir of the jubilee celebrations . . .* (Manchester 1901), p. 3.

109 Anon., *The Coronation history of the Barnsley British Co-operative Society Ltd., 1862–1902* (Manchester 1903), pp. 6, 93–7. Similar treatments can be found in the histories of various Yorkshire societies seriously affected by the 1893 dispute. See, for example, Boydell, *Leigh*, pp. 275–6; Cotterill, *Pendleton*, p. 114; Jones and Rhodes, *Hyde*, p. 83. However, the record was not one of unwavering support. The Congleton Society, for example, revised their rules in 1892, following a debate over a donation made to striking fustian cutters the previous year and debarred the disposal of profits on strikes, lockouts, or for religious and political objects. See A. Cooke and J. Cooke, *The Jubilee History of the Congleton Equitable and Industrial Society Ltd. 1860–1910* (Manchester 1910), pp. 99–100. Societies which were largely dependent on a single industry, like the one in Barnsley, exhibited solidarity more readily.

110 See the figures in G. D. H. Cole, *A Century of Co-operation* (Manchester 1945), pp. 155, 177.

111 John Baldwin and Joseph Bennett, *Jubilee History 1860–1910 of the City of Bradford Co-operative Society* (Bradford 1911), pp. 234–5.

112 Malcolm Chase, 'From Millenium to Anniversary: The Concept of Jubilee in Late Eighteenth and Nineteenth Century England', *Past and Present*, 129, 1990, pp. 132–47. Some of the chapel histories were very radical: for an excellent example see Rev. William Tonks, *Victory in the Villages: The History of the Britsworth Circuits* (1907), pp. 13, 75. Chase

('From Milienium', pp. 146–7) notes the usage by co-operative societies but does not discuss their attempted reworking of the term and concludes that the evidence points to 'the redundancy of jubilee as a distinctive part of the political vocabulary'. All in all, his judgement is probably correct. For the jubilee and the monarchy see David Cannadine, 'The Context, Performance and Meaning of Ritual: The British Monarchy and the "Invention of Tradition" *c.* 1820–1977', in Hobsbawm and Ranger (eds), *The Invention of Tradition*.

113 Cotterill, *Pendleton*, p. 5; Kenworthy, *Stocksbridge*, title page; Jones and Rhodes, *Hyde*, p. 140.

114 Simpson, *Cramlington*, p. 7. See also C. J. Beckitt, *Darwen Industrial Co-operative Society, 1860–1910; Souvenir in commemoration of its jubilee* (Manchester 1910), p. 114.

115 W. R. Rae, reported in *Co-operative Congress Report*, 1912, p. 459. For the links between rhetoric and militancy during this phase see Bernard Waites, 'The Language and Imagery of "Class" in Early Twentieth-Century England', *Literature and History*, 4, 1976, p. 43.

116 For the internal relationship between history and politics see Johnson et al., *Making Histories*, p. 244.

117 *Wheatsheaf*, December 1911, p. 81.

Chapter six: The middle-class embrace

1 *Encyclopedia Britannica* (9th edn, Edinburgh 1877).

2 A. E. Bestor, 'The Evolution of the Socialist Vocabulary', *Journal of the History of Ideas*, 9, 1948, pp. 259–302.

3 *Quarterly Review*, 114, 1863, p. 418. See also the entry in the *Oxford English Dictionary on Historical Principles* (Oxford 1933).

4 See John Seed, 'Unitarianism, Political Economy and the Antinomies of Liberal Culture in Manchester 1830–1850', *Social History*, 7/1 (1982); Seed, 'Theologies of Power: Unitarianism and the Social Relations of Religious Discourse, 1800–1850', in R. J. Morris (ed.), *Class, Power and Social Structure in British Nineteenth-Century Towns* (Leicester 1986); R. J. Morris, *Class, Sect and Party: The Making of the British Middle Class, Leeds 1820–1850* (Manchester 1990); Leonore Davidoff and Catherine Hall in *Family Fortunes: Men and women of the English Middle Class, 1780–1850* (1987).

5 The key text here is Martin Weiner's *English Culture and the Decline of the Industrial Spirit 1850–1980* (Cambridge 1981). For a useful critique from a large literature see Michael Barratt Brown, 'Away With All the

Great Arches: Anderson's History of British Capitalism', *New Left Review*, 167, 1988, pp. 22–51.

6   See the well known section entitled, 'The Probable Futurity of the Labouring Classes' in Book II. Mill's views had been shaped by the propagandism of G. J. Holyoake.

7   Raymond Williams, *Marxism and Literature* (Oxford 1977) drawing on V. N. Volosinov, *Marxism and the Philosophy of Language* (1930, New York 1973); See also Pierre Bourdieu, *Language and Symbolic Power* (Oxford 1991).

8   Pierre Bourdieu, *In Other Words: Essays Towards a Reflexive Sociology* (Oxford 1990) p. 54. From a rapidly expanding literature on the social history of language see William Sewell, *Work and Revolution in France. The Language of Labour from the Old Regime to 1848* (Cambridge 1980); Gareth Stedman Jones, 'Rethinking Chartism' in his *Languages of Class* (1983) and John Foster's insightful response, 'The Declassing of Language', *New Left Review*, 150, 1985, pp. 29–45; J. E. Cronin, 'Language, Politics and the Critique of Social History', *Journal of Social History*, 20, 1986–7, pp. 177–83; J. W. Scott, 'On Language, Gender and Working-Class History', in *Gender and the Politics of History* (New York 1988); Robert Gray, 'The Languages of Factory Reform in Britain, c. 1830–1860' in Patrick Joyce (ed.), *The Historical Meanings of Work* (Cambridge 1987); Peter Burke & Roy Porter (eds), *The Social History of Language* (Cambridge 1987); Patrick Joyce, *Visions of the People: Industrial England and the question of class 1848–1914* (Cambridge 1991).

9   For the relationship between this general sense of co-operation and capitalist development see Marx, *Capital* vol. I (1867, 1976), ch.13, pp. 439–54 especially p. 454: 'Co-operation remains the fundamental form of the capitalist mode of production . . . .' Marx also ridiculed what I term in this chapter the middle-class embrace. See, for example, his comments on p. 449 fn. 15.

10   Alisdair Macintyre, 'The essential contestability of some social concepts', *Ethics*, 84, 1973, pp. 1–9.

11   On the Christian Socialist connection see T. Christensen, *Origin and History of Christian Socialism, 1848–1854* (Copenhagen 1962); N. C. Masterman, *J. M. Ludlow. The Builder of Christian Socialism* (1963); Philip Backstrom, *Christian Socialism and Co-operation in Victorian England* (1974). J. Saville, 'The Christian Socialists of 1848' in J. Saville (ed.), *Democracy and the Labour Movement* (1954) remains a useful critique.

12   See Nigel Todd, *The Militant Democracy: Joseph Cowen and Victorian Radicalism* (1991), pp. 105–12. Cowen's real hobby-horse was

profit-sharing and Todd, in his otherwise insightful study, fails to unravel critically Cowen's thinking here. Thus his later disillusionment with the consumers' movement (cited on p. 162) can be interpreted merely as yet another quirk of old age.

13 On this important theme see Philip Abrams, *The Origins of British Sociology 1834–1914* (Chicago 1968); Raymond Williams, *Politics and Letters* (1979), pp. 170–72; Philip Corrigan & Derek Sayer, *The Great Arch: English State Formation as Cultural Revolution* (1985), pp. 129, 134–5.

14 Lawrence Goldman, 'A Peculiarity of the English? The Social Science Association and the Absence of Sociology in Nineteenth Century Britain', *Past and Present*, 114, February 1987, pp. 133–71. See also, by the same author, 'The Social Science Association, 1857–86: A Context for Mid-Victorian Liberalism', *English Historical Review*, 101, 1986, pp. 95–134. There is a short illuminating discussion of the SSA's attitude to co-operation in E. M. Yeo, 'Social Science and Social Change: A Social History of Some Aspects of Social Science and Social Investigation in Britain, 1830–1890' (Unpublished DPhil thesis, University of Sussex, 1972) pp. 271–4.

15 Henry Travis, *A Manual of Social Science for the Working Classes* (1877), pp. 9–10.

16 *Transactions of the National Association for the Promotion of Social Science* (*TNAPSS*), Dublin, 1861, p. 15. Brougham praised co-operation in his presidential addresses in 1862, 1863 and 1864.

17 *TNAPSS*, 1866, p. 778; *TNAPSS* 1871 p. 572.

18 *TNAPSS*, Glasgow 1874, p. 13.

19 J. M. Ludlow and Lloyd Jones, The *Progress of the Working Classes, 1832–1867* (1867, New York 1973), p. 227.

20 *Ibid.*, pp. 142–3.

21 For the debate on profit-sharing see Backstrom, *Christian Socialism* and Percy Redfern, *The Story of the C.W.S.* (Manchester 1913).

22 Ben Jones, *Co-operative Production* (Oxford 1894), pp. 757–8; C. R. Fay, *Co-operation at Home and Abroad* (1936), p. 223 and the same author's *Co-partnership in Industry* (1913).

23 *TNAPSS*, Sheffield, 1865 pp. 480–86.

24 *TNAPSS*, Manchester, 1866, p. 704.

25 *Ibid.*, p. 708.

26 See R. A. Church, 'Profit-sharing and Labour Relations in England in the Nineteenth Century', in *International Review of Social History*, 16, 1971, pp. 2–16; Edward Bristow, 'Profit-Sharing, Socialism and Labour Unrest', in K. D. Brown (ed.), *Essays in Anti-Labour History* (1974); and Sidney Pollard and Robert Turner, 'Profit-Sharing and Autocracy: The

Case of J. T. and J. Taylor of Batley Woollen Manufacturers, 1892–1966',
Business History, 18, 1976, pp. 4–34.
  27 *TNAPSS*, 1872, p. 458.
  28 *Ibid.*, p. 459.
  29 John Ruskin, *Time and Tide by Weare and Tyne: Twenty Five Letters to a Working Man of Sunderland* (1867) in E. T. Cook and A. Wedderburn (eds), *The Works of John Ruskin*, vol. XVII (London 1905), p. 319. Holyoake sent Ruskin a copy of his two-volume *History of Co-operation* over a decade later, which provoked this curt dismissal: 'All political movement among such animals I call essentially fermentation and putrifaction – not Co-operation'. Cited by J. T. Taylor in *Jubilee Co-operation in Oldham: the jubilee history of the Oldham Industrial Co-operative Society Ltd., 1850–1900* (Manchester 1900), p. 11. Many co-operators warmed to Ruskin's moral critique of industrial capitalism and were fond of quoting his dictum (taken from *Unto the Last*) that 'Government and Co-operation are . . . the Laws of Life. Anarchy and Competition the Laws of Death.' Ruskin's undemocratic prescriptions, however, were either ignored or rejected.
  30 *TNAPPS*, Birmingham, 1868, p. 19. Sir William Armstrong also advised trade unions to invest in co-operative production of the 1870 meeting (p. 80) and looked forward to the creation of 'little capitalists'.
  31 In 1860 Sir James Emmerson Tennent argued that co-operation should stick to supplying its own members and recommended 'caution in the extension of the co-operative principle so far as regards its application to "new" fields of enterprise.' Large-scale factory production should not be contemplated. *TNAPSS*, 1860, p. 148. For similar statements see *TNAPSS*, 1870, p. 498; *TNAPSS*, 1873, p. 516; *TNAPSS*, 1881, p. 679.
  32 *TNAPSS*, 1873, p. 520.
  33 *Ibid.*, p. 516.
  34 William Booth, *In Darkest England and the Way Out* (1890), p. 142. An account of 'The Co-operative Experiment at Ralahine' appeared as an appendix to this work. Booth perversely linked Craig's attempt to establish a 'Community' with his own advocacy of labour colonies! For the Owenite phase see E. T. Craig, *The Irish Land and Labour Question, Illustrated in the History of Ralahine and Co-operative Farming* (Manchester 1882); V. Geoghegan, 'Ralahine: an Irish Owenite community (1831–1833)', *International Review of Social History*, 36, 1991, pp. 377–411.
  35 *Fourth Report of the Royal Commission on Labour, 1893* (Shannon, Co. Clare 1970), vol. 43, p. 19.
  36 *Ibid.*, p. 22. The commission discussed profit-sharing extensively

and included a comprehensive bibliography of the relevant literature in its published report. See pp. 401–6 and 518–32.

37   *Co-operative News*, 11 December 1886, p. 126 for a good example.

38   R. Schatz, 'Co-operative Production and the Ideology of Co-operation in England, 1870–1895' (Unpublished paper, University of Pittsburg 1973), pp. 72–5. Thanks to Dr Neville Kirk for providing me with a copy of this paper. A letter from George Quirk in the *Co-operative News* expressed the dominant attitude succinctly. Quirk wrote that 'our social salvation must be sought not in an indefinite number of co-partnership industries, but in the common ownership of all production by co-operation . . .', best achieved through the Wholesales. 3 January 1903, p. 22.

39   *Labour Co-partnership*, September 1900, p. 158.

40   *Wheatsheaf*, September 1900, p. 45. The paper also noted that the 'noble' Earl had once been the Administrator of Rhodesia and published instructions concerning labour in mines, which proved that he had cunningly exploited black workers!

41   Quoted by Charles Wilson in *The History of Unilever: A Study in Economic Growth and Social Change* (1954), pp. 146–7.

42   W. H. Lever, *Co-partnership, An Address Spoken to the Woolwich Chamber of Commerce* (Port Sunlight 1909), p. 13.

43   *Ibid.*, p. 14.

44   See Corrigan and Sayer, *The Great Arch*, chs. 6 and 7.

45   J. R. Hay, 'Employers' Attitudes to Social Policy and the Concept of Social Control, 1900–1920', in Pat Thane (ed.), *The Origins of British Social Policy* (1978), p. 110.

46   W. H. Lever, *Co-partnership and Efficiency: An address delivered at a meeting convened by the Consultative Council of the Labour Co-partnership Association* (Port Sunlight 1912), p. 11. For more on Lever's attitudes see his *Partnership Scheme: Meeting of Employees of Lever Brothers Limited* (Supplement to *Progress*, April 1909); *Co-partnership: An address to members of the Agricultural and Horticultural Association* (Port Sunlight 1912); *Co-partnership: laying the three ghosts, unemployment, sickness, death* (Port Sunlight 1922).

47   *Plymouth Co-operative Record*, September 1912, p. 210.

48   D. H. MacGregor, *The Evolution of Industry* (1911), pp. 230–31. See also MacGregor's paper to the Bradford Congress in 1910 on 'Co-operation in Relation to the Trust Movement', *Co-operative Congress Report*, 1910, pp. 492–510.

49   Collini, *Liberalism and Sociology* (Cambridge 1979) pp. 29–31.

50   *TNAPSS*, 1862, pp. 803–4. On Mechanics Institutes see E. Royle,

'Mechanics Institutes and the Working Classes', *The Historical Journal*, 12, 1971, pp. 306–21.

51 *TNAPSS*, 1865, pp. 529–30.

52 Henry Solly, *These Eighty Years: Or, the Story of an Unfinished Life* (1893), vol. II, pp. 170–71.

53 The Commissioners represented female agricultural workers as brutalised creatures, sensuous and 'masculine', and believed that Co-operation would help establish 'natural' relations between the sexes. See the 'First Report from the Commissioners of the Employment of Children, Young Persons and Women in Agriculture' 1867. *Parliamentary Papers* (Shannon 1968), vol. 10, pp. 46–50. Thanks to Dr Mandy Morris for pointing me towards Fraser.

54 *Hansard's Parliamentary Debates*, 3rd series, vol. 182, 12 March 1866, 37–8. On the construction of the 'Rochdale Man' see Royden Harrison, *Before the Socialists: Studies in Labour and Politics, 1861–1881* (1965), pp. 113–19; M. E. Rose, 'Rochdale Man and the Stalybridge Riot: Poor Relief during the Lancashire Cotton Famine 1861–5', in A. P. Donajgrodski (ed.), *Social Control in Nineteenth-Century Britain* (1977). For the gendered nature of politics see J. W. Scott, 'Gender: A Useful Category of Historical Analysis', in *Gender and the Politics of History* (New York 1988), pp. 46–50.

55 The evidence suggests that many male co-operators shared this patriarchal vision of co-operation by the late nineteenth century. See, for example, the pamphlet by the Manchester co-operator William Marcroft, *The Inner Circle of Family Life* (Manchester 1886); and Margaret Llewelyn Davies' remarks in *Co-operative News*, 29 June 1907, p. 789.

56 *TNAPSS*, 1872, p. 454. On this theme see Judith Walkowitz, *City of Dreadful Delight: Narratives of Sexual Danger in Late-Victorian London* (1992), pp. 46–50.

57 *TNAPSS*, 1870, p. 80; *ibid.*, p. 499; *TNAPSS*, 1871, p. 571.

58 *Co-operative Congress Report*, 1890, p. 8.

59 G. J. Holyoake, *The Co-operative Movement Today* (1891, 4th edn 1905), p. 74; Edward Jackson, *A Study in Democracy; being an account of the rise and progress of Industrial Co-operation in Bristol* (Bristol 1911), p. 441. For another excellent example see Thomas Redshaw, *Jubilee History of Bishop Auckland Industrial Co-operative Flour and Provision Society Limited from 1860–1910* (Manchester 1910), p. 78.

60 At the Co-operative Congress at Ipswich in 1889. Hines went on to recommend independent political action. *Co-operative Congress Report*, 1889, p. 93.

61 Peter Bailey, *Leisure and Class in Victorian England* (1978), p. 178. See also Bailey's article, '"Will the Real Bill Banks Please Stand Up?" Towards a Role Analysis of Mid-Victorian Working-Class Respectability', *Journal of Social History*, 12, 1978, pp. 336–53.

62 *Co-operative Congress Report*, 1892, p. 125.

63 Presidential address at the society's Annual Tea Party, reported in the *Bolton Co-operative Record*, April 1918, p. 23.

64 *TNAPSS*, 1860, p. 753.

65 *TNAPSS*, 1863, p. 752.

66 *Ibid.*, p. 754.

67 Quoted in Thomas Rigby, *The origin and history of Co-operation in Bury* (Bury 1905), p. 42.

68 Ludlow and Jones, *Progress*, pp. 296–7.

69 *TNAPSS*, 1863, p. 756.

70 *Co-operative Congress Report*, Newcastle-upon-Tyne 1880, p. 5.

71 Gareth Stedman Jones, *Outcast London: A study in the relationship between classes in Victorian society* (Oxford 1971, 1984 edn), p. 290.

72 *TNAPSS*, 1881, p. 683.

73 *Ibid.*, p. 687.

74 *Ibid.*, p. 688.

75 *Co-operative Congress Report*, Oxford 1882, p. 3.

76 *Ibid.*, p. 7. Note also the presidential address given by the Earl of Morley at the Plymouth Congress in 1886, in which he violently attacked socialism and the 'ideal' side of co-operation – defended in the discussion which followed by Mr Rule of the Gateshead Society; *Co-operative Congress Report*, 1886, pp. 6–11.

77 *Co-operative Congress Report*, Glasgow 1890, p. 7.

78 In 1894 Spencer subscribed 2 guineas, following a personal request from Holyoake, to the co-partnership cause: 'I feel bound to aid all efforts to encourage the only type of industrial civilisation which holds out any hope of better things' – he wrote to Holyoake. Quoted in David Duncan, *The Life and Letters of Herbert Spencer* (1908), p. 359. See also Herbert Spencer, *An Autobiography* (1904), vol. II, p. 369; Beatrice Webb's recollections in *My Apprentiship* (1926, Cambridge 1979); Holyoake's eulogy in *Bygones Worth Remembering* (1905), vol. II. Note also Spencer's firm belief in the capitalist principle of authority in *Principles of Sociology* (1882, 1893 edn).

79 *Co-operative Record of the Birmingham District*, 15 March 1896, p. 11.

80 *Co-operative Congress Report*, Plymouth 1886, p. 14.

81 *Ibid.*, 1892, p. 9.

82 See the pamphlet by E. O. Greening and E. V. Neale, *Proposals for an International Alliance of the Friends of Co-operative Production* (1892).

83 Pamphlet by E. O. Greening, *International Co-operation and the Constitution of the International Co-operative Alliance* (1895).

84 *Co-operative Congress Report*, 1901, p. 16. See also my chapter, '"A Higher State of Civilisation and Happiness": Internationalism in the British Co-operative Movement between *c.* 1869–1918', in Frits Van Holthoon and Marcel Van der Linden (eds), *Internationalism in the Labour Movement 1830–1940* (Leiden 1988), pp. 560–64; and Arnold Bonner, *British Co-operation* (1961), pp. 423–9.

85 *Co-operative News*, 6 June, 1914 p. 727.

86 Pierre Bourdieu, *In Other Words*, p. 138.

87 This contradicts the view presented by Paul Johnson in 'Conspicuous Consumption and Working-Class Culture in Late-Victorian and Edwardian Britain', *Transactions of the Royal Historical Society*, 38, 1988, pp. 27–42, who concludes that 'this study of the actions of workers and their families in spending and consuming highlights not the solidarity of workers but the degree of competition within their ranks.' The evidence on which this view is based is thin, and Johnson perversely ignores the Co-operative movement entirely. He also employs Veblen's reading of consumption as a form of 'social emulation' in a simplistic, uncritical manner. For an acute summary of the problems with Veblen's analysis see Colin Campbell, *The Romantic Ethic and the Spirit of Modern Consumerism* (Oxford 1987), pp. 49–57.

Chapter seven: Socialists, co-operators and the state

1 The socialists split from the Co-operative Union in France in 1895 but rejoined in 1912. Detailed accounts can be found in Jean Gaumont, *Histoire Générale de la Co-operation en France: les idées et les faits, les hommes et les oeuvres* (Paris 1924); Ellen Furlough, *Consumer Co-operation in France: The Politics of Consumption, 1834–1930* (Ithaca, NY 1991).

2 Karl Marx, *Inaugural Address of the Working Men's International Association* (1864) in Karl Marx and Frederick Engels, *Articles on Britain* (Moscow 1971), p. 343–4.

3 For this debate see R. C. N. Thornes, 'The Early Development of the Co-operative Movement in West Yorkshire, 1827–63' (Unpublished DPhil thesis, University of Sussex, 1984), pp. 255–68.

4   Bill Lancaster, *Radicalism, Co-operation and Socialism: Leicester working-class politics, 1860–1906* (Leicester 1987), pp. 134–49. In *The Evolution of the Labour Party 1910–24* (Oxford 1974), pp. 44–7, Ross McKibbin notes the friendly relations which existed between Labour Representaion Committees and co-operative societies in Clitheroe and Plymouth as well as Leicester, but also stresses, quite rightly, the 'fragmented' nature of working-class consciousness before the First World War.

5   The literature on this subject is voluminous but major works include Henry Pelling, *The Origins of the Labour Party 1880–1900* (Oxford 1965); Peter Clarke, *Lancashire and the New Liberalism* (Cambridge 1971); McKibbin *Evolution of the Labour Party*; David Howell, *British Workers and the Independent Labour Party 1888–1906* (Manchester 1982): Keith Laybourn and Jack Reynolds, *Liberalism and the Rise of Labour 1890–1918* (1984). Only McKibbin pays any attention to the Co-operative movement.

6   The best treatment of this theme is by Bertell Ollman, in *Alienation, Marx's Critique of Man in Capitalist Society* (Cambridge 1971). Various scholars have stressed Marx's productivist bias including Marshall Berman, *All That is Solid Melts Into Air* (1982), pp. 126–7; Raymond Williams, *Towards 2000* (1983), pp. 264–6. It was also emphasised by the French co-operator, Ernest Poisson, who called for 'a political economy of consumption . . . as opposed to a political economy of production' in his influential text, *The Co-operative Republic* (Paris 1920; translated by W. P. Watkins, Manchester 1925), p. 70.

7   Karl Marx, *Capital: A Critique of Political Economy*, vol. I (1867, Penguin 1976), p. 717. In his unpublished working notes Marx acknowledged that production and consumption were two sides of an indissoluble social process, a view which was suppressed from the published text. See *Grundrisse: Foundations of the Critique of Political Economy* (New York 1973), p. 93.

8   *Co-operative Congress Report*, 1894, p. 795.

9   Noel Thompson, *The Peoples' Science* (Cambridge 1984), pp. 89, 110, 135. See also Gregory Claeys, *Machinery, Money and the Millenium: From Moral Economy to Socialism, 1815–1960* (Princeton, NJ 1987), pp. 94–8; and Claeys, *Citizens and saints: Politics and anti-politics in early British socialism* (Cambridge 1989), pp. 148–50, 159–61.

10   *Justice*, 27 August 1898, p. 4.

11   *Clarion*, 11 June 1898, p. 187.

12   *Justice*, 7 June 1890, p. 1. See also *Clarion*, 22 September 1900, p. 302; *Labour Leader*, 31 January 1908, p. 6.

13 G. D. H. Cole, *A Century of Co-operation* (Manchester 1945), pp. 336–8, 339–4.

14 William Paine, *Shop Slavery and Emancipation: A Revolutionary Appeal to the Educated Young Men of the Middle Class* (1912), p. 50. Similar criticisms were made by Teresa Billington Greig in *The Consumer in Revolt* (1912), pp. 82–4. Pressure from the AUCE during the First World War improved pay and conditions. See the ILP report, *The Co-operative Movement and Socialism* (1928), pp. 29–30.

15 *Co-operative News*, 19 June 1886, p. 581.

16 *Ibid.*, 11 December 1886, pp. 1214–16; 12 March 1887, pp. 245–7.

17 Percy Redfern, *The Story of the C.W.S.* (Manchester 1913), pp. 172–4 and *passim* ; Lancaster, *Radicalism*, pp. 140–41 and 145.

18 Ben Jones, *Co-operative Production* (Oxford 1894), pp. 747.

19 *Justice*, 28 April 1888, p. 4; 23 June 1888, p. 7; 27 August 1892, p. 2.

20 *Ibid.*, 19 Sept. 1891, p. 4; 21 November 1896, p. 1; 24 April 1897, p. 3; 1 February 1913 p. 1; *Labour Leader*, 1 October 1898, p. 325.

21 Laybourn and Reynolds, *Liberalism and the Rise of Labour*, pp. 41–2. On the role of conflict see also Alun Howkins, 'Edwardian Liberalism and Industrial Unrest: A Class View of the Decline of Liberalism', *History Workshop Journal*, 4, 1977, pp. 143–61.

22 Gareth Stedman Jones, 'Utopian Socialism Reconsidered', in Raphael Samuel (ed.), *People's History and Socialist Theory* (1981) p. 141.

23 *Co-operative Congress Report*, 1899, p. 151.

24 See the excellent discussion in Gareth Stedman Jones, *Outcast London: A Study in the Relationship Between Classes in Victorian Society* (Oxford 1971; 1984 edn), pp. 344–5.

25 *Justice*, 27 October 1894, p. 5; 1 May 1897, p. 3.

26 *Ibid.*, 20 September 1884, p. 4; 10 December 1887, p. 2.

27 *Ibid.*, 1 January 1898, p. 6.

28 *Co-operative News*, 12 November 1910, p. 1470.

29 *Ibid.*, 23 March 1912, p. 362; 30 March 1912, p. 384.

30 *Wheatsheaf*, May 1912, pp. 161–2; June 1912, p. 177. For a summary of co-operative support see the pamphlet by F. M. Eddie, *Co-operation and Labour Uprisings* (Manchester 1912).

31 *Millgate Monthly*, August 1911, p. 679.

32 *Ibid.*, September 1911, pp. 744–6. The editor was soon advocating nationalisation of the railways, October 1911, p. 7; and the mines, April 1912, p. 462.

33 *Ibid.*, July 1912, p. 598. The journal reported the Dublin strike

sympathetically in 1913, criticised the increasing internationalisation of capital and declared that there 'is a war between labour and capital.' November 1913, pp. 66–7.

34 *Ibid.*, October 1913, pp. 1–4. The children's magazine *Our Circle* consistently supported the unions during the labour unrest of this period and also set up a relief fund.

35 'Co-operation and Socialism', from *Subjects of the Day*, August 1890, p. 101. For a discussion of Holyoake's anti-statism see my contribution, 'George Jacob Holyoake: Socialism, Association and Co-operation in Nineteenth Century England', in Stephen Yeo (ed.), *New Views of Co-operation* (1988) pp. 62–3.

36 See the pamphlet, *Co-operation v. Socialism: Being a Report of a Debate between Mr H. H. Champion and Mr Ben. Jones* (Manchester 1887), pp. 7, 11, 16, 22.

37 Pamphlet by Harry Quelch and William Simpson, *State Socialism: Is it Just and Reasonable? (Report of a debate . . . at the Corporation Hall, Burnley 1893, reprinted from the 'Burnley Gazette')* (1893), p. 19.

38 For Reading see Stephen Yeo, *Religion and Voluntary Organisations in Crisis* (1976), pp. 274–5.

39 See Ian Bullock, 'Socialists and Democratic Form in Britain 1880–1914: Positions, Debates and Conflicts', (Unpublished DPhil thesis, Sussex University 1981), p. 157.

40 Pat Thane, 'The Working Class and State "Welfare" in Britain, 1880–1914', *The Historical Journal*, 4, 1984, pp. 282–3.

41 Beatrice Webb, *My Apprenticeship* (1926, Cambridge 1979), pp. 355–87; for a dissection of their views see Derek C. Jones, 'British Producer Co-operatives', in Ken Coates (ed.), *The New Worker Co-operatives* (Nottingham 1976), pp. 34–68.

42 Harry Snell, *Socialism and Co-operation: their fundamental unity: an appeal to co-operators* (Huddersfield 1908), p. 9. See also Snell's autobiography, *Men, Movements and Myself* (1936).

43 Neal Blewitt, 'The Franchise in the United Kingdom, 1885–1914', *Past and Present*, 32, 1965, pp. 27–56.

44 Snell, *Socialism and Co-operation*, p. 10. For analyses of Fabianism and the state see A. M. McBriar, *Fabian Socialism and English Politics 1884–1918* (Cambridge 1966), pp. 72–5; Stephen Yeo, 'Notes on Three Socialisms, Mainly in Late-nineteenth and Early-twentieth-century Britain', in Carl Levy (ed.), *Socialism and the Intelligensia* (1987), pp. 245–6.

45 Reported in the *Co-operative News*, 29 April 1905, p. 493.

46 See Bernard Barker (ed.), *Ramsay MacDonald's Political Writings*

(1972), pp. 17–20.

47 Ramsay MacDonald, *Socialism and Society* (1905), in Barker, p. 86. Fifteen years later, in *Parliament and Democracy*, MacDonald went further and declared that 'in the end the Co-operative movement would become what it was intended to be – a function in the industrial State . . . .' See Barker, *MacDonald's Political Writings*, p. 256.

48 Keir Hardie, *From Serfdom to Socialism* (1907), pp. 6–7.

49 *Ibid.*, p. 96. The best recent biography of Hardie, K. O. Morgan's *Keir Hardie: Radical and Socialist* (1975), does not discuss Hardie's attitude to either the Co-operative movement or the state.

50 Carl Levy, 'Education and Self-education: Staffing the Early ILP', in Levy, *Socialism and the Intelligentsia* (1987), pp. 190–91.

51 *Co-operative Record of the Birmingham District*, April 1895, p. 16.

52 Tom Mann, 'Trades Unionism and Co-operation', in Edward Carpenter (ed.), *Forecasts of the Coming Century* (Manchester 1897), p. 40.

53 Quoted in Chushichi Tsuzuki, *Tom Mann, 1856–1941. The Challenges of Labour* (Oxford 1991), p. 193.

54 Patrick Joyce, *Visions of the People: Industrial England and the Question of Class* (Cambridge 1991), p. 79. A useful overview of these themes can be found in Geoffrey Foote, *The Labour Party's Political Thought: A History* (1985).

55 See R. D. Sutton, 'Co-operation and the Poor, 1890–1908' (MA thesis, University of York 1985).

56 *Manchester and Salford Co-operative Herald*, October 1902, p. 155.

57 *Co-operative Congress Report*, 1899, p. 10. For the general lack of working-class enthusiasm for social reform see Pat Thane, 'Working Class and state "Welfare"'; Henry Pelling, 'The Working Class and the Welfare State', in *Popular Politics and Society in Late-Victorian England* (1968).

58 *Co-operative News*, 7 January 1911, p. 14; 24 June 1911, pp. 809–10; *Wheatsheaf*, August 1912, p. 22; November 1912, p. 66.

59 *Millgate Monthly*, August 1912, p. 664; September, 1912 pp. 721–3. For the threat to friendly societies see Stephen Yeo, 'Working-class Association, Private Capital and the State', in N. Parry, M. Rustin and C. Satyamurti (eds), *Social Work, Welfare and the State* (1979).

60 *Millgate Monthly*, Feburary, 1914 p. 280.

61 Nicos Poulantzas, *Political Power and Social Classes* (1973).

62 *Co-operative Congress Report*, 1911, pp. 23–4.

63 See especially Philip Corrigan and Derek Sayer, *The Great Arch: English State Formation as Cultural Revolution* (1985), p. 179; Stuart Hall and Bill Schwarz, 'State and Society, 1880–1930', in Mary Langan and Bill Schwarz (eds), *Crises In The British State 1880–1930* (1985), pp. 7–32.

64   Stefan Collini, *Liberalism and Sociology: L. T. Hobhouse and Political Argument in England 1880–1914* (Cambridge 1979), p. 15.

65   McBriar, *Fabian Socialism*, pp. 98–118, *passim*.

66   Stephen Yeo, 'A New Life: The Religion of Socialism in Britain, 1883–1896', *History Workshop Journal*, 4, 1977, pp. 5–56.

67   Thomas Kirkup, *A History of Socialism* (1887, 1906 edn), p. 335. In the 1913 edition, which was largely rewritten by Edward Pease, secretary and early historian of the Fabian Society, this passage was cut and replaced by a statement of support for consumer co-operation and an attack on producer co-ops which were 'not in accordance with the principles of socialism'. A review of Kirkup's original in the *Co-operative News* pointed out that his views were very close to those of co-operators. See 28 January 1888, pp. 84–5.

68   Quoted in the anonymous pamphlet, *Is Co-operation Beneficial to the Community?* (Manchester 1886).

69   Samuel and Henrietta Barnett, *Practicable Socialism* (1888); Charles Booth, *Life and Labour of the People of London* vol. 1, (1889). See also Gareth Stedman Jones's useful discussion in *Outcast London*, p. 308.

70   *Leeds Co-operative Record*, January 1892; W. T. Carter, *Co-operation is Reasonable Socialism* (Manchester 1894); *Labour Co-partnership*, June 1895; *Reynold's News*, 13 June 1897; *Comradeship*, February 1906; *Leeds Co-operative Record*, February 1907; *Millgate Monthly*, March 1908.

71   *Co-operative News*, 24 October 1903, p. 1298.

72   See Eric Bristow, 'Profit-sharing, Socialism and the Labour Unrest', in K. D. Brown (ed.), *Essays in Anti-Labour History* (1974), p. 271; G. J. Holyoake, *The History of Co-operation* (1906 edn), p. 666.

73   Joyce, *Visions*, p. 79.

74   For the Tariff Reform League see the interesting analysis by Bill Schwarz, 'Conservatism and "caesarism", 1903–22', in Langan and Schwarz, pp. 33–62; Quelch's comment is from *Justice*, 10 April 1909, p. 6.

75   Ross McKibbin, *The Ideologies of Class: Social Relations in Britain, 1880–1950* (Oxford 1990), pp. 31–2.

76   *Co-operative News*, 12 December 1908, p. 1508.

77   Joseph Baldwin and John Bennett, *City of Bradford Co-operative Society Limited, Jubilee History, 1860–1910* (Bradford 1911), pp. 224–5.

78   Redfern's article was 'The Conflict of Capitalism and Democracy', in *C.W.S. Annual, 1910*..

79 Redfern, 'The Story of the C.W.S.'. p. 187.

80 *Ibid.*, p. 313.

81 Sidney Pollard stressed the gradual nature of this shift in his seminal essay on 'The foundation of the Co-operative Party', in Asa Briggs and John Saville (eds), *Essays in Labour History 1886–1923* (1971). Tony Adams in 'The Formation of the Co-operative Party Reconsidered', *International Review of Social History*, I, 1987, has argued for the catalytic effects of the First World War. Not surprisingly, both views contain some truth.

82 *Justice*, 3 November 1894, p. 3.

83 *Clarion*, 11 June 1898, p. 187; *Labour Leader*, 4 June 1898, p. 189; 28 April 1900, p. 132.

84 *Justice*, 8 June 1901, p. 1; 3 June 1905, p. 1; *Wheatsheaf*, March 1906, p. 129. For a narrative of these debates see G. D. H. Cole, *A Century of Co-operation* (Manchester 1945), pp. 310–18. Only one society (Tunbridge Wells!) affiliated to the Labour Party before 1914.

85 *Justice*, 10 May 1913, p. 7. Maclean was a member of the Pollokshaws Society and, according to his biographer, was 'devoted in his attendance at the quarterly meetings.' See Nan Milton, *John Maclean* (1973), p. 64.

86 *Justice*, 19 April 1913, p. 1.

87 Reported in the *Chorley Co-operative Record*, May 1914, p. 15.

Chapter eight: The politics of working-class consumption

1 W. D. Rubinstein, 'Wealth, Elites and the Class Structure of Modern Britain', *Past and Present*, 76, 1977, p. 102; J.B.Jefferys, *Retail Trading in Britain 1850–1950* (Cambridge 1954), p. 25; W. H. Fraser, *The Coming of the Mass Market, 1850–1914* (1981); M. J. Winstanley, *The Shopkeeper's World 1830–1914* (Manchester 1983). Note Harold Perkin's incisive criticism and reworking of Rubinstein's data in *The Rise of Professional Society* (1989), pp. 257–8.

2 Michel Aglietta develops this concept in *A Theory of Capitalist Regulation: The US Experience* (1979) p. 151, but as I noted in the Introduction his functionalist approach leads him to ignore conflict.

3 E. P. Thompson, *The Making of the English Working Class* (1963), p. 803.

4 At a quarterly meeting of the CWS reported in the *Co-operative News*, 11 December 1880, p. 809.

5 See Marshal Berman, *All That Is Solid Melts Into Air: The Experi-*

ence of Modernity (1983), p. 238.

6   Pamphlet by James Cheyne, *Co-operative Advertising* (Glasgow 1903), p. 11.

7   Thomas Armstrong, 'Advertising and the Co-operative Movement', *C.W.S. Annual* (Manchester 1916), pp. 479–510; H. W. Atkins, *Advertising for Co-operative Societies* (Leicester 1933); Percy Redfern, *The New History of the C.W.S.* (Manchester 1937) pp. 429–30; *Co-operative Congress Report*, 1920, p. 510. See also *Co-operative Congress Report*, 1923 p. 368.

8   For the 'consumer' as stomach see Raymond Williams, *The Long Revolution* (1961; Pelican 1965), p. 322.

9   Thomas Richards, *The Commodity Culture of Victorian England: Advertising and Spectacle, 1851–1914* (1991).

10   Charles Wilson, *The History of Unilever: A Study in Economic Growth and Social Change* (1954), pp. 21, 43. Some modern social historians have grossly underestimated the importance of advertising, especially James Obelkevich in an unpublished paper to the Social History Society Conference, January 1993 and John Benson in *The Rise of Consumer Society* (1994), p. 78.

11   Peter Mathias, *Retailing Revolution: A History of Multiple Retailing in the Food Trades* (1967), pp. 41, 100, 108, 112.

12   Thomas Lipton, *Leaves From The Lipton Log* (1931), pp. 121, 216–21; Mathias, *Retailing Revolution*, pp. 107, 115.

13   Dana Frank, '"Food Wins All Struggles": Seattle Labor and the Politicization of Consumption', *Radical History Review*, 51, 1991; Ellen Furlough, *The Politics of Consumption: The Consumer Co-operative Movement in France, 1834–1930* (Ithaca, NY 1992). See also Martin Pugh, 'Women, Food and Politics, 1880–1930', *History Today*, 41, March 1991, pp. 14–20.

14   Geoffrey Crossick, 'Shopkeepers and the State in Britain, 1870–1914', in G. Crossick and G. Haupt (eds), *Shopkeepers and Master Artisans in Nineteenth Century Europe* (1980). See also Winstanley, *Shopkeeper's World*, pp. 83–88.

15   Percy Redfern, *The Story of the C.W.S.* (Manchester 1913), pp. 42–4.

16   *The Scottish Co-operator*, 34 February 1896, cited by Leonard Campbell, 'Retail Co-operation in the Greater Glasgow Area *c.* 1860–1914' (Unpublished PhD thesis, University of Strathclyde 1983) p. 351.

17   James Deans, 'The Private Traders' Anti-Co-operative Movement',

C.W.S. Annual (Manchester 1899), p. 295. For a detailed account see J. Kinloch and J. Butt, *History of the Scottish Co-operative Wholesale Society Limited* (Glasgow 1981), ch. 11; Campbell, 'Retail Co-operation' (thesis), pp. 347–53.

18 See G. D. H. Cole, *A Century of Co-operation* (Manchester 1945), p. 122.

19 *Co-operative Congress Report*, 1903, pp. 105–8.

20 C. L. Laker, 'Co-operative Stores and Private Traders in Preston 1870–1906' (MA thesis, University of Lancaster 1981), pp. 27–8.

21 *Preston Argus*, 26 May 1905, cited by Laker, 'Co-operative Stores' (thesis), pp. 36–7.

22 *Co-operative Congress Report*, 1906, p. 126.

23 *Ibid.*, p. 336.

24 David S. Landes, *The Unbound Prometheus: Technological Change and Industrial Development in Western Europe from 1750 to the Present* (Cambridge 1969), p. 247.

25 Leslie Hannah, *The Rise of the Corporate Economy* (1976), p. 23.

26 Bill Schwarz, 'The Corporate Economy, 1890–1929', in M. Langan and B. Schwarz (eds), *Crises in the British State, 1880–1930* (1985), p. 80.

27 *C.W.S. Annual* (Manchester 1890), pp. 210–11.

28 *Wheatsheaf*, July 1901, p. 11.

29 *Co-operative Congress Report*, 1903, pp. 176, 345–6. See also Teresa Billington Greig, *The Consumer in Revolt* (1912), pp. 42–3.

30 Wilson, *History of Unilever*, chapter 8.

31 *Justice*, 30 March 1889, p. 1. See also *ibid.*, 15 November 1902, p. 4; and the pamphlet by Harry Quelch and William Simpson, *State Socialism: Is it Just and Reasonable?* (Burnley 1893), p. 18.

32 For Maclean's criticisms see his pamphlet *Co-operation and the Rise in Prices* (Glasgow 1912).

33 See the review in *Justice*, 10 July 1909, p. 5.

34 Philip Snowden, *Socialism and Syndicalism* (1913), pp. 106–7.

35 Landes, *Unbound Prometheus*, pp. 248.

36 Percy Redfern, *The Story*, pp. 241–3.

37 Quoted in W. H. Oliver (ed.), *Jubilee History of the Coventry Perseverance Society* (Coventry 1917), pp. 244–5.

38 For details see Wilson, *History of Unilever*, pp. 21–55.

39 See Jackson Lears' essay, 'From Salvation to Self-Realization. Advertising and the Therapeutic Roots of the Consumer Culture, 1880–1930' in R. Wightman Fox and T. J. Jackson Lears (eds), *The Culture of Consumption: Critical Essays in American History, 1880–1980* (New York

1983).

40 *Co-operative News*, 6 January 1906, p. 15. There is a 'whiggish', over-optimistic treatment of adulteration in John Burnett, *Plenty and Want: A social history of diet in England from 1815 to the present day* (1966; 1968 edn), pp. 240–67.

41 *Co-operative News*, 14 April 1906, pp. 416–17. See also the sympathetic reviews of Sinclair's work in *Justice*, 9 June 1906, p. 1; *Clarion*, 15 June 1906, p. 5.

42 See Peter Clarke, *Lancashire and the New Liberalism* (Cambridge 1971), pp. 222–3; Wilson, History of Unilever, p. 148.

43 Redfern, *The Story*, pp. 245–251.

44 *Co-operative News*, 9 March 1912, p. 279.

45 *Co-operative Congress Report*, 1903, p. 347.

46 Wilson, *History of Unilever*, p. 168.

47 *Co-operative News*, 27 June 1914, p. 835. See also 27 August 1910, pp. 1118–19.

48 See S. J. Hurwitz, *State Intervention in Great Britain: A Study of Economic Control and Social Response 1914–1919* (1949).

49 Cole, *A Century*, p. 265.

50 *Ibid.*, p. 371; Jefferys, *Retail Trading*, p. 58.

51 *Co-operative News*, 3 July 1915, p. 906.

52 *Millgate Monthly*, July 1915, p. 586.

53 *Plymouth Co-operative Record*, July 1916 p. 228. For Greening see *Millgate Monthly*, August 1916 pp. 706–8

54 *Co-operative News*, 5 August 1916, p. 815. The notion of a 'Servile State' derived of course from Hilaire Belloc's *Servile State* (1912), a popular work in co-operative circles. T. W. Mercer wrote extensively on the limitations of statist social reform at this time. See *Plymouth Co-operative Record*, February 1916, p. 48; December 1916, p. 404.

55 *Bolton Co-operative Record*, October 1915, p. 7.

56 *Plymouth Co-operative Record*, April 1916, p. 119.

57 *Ibid.*, August 1916, p. 268.

58 *See Co-operative Congress Report*, 1917.

59 Cole, *A Century*, p. 267.

60 Sidney Pollard, 'The Foundation of the Co-operative Party', in Asa Briggs and John Saville (eds), *Essays in Labour History 1886–1923* (1971); Tony Adams, 'The Formation of the Co-operative Party Reconsidered', *International Review of Social History*, 1987, I, pp. 48–68. As noted in the last chapter (n.81), in accounting for this shift Adams places greater emphasis on the impact of the war.

61 L. Margaret Barnett, *British Food Policy During the First World War* (1985). Two older works remain useful: W. H. Beveridge, *British Food Control* (1928) and F. H. Coller, *A State Trading Adventure* (1925).

62 See *Bolton Co-operative Record*, February 1917, p. 1. Some 860 delegates attended, representing trade unions, Labour Party branches, Trades Councils and the Women's Co-operative Guild.

63 *Co-operative News*, 28 April 1917, p. 401. Devonport was a successful wholesaler, hardly an unbiased choice!

64 *Ibid.*, 10 June 1917, p. 583.

65 *Ibid.*, 11 August, 1917, pp. 759, 763; 25 August, 1917 pp. 797, 805; 1 September, p. 817.

66 Quoted in Barnett, *British Food Policy*, p. 130.

67 *Co-operative News*, 1 September, 1917 pp. 822–3.

68 Bernard Waites, *A Class Society at War: England 1914–18* (Leamington Spa 1987), p. 222. See also Barnett, *British Food Policy*, pp. 124–3.

69 *Co-operative News*, 22 September 1917, p. 900; Mr Bradley in the *Bolton Co-operative Record*, November, 1917 pp. 14–15.

70 *Co-operative News*, 8 September, 1917 p. 842.

71 *Ibid.*, 20 October 1917, p. 984.

72 See Percy Redfern, *New History*, p. 153, *passim*.

73 *Co-operative News*, 10 November 1917, p. 1060.

74 See Patrick Maguire, 'Co-operation and Crisis: Government, Co-operation and Politics 1917–22', in Stephen Yeo (ed.), *New Views of Co-operation* (1988), p. 194. The dialogue between British and Russian co-operators, noted in chapter four above, no doubt heightened fears at this time.

75 Barnett, *British Food Policy*, p. 142.

76 *Ibid.*, p. 144; Waites, *A Class Society*, pp. 230–31.

77 Waites, *A Class Society*, pp. 229–30.

78 *Co-operative News*, 7 February 1925, p. 10.

79 *Ibid.*, 19 January 1918, p. 51.

80 Cited by Redfern, *New History*, p. 162. According to Redfern at least 27 CWS officials participated in food and other controls. William Dudley was knighted in 1926.

81 *Manchester and Salford Co-operative Herald*, April 1919, p. 40.

82 Interviewed by author, Roe Green, Manchester, April 1986.

83 R. H. Tawney, 'The Dismantling of Controls after 1918', *Economic History Review*, 1943. See also Philip Abrams, 'The Failure of Social Reform after the First World War', *Past and Present*, 1963.

84 *Report of Committee on Trusts* [Cd.9236] 1919, pp. 11–14. A

précis of the report appeared in the *People's Year Book* (Manchester 1920), pp. 232–38.

85   *Co-operative News*, 27 August 1910, p. 118; 24 February 1912, p. 219.

86   Mathias, *Retailing Revolution*, pp. 118–20.

87   See Neil Killingback, 'Limits to Mutuality: Economic and Political Attacks on Co-operation during the 1920s and 1930s', in S. Yeo (ed.), *New Views*, p. 214; Redfern, *New History*, p. 241.

88   Excellent examples can be found in *Manchester and Salford Co-operative Herald*, April 1920, p. 67; January 1923, p. 8.

89   *Co-operative Congress Report*, 1923, p. 90.

90   *Co-operative Congress Report*, 1920, pp. 509–10.

91   *Co-operative Congress Report*, 1930 p. 447; Jefferys, *Retail Trading*, pp. 53–4; B. S. Yamey (ed.), *Resale Price Maintenance* (1966).

92   C. L. Mowat, *Britain Between the Wars* (1956), p. 121. See also James Hinton, *The First Shop Stewards' Movement* (1973).

93   Quoted by Chris Wrigley, *Lloyd George and the Challenge of Labour* (1990), p. 160. Lloyd George also recommended the seizure of motor lorries belonging to co-operative societies to ensure that miners would not be fed.

94   Quoted by Maguire in 'Co-operation in Crisis', p. 199.

95   Patrick Gallagher, *My Story by Paddy the Cope* (1939), pp. 212–13, 217–19.

96   *Co-operative Congress Report*, 1921, pp. 437–52.

97   *Western Mail*, 15 April 1921, p. 5; 26 April 1921, p. 5.

98   *Co-operative Congress Report*, 1926, pp. 51–2; J. Stevens, 'The Coalmining Lockout of 1926, with particular reference to the Co-operative Movement and the Poor Law' (Unpublished PhD thesis, Sheffield University 1984), p. 208.

99   Cole, *A Century*, p. 321; T. P. Carbery, *Consumers in Politics* (Manchester 1969).

100   *Co-operative Congress Report*, 1923, p. 370.

101   Alf Barnes, 'The Co-operator in Politics', in Leonard Woolf (ed.), *Fabian essays on Co-operation* (1923), p. 6. Barnes went on to document exhaustively the commercial and professional interests of MPs.

102   *Times*, 16 October 1924, p. 8; 21 October 1924, p. 10.

103   *Ibid.*, 5 December 1924, p. 8. For the patriotic dimension see Hugh Cunningham, 'The Conservative Party and patriotism', in Robert Colls and Philip Dodd (eds), *Englishness: Politics and Culture 1880–1920* (1986), pp. 283–307. See also Baldwin's speech at another victory gala the

following summer (the Conservatives celebrated for a long time – such was the relief), in which he admited that food had been a vital issue in the election and stated that a Food Council was necessary to assure the long-term defeat of socialism, 'because these evil doctrines are really begotten of a sense of social injustice out of ignorance, and it is our duty to expel both.' Reported in *The Times*, 2 June 1925, p. 17.

104 Ross McKibbin, 'Class and Conventional Wisdom: The Conservative Party and the "Public" in Inter-war Britain', in his book, *The Ideologies of Class: Social Relations in Britain, 1880–1950* (Oxford 1990), pp. 259–93.

105 *First Report of the Royal Commission on Food Prices*, [Cmd.2390], vol. II, Minutes of Evidence 1925, p. 182.

106 *Ibid.*, pp. 188–90. Alexander launched a damning attack on trusts in a pamphlet published in February entitled *Is Co-operation a Social Menace?* (Manchester 1925), pp. 16–17.

107 *Royal Commission on Food Prices*, p. 220.

108 As a gesture to the female consumer the commission took evidence from two working-class women from north London who both testified to the increased cost of food since before the war. Mrs Wilson delivered an anti-co-operative tirade and was later rewarded with a place on the Food Council. See *ibid.*, pp. 337–42.

109 *Clarion*, 30 January 1925, p. 7. In an editorial a few weeks later A. M. Thompson stated: 'There is the control of national finance . . . There is the control of the mines . . . But the Food problem comes first.' 13 February 1925, p. 6. See also *Co-operative News*, 24 January 1924, p. 8.

110 *Hansard's Parliamentary Debates*, 4 March 1925, 553.

111 *Ibid.*, 579–95. See also the report in *The Times*, 5 March 1925, p. 8.

112 *Times*, 2 March 1925, p. 16.

113 *Co-operative News*, 7 February 1925, p. 5. Hugh Dalton and James Maxton were also arguing that the state would take over co-operative concerns, a view criticised in *ibid.*, 18 April 1925, p. 1.

114 *Clarion*, 13 February 1925, pp. 1,7. For friction between local Co-operative and Labour Parties see Ross McKibbin, *The Evolution of the Labour Party 1910–1924* (Oxford 1974), pp. 178–91; Chris Shelley, 'Birmingham Co-operative Party in the 1930s: Co-operation and Labour Movement Politics' (MA thesis, University of Warwick 1987).

115 *First Report of the Royal Commission on Food Prices*, vol. I, 1925 p. 2.

116 *Ibid.*, p. 175–6. As Smith pointed out, Vesty's company routinely

practiced forestalling and hoarded meat until consumer demand peaked.

117 *Times*, 11 May 1925, p. 7; 12 May 1925, p. 16.

118 *Co-operative News*, 16 May 1925, p. 10; 30 May 1925, p. 8; *Hansard*, 17 February 1925, 878–82; *Co-operative Congress Report*, 1926, pp. 90, 440.

119 *Times*, 29 July 1925, p. 11. Out of twelve members only one right-wing trade unionist and one co-operator were included (F. W. Birchenough of the Oldham Cotton Spinners and W. E. Dudley of CWS); the rest were civil servants and businessmen apart from the anti-co-operative housewife, Mrs Wilson.

Chapter nine: The experience of defeat

1 *Co-operative Congress Report*, 1926, p. 409.

2 For a good example see *Bolton Co-operative Record*, May 1925, p. 15. This alarmism was partially justified as the Communist official J. T. Murphy admitted in the *Co-operative News*, 3 January 1925, p. 3. See also the editorial the following week entitled 'Hands Off Our Movement!', p. 8.

3 *Co-operative News*, 28 March 1925, pp. 8, 10; 4 April, pp. 4–5, 8; 11 April, p. 8; *Bolton Co-operative Record*, April 1925, pp. 11–15.

4 *Co-operative Congress Report*, 1926, p. 446.

5 See J. Stevens, 'The Coalmining Lockout of 1926, with particular reference to the Co-operative Movement and the Poor Law' (Unpublished PhD, University of Sheffield 1984), p. 139. On the question of permits see R. W. Postgate, E. Wilkinson and J. F. Horrabin, *A Workers' History of the Great Strike* (1927), pp. 35–6.

6 *Derby Co-operative Record*, June 1926, p. 2. For the experience of another local society which was adversely affected see *Bolton Co-operative Record*, July 1926, pp. 1–2.

7 *Co-operative Congress Report*, 1927, pp. 51–2.

8 *Ibid.*, pp. 53–5.

9 *Co-operative Congress Report*, 1928, p. 427.

10 *Co-operative Congress Report*, 1929, pp. 437–8.

11 Percy Redfern, *The New History of the C.W.S.* (Manchester 1938), pp. 359–60, 392–3 and 396–7.

12 Fred Longden, *Co-operative Politics inside Capitalist Society* (Birmingham 1941), pp. 136–7. This book was a scathing critique of the study written by A. M. Carr-Saunders et al., *Consumers' Co-operation in Great Britain* (1938), which largely ignored the hostile political context within which co-operation operated.

13 *Co-operative Congress Report*, 1932, p. 39.

14 As Fred Hayward pointed out at the Annual Conference of the Co-operative Party in 1930 in a speech which later appeared as a pamphlet entitled *The Co-operative Boycott* (Manchester 1930).

15 See Neil Killingback, 'Limits to Mutuality: Economic and Political Attacks on Co-operation during the 1920s and 1930s' in Stephen Yeo (ed.), *New Views of Co-operation* (1988), pp. 207–28. The legislation introduced in the 1933 Budget was a compromise. Co-op societies did not have to pay tax on 'divi' but were liable to an increased burden under Schedules C and D of the Income Tax which meant that reserves were taxed Sums involved were not inconsiderable but neither were they crippling.

16 William Mellor, 'The Co-operative Movement and the Fight For Socialism', in G. D. H. Cole et al., *Problems of the Socialist Transition* (1934) p. 141.

17 Percy Redfern, *Co-operation For All* (Manchester 1914), p. 118.

18 Pamphlet by J. Deans, *The Amalgamation of Societies as a Means of Consolidating the Co-operative Movement* (Glasgow 1903), p. 9.

19 *Co-operative Independent Commission Report* (Manchester 1958), p. 3.

20 See, for example, *Co-operative Congress Report*, 1929, p. 48; J. A. Hough, *Co-operative Retailing, 1914–1945: A Statistical Analysis of the Development of Retailing in the British Co-operative Movement* (1949), p. 97.

21 G. D. H. Cole, *A Century of Co-operation* (Manchester 1945), pp. 371–2.

22 Gill Scott, '"The Working Class Women's Most Active and Democratic Movement": the Women's Co-operative Guild, 1883–1950' (Unpublished DPhil thesis, University of Sussex 1988), pp. 220–30 and 326–7.

23 M. B. Miller, *The Bon Marché: Bourgeois Culture and the Department Store, 1869–1920* (1981).

24 See R. H. Williams, *Dream Worlds: Mass-Consumption in Late 19th Century France* (1982); Susan Buck-Morss, *The Dialectics of Seeing: Walter Benjamin and the Arcades Project* (1989).

25 Asa Briggs, *Friends of the People: The Centenary History of Lewis's* (1956), pp. 37–8, 122.

26 *Ibid.*, pp. 46–59.

27 *Ibid.*, pp. 157–8. The opportunities opened-up by the department store are discussed in the stimulating article by W. R. Leach, 'Transformations in a Culture of Consumption: Women and Department Stores, 1890–1925', *The Journal of American History*, vol. 71, 2, 1984.

28   Mass-Observation Archive, Worktown Collection, Box 32D, MS entitled 'The Co-operative Movement in Worktown', p. 4.

29   See C. L. Mowat, *Britain Between the Wars* (1956), pp. 451–5; John Stevenson and Chris Cook, *The Slump: Society and Politics during the Depression* (1979), pp. 15–16. This phenomenon was also noted by observers like Priestley and Orwell at the time, the latter suggesting, half-seriously, that this was why Britain had not experienced a revolution. See J. B. Priestley, *English Journey* (1934), pp. 401–2; George Orwell, *The Road to Wigan Pier* (1937), pp. 79–81.

30   Jane Southern, 'The Co-operative Movement in the Inter-war Period: Cleatormoor – a case study' (MA thesis, University of Lancaster 1990), pp. 54–6.

31   *Coventry Wheatsheaf*, March 1926, p. ii.

32   *Ibid.*, February 1926, p. ii.

33   *Ibid.*, December 1926, p. v; May 1927, p. i.

34   On the rise of the young consumer in this period see David Fowler, 'Teenage Consumers? Young Wage-Earners and Leisure in Manchester, 1919–1939', in Andrew Davies and Stephen Fielding (eds), *Workers' Worlds: Cultures and Communities in Manchester and Salford, 1880–1939* (Manchester 1992) p. 150.

35   *Co-operative Congress Report*, 1929, p. 397.

36   M.O. Archive, 'Co-op Movement in Worktown', p. 16. For the role of film see Alan Burton, *The People's Cinema: Film and the Co-operative Movement* (1994).

37   M.O. Archive, 'Co-op Movement in Worktown', pp. 7, 11–12.

38   See Hough, *Co-operative Retailing*, p. 7; Cole, *A Century*, p. 372.

39   E. A. Alcock, 'The Liverpool Co-operative Society 1886–1939: Its Growth, Aims and Social Structure' (MA thesis, University of Lancaster 1986); Southern, 'Cleatormoor'; M.O. Archive, 'Co-op Movement in Worktown', *passim*.

40   G. D. H. Cole, *The British Co-operative Movement in a Socialist Society* (1951), p. 22.

41   *Co-operative Independent Commission Report*, pp. 237–53. The theme of 'democracy' versus 'efficiency' is pursued by Malcolm Hornsby in his unpublished MPhil thesis, 'The Consumers' Co-operative Movement in the Twentieth Century' (University of York 1989).

42   Charles Sabel and Johnathan Zeitlin, 'Historical Alternatives to Mass Production: Production, Politics, Markets and Technology in Nineteenth Century Industrialization', *Past and Present*, 108, 1985.

43   Erik Olin Wright, 'Class Analysis, History and Emancipation',

New Left Review, 202, 1993, pp. 24–5.

44   Peter Mathias, *Retailing Revolution: A History of Multiple Retailing in the Food Trades* (1967) pp. 113–14, 195–257; Charles Wilson, *The History of Unilever: A Study in Economic Growth and Social Change* (1954), pp. 119, 128–40, 207–9, 257–8, 269.

45   See G. D. H. Cole's comments in *British Co-operative Movement*, pp. 15–16. The movement was represented on the National Council of Labour from 1927 but was not properly consulted by the Labour Party even on issues which directly affected its future. This lack of co-ordination and sympathy is nicely symbolised by the nationalisation of the co-operative colliery at Shilbottle by the Labour government after the Second World War. See F. W. Leeman, *Co-operation in Nottingham: A History of 100 Years of Nottingham Co-operative Society Limited* (Nottingham 1963), pp. 162–4.

Bibliography

(The place of publication is London, unless otherwise stated).

1 Newspapers and periodicals

Bolton Co-operative Record
Burnley Co-operative Record
Chorley Co-operative Record
Clarion
Comradeship
Co-operative News and Journal of Associated Industry
Co-operative Record of the Birmingham District
Co-operator
Coventry Wheatsheaf
C.W.S. Annual
Derby Co-operative Record
Economic Review
Failsworth Co-operative Messenger
Fortnightly Review
International Co-operative Bulletin
Justice
Labour Co-partnership
Labour Leader
Leeds Co-operative Record
Liberty Review
Manchester and Salford Co-operative Herald
Middlesbrough Co-operative Record
Millgate Monthly
Northern Star

Notes to the People
Oldham Industrial Co-operative Society Record
Our Circle
Pendleton Co-operative Record
People's Year Book
Plymouth Co-operative Record
Progressive Review
Quarterly Review
Review of Reviews
Reynold's News
Russian Co-operator
Subjects of the Day
The Times
Western Mail
Wheatsheaf

2 Official government publications

First Report from the Commissioners of the Employment of Children, Young Persons and Women in Agriculture 1867 (Shannon, Co. Clare 1968).
Fourth Report of the Royal Commission on Labour 1893 (Shannon, Co. Clare 1970).
Report of Committee on Trusts 1919 [Cd.9236].
First Report of the Royal Commission on Food Prices 1925 [Cmd.2390].
Hansard's Parliamentary Debates.

3 Annual reports and proceedings

Co-operative Congress Reports.
Report of the Proceedings of the 7th Congress of the I.C.A. held at the Cremona, 1907 (1908).
Transactions of the National Association for the Promotion of Social Science (TNAPSS).

4 Jubilee histories of co-operative societies

Anon., *The Coronation history of the Barnsley British Co-operative Society Ltd., 1862-1902* (Manchester 1903).
Anon., *Jubilee history of Bedlington Equitable and Industrial Co-operative*

Society Ltd., 1861-1911 (signed by the 'Book Committee', Manchester 1911).

Baldwin, J. and Bennett, J., *Jubilee History 1860-1910 of the City of Bradford Co-operative Society* (Bradford 1911).

Balmforth, O., *A history of fifty years progress, 1860-1910, of Huddersfield Industrial Society Ltd.* (Manchester 1910).

Beckitt, C. J., *Darwen Industrial Co-operative Society, 1860-1910; Souvenir in commemoration of its jubilee* (Manchester 1910).

Blatchford, M., *The history of Halifax Industrial Society for the first fifty years, to commemorate the celebration of its Jubilee in January 1901: 1851-1901* (Halifax 1901).

Boydell, T., *The Jubilee history of the Leigh Friendly Co-operative Society Ltd., 1857-1907* (Manchester 1907).

Briggs, G., *Jubilee history of the York Equitable Industrial Society Ltd., established August 26th 1858* (Manchester 1909).

Caldwell, J., *History of Brighouse and its Co-operative Society* (Brighouse 1899).

Childe, W. H., *Batley Co-operative Society Ltd.: a brief history of the Society, 1867-1917* (Manchester 1919).

Cooke, A. and Cooke, J., *The Jubilee History of the Congleton Equitable and Industrial Society Ltd., 1860-1910* (Manchester 1910).

Cottrell, W. F., *The Jubilee Record of the Pendleton Co-operative Industrial Society Limited: 1860-1910* (Manchester 1910).

Hartley, W., *Fifty Years of Co-operation in Bingley; a Jubilee record of Bingley Industrial Co-operative Society Ltd.* (Bingley 1900).

Haslam, J., *A History of fifty years progress of Eccles Provident Industrial Co-operative Society Ltd: Jubilee souvenir, 1857-1907* (Manchester 1907).

Haslam, J., *A History of fifty years of progress of Accrington and Church Industrial Co-operative Society Ltd., a souvenir of the Society's Jubilee: 1860-1910* (Manchester 1910).

Hodgson, H., *Fifty Years of Co-operation in Great Horton and District, being the Jubilee history of the Great Horton Industrial Society, 1859-1909* (Manchester 1909).

Holyoake, G. J., *Leeds Industrial Co-operative Society Ltd., 1847-1897: traced year by year* (Manchester 1897).

Holyoake, G. J. and Scotton, A., *The Jubilee history of Derby Co-operative Provident Society 1850-1900* (Manchester 1900).

Hudson, B., *History of Co-operation in Cainscross and District: a souvenir in commemoration of the Jubilee of Cainscross and Ebley Co-operative*

Society, 1863-1913 (Manchester 1913).

Jackson, E., *A Study in Democracy; being an account of the rise and progress of Industrial Co-operation in Bristol* (Bristol 1911).

Jones, T. and Rhodes, J., *Jubilee history of the Hyde Equitable Co-operative Society Ltd., 1862-1912* (Manchester 1912).

Kenworthy, J., *History of the Stocksbridge Band of Hope Industrial Co-operative Society Ltd., 1860-1910* (Manchester 1910).

McClean, J. and Hewitt, A., *Fifty Years' history of the Compstall Co-operative Industrial Society Ltd., 1851-1901: A Souvenir of the jubilee celebrations* . . . (Manchester 1901).

McInnes, D., *History of Co-operation in Lincon, 1861-1911* (Manchester 1911).

Ogden, J. H., *Failsworth Industrial Co-operative Society Ltd: jubilee history 1859-1909* (Manchester 1909).

Oliver, W. H. (ed.). *Coventry Perseverance Co-operative Society Limited, Jubilee History, 1867-1917* (Coventry 1917).

Oxberry, J., *Windy Nook village, its inhabitants and their Co-operative store: a jubilee tribute and historical sketch* (Pelaw-on-Tyne 1924).

Peaples, F. W., *History of the Great and Little Bolton Co-operative Society; showing fifty years of progress, 1859-1909: A souvenir in commemoration of the Society's Jubilee* (Manchester 1909).

Pickles, F., *Jubilee History of the Bridge End Co-operative Society Limited: From 1847 to 1901* (Manchester 1902).

Purnell, F. and Williams, H., *Jubilee History of the Gloucester Co-operative Industrial Society, 1860-1910, established 10th July 1860* (Gloucester 1910).

Redshaw, T., *Jubilee History of Bishop Auckland Industrial Co-operative Flour and Provision Society Ltd. from 1860-1910* (Manchester 1910).

Rhodes, J., *Half a century of Co-operation in Keighley, 1860-1910: Jubilee history* (Manchester 1911).

Rigby, T., *The origin and history of Co-operation in Bury; written in commemoration of the Jubilee of the Bury District Co-operative Society Ltd., 1855-1905* (Bury 1905).

Simpson, W., *Jubilee Souvenir; a short history of Cramlington District Co-operative Society, 1861-1911* (Manchester 1912).

Taylor, J. T., *Jubilee Co-operation in Oldham: the jubilee history of the Oldham Industrial Co-operative Society Ltd., 1850-1900* (Manchester 1900).

5 Autobiographies and biographies

Bentley, M., *Born 1896. Childhood in Clayton and Working in Manchester and Cheshire* (Manchester 1985).

Carpenter, L. P., *G. D. H. Cole: An Intellectual Biography* (Cambridge 1973).

Cole, M., *The Life of G. D. H. Cole* (1972).

Cooper, T., *The Life of Thomas Cooper* (1872, Leicester 1971).

Crime, T., E. O. *Greening: A Maker of Modern Co-operation* (Manchester 1923).

Duncan, D., *The Life and Letters of Herbert Spencer* (1908).

Gallagher, P., *My Story by Paddy the Cope* (1939).

Grugel, L., *George Jacob Holyoake: A Study in the Evolution of A Victorian Radical* (Philadelphia 1976).

Gutteridge, J., *Lights and Shadows in the Life of an Artisan* (published in serial form in the *Coventry Herald and Free Press* 1891).

Harrison, J. F. C., *Robert Owen and the Owenites in Britain and America* (1969).

Holyoake, G. J., *Life and Character of Henry Hetherington* (pamphlet, 1849).

—— *Life of Joseph Rayner Stephens* (1881).

—— *Sixty Years of an Agitators Life* (1892).

Lawton, J., *A Man's Life* (1932).

Lipton, T., *Leaves From The Lipton Log* (1931).

Llewelyn-Davies, M. (ed.), *Life As We Have Known It* (1930, 1977 edn).

McCabe, J., *Life and Letters of George Jacob Holyoake* (2 vols., 1908).

—— *George Jacob Holyoake* (1922).

Maitland, S., *Vesta Tilley* (1986).

Masterman, N. C., *J. M. Ludlow: The Builder of Christian Socialism* (1963).

Milton, N., *John Maclean* (1973).

Morgan, K. O., *Keir Hardie. Radical and Socialist* (1975).

Murray, A. D. (ed.), *J. M. Ludlow: The Autobiography of a Christian Socialist* (1981).

Seabrook, J., *Working-Class Childhood* (1982).

Snell, H., *Men, Movements and Myself* (1936).

Solly, H., *These Eighty Years; Or, the Story of an Unfinished Life* (1893).

Spencer, H., *An Autobiography* (1904).

Thew, L. M., *The Pit Village and the Store* (1985).

Todd, N., *The Militant Democracy: Joseph Cowen and Victorian*

Radicalism (Tyne and Wear 1991).

Tsuzuki, C., *Tom Mann, 1856-1941: The Challenges of Labour* (Oxford 1991).

Webb, B., *My Apprenticeship* (Cambridge 1926, 1979).

Weir, M., *Shoes were for Sunday* (1970).

Woolf, L., *Beginning Again: An Autobiography of the years 1911-1918* (1964).

6 Books published before 1945

Acland, A. H. D. and Jones, B., *Working Men Co-operators* (1884).

Atkins, H. W., *Advertising for Co-operative Societies* (Leicester 1933).

Bamford, W. M., *Our Fifty Years, 1871-1921* (Manchester 1921).

Barnett, S. and H., *Practicable Socialism* (1888).

Belloc, H., *The Servile State* (1912).

Beveridge, W. H., *British Food Control* (1928).

Billington Greig, T., *The Consumer in Revolt* (1912).

Blandford, T. and Newell, G., *History of the Leicester Co-operative Hosiery Manufacturing Society Limited* (Leicester 1898).

Booth, C., *Life and Labour of the People of London* (vol. I, 1889).

Booth, W., *In Darkest England and the Way Out* (1890).

Brown, W. H., *The Co-operative Manager: Being the Silver Jubilee History, 1912-1937, of the National Co-operative Manager's Association* (Manchester 1937).

Carpenter, E. (ed.), *Forecasts of the Coming Century* (Manchester 1897).

Carr-Saunders, A. M. et al. *Consumers' Co-operation in Great Britain* (1938).

Cole, G. D. H., *The World of Labour* (1913, Brighton 1973).

—— *Self-Government in Industry* (1917, 1972).

—— *The World of Labour* (1919).

—— *Guild Socialism Re-stated* (1920).

Cole, G. D. H., et al., *Problems of the Socialist Transition* (1934).

Coller, F. H., *A State Trading Adventure* (1925).

Craig, E. T., *The Irish Land and Labour Question, Illustrated in the History of Ralahine and Co-operative Farming* (Manchester 1882).

Fay, C. R., *Co-partnership in Industry* (1913).

—— *Co-operation at Home and Abroad* (1936).

Gammage, R. G., *History of the Chartist Movement* (1854).

Gaumont, J., *Histoire Générale de la Co-operation en France: les idées et les faits, les hommes et les oeuvres* (Paris 1924).

Gibbins, H. de B., *Industrial History* (1892).

Green, J. R., *Short History of the English People* (1877).

Greening, E. O., *Co-operative Life* (1889).

Gronlund, L., *The Co-operative Commonwealth* (1886).

Hall, F., *The History of the Co-operative Printing Society, 1869-1919* (Manchester 1919).

Hall, F., and Watkins, W. P., *Co-operation: A Survey of the History, Principles and Organisation of the Co-operative Movement in Great Britain and Ireland* (Manchester 1937).

Hardie, K., *From Serfdom to Socialism* (1907).

Haslam, J., *The Hand-Loom Weaver's Daughter* (Manchester 1904).

Hobson, J. A., *The Evolution of Modern Capitalism* (1894; 1917 edn).

Holyoake, G. J., *Self-Help by the People: History of Co-operation in Rochdale* (1858).

—— *The History of Co-operation in Halifax* (1867).

—— *The Co-operative Movement Today* (1891, 4th edn 1905).

—— *Bygones Worth Remembering* (1905).

—— *The History of Co-operation in England* (first vol. 1875, complete edn 1906).

Hughes, T. and Neale, E. V., *A Manual for Co-operators* (1881).

Jones, B., *Co-operative Production* (Oxford 1894).

Kirkup, T., *A History of Socialism* (1887, 1906 edn).

Kropotkin, P., *Fields, Factories and Workshops* (1899, C. Ward edn, 1974).

—— *Mutual Aid; A Factor of Evolution* (1902, 1910 ed.).

Lloyd, H. D., *Labour Co-partnership* (New York 1898).

Longden, F., *Co-operative Politics inside Capitalist Society* (Birmingham 1941).

Ludlow, J. M. and Jones, L., *The Progress of the Working Classes* (1867).

MacGregor, D. H., *The Evolution of Industry* (1911).

Macrosty, H., *Trusts and the State* (1901).

Mansbridge, A., *An Adventure in Working-Class Education* (1920).

Marx, K., *Capital: A Critique of Political Economy* (1867, Penguin 1976).

Massingham, H. W. (ed.), *Labour and Protection* (1903).

Mercer, T. W., *Towards the Co-operative Commonwealth* (Manchester 1937).

Michels, R., *Political Parties* (1915).

Mill, J. S., *Principles of Political Economy* (1848, 5th edn 1862).

Nicholson, I., *Our Story* (Manchester 1903).

Orwell, G., *The Road to Wigan Pier* (1937).

Paine, W., *Shop Slavery and Emancipation: A Revolutionary Appeal to the Educated Young Men of the Middle Class* (1912).

Peaples, F. W., *History of the Educational Department of the Bolton Co-operative Society Limited, 1861-1914* (Manchester 1915).

Peel, F., *The Risings of the Luddites, Chartists and Plug-Drawers* (1880; fourth edn 1968).

Poisson, E., *The Co-operative Republic* (Paris, 1920; trans. Manchester 1925).

Postgate, R. W., Wilkinson, E. and Horrabin, J. F., *A Workers' History of the Great Strike* (1927).

Potter, B., *The Co-operative Movement in Great Britain* (1891).

Priestley, J. B. *English Journey* (1934).

Redfern, P. *The Story of the C.W.S.* (Manchester 1913).

—— *Co-operation For All* (Manchester 1914).

—— *The New History of the C.W.S.* (Manchester 1938).

Rothstein, T., *From Chartism to Labourism* (1929).

Ruskin, J., *Works* (ed. E.T. Cook and A. Wedderburn), vol. XVII (1905).

Sinclair, U., *The Jungle* (1906).

Snowden, P., *Socialism and Syndicalism* (1913).

Spencer, H., *Principles of Sociology* (1882, 1893 edn).

Rogers T., *Six Centuries of Work and Wages* (1884).

Tonks, W., *Victory in the Villages: The History of the Britsworth Circuits* (1907).

Toynbee, A., *The Industrial Revolution* (1884).

Travis, T., *A Manual of Social Science for the Working Classes* (1877).

Volosinov, V. N., *Marxism and the Philosophy of Language* (1930, New York 1973).

Webb, C., *The Woman With the Basket* (Manchester 1927).

Webb, C., (ed.). *Industrial Co-operation: The Story of a Peaceful Revolution* (Manchester 1904; third edn 1907).

Williams, A., *Co-partnership and Profit-Sharing* (1913).

Woolf, L., *Co-operation and the Future of Industry* (1918).

—— *Co-operation and Socialism* (1921).

Woolf, L. (ed.), *Fabian essays on Co-operation* (1923).

7 Pamphlets published before 1945

Alexander, A. V., *Is Co-operation a Social Menace?* (Manchester 1925)..

Anon. *Is Co-operation Beneficial to the Community?* (Manchester 1886).

Carter, W. T., *Co-operation is Reasonable Socialism* (Manchester 1894).

Champion, H. H. and Jones, B., *Co-operation v. Socialism: Being a Report of a Debate between Mr H.H.Champion and Mr Ben. Jones* (Manchester 1887).

Cheyne, J., *Co-operative Advertising* (Glasgow 1903).

Co-op Union, *250 Good Books for Co-operative Libraries* (Manchester 1894).

—— *Songs and Readings for Co-operators* (Manchester 1896).

Deans, J., *Co-operation versus Private Trading* (Manchester 1889).

—— *The Amalgamation of Societies as a Means of Consolidating the Co-operative Movement* (Glasgow 1903).

Eddie, F. M., *Co-operation and Labour Uprisings* (Manchester 1912).

Enfield, A. H., *International Co-operative Trade* (Manchester n.d.).

Garnett, F. *Co-operative Classes; How to Make Them More Attractive and Successful* (Manchester 1892).

Greening, E. O., *International Co-operation and the Constitution of the International Co-operative Alliance* (1895).

Greening, E. O. and Neale, E. V., *Proposals for an International Alliance of the Friends of Co-operative Production* (1892).

Greenwood, A., *The Educational Department of the Rochdale Equitable Pioneers' Society Limited* (Manchester 1877).

Hall, F., *The Co-ordination and Extension of Co-operative Education and the Part of the Co-operative College Therein* (Manchester 1914).

Hayward, F., *The Co-operative Boycott* (Manchester 1930).

Holyoake, G. J., *Rationalism: A Treatise for the Times* (1845).

—— *Practical Grammar* (1846).

—— *The Life and Character of Henry Hetherington* (1849).

—— *Public Speaking and Debate* (1849).

—— *The Liberal Situation: necessity for a Qualified Franchise* (1865).

—— *The Logic of Co-operation* (1873).

—— *The Opportunity of Ireland* (1886).

—— *Essentials of Co-operative Education* (Manchester 1898).

ILP, *The Co-operative Movement and Socialism* (1928).

Lee, H. W., *The Triumph of the Trust Under Free Trade* (1908).

Lever, W. H., *Co-partnership, An Address Spoken to the Woolwich Chamber of Commerce* (Port Sunlight 1909).

—— *Partnership Scheme: Meeting of Employees of Lever Brothers Limited* (supplement to *Progress*, April 1909).

—— *Co-partnership and Efficiency: An address delivered at a meeting convened by the Consultative Council of the Labour Co-partnership Association* (Port Sunlight 1912).

—— Co-partnership: An address to members of the Agricultural and Horticultural Association (Port Sunlight 1912).

—— Co-partnership: laying the three ghosts, unemployment, sickness, death (Port Sunlight 1922).

Lowery, R., Address to the Fathers and Mothers, Sons and Daughters of the Working Classes, on the System of Exclusive Dealing, and the Formation of Joint Stock Provision Companies (Newcastle-upon-Tyne 1839).

Maclean, J., Co-operation and the Rise in Prices (Glasgow, 1912).

McInnes, D., Co-operative Education and the Sectional Choral Association (Manchester 1914).

Marcroft, W., The Inner Circle of Family Life (Manchester 1886).

Marx, K., Inaugural Address of the Working Men's International Association (1864) in K. Marx and F. Engels, Articles on Britain (Moscow 1971).

Maxwell, W., The I.C.A.: its claims (Glasgow 1909).

Pilkington, E., The Dawn (1909).

Quelch, H. and Simpson, W., State Socialism: Is it Just and Reasonable? (Report of a debate . . . at the Corporation Hall, Burnley) (1893).

Snell, H., Socialism and Co-operation: their fundamental unity: an appeal to co-operators (Huddersfield 1908).

Twigg, H. J., An Outline History of Co-operative Education (Manchester 1924).

8 Books published from 1945 onwards

Abrams, P., The Origins of British Sociology 1834-1914 (Chicago 1968).

Aglietta, M., A Theory of Capitalist Regulation. The US Experience (1979).

Attfield, J., With Light of Knowledge (1981).

Backstrom, P., Christian Socialism and Co-operation in Victorian England (1974).

Bailey, P., Leisure and Class in Victorian England: Rational Recreation and the Contest for Control, 1830-1885 (1978).

Bailey, P. (ed.), Music Hall: The Business of Pleasure (Milton Keynes 1986).

Barker, K. (ed.), Ramsay MacDonald's Political Writings (1972).

Barnett, L. M., British Food Policy During the First World War (1985).

Barrow, L., Independent Spirits: Spiritualism and English Plebeians 1850-1910 (1986).

Benjamin, W., *One Way Street* (1979).

Benson, J., *The Rise of Consumer Society in Britain, 1880-1980* (1994).

Berg, M., *The Age of Manufactures: Industry, Innovation and Work in Britain 1700-1820* (1985).

Berman, M., *All That Is Solid Melts Into Air: The Experience of Modernity* (1982).

Bettelheim, C., *Class Struggles in the USSR* (Brighton 1976).

Biagini, E., *Liberty, Retrenchment and Reform: Popular Liberalism in the Age of Gladstone, 1860-1880* (Cambridge 1992).

Biagini, E. and Reid, A. (eds), *Currents of Radicalism: Popular Radicalism, Organised Labour and Party Politics in Britain, 1850-1914* (Cambridge 1991).

Birchall, J., *Co-op: The People's Business* (Manchester 1994).

Bonner, A., *British Co-operation: The History, Principles and Organisation of the British Co-operative Movement* (1961).

Booth, W., *In Darkest England and the Way Out* (1890).

Bourdieu, P., *Homo academius* (Cambridge 1988).

—— *In Other Words: Essays Towards a Reflexive Sociology* (Oxford 1990).

—— *Language and Symbolic Power* (Cambridge 1991).

Briggs, A., *Friends of the People: The Centenary History of Lewis's* (1956).

—— *Mass Entertainment: The Origins of a Modern Industry* (Adelaide 1960).

Buck-Morss, S., *The Dialectics of Seeing: Walter Benjamin and the Arcades Project* (1989).

Burke, P. and Porter, R. (eds), *The Social History of Language* (Cambridge 1987).

Burnett, J., *Plenty and Want: A Social History of Diet in England from 1815 to the Present Day* (1966).

Burton, A., *The People's Cinema: Film and the Co-operative Movement* (1994).

Campbell, C. B., *The Romantic Ethic and the Spirit of Modern Consumerism* (Oxford 1987).

Carbery, T. P., *Consumers in Politics* (Manchester 1969).

Carr, E. H., *The Bolshevik Revolution, 1917-23, vol. II* (1952).

—— *Socialism in One Country, 1924-26, vol. I* (1958).

Chancellor, V., *History for their Masters* (1970).

Christensen, T., *Origin and History of Christian Socialism 1848-54* (Copenhagen 1962).

Church, R., *Economic and Social Change in a Midland Town. Victorian*

Nottingham 1815-1900 (1966).

Claeys, G., *Machinery, Money and the Millennium: From Moral Economy to Socialism, 1815-1960* (Princeton, NJ 1987).

—— *Citizens and Saints: Politics and Anti-politics in Early British Socialism* (Cambridge 1989).

Clarke, J. and Critcher, C., *The Devil Makes Work: Leisure in Capitalist Britain* (1985).

Clarke, J., Critcher, C. and Johnson, R. (eds), *Working Class Culture: Studies in History and Theory* (1979).

Clarke, P., *Lancashire and the New Liberalism* (Cambridge 1971).

Cole, G. D. H., *A Century of Co-operation* (Manchester 1945).

—— *The British Co-operative Movement in a Socialist Society* (1951).

Collini, S., *Liberalism and Sociology: L. T. Hobhouse and Political Argument in England 1880-1914* (Cambridge 1979).

Colls, R., *The Collier's Rant: Song and Culture in the Industrial Village* (1977).

—— *The Pitmen of the Northern Coalfield: Work, culture and protest, 1790-1850* (Manchester 1987).

Co-op Union, *Co-operative Independent Commission Report* (Manchester 1958).

Corrigan, P. and Gillespie, V., *Class-struggle, Social Literacy and Idle Time* (Brighton 1977).

Corrigan, P. and Sayer, D., *The Great Arch: English State Formation as Cultural Revolution* (1985).

Craik, W. W., *The Central Labour College 1909-29* (1964).

Cross, G., *A quest for time: the reduction of work in Britain and France, 1840-1940* (Berkeley, Cal. 1989).

—— *Time and Money: The Making of Consumer Culture* (1993).

Crossick, G. *An Artisan Elite in Victorian Society* (1978).

Cunningham, H., *Leisure in the Industrial Revolution, 1780-1880* (1980).

Davidoff, L. and Hall, C., *Family Fortunes: Men and women of the English Middle Class, 1780-1850* (1987).

Davies, A., *Leisure, gender and poverty: Working-class culture in Salford and Manchester, 1900-1939* (Buckingham 1992).

Dellheim, C. *The Face of the Past: The Preservation of the Medieval Inheritance in Victorian England* (Cambridge 1982).

Douglas, M. and Isherwood, B., *The World of Goods: Towards an Anthropology of Consumption* (1979).

Foote, G., *The Labour Party's Political Thought: A History* (1985).

Foster, J., *Class Struggle and the Industrial Revolution* (1974).

Fraser, W. H., *The Coming of the Mass Market, 1850-1914* (1981).

Furlough, E., *The Politics of Consumption: The Consumer Co-operative Movement in France, 1834-1930* (Ithaca, New York 1992).

Gaffin, J. and Thoms, D., *Caring and Sharing: The Centenary History of the Co-operative Women's Guild* (Manchester 1983).

Gardiner, P., *The Lost Elementary Schools of Victorian England* (1986).

Gray, R., *The Labour Aristocracy in Victorian Edinburgh* (Oxford 1976).

—— *The Aristocracy of Labour in Nineteenth-century Britain, 1850-1914* (1981).

Gustav Klaus, H., (ed.). *The Rise of Socialist Fiction 1880-1914* (1987).

Hannah, L., *The Rise of the Corporate Economy* (1976).

Harrison, J. F. C., *Learning and Living 1790-1960: A Study of the History of the English Adult Education Movement* (1961).

Harrison, R., *Before the Socialists: Studies in Labour and Politics, 1861-1881* (1965).

Hinton, J., *The First Shop Stewards' Movement* (1973).

Hoare, Q. and Nowell-Smith, G. (eds), *Selections from the Prison Notebooks of Antonio Gramsci* (1971).

Hobsbawm, E. and Ranger, T. (eds), *The Invention of Tradition* (Cambridge 1983).

Hoggart, R., *The Uses of Literacy* (1957).

Hough, J. A., *Co-operative Retailing, 1914-1945. A Statistical Analysis of the Development of Retailing in the British Co-operative Movement* (1949).

Howell, D., *British Workers and the Independent Labour Party 1888-1906* (Manchester 1982).

Humphries, S., *Hooligans or Rebels? An Oral History of Working-Class Childhood and Youth 1889-1939* (1981).

Hurwitz, S. J., *State Intervention in Great Britain: A Study of Economic Control and Social Response 1914-1919* (1949).

Jefferys, J. B., *Retail Trading in Britain 1850-1950* (Cambridge 1954).

Jenkins, K., *Re-Thinking History* (1991).

Jenkins, M., *The General Strike of 1842* (1980).

Johnson, P., *Saving and Spending: The Working-class Economy in Britain 1870-1939* (Oxford 1985).

Jones, S. G., *Workers at play: A social and economic history of leisure 1918-1939* (1986).

Joyce, P., *Work, Society and Politics* (Brighton 1980).

—— *Visions of the People. Industrial England and the question of class 1848-1914* (Cambridge 1991).

Kaye, H. J., *The British Marxist Historians: An Introductory Analysis* (Cambridge 1984).

Kinloch, J. and Butt, J., *History of the Scottish Co-operative Wholesale Society Limited* (Glasgow 1981).

Kirk, N., *The Growth of Working-Class Reformism in Mid-Victorian England* (1985).

LaCapra, D,, *History & Criticism* (Ithaca, NY 1985).

Lancaster, B., *Radicalism, Co-operation and Socialism: Leicester working-class politics, 1860-1906* (Leicester 1987).

Landes, D. S., *The Unbound Prometheus. Technological Change and Industrial Development in Western Europe from 1750 to the Present* (Cambridge 1969).

Langan, M. and Schwarz, B. (eds), *Crises In The British State 1880-1930* (1985).

Laybourn, K. and Reynolds, J., *Liberalism and the Rise of Labour 1890-1918* (1984).

Leeman, F. W., *Co-operation in Nottingham: A History of 100 Years of Nottingham Co-operative Society Limited* (Nottingham 1963).

Levy, C. (ed.), *Socialism and the Intelligentsia* (1987).

Lidtke, V., *The Alternative Culture* (Oxford 1985).

Lowerson, J. and Myerscough, J., *Time to Spare in Victorian England* (Brighton 1977).

Mackenzie, J. M., *Propaganda and Empire: the manipulation of British public opinion* (Manchester 1984).

Mackenzie, J. M. (ed.), *Imperialism and Empire* (Manchester 1986).

Mandel, E., *Late Capitalism* (1975).

Martin, B., *A Sociology of Contemporary Cultural Change* (Oxford 1981).

Marx, K., *Grundrisse: Foundations of the Critique of Political Economy* (New York 1973).

Mason, T., *Association Football and English Society 1863-1915* (Hassocks, Sussex 1980).

Mathias, P., *Retailing Revolution: A History of Multiple Retailing in the Food Trades* (1967).

McBriar, A. M., *Fabian Socialism and English Politics 1884-1918* (Cambridge 1966).

McKibbin, R., *The Evolution of the Labour Party 1910-24* (Oxford 1974).

—— *The Ideologies of Class. Social Relations in Britain, 1880-1950* (Oxford 1990).

Meacham, S., *A Life Apart: the English Working Class, 1880-1914* (1977).

Meller, H., *Leisure and the changing city, 1870-1918* (1976).

Miller, D., *Material Culture and Mass Consumption* (1987).

Miller, M. B., *The Bon Marché: Bourgeois Culture and the Department Store, 1869-1920* (1981).

Morris, R .J., *Class, sect and party: The making of the British middle class, Leeds 1820-1850* (Manchester 1990).

Mowat, C. L., *Britain Between the Wars* (1956).

Ollman, B., *Alienation, Marx's Critique of Man in Capitalist Society* (Cambridge 1971).

Pelling, H., *The Origins of the Labour Party 1880-1900* (Oxford 1965).

Perkin, H., *The Origins of Modern English Society* (1969).

—— *The Rise of Professional Society* (1989).

Poulantzas, N., *Political Power and Social Classes* (1972).

Price, R., *An Imperial War and the British Working Class: Working-Class Attitudes and Reactions to the Boer War, 1899-1902* (1972).

Reid, A., *Social Classes and Social Relations in Britain, 1850-1914* (1992).

Richards T., *The Commodity Culture of Victorian England. Advertising and Spectacle, 1851-1914* (1991).

Roth, G., *The Social Democrats in Imperial Germany: A Study in Working Class Isolation and National Integration* (1963).

Royle, E., *Radicals, Secularists and Republicans: Popular Freethought in Britain, 1866-1915* (Manchester 1980).

Russell, D., *Popular Music in England, 1840-1914* (Manchester 1987).

Samuel, R. (ed.), *People's History and Socialist Theory* (1981).

Samuel, R., MacColl, E. and Cosgrove, S. (eds), *Theatres of the Left 1880-1935* (1985).

Savage, M., *The Dynamics of Working-class Politics: The Labour Movement in Preston, 1880-1940* (Cambridge 1987).

Saville, J., *1848: The British state and the Chartist movement* (Cambridge 1987).

Saville, J. and Bellamy, J., *Dictionary of Labour Biography* (1972, 1974).

Scott, J.W., *Gender and the Politics of History* (New York 1988).

Sewell, R. H., *Work and Revolution in France. The Language of Labour from the Old Regime to 1848* (Cambridge 1980).

Silver, H., *The Concept of Popular Education* (1965).

Simon, B., *Studies in the History of Education, 1780-1870* (1960).

—— *Education and the Labour Movement, 1870-1920* (1965).

Snell, K., *Annals of the Labouring Poor: Social Change and Agrarian England, 1660-1900* (Cambridge 1985).

Sontag, S., *On Photography* (1978).

Stallybrass, P. and White, A., *The Politics and Poetics of Transgression*

(1986).

Stedman Jones, G., *Outcast London: A study in the relationship between classes in Victorian society* (Oxford 1971, 1984).

—— *Languages of Class: Studies in English Working-Class History 1832-1982* (Cambridge 1983).

Stevenson, J. and Cook, C., *The Slump: Society and Politics during the Depression* (1979).

Taylor, B., *Eve and the New Jerusalem* (1983).

Tholfsen, T., *Working-Class Radicalism in Mid-Victorian England* (1976).

Thompson, D., *The Early Chartists* (1971).

Thompson, E. P., *The Making of the English Working Class* (1963).

—— *Witness Against the Beast: William Blake and the Moral Law* (Cambridge 1993).

Thompson, N., *The Peoples' Science* (Cambridge 1984).

Vicinus, M., *The Industrial Muse* (1974).

Vincent, D., *Bread, Knowledge and Freedom* (1981).

—— *Literacy and popular culture: England 1750-1914* (Cambridge 1989).

Vincent, J., *The Formation of the Liberal Party 1857-68* (1966).

Waites, B., *A Class Society at War: England 1914-18* (Leamington Spa 1987).

Walkowitz, J., *City of Dreadful Delight: Narratives of Sexual Danger in Late-Victorian London* (1992).

Waters, C., *British Socialists and the Politics of Popular Culture, 1884-1914* (Manchester 1990).

Watkins, W. P., *The International Co-operative Alliance, 1895-1970* (Manchester 1970).

Webb, R. K., *Modern England: From the Eighteenth Century to the Present* (1969).

Weiner, M., *English Culture and the Decline of the Industrial Spirit 1850-1980* (Cambridge 1981).

White, H., *The Content of the Form* (Baltimore 1987).

Williams, R., *Culture and Society 1780-1950* (1958).

—— *The Long Revolution* (1961).

—— *Keywords* (1976).

—— *Marxism and Literature* (Oxford 1977).

—— *Politics and Letters. Interviews with New Left Review* (1979).

—— *Problems in Materialism and Culture* (1980).

—— *Culture* (Glasgow 1981).

—— *Towards 2000* (1983).

Williams, R. H., *Dream 3 Worlds: Mass-Consumption in Late 19th*

Century France (1982).

Wilson, C., *The History of Unilever: A Study in Economic Growth and Social Change* (1954).

Winstanley, M., *The Shopkeeper's World 1830-1914* (Manchester 1983).

Winter, J. (ed.), *The Working Class in Modern British History* (Cambridge 1983).

Wrigley, C., *Lloyd George and the Challenge of Labour* (1990).

Yamey, B. S.(ed.), *Resale Price Maintenance* (1966).

Yeo, S., *Religion and Voluntary Organisations in Crisis* (1976).

Yeo, S., (ed.). *New Views of Co-operation* (1988).

9   Articles and contributions

Abrams, P., 'The Failure of Social Reform after the First World War', *Past and Present*, 1963.

Adams, T., 'The Formation of the Co-operative Party Reconsidered', *International Review of Social History*, 1987, I.

Anderson, P., 'Origins of the Present Crisis', *New Left Review*, 23, 1964.

Bailey, P., '"Will the Real Bill Banks Please Stand Up?" Towards a Role Analysis of Mid-Victorian Working-Class Respectability', *Journal of Social History*, 12, 1978.

Barratt Brown, M., 'Away With All the Great Arches: Anderson's History of British Capitalism', *New Left Review*, 167, 1988.

Beetham, D., 'From socialism to fascism: the relation between theory and practice in the work of Robert Michels', *Political Studies*, 25, 1977.

—— 'Reformism and the "Bourgeoisification" of the labour movement', in Carl Levy (ed.), *Socialism and the Intelligentsia 1880-1914* (1987).

Berger, J., 'Ways of Remembering', *Camerawork*, 10, 1978.

Bestor, A. E., 'The evolution of the socialist vocabulary', *Journal of the History of Ideas,* 1948.

Blanch, M. D., 'British society and the war', in P. Warwick (ed.), *The South African War* (1980).

Blewitt, N., 'The Franchise in the United Kingdom, 1885-1914', *Past and Present*, 32, 1965.

Bond, R., 'Cinema in the Thirties: Documentary Film and the Labour Movement', in John Clark et al. (eds), *Culture and Crisis in Britain in the 30s* (1979).

Bourdieu, P., 'Doxa and Common Life', *New Left Review*, 191, 1992.

Breen, T. H., '"Baubles of Britain": The American and Consumer Revolutions of the 18th Century', *Past and Present*, 119, 1988.

Brehony, K., 'Popular control or control by experts? Schooling between 1880 and 1902', in Langan, M. and Schwarz, B. (eds), *Crises in the British State 1880-1930* (1985).

Breuilly, J., 'The Labour Aristocracy in Britain and Germany 1850-1914: A Review Article', in K. Tenfelde (ed.), *Arbeiter und Arbeiterbewegung im Vergleich* (Munich 1986).

Briggs, A., 'The Language of "Mass" and "Masses" in Nineteenth-Century England', in Martin, D. and Rubinstein, D. (eds), *Ideology and the Labour Movement* (1979).

Bristow, E., 'Profit-Sharing, Socialism and Labour Unrest', in K. D. Brown (ed.), *Essays in Anti-Labour History* (1974).

Cannadine, D., 'The Context, Performance and Meaning of Ritual: The British Monarchy and the "Invention of Tradition" *c.*1820-1977', in E.Hobsbawm and T. Ranger (eds), *The Invention of Tradition* (Cambridge 1983).

Chase, M., 'From Millenium to Anniversary: The Concept of Jubilee in Late Eighteenth and Nineteenth Century England', *Past and Present*, 129, 1990.

Church, R. A., 'Profit-sharing and Labour Relations in England in the Nineteenth Century', *International Review of Social History*, 16, 1971.

Cronin, J. E. 'Language, Politics and the Critique of Social History', *Journal of Social History*, 20, 1986-7.

Crossick, G., 'Shopkeepers and the State in Britain, 1870-1914', in G. Crossick and G. Haupt (eds), *Shopkeepers and Master Artisans in Nineteenth Century Europe* (1980).

Cunningham, H., 'The language of Patriotism', *History Workshop Journal*, 12, 1981.

—— 'The Conservative Party and patriotism', in R. Colls and P. Dodd (eds*)*, *Englishness: Politics and Culture 1880-1920* (1986).

Featherstone, M., 'Perspectives on Consumer Culture', *Sociology*, 24/1, 1990.

Foster, J., 'The Declassing of Language', *New Left Review*, 150, 1985.

Fowler, D., 'Teenage Consumers? Young Wage-Earners and Leisure in Manchester, 1919-1939', in A. Davies and S. Fielding (eds), *Workers' Worlds: Cultures and Communities in Manchester and Salford, 1880-1939* (Manchester 1992).

Frank, D., '"Food Wins All Struggles": Seattle Labor and the Politicization of Consumption', *Radical History Review*, 51, 1991.

Gazeley, I., 'The cost of living for urban workers in late Victorian and Edwardian Britain', *Economic History Review*, 42/2 (1989).

Geoghegan, V., 'Ralahine: an Irish Owenite community (1831-1833).', *International Review of Social History*, 36, 1991.

Goldman, L., 'The Social Science Association, 1857-86: A Context for Mid-Victorian Liberalism', *English Historical Review*, 100, 1986.

—— 'A Peculiarity of the English? The Social Science Association and the Absence of Sociology in Nineteenth Century Britain', *Past and Present*, 114, 1987.

Gray, R., 'The Languages of Factory Reform in Britain, *c.* 1830-1860' in P.Joyce (ed.), *The Historical Meanings of Work* (Cambridge 1987).

—— 'Class, politics and historical "revisionism"', *Social History*, 19/2, 1994.

Gurney, P. J., 'George Jacob Holyoake: Socialism, Association and Co-operation in Nineteenth-Century England', in S.Yeo (ed.), *New Views of Co-operation* (1988).

—— '"A Higher State of Civilisation and Happiness": Internationalism in the British Co-operative Movement Between *c.* 1869-1918', in Van Holthoon, F. and Van der Linden, M. (eds), *Internationalism in the Labour Movement 1830-1940* (Leiden 1988).

—— 'Heads, Hands and the Co-operative Utopia: an Essay in Historiography', *North West Labour History*, 1994.

—— 'The Middle-Class Embrace: language, representation and the contest over co-operative forms in Britain, 1860-1914', *Victorian Studies*, Winter, 1994.

Hall, S. and Schwarz, B., 'State and Society, 1880-1930', in M. Langan and B. Schwarz (eds), *Crises In The British State 1880-1930* (1985).

Harding, K., '"The Co-operative Commonwealth": Ireland, Larkin, and the *Daily Herald*', in S. Yeo (ed.), *New Views of Co-operation* (1988).

Hay, J. R. 'Employers' Attitudes to Social Policy and the Concept of Social Control, 1900-1920', in P. Thane (ed.), *The Origins of British Social Policy* (1978).

Hobsbawm, E., 'The Labour Aristocracy in Nineteenth Century Britain', in *Labouring Men: Studies in the History of Labour* (1964).

—— 'Artisans and Labour Aristocrats', *Worlds of Labour* (1984).

Howkins, A., 'Edwardian liberalism and industrial unrest: a class view of the decline of Liberalism', *History Workshop Journal*, 4, 1977.

Jackson Lears, T. J. 'From Salvation to Self-Realization: Advertising and the Therapeutic Roots of the Consumer Culture, 1880-1930' in R. Wightman Fox and T. J., Jackson Lears (eds), *The Culture of Consumption: Critical Essays in American History, 1880-1980* (New York 1983).

Johnson, P., 'Conspicuous Consumption and Working-Class Culture in Late-Victorian and Edwardian Britain', *Transactions of the Royal Historical Society*, 38, 1988.

Johnson, R., 'Culture and the historians', in Clarke, J., Critcher, C. and Johnson, R. (eds), *Working Class Culture. Studies in history and theory* (1979).

——— '3 Problematics: elements of a theory of working-class culture', in Clarke, J., Critcher, C., and Johnson, R.(eds), *Working Class Culture*.

——— '"Really Useful Knowledge": radical education and Working-Class Culture, 1790-1848', in Clarke, J., Critcher, C. and Johnson, R. (eds), *Working Class Culture*.

Jones, D. C., 'British Producer Co-operatives', in Ken Coates (ed.), *The New Worker Co-operatives* (Nottingham 1976).

Killingback, N., 'Limits to Mutuality: Economic and Political Attacks on Co-operation during the 1920s and 1930s', in S. Yeo (ed.), *New Views of Co-operation* (1988).

Kirk, N., '"Traditional" working-class culture and the "rise of Labour": some preliminary questions and observations', *Social History*, 16/2, 1991.

Kusamitsu, T., 'Great Exhibitions before 1851', *History Workshop Journal*, 9, 1980.

Lash, S. and Urry, J., 'The New Marxism of Collective Action: A Critical Analysis', *Sociology*, I, 1984.

Leach, W. R., 'Transformations in a Culture of Consumption: Women and Department Stores, 1890-1925', *The Journal of American History*, 71/2, 1984.

Levine, D., 'Recombinant family formation strategies', *Journal of Historical Sociology*, June 1989.

Levy, C., 'Education and self-education: staffing the early ILP', in C. Levy (ed.), *Socialism and the Intelligensia* (1987).

Lidtke, V., *The Alternative Culture* (Oxford 1985).

Linebaugh, P., 'From the Upper West Side to Wick Episcopi', *New Left Review*, 201, 1993.

Macintyre, A., 'The essential contestability of some social concepts', *Ethics*, 84, 1973

Maguire, P., 'Co-operation and Crisis: Government, Co-operation and Politics 1917-22', in S. Yeo (ed.), *New Views of Co-operation* (1988).

Mayfield, D. and Thorne, S., 'Social history and its discontents: Gareth Stedman Jones and the politics of language', *Social History*, 17/2, 1992.

McWilliam, R., 'Radicalism and popular culture: the Tichborne case and the politics of "fair play", 1867-1886', in E. Biagini and A. Reid (eds), *Currents of Radicalism:. Popular radicalism, organised labour and party politics in Britain, 1850-1914* (Cambridge 1991).

Moorhouse, H. F., 'The Marxist Theory of the Labour Aristocracy', *Social History*, 3, 1978.

Nairn, T., 'The English Working Class?', *New Left Review*, 24, 1964.

Nettl, P., 'The German Social Democratic Party 1890-1914 as a Political Model', *Past and Present*, 30, 1965.

Payne, P. L., 'The Emergence of the Large-Scale Company in Britain 1870-1914', *Economic History Review*, 3, 1967.

Pelling, H., 'The working class and the welfare state', in *Popular politics and society in late-Victorian England* (1968).

Phillips, A. and Putnam, T., 'Education for emancipation: the movement for independent working class education', *Capital and Class*, 10, 1980.

Pollard, S., 'Nineteenth-Century Co-operation: From Community Building to Shopkeeping', in Briggs, A. and Saville, J. (eds), *Essays in Labour History* (1960).

—— 'The Foundation of the Co-operative Party', in Briggs, A. and Saville, J. (eds), *Essays in Labour History 1886-1923* (1971).

Pollard, S. and Turner, R., 'Profit-Sharing and Autocracy: The Case of J T. and J. Taylor of Batley Woollen Manufacturers, 1892-1966', *Business History*, 18, 1976.

Popular Memory Group, 'Popular Memory: theory, politics, method', in R. Johnson et al., *Making Histories: Studies in history-writing and politics* (1982).

Pugh, M., 'Women, Food and Politics, 1880-1930', *History Today*, 41, March 1991.

Purvis, J., 'Working-class Women and Adult Education in Nineteenth Century Britain', *History of Education*, 3, 1980.

Purvis, M., 'Co-operative retailing in England, 1835-1850: developments beyond Rochdale', *Northern History*, 1986.

—— 'The development of co-operative retailing in England and Wales, 1851-1901: a geographical study', *Journal of Historical Geography*, 16, 3, 1990.

—— 'Co-operative retailing in Britain', in John Benson and Gareth Shaw (eds), *The evolution of retail systems, c. 1800-1914* (Leicester 1992).

Reid, A., 'Old Unionism reconsidered: the radicalism of Robert Knight, 1870-1900', in E. Biagini and A. Reid (eds), *Currents of Radicalism: Popular radicalism, organised labour and party politics in Britain, 1850-1914* (Cambridge 1991).

Ritter, G., 'Workers' Culture in Imperial Germany', *Journal of Contemporary History*, vol.13/2, 1978.

Rose, M. E., 'Rochdale Man and the Stalybridge Riot: Poor Relief during the Lancashire Cotton Famine 1861-5' in A. P. Donajgrodski (ed.), *Social Control in Nineteenth-Century Britain* (1977).

Ross, E., 'Women's Survival Networks: Neighbourhood Sharing Before WWI', *History Workshop Journal*, 5, 1983.

Royle, E., 'Mechanics Institutes and the Working Classes', *The Historical Journal*, 12, 1971.

Rubinstein, W. D., 'Wealth, Elites and the Class Structure of Modern Britain', *Past and Present*, 76, 1977.

Sabel, C. and Zeitlin, J., 'Historical Alternatives to Mass Production: Politics, Markets and Technology in Nineteenth Century Industrialization', *Past and Present*, 108, 1985.

Samuel, R., 'Workshop of the World: Steam Power and Hand Technology in Mid-Victorian Britain', *History Workshop Journal*, 3, 1977.

—— 'British Marxist Historians, 1880-1980: Part I', *New Left Review*, 120, 1980.

Saville, J., 'The Christian Socialists of 1848' in J.Saville (ed.), *Democracy and the Labour Movement* (1954).

Seed, J., 'Unitarianism, Political Economy and the Antinomies of Liberal Culture in Manchester 1830-1850', *Social History*, 7/1, 1982.

—— 'Theologies of Power: Unitarianism and the Social Relations of Religious Discourse, 1800-1850', in R. J. Morris (ed.), *Class, Power and Social Structure in British Nineteenth-Century Towns* (Leicester, 1986).

Schwarz, B., 'Conservatism and "caesarism", 1903-22', in M. Langan and B. Schwarz (eds), *Crises In The British State 1880-1930* (1985).

—— 'The corporate economy, 1890-1929', in M. Langlan and B. Schwarz (eds), *Crises in the British State, 1880-1930* (1985).

Smith, J. and Walton, J. K., 'Property, Employment and the Co-operative Movement: The Social Structure of Co-operation in Sabden, 1923', *The Historic Society of Lancashire and Cheshire*, vol. 134, 1985.

Stedman Jones, G., 'Working-Class Culture and Working-Class Politics in London, 1870-1900: Notes on the remaking of a working class', *Journal of Social History*, 7, 1974.

—— 'Class Struggle and the Industrial Revolution', *New Left Review*, 90, 1975.

—— 'Utopian Socialism Reconsidered' in R. Samuel (ed.), *People's History and Socialist Theory* (1981).

Supple, B., 'A Framework for British Business History', in Supple, B. (ed.),

Essays in British Business History, (Oxford 1977).

Tann, J., 'Co-operative Corn Milling: Self-help During the Grain Crisis of the Napoleonic Wars', *Agricultural History Review*, 28, 1980.

Tawney, R. H., 'The Dismantling of Controls after 1918', *Economic History Review*, 1943.

Thane, P., 'The Working Class and State "Welfare" in Britain, 1880-1914', *The Historical Journal*, 4, 1984.

Thompson, E. P., 'The Peculiarities of the English' in Ralph Miliband and John Saville, *The Socialist Register*, 2, 1965.

—— 'The Moral Economy of the English Crowd in the Eighteenth Century', *Past and Present*, 50, 1971.

Thornes, R., 'Change and Continuity in the Development of Co-operation, 1827-1844' in S. Yeo (ed.), *New Views of Co-operation* (1988).

Tiller, K., 'Late Chartism: Halifax 1847-1858', in D. Thompson, & J. Epstein (eds), *The Chartist Experience* (1982).

Waites, B., 'The Language and Imagery of 'Class' in Early Twentieth-Century England', *Literature and History*, 4, 1976.

Walton, J. K., 'The demand for wo.rking-class seaside holidays in Victorian England', *Economic History Review*, 34, 1981.

—— 'Co-operation in Lancashire, 1844-1914', *North West Labour History*, 19, 1994/5.

Wright, E. O., 'Class Analysis, History and Emancipation', *New Left Review*, 202, 1993.

Yeo, E., 'Culture and Constraint in Working-Class Movements, 1830-55', in E. and S. Yeo (eds), *Popular Culture and Class Conflict 1590-1914: Explorations in the History of Labour and Leisure* (Brighton 1981).

Yeo, E. and S., 'Perceived Patterns: Competition and Licence vs. Class and Struggle', in E. and S. Yeo (eds), *Popular Culture*.

Yeo, S., 'On the uses of "Apathy"', *Archives Européenes de Sociologie*, 15 (1974).

—— 'A new life: the religion of socialism in Britain, 1883-1896', *History Workshop Journal*, 4, 1977.

—— 'Working-class association, private capital and the state', in N. Parry, M. Rustin and C. Satyamurti (eds), *Social Work, Welfare and the State* (1979).

—— 'Notes on Three Socialisms, mainly in late-nineteenth and early-twentieth-century Britain', in C. Levy (ed.), *Socialism and the Intelligensia* (1987).

10 Unpublished work

Adams, T., 'Working-Class Organisation, Industrial Relations and the Labour Unrest, 1914-1921'. PhD thesis, University of Leicester 1988.

Alcock, E. A., 'The Liverpool Co-operative Society 1886-1939: Its Growth, Aims and Social Structure'. MA thesis, University of Lancaster 1986.

Bullock, I., 'Socialists and Democratic Form in Britain 1880-1914: Positions Debates and Conflicts'. DPhil thesis, University of Sussex 1981.

Campbell, L., 'Retail Co-operation in the Greater Glasgow Area *c.* 1860-1914'. PhD thesis, University of Strathclyde 1983.

Darvill, P. A., 'The Contribution of Co-operative Retail Societies to Welfare within the framework of the North East Coast area'. MLitt thesis, University of Durham 1954.

Holyoake Collection Co-operative Union Archive, Manchester.

Hornsby, M., 'The Consumers' Co-operative Movement in the Twentieth Century'. MPhil thesis, University of York 1989.

Laker, C. L., 'Co-operative Stores and Private Traders in Preston 1870-1906'. MA thesis, University of Lancaster 1981.

McCann, W. P., 'Trade Unionist, Co-operative and Socialist Organisations in Relation to Popular Education, 1870-1902'. PhD thesis, University of Manchester 1960.

Obelkevich, J., 'Men's Toiletries and Men's Bodies in Britain, 1950-1980', paper read at the Annual Social History Conference, Roehampton Institute 1993.

Schatz, R., 'Co-operative Production and the Ideology of Co-operation in England, 1870-1895.' Unpublished MS, University of Pittsburgh, 1973.

Scott, G., '"The working class women's most active and democratic movement": the Women's Co-operative Guild, 1883-1950'. DPhil thesis, University of Sussex 1988.

Shelley, C., 'Birmingham Co-operative Party in the 1930s: Co-operation and Labour Movement Politics'. MA thesis, University of Warwick 1987.

Southern, J., 'The Co-operative Movement in the inter-war period: Cleatormoor - a case study'. MA thesis, University of Lancaster 1990.

Stevens, J., 'The Coalmining Lockout of 1926, with particular reference to the Co-operative Movement and the Poor Law'. PhD thesis, University of Sheffield 1984.

Sutton, R. D., 'Co-operation and the Poor, 1890-1908'. MA thesis, University of York 1985.

Thornes, R. C. N., 'The Early Development of the Co-operative Movement in West Yorkshire, 1827-1863'. DPhil thesis, University of Sussex 1984.

Worktown Collection Mass Observation Archive, University of Sussex, Brighton.

Yeo, E. M., 'Social Science and Social Change: A Social History of Some Aspects of Social Science and Social Investigation in Britain, 1830–1890'. DPhil thesis, University of Sussex 1972.

Yeo, S., 'Who was J. T. W. Mitchell?' Unpublished MS, University of Sussex 1987.

Index